SUBTLE WHISPERS

TO A SELF-DISCOVERING YOUNG ADULT

LAURA JAMES

 FriesenPress

Suite 300 - 990 Fort St
Victoria, BC, V8V 3K2
Canada

www.friesenpress.com

ISBN
978-1-5255-7213-5 (Hardcover)
978-1-5255-7212-8 (Paperback)
978-1-5255-7214-2 (eBook)

1. BIOGRAPHY & AUTOBIOGRAPHY, PERSONAL MEMOIRS

Distributed to the trade by The Ingram Book Company

ACKNOWLEDGMENT TO SPIRIT

Nudged by my Spirit Guide and before I sat down to continue writing this second book, I took her advice and re-read *Subtle Whispers: To an Innocent Child*. I had written the book, lived the life, and knew the story. In fact, I had no desire to relive it again, and I wanted to move on with my writing. Reluctantly, I picked up the published book, made a cup of coffee, and sat down to read it as my Spirit Guide suggested.

After finishing the first few chapters, I realized that I was no longer the author of this book, but a new reader for the first time. Spiritual teachings were jumping off the pages and correlating to the exact moments in my life that they were applicable to. The first twenty years of my life was presenting itself with defined logic. I was not experiencing reactions or emotions like I had when I was writing the book. My state of mind was one of analyzing, reframing, and attempting to abandon other souls' actions and judgments. My *Spiritual Self* (soul) was reading the book, not my physical self. As I finished reading the last page, I heard:

Expect the unexpected. This is your moment of connection to the Divine in your own personal nature.

In order to be true to myself and to my readers, I meditate prior to writing. When my mind empties and becomes still, my Spirit Guide takes me back to the exact time and place that I am writing about. I relive the emotion. I remember precise conversations with humans. I am made aware of my thought process at the time, as well as the words of my Spirit World speaking to me. I am humbled by such an extraordinary blessing.

A new understanding has been received from re-reading my first book and I have clarity. Thank you Spirit World for a heightened sense of my own well-being as I continue to write. Please guide me and bless me with your knowledge through the next twenty years.

Embrace your journey where what is above and what is below are becoming united and of one mind.

INTRODUCTION

DOES A CREATOR EXIST?

Does what we do in a lifetime depend on whether or not we believe there is an afterlife and whether or not we believe that we are accountable to a Higher Power for the evolution of our souls?

If a Creator does exist, would it change everything? In contrast, if a Creator does not exist, would our life be of no consequence at all as we make our journey?

Do we all need to believe in a Higher Power in order to navigate a physical existence and survive the tragedies of life – a power that helps us to carry on and make life worth living?

Scientifically, we already know that the Universe works on balance. We experience it every day. How does a soul endure life's pain and turmoil without a belief system? Does lack of belief result in suicide idealization?

Does how we choose to behave towards other souls depend on whether or not we believe a Creator exists? If a soul behaves morally and a Creator does exist, would we stand to win everything in the end? What if we behave morally and a Creator does not exist, would we stand to lose anything?

Subtle Whispers: To an Innocent Child is the inception to this trilogy and depicts the first twenty years of my biography. It is a suggested read to understand and relate to the characters of this second book. Based on reviews, my first novel will captivate a reader as a forthright, insightful, and a powerful account of a difficult journey. I was a young girl living an abusive physical existence while still remaining connected to the world I arrived from.

As my words come to life in the next twenty years of my memoirs, those words will unveil many soul-shattering experiences. Most, I withstand with help and information from the Spirit World until one experience results in a decision to disconnect from Spirit. That choice produces a downward spiral of dysfunctional behavior as I grapple to recover from it.

My memoirs are designed with a unique structure. Each chapter takes a reader through my actual life experiences. Italicized sentences are my thoughts in that specific point of time. Bolded sentences are messages from Spirit. At the end of each chapter, a reflection channeled from my Spirit Guide enlightens readers on how the evolution of the soul is meant to transpire and the lessons that need to be learned or have been learned specific to my personal journey.

To all my readers who will make the journey with me throughout this second book, my hope is that you will find a part of yourself that can relate to my experiences and that you will walk away with a different perspective on your own personal healing and journey. As the writer, I am learning valuable information after the fact. As the reader, you are learning valuable information in real time.

CHAPTER 1

IN THE NAME OF LOVE

The first twenty years of my life had left me mentally and emotionally unprepared to function on my own as a young adult in the world. Not being wanted as a child had left scars and deep wounds that only time and true love could potentially heal.

Most of my childhood growing up had been one of rejection, isolation, unjustifiable grueling punishments, and lack of love. When my mother walked out of my life at two years old, her absence persisted until I left home and sought her out. My father remarried several years after my mother left. That was my beginning to the abuse that would define me for many years to come. I was removed from the love of an extended family and forbidden from having friends. My acceptance as a lovable soul was dependent on a psychotic stepmother with a skewed view on the value of loving and nurturing her children and an absent father, who was constantly working to provide for his family. Our household environment was one riddled with fear, anxiety, and abuse on a daily basis.

The ability to survive my childhood existence was a result of my connection to the Spirit World, the world that I had arrived from. At the age of five, I discovered that I could hear the subtle whispers from beyond and they were guiding me with each thought or prayer I prayed. My Creator removed the fear and anxiety each night and filled my spirit with the hope of a better tomorrow. My Spirit Guide blessed me with the ability to cope in my environment during the day with thought-provoking messages of guidance. My Angel guarded my heart and mind during tumultuous times of starvation and physical beatings in order to fight the forces of spiritual darkness. I had survived my childhood, but I was far from being the soul I had been created to be.

The deep pit of feeling repulsive to others plagued me in my teen years. Was I lovable by other souls? Was I truly worthy of acceptance for who I was? I was so desperate to be loved that I made poor choices. Multiple forms of abuse had left me with chronic low self-esteem, the inability to communicate to others effectively, and mistrust of other souls' intentions. I was looking for love with no idea what love looked like or the ability to recognize healthy, meaningful relationships.

After a failed relationship with my first love at seventeen years old, I shied away from having another. Even though I desperately wanted to be loved, I had not been willing to take the risk of experiencing the pain of rejection again. Perhaps we are hardwired to be individuals, separate and distinct from all other souls, without the need for love from another physical being. The thought had crossed my mind many times after my first love.

Are we all searching for a source of love from the moment we arrive in physical form? Maybe a great love already exists within us, the Divine Love of our Creator, but we cannot remember that love when we leave the Spirit World. If we are filtering that love through a human lens, is it possible that it suddenly becomes limited or skewed as something specific, such as romantic love, passionate love, or a mother's love? Or is love just that: love?

My days were meaningful, and I enjoyed my work with the Naval Reserves at Albert Head, but more times than not, my nights were lonely in my apartment by myself. I missed being in a relationship. I missed intimacy and waking up with someone beside me each morning. I missed having conversation during a meal. I missed taking a walk with someone and holding hands. I was happy for the most part, but I was empty at the same time. Maybe I was finally ready for another relationship, but that thought was more than a little worrisome. Not being wanted as a young adult was just as debilitating as not being wanted as a child.

Why are relationships so challenging? Trust was a huge barrier for me and I knew it. Combined with my inability to communicate my true feelings to another human, was I self-sabotaging the potential for any relationship to be successful? Being vulnerable, honest, and leaving myself open to rejection was something that my soul was not capable of at this point in my journey. I was a damaged soul and I knew it. I also knew that I needed to move on from Lloyd (my first love) and stop living in his memory. I just did not know how to go about that. *Please, Spirit, I think I am ready. Help me find someone to love again.*

In my quest to find love again, I made a conscious decision to bury my feelings from the past deep in my soul and lock away the memories in the far reaches of my mind, with a plan to never revisit them again. It was only logical that I would make this choice and try to carry on with a new beginning because, sadly, I knew no other way. It had become my coping mechanism from a noticeably young age to bury life's disappointments and move on. Only the first twenty years of my life were a lot harder to bury than I had imagined as those memories continued to resurface unexpectedly.

Maybe experiences with other humans are like icebergs. We can see the top of the iceberg but not the danger that is lurking below the water. Do we search for love with only what we see on the surface, or do we let what is below the water disrupt us, shake us to our core, and teach our souls? The first choice is always the easier. The first choice was the one that I was about to make.

Three months before my yearlong contract with the Naval Reserves was due to end, I met Tim. He was not in the military but was on the base as part of the Katimavik Military Option Program. Katimavik is a nine-month volunteer program that exposes youth to various aspects of life with a $1000 paycheck at the end of the experience. The last three months of Tim's contract was to experience the military option at CFB Esquimalt, British Columbia.

Tim was a year younger than me and of Swedish descent - tall with blond hair and beautiful blue eyes. He came from a well-to-do family, enjoying a privileged life. His mother was a psychologist and his father was the Vice-President for the Canadian Division of the Volkswagen Corporation. Tim was a spoiled child who had arrived much later than his other two siblings. Unfortunately, his father died of a heart attack when he was only twelve years old. With the best of intentions, his mother sent him to a private boarding school in Winnipeg, Manitoba, a school with a focus on outdoor adventure. That decision remained a thorn in Tim's side while growing up. He saw himself as the child that was thrown away after his father's death. Tim's older brother, Jim, was an executive with Avco Finance, and his sister, Kim, was a marine biologist in Halifax. Tim was the lost soul of his family without any direction in life.

Tim and I spent the next three months dating and quickly became close. Everywhere we went together, I noticed that women were instantly attracted to him. Perhaps it was his boyish charm and good looks. What I failed to recognize, at the time, was that he was as lost as I was. We were two souls wandering aimlessly together trying to figure out life.

In the beginning, Tim and I were basking in the excitement and glow of new love. We partied with friends, often to excess, and nursed hangovers more often than we should have. I bought a second-hand 1969 Chevy van from the Chief Warrant Officer that I was working for. It became our pastime to explore Vancouver Island. When the weekend rolled around, it was not unusual for us to throw a change of clothes into the van and let the road take us on an adventure. The van was equipped with a double bed in the back, so we stopped wherever our hearts desired, most often staying at beach parking lots for the night. Thetis Lake became one of our favorite destinations. My attraction was the panoramic view of water and rolling hills, while Tim enjoyed the hiking trails. Life was fun and free of responsibility.

After a long conversation at dinner one night, we both decided we wanted to see where the relationship was going to take us. I was twenty years old when Tim finished the Katimavik Program and he was nineteen. Instead of going back to Ontario, he decided to stay in Esquimalt with me and moved his things over to my apartment. My lease on the apartment was ending in two weeks, as well as my employment with the Reserves. If we were going to figure out a future together, we had little more than a week to do so. We needed a plan.

We decided to let go of the apartment I was currently renting and rent another apartment together in Victoria. I found a job working as an underwriter for a life insurance company, and Tim began working with a security company. Tim's mother was not happy about his decision. She wanted him to come home and go to university. Tim refused to listen. He was going to live his life his own way, on his own terms. Neither of us knew where life was taking us, but we were happy in the moment. In reality, we were both running against the wind, running from our pasts, and it would only be a matter of time before we ran out of breath. Life was about to start unraveling before we knew it, as we brought our baggage to the relationship.

Five months had passed with us blissfully living together when we received news that Tim's brother, Jim, was transferred to the city of Vancouver on the mainland. Tim was excited at the prospect of seeing family again. A passenger/vehicle ferry links Vancouver Island to the Mainland, so we packed the van one weekend and made a trip to visit them. Jim and his wife Judy were several years older than us, established in life, and had been trying to start a family for the past two years. I liked them on first impression, and I was happy for Tim to have family close at hand.

When the HMCS *Terra Nova* returned to port after a six-month sail to China, my youngest brother, Rick, and I finally managed to meet up. Rick was a cook onboard the ship and invited me to join him for dinner one night after the rest of the crew had been fed. I had been estranged from my siblings when I left home. We usually found out what was going on in each other's lives through conversations with my father. He was the connection that kept the family together. One of the scars that I had been left with from my childhood was thinking that my brothers did not want to hear from me. I had taken on the responsibility for being the one who had ruined their childhood. I had convinced myself that they must be happy to be free from me. Truth be told, our relationships were damaged for each and every one of us, and it would take us well into adulthood to recover. Perhaps having to witness abuse can be just as damaging as being on the receiving end of it.

Rick and I spent several hours catching up on the past few years, as I enjoyed a delicious meal that he had prepared for the ship's crew that night. I learned that he was living with a girl named Catherine when he was not at sea, and they were renting a two-bedroom apartment together. They were renting out their second bedroom to a sailor Rick knew from another ship in order to help with expenses and give Catherine company when Rick was away from home. He took me on a tour of the ship, and it brought back memories of my earlier days in Halifax. The end of his five-year contract was approaching, and we talked about him getting out of the military and what he might do after that. All in all, he seemed happy with life in general. I enjoyed the time I spent with him that night. It was a beginning to re-establishing a relationship, this time as adults.

By August of 1980, the family was planning to get together in Victoria to celebrate Rick and Catherine's decision to get married. I was not sure how I felt about seeing my family again. On one hand, I was apprehensive, especially of my stepmother, Joan, and my oldest brother, Bob. *Can we all be together again as adults without fighting? Surely, the happiness of a wedding taking place will set the right tone.* That thought quelled my apprehension somewhat, along with the fact that we were all living our own lives. We could make our own choices on whether to engage or disengage from drama. Having Tim by my side was also reassuring to me. On the other hand, life had always been extremely unpredictable whenever it involved Joan.

The family reunion for the wedding went smoothly. We spent a day fishing for salmon, leaving empty handed because we were too busy drinking and partying on the boat. More drinking ensued as we carried on that evening with the rehearsal dinner. The next day, Rick was late for his wedding. He and my brothers got lost on their way to the church, arriving ten minutes past the time the wedding was scheduled to start. Short of that hiccup, the weekend went off without a glitch, the marriage took place, and everyone returned to their own lives again.

The night of the wedding reception, I drank very little. I had partied so much the day before that I decided to coast. One can be very observant if you are the only sober one in the room. It was obvious that my father and Joan liked Tim. In fact, Joan seemed a little too cozy with my man. *Maybe I am reading too much into their attraction. Maybe they just like each other and are having fun dancing together.* I was not convinced. I was hoping that Joan did not have an agenda with him, but her actions were saying otherwise. I knew her too well. She was on a mission of some kind. I just had no idea at the time what it was nor could I have even prepared for what was coming.

Our first-year anniversary of being together was quickly approaching, so I decided to buy Tim a ring. I chose a black onyx stone that had been flattened and polished, with a gold "T" on top and 2 diamonds. I prepared a special candlelight dinner. I showered, put on lingerie, did my hair and makeup, and went about preparing for a special night - one to remember. When Tim walked through the door from work, his reaction said it all. "What's all this?" he asked. He had an awkward look, like a deer caught in the headlights. I was the Queen of Awkward and recognized that look immediately. "We have been together for a year now, and I wanted to do something special to celebrate the occasion," I replied. What I wanted was a romantic evening, and what Tim wanted was to get away from me as fast as he could. The evening was a total bust and not one that I cared to remember.

Three days later, I walked in the door from work to an empty apartment. Tim's personal things were gone, and there had been no goodbye. No note. No phone call. Nothing! I had no idea where he was or if he was ever coming back. He had disappeared like a thief into the night. I was devastated and began sobbing. *How did I not see this coming? I do not understand. Why? Where is he?* Was I on the receiving end of how running away feels to someone who loves you? The thought had entered my mind. Was I being taught a lesson? There was no comparison. My running away was not the same. I had run in the past as a survival mechanism - when I was not happy or I was afraid. *Is Tim not happy? Has he ever been happy? Is he tired of playing house? Is he afraid of where life is taking us? Is that why he ran?*

The truth can be painful, but a lie is much more damaging.

Go away please. **You asked.** The decision to not listen in that moment of truth was one that I would live to regret.

Friday night and most of Saturday had gone by with no word from Tim. I needed something - anything. I decided to call Tim's brother. "Jim, I can't find Tim. The last time I talked to him was Friday morning before I left for work. Please tell me you have heard from him. I am so worried," I said as he answered the phone.

"Stop worrying. He is here with us," Jim replied. "We are getting on the ferry tomorrow morning. We will see you soon." He hung up the phone before I could ask to speak to Tim. I was angry as I began redialing Jim's phone number. **Patience is a virtue**. I hung up the phone before the number connected.

At 2:00 p.m. Sunday afternoon, Jim, Judy, and Tim showed up at the apartment. I watched with conflicting emotion as Tim set his luggage down in the doorway and removed his shoes. I was happy to see him, but I was furious at what he had put me through. The air was heavy with uneasiness for all four of us. "I think we all need to sit down and talk," Jim said.

"I will make a pot of coffee," I replied as I tried to busy myself while sorting through my overwhelming emotions. *Please don't cry, Laurie. He has his suitcase with him. That is a good sign.* As much as I had reassured myself with that thought, I did not know where the conversation was going to take us. I was no longer angry, and I was losing my courage to speak. *Why do I always have to be mad to voice my opinion or feelings? I need to learn to speak up. My thoughts and feelings are important and should matter.* I sat at the dining room table without uttering a single word throughout the entire conversation.

That day, Tim and I got back together as a couple with the decision to move to the Mainland to start over. We gave one month's notice to the landlord and put an advertisement in the newspaper to sell our furniture. We both gave notice at work, but the whole time we were going through the motion of preparing to relocate, I could not expel the nagging feeling I had inside of me. I still did not know why Tim had left to begin with. Worse, he was not wearing his ring. After two weeks, I finally mustered up the courage to ask Tim where his ring was. "I threw it over the railing of the ferry on my way to Vancouver," he said, "a decision that I now regret."

I was hurt. *Is that what my token of love had meant to him? So easily discarded and now lying at the bottom of the Strait of Georgia.* I had regret too. Regret for even buying it.

I honestly could not tell you why I made the decision to leave Victoria with Tim. Maybe going with him was better than the fear of being alone. Fear can be so crippling. Maybe it was the fear of abandonment in the back of my mind. Going with him seemed to be the better option than staying behind. I was exhausted from fighting battles in my mind, heart, and soul.

For a few weeks, we stayed in the spare room in Jim and Judy's condo while we searched for jobs and a place of our own to live. All of our worldly possessions occupied a van down in the parking lot. We were starting from scratch. I interviewed for three jobs within our first two days there, and five days later, I was offered two positions of the three I had previously interviewed for. I chose the job working for Transport Canada at the Vancouver International Airport as an accounts receivable clerk. The thought of working at an airport was different and enticing, and the job offer felt right in the moment. By the end of the week, Tim had found a job back in the security industry. We were on our way to settling down again. Now that we both had a means of income, we decided to rent the main floor of a house in Richmond, a municipality of Metro Vancouver with five-minute access to the airport. We were both working now and had our own place to live. Our new life on the Mainland had begun.

We muddled through our change with good and bad moments, but nothing abnormal for young couples. We were content, and we seemed to have made it through the storm. As I sat out in the backyard one night after Tim had left for work, I was filled with questions. I am sure my Spirit Guide must have been tired of listening to the constant chatter in my head. *Is the writing on the wall? Are we both doomed to fail at this relationship because we are so young? He has already run from me once before. I can't seem to let it go. Is that because he is going to run again? Can I even trust him or should I just move on now? I feel so empty. Are you trying to tell me something with the way I am feeling?*

Spiritual growth is letting go of something so that something new can be born. Not every soul is a loss.

By June, I had picked up a virus that had been circulating through our office. After a visit to the doctor and two weeks of antibiotics, I awoke one morning feeling worse. My throat and chest felt better, but I was constantly vomiting and feeling lethargic. I went again to the doctor's office days later, after the bloodwork and urine test results were received from the lab.

"The reason you have been feeling so sick, Laurie, is because you are pregnant." The first words out of the doctor's mouth took a few seconds to register, as I sat down in the chair beside his desk.

"That's not possible," I replied. "I am on the pill and I have taken it faithfully at the exact same time every day."

"Did you take extra precautions while you were on your antibiotics?" he asked.

How would I know that antibiotics counteract with birth control? He should have told me that when he prescribed the pills. We are not ready for a baby. We are sleeping on mattresses on a floor. Our furniture consists of a living room couch. How could this be happening?

I was unsure in that initial moment whether I even wanted a baby. The timing was all wrong. The doctor continued. "I am going to send you for an ultrasound. There is a possibility that your fetus could be deformed from using birth control for so long. It causes a hormonal imbalance in the body that can result in birth defects. The earlier we find out, the better, so there is time to abort if need be."

Wait a minute! You are talking about potentially killing my baby. In that instant, I wanted my baby more than life itself. I prayed for that little soul growing inside of me to be perfect. I did not have my knight in shining armor, but I was on my way to the greatest blessing life has to offer. I was bringing another soul into existence by the Grace of my Creator.

Spiritual Beings on a Human Experience

A soul will only come to a point of clarity when it is freed of the burdens that have been weighing it down. Laurie's soul needs to move through her sacred transformational experience; move through her pain and broken psyche in order to feel at peace with herself, love herself, and trust her judgment as she continues her physical life. If she does not learn to purge her burdens, her experiences will continue to build up over time and become toxic to her soul and her growth.

In order for any soul to evolve and for it to heal from traumatic experiences, it needs to face the feelings it has buried. The soul needs to be in the moment with the emotions surrounding the experience, own what is that soul's part to own, ask the Creator for forgiveness for the part they have played, and give back to Him what a soul has no control over (another soul's actions). That is the intended healing process – a process many souls on a human experience never figure out.

Laurie's soul has endured many tragedies that have left her unable to give her whole heart to another soul. She feels betrayed by other souls, is unable to trust, usually withdraws, and is becoming dangerous to herself. It is only the soul that can pull itself from the darkness and learn to let go. Right now she is comfortable with another soul who is lost. Her Spirit Guide and Angel keep speaking to her, trying to relay the message that the union of these two souls is headed for doom. Her fear of letting go, combined with her desire to be loved, is keeping her locked in a vicious cycle of stagnation that is unfulfilling.

This soul's baby is a Divine gift from her Heavenly Father and spirituality is the child's birthright. God has a plan for her life, as well as her baby's life, and will continue to give her the strength and the wisdom that she needs to care for this special blessing. He is hoping she is open to His wonder, amidst the mess of her reality. He wants to provide her with the experience of a nourishing human connection.

CHAPTER 2

A TIME FOR EVERY PURPOSE

"Tim, I have news and I am not sure how you are going to feel about it, so I will just tell you outright. I am pregnant."

"Are you sure?" he asked.

"Of course, the doctor just told me. I want this baby, with or without you by my side. Just so you know," I replied.

His expression quickly changed from shock to excitement. "I can't believe this. Wow! You're pregnant! Don't worry. We still have lots of time to prepare," he said, as he stood up, walked over, and hugged me. He seemed to be excited about this baby, and I felt relieved.

Tim was twenty-one years old, I was twenty-two, and we had a baby on the way. Neither of our families welcomed the news with enthusiasm. Tim's mother felt he was much too young. She was right. Joan berated me for getting pregnant out of wedlock. "Your father will be so disappointed when I tell him. Do you realize you robbed him of the chance to walk his only daughter down the aisle? Are you even capable of raising a baby? What were you thinking? Once again, you don't think about anyone but yourself."

I sat quietly until Joan was finished ranting, and then I hung up the phone, feeling less than adequate once again. *Does she really think I did this on purpose? She is so annoying. I don't know why I even bother to talk to her. She is incapable of any compassion or understanding. I should have just waited to talk to my father and tell him the news myself.*

Some humans can get lost on their way to a miracle. Accept this gift with your whole heart and He will handle all the complications.

On Friday night, we were invited to Jim and Judy's for supper. They always prepared such wonderful meals. Perhaps that was due to all the corporate entertaining that Jim did as part of his job, but I did not want to go that night. I was repulsed by food and not in the mood to tell anyone else about the pregnancy.

"Let's just go and get it over with," Tim said. I was nervous. They were a couple trying to have a baby, and they were financially prepared to welcome one. We were not trying to have a baby nor were we remotely ready. The news would be less than joyous to them. I was sure of it. The topic of my pregnancy was not brought up that night, and my nausea was explained away as not feeling well. Tim had decided that he wanted to tell his brother the news alone and in his own time.

My ultrasound results came back as *normal*. Some women glow through their pregnancy and enjoy the experience. I was not so lucky. My first two trimesters were consumed with morning, noon, and night sickness. I could not get out of bed without crackers and water, which came back up as quickly as they went down. The smell of food cooking was nauseating, especially meat of any kind, which would send me running to the bathroom once again. Tim was surviving on peanut butter and jam sandwiches or eating out at restaurants. While I was at work, I constantly had my head in my garbage pail while running down the hallway to the bathroom. I had lost fourteen pounds by my sixth month of pregnancy, and the doctor was concerned during my last visit. He prescribed a thyroid pill to slow down my metabolism and enable my baby to get some nourishment. Knowing how much I loved Dairy Queen, Tim came home with a dish of ice milk one night. I was able to keep it down, and it felt good. It was quelling my heartburn and taking away the nausea. A steady diet of ice milk resulted in a weight gain of thirty pounds in my last trimester, but I did not care. This baby was going to be worth every pound gained.

One night after work, Tim and his brother decided to go out for a few beers and Tim filled me in on their conversation when he returned home. "I think we should get married, Laurie. Jim suggested a Justice of the Peace, and he and Judy will be our witnesses. Let's make it official for this baby," he said. This was not how I had imagined a marriage proposal. *Nothing in my life has ever turned out the way I have imagined it should be. Is there a reason for that? Am I living in my own fairy-tale world instead of reality? Where is the romance?*

I knew in my heart that I was heading into a danger zone, but I could not stop myself. Against my better judgment, we were married in August of 1981 in Maple Ridge, British Columbia, with Jim and Judy as our witnesses. After the ceremony, they took us to Granville Island to a very high-end restaurant to celebrate. This was not how I had envisioned getting married, and Tim was not the man of my dreams. His marriage proposal was about needing to do the right thing, not about love. *What have I done?*

Nothing that cannot be undone. Little did I know at the time just how powerful those words were going to be in a few years.

For the next few months, we were preoccupied with setting up the nursery. On garbage day, we found an old dresser on the side of the road and took it home. We cleaned it up, painted it white, and put Disney stickers on the drawers. Besides being a dresser, it also doubled as the bath and change table. Tim's grandparents bought us a crib and a washer and dryer. The girls at work had a baby shower for me that resulted in most of our essential needs being met. We were finally ready for this new little soul to arrive and just in the nick of time.

At 10:00 a.m. on March 15, my water broke. The last two weeks had been extremely uncomfortable with the baby constantly kicking under my ribcage and knocking the wind out of me. I did not enjoy pregnancy and was looking forward to it all being over. Looking back, it was probably a blessing that I had no idea just how challenging labor was going to be. When I arrived at the hospital several hours later, the pain was so intense and I was only five centimeters dilated. The doctor made the decision to give me an epidural to help me relax. Now I was numb from the waist down, but this little soul was taking its time, and I lay there alone for many more hours. Tim had gone to the bar with his brother, and Judy was their driver. This was not how I had envisioned having a baby either. I was all alone - just me and my Spirit World.

I was fully dilated by midnight, but the baby was struggling. He began his descent down the birth canal facing the ceiling instead of the floor. His face and forehead were taking all the pressure of descension instead of the crown of his head. The doctor decided to try and turn him around the right way by using forceps, but the forceps caught him in the left eye. He immediately went into fetal distress.

"I have lost the heartbeat, doctor."

"Everyone prepare for a C-section," he replied.

Oh dear God, please don't take my baby now. Please I beg you. If you have to take this baby, take me too. I don't want to live without this little soul. As I uttered those words, I could feel His power and His grace as a wave of calm flooded me.

I watched the anesthesiologist inject a needle into the tube on my hand. I could feel my heartbeat slowing down, and it was becoming impossible to breathe. He told me to start counting from ten backwards, but all I felt was panic as I lay there wide awake. "I can't breathe. So hard to breathe," I muttered.

He had administered the wrong drug, and realizing his mistake when I was still awake and my vitals had dropped, he quickly gave me another drug to counteract the effects of the first one. I began lapsing in and out of consciousness sporadically. I watched the scalpel start to cut my stomach. Then I faded out. When I regained consciousness, they were removing my child. *I don't hear any crying. Why is my baby not crying? Why does he look like that?* I could see that he had no forehead. The center of his left eye was all red, and there was so much bruising. I could hear them all talking until their voices suddenly became drowned out by the sounds of a baby crying. *He is alive! Oh Father, thank you, thank you, thank you.*

"Laurie, you have a baby boy, and he is doing fine. His head will reshape very quickly. Don't worry. We are taking you to recovery now for a few hours. You will see your baby soon." Those were the last words I heard, as they wheeled me out of the delivery room and I drifted off to sleep.

Two hours later, Tim was sitting in the chair beside the bed when I returned to the room. It was March 16, and we had been blessed with a son. Other than the trauma of the birthing process, he was healthy and perfect. "He is amazing, Laurie," were Tim's first words. He kissed my forehead and then sat beside the bed, holding my hand. I really wanted to see my baby. I wanted to hold him. The nurse entered the room, took my pulse, asked how I was feeling and then left again. She returned with my little boy, removed him from his infant bed, and placed him at my breast. As he began feeding, I looked into his eyes. I knew, in that very moment, that we would have a special bond for life. If I were never to become anything more than a mother, it would be enough. In fact, it would be everything.

Tim stayed another hour as we wallowed in the joy of this new soul. Before leaving to go home, his final words left me quite unsettled. "Jim and Judy want our baby, and they are willing to pay us for him. We are young, and we can have more babies, but they can't get pregnant. Think about it." I did not need to think about it. That was never going to happen as long as I had breath in my body.

Born at seven pounds, seven ounces and twenty inches in length, our son was named Timothy James - "TJ" for short. A few hours later, once I had figured out the time change, I called my father and Joan to give them the news. The conversation went well, and we made plans for a trip back to Windsor to have TJ baptized in the next two months. My second call was to my mother to give her the news. She was overjoyed at being a grandmother and looking forward to meeting him. I mentioned that we would be in Ontario for the christening, and I would speak to my father about her being added to the guest list, along with the rest of my mother's side of the family. I should have known better. Joan refused to have my mother involved in any way, shape, or form. Laura was not welcome, nor was that side of the family. It broke my mother's heart when I called her back to tell her that she could not be included in the celebration because of Joan's decision. Even as an adult, I was not capable of standing up to Joan. I was still a wounded child that obeyed her every word for fear of the repercussions.

That May, TJ was baptized in Windsor, with my brother Steve and his wife Grace accepting the role as godparents. I had missed my brother's wedding due to my pregnancy. The doctor did not recommend traveling at that point. It was too risky. Grace was no stranger to me though. We went to high school together. As a christening present, she made TJ's gown and cap that he wore that day. A reception followed the christening with a guest list that Joan had designed – a list that excluded any people that I wanted to share my joy with. Tim and I received beautiful gifts that day to help us provide for our new bundle of joy. On one hand, I was extremely grateful.

On the other hand, I was troubled once again as I watched the interaction between Tim and Joan. Her entire attention was focused on my husband as she turned on her charm to seduce him. Our return to Vancouver could not come fast enough for me.

After the baptism, we decided to move from the place we were living and began renting a house by ourselves, with no one living above us or below. We traded the van in for a car that could accommodate a baby car seat, leaving us with a $12,000 loan for the vehicle. For the first year and a half, this precious little boy was our whole world. Tim and I had found a new bond, and we were happy being parents.

In 1983, the family gathered again - this time in Calgary to celebrate my brother Jimmy's marriage. Jimmy and Jaimie's wedding was not traditional or formal. It was one big party with lots of alcohol and homemade food that was constantly being replenished throughout the evening. People ate when they chose to and as often as they wanted. This was the first time I had seen my brother Bob on his home turf. He was living a lavish life-style, driving a brand-new Cadillac, and had a beautiful girlfriend from Guyana, South America. I would discover that weekend that Bob's income was being derived from a prostitution ring he had established as a business. It was a business that was high end and pricey, made up of exotic, dark-skinned women. Little did Bob know the price he would pay for that business within a few short years.

By early fall, Tim was let go from his job, and we started to struggle on my salary alone. Each month that went by was getting worse. By November, we were surviving on a fifty-pound bag of potatoes, along with dairy products that were delivered to our door by a milk truck. I said nothing to anyone about our situation. We had not been to a grocery store in months. Christmas came and went without a tree or presents, but we had one saving grace that made that Christmas special.

I was responsible for processing the payroll for all the public service employees working at the airport. I made it my priority to prepare the paychecks for the firehall first because they were shift workers. Four days before Christmas, while picking up their paychecks, the shift supervisor from the firehall arrived at my desk with a beautifully wrapped basket of food. "This is from the guys at the firehall for all the special attention you give us with the payroll and our overtime cheques. Make sure that you refrigerate it. Merry Christmas, Laurie" he said. After he left the office, I looked in the basket. We had a turkey, cranberries, canned vegetables, a box of stuffing, a bottle of wine, crackers, cheese, chocolates, and cookies. I was choked up and teary-eyed as I looked at all the food in that basket. In the spirit of Christmas, we decided to invite another couple that was struggling like we were to join us for dinner. That Christmas basket of food was the best Christmas present ever. It was a Divine blessing at a time when food banks did not exist. *Thank you, Heavenly Father. Merry Christmas!*

By February, we needed to revisit our situation. Tim had still not found work, and we were sinking financially. We had enough money saved for two more months of rent and then we would end up homeless. While talking to my father one day in March, I finally broke down and told him about Tim losing his job. He suggested that we consider moving to Windsor, and he would help us get back on our feet again. "Tim can come right away, stay with us, and look for work while you get things sorted out on your end. Everything should fall into place perfectly by the time you get here." His plan made sense, and I was tired of struggling to make ends meet.

My father and Joan had moved into a mobile home park in Tecumseh when he was transferred to the Lauzon Road Police Precinct. There were several homes in the park that were available to rent or to purchase, and we were excited at the prospect of starting over again somewhere that we could afford to live. Vancouver was becoming way too expensive.

Tim left for Windsor in April, but not before we had a long talk about Joan. He knew my past with her, but I felt I needed to remind him. "Be careful with her, Tim. She is a wolf in sheep's clothing. Whatever you do, do NOT trust her. She always has an agenda where I am concerned," I said.

"You worry too much," was his reply. He kissed me goodbye and was on his way out the door.

After Tim left, my first priority was to have the car shipped to Ontario. I spoke with one of the girls at work, and we agreed to carpool for my last two weeks of work and I would pay for her gas. That way, Tim would have a vehicle to get back and forth from work once he found a job, and the car would already be in Ontario when I arrived. The car was on its way to Windsor one day later, and I had paid them in cash when they picked it up.

For the next two weeks that I remained behind in Vancouver, I had little time to rest and relax. I was still working full time, taking care of TJ when he was not with the babysitter, packing up the essentials that we would need to start over again at the other end, selling the furniture we did not want to move, and arranging for a moving company. When I went to the bank to close my account the day before I left, I walked away with a little more than $5500 between the things I had sold and cashing my final paycheck. It would be enough to pay the moving company at the other end, with some money left over to start our lives again.

I requested a leave of absence from my job. My boss wrote me a glowing letter of recommendation and assured me I would be on the priority list for any public service positions I qualified for, ahead of the general public. I thanked him for the letter and his time, and then left his office. I was going to miss my job and the friends I had made in the office. It was hard to say goodbye to a job and co-workers that had become such a huge part of my life for the past three years.

When I got off the plane in Windsor, Tim was at the airport to meet me, but his reaction to seeing us was not normal. He did not hug or kiss me, or his son for that matter. In fact, he was acting indifferent, aloof. I knew something was terribly wrong, but I was too exhausted at the time to question it. *Maybe it is because I am covered in baby barf.* I chose to let his behavior slide for the time being. When we arrived at the trailer, I could smell liver cooking. I gagged as I walked in the door and immediately did a one eighty and exited back outside. Tim and my father followed me. "Do not include me in this meal," I said. "I will order a pizza or go to McDonalds. I am NOT eating liver."

"Stop it, Laurie! You are acting like a baby," was Tim's reaction. We started fighting after my father went back inside. During the lull in our fighting, I could hear my father's conversation with Joan through the open kitchen window.

"Joan, why would you make liver for her first meal home? You know it makes her sick. What is wrong with you?" my father asked.

"If she does not like liver, she does not have to eat it. We are having liver. End of conversation." I was back in Joan's world again and things were off to a bad start. Even though I was twenty-five years old, it was her home.

She had the control and she was not shy about exercising it. Tim handed me the car keys, and I drove to McDonalds for supper by myself. *Please Father, I need to get out from under Joan's roof. Please help me make that happen as quickly as possible.* My prayer was heard, and it was about to be answered much faster than I had ever anticipated.

I was lost in thought as I ate my hamburger. *What has Tim been doing all this time? He was supposed to start working and find us a place to live. He hasn't done anything, and he is totally unfazed by it all. I don't understand where his head is at.*

Those who think they have nothing to lose are in the most danger of losing it all.

I hated living with Joan again, and I was on a mission to get out of there – the sooner, the better. My father talked to the owner of Franco's Pizzeria, and I began a waitressing job, as I tried to figure out my next step. If Tim was not going to work, he could make himself useful by babysitting. That plan backfired within the first two days. While my father and I were busy working, Tim and Joan were going out to the bars, drinking, dancing, and God only knows what else, leaving TJ with a babysitter. When I got home at night, my tip money was leaving my hands as quickly as I had earned it to pay babysitters or repay money that Tim had borrowed from Joan to buy drinks. I was angry with him and did not hesitate to let that anger fly. "What is it with you and Joan? I am not giving you any more of my hard-earned money for you to go out and have a good time. Don't ask me again. I am done with your bullshit. You need to grow up and find a damn job." I went to bed alone, and he slept on the couch.

Since my arrival five days earlier, any form of attention or intimacy was still non-existent between Tim and I, so I made it my mission to pay closer attention to Joan and Tim's relationship. They were acting very friendly with each other - too friendly. I was catching the looks they were exchanging between themselves when they thought no one was looking. One night at supper, I caught them playing footsie with each other under the dining table. Tim was teaching Joan how to drive, so they were disappearing together for hours at a time for quote "driving lessons". All the while this was going on, our relationship had not returned to normal. There was no handholding, no hugs, and no interest by him in the slightest. Alarm bells were going off in my head, and I had every right to be suspicious by his lack of attention. This was definitely not normal for us.

Two weeks had gone by, and I had a night off from work. My father suggested that Tim and I get out of the house together; maybe go see a movie or go out for dinner. "Take some quality time for yourselves. We will babysit," he said. Tim was not in the mood. He had not been in the mood to do anything with me since I had arrived. That was very obvious. "Let's call the babysitter then. We can all go down to HMCS *Hunter* for a few drinks together. How does that sound? Laurie probably needs to get out for a night of fun." Tim was on board to do that because it involved Joan, but this was going to be the furthest thing from a night of fun for me.

When we arrived at HMCS *Hunter*, Tim asked me if I wanted to play a game of pool. I was shocked. He actually wanted to do something with me alone. We grabbed our drinks from the bar and made our way to the pool table. Within a matter of five minutes, my entire world came crashing down around me. "I want a divorce, Laurie. I don't love you anymore," he said, as he called his next shot.

I was speechless, standing in shock and disbelief at the words that had just come out of his mouth and the lack of affect he was displaying while saying them. I knew our relationship was strained, but I had never imagined it had gone that far. I set my pool cue on the table and then retreated to the women's washroom. I was not going to give him the satisfaction of crying in front of him.

A few minutes later, Joan walked into the washroom. "What's wrong?" she asked.

"Tim just asked me for a divorce," I replied.

"I'll go get your father," was her response to my comment. *What the hell! Get my father? Why?* Her response solidified my suspicion. She was guilty and needed to be alone with Tim. She needed to find out exactly what had happened while we were playing pool and what he had revealed to me.

My father came into the women's washroom, totally unaware of where he was. I began sobbing onto his chest, as he wrapped his arms around me. "Tim just asked me for a divorce. I think he and Joan are having an affair," I blurted out, in between sobs.

"Laurie, you are over-reacting," he said. "I am sure it is nothing like that. Wash your face, honey. Stop crying and come back to the table. We will talk about this together and I will get to the bottom of what is going on with Tim."

Deep in my soul, I knew different. Our relationship was over. He did not love me anymore. Maybe he never had.

Spiritual Beings on a Human Experience

God is present in the creation of every human life with a plan and a purpose for every soul, regardless of the means of conception, accidental or not. His breath of life into this soul child will create a bond between mother and child. LOVE will be the bond that they will hold closest and apply the most to their own hearts as they make the journey together. The Spirit World rejoices at her decision to accept her child wholeheartedly as he is her introduction to pure soul-to-soul love.

Although these two adult souls believe they are in love, it is not a love that will sustain the test of time. Both souls know this love does not feel right. The soul is created for the connection to what is sacred, for the touch of authentic love. That is not possible when souls are lost and attaching themselves to what they believe will make them happy. This union is unfulfilling and as evil enters into their union, they have no hope of making the relationship work. This evil is manipulating and self-serving and will devastate both of them as they try to pick up the pieces of their shattered worlds.

CHAPTER 3

I CAN OF MY OWN SELF DO NOTHING

A gaping sinkhole had just opened up and swallowed me whole. I was filled with so many emotions - devastation, disbelief, anger, confusion, worthlessness, and resentment, just to mention a few. Certainly, I had to be wrong. *Oh dear God, please let me be wrong.* When I returned to the table from the washroom, the decision had been made to go home and discuss Tim's resolve to end the marriage in a private setting. As soon as we pulled into the driveway, Tim and Joan went into the house and straight to bed, with the excuse that they were too tired to talk. My father and I sat at the kitchen table trying to make sense of everything that had just happened. He was still in denial about the affair. Perhaps it was because the reality of Joan doing this to him was too overwhelming to even consider. Or perhaps he genuinely thought I was over-reacting and reading too much into Joan and Tim's relationship. I could tell that he still did not believe me.

"You need to get some sleep, honey. Things will look different in the morning once the shock wears off," he said.

"I can't sleep. I can't shut my mind off," I replied.

"I will get Joan's sleeping pills. Take one, and it will help you relax. Your son will be up in another few hours, and he will want his mother." My father brought me Joan's pills and then went to bed.

I stood at the kitchen sink with the bottle of sleeping pills in my hand. I opened the container and swallowed one. Then I contemplated taking another. *One more won't hurt. I really need to sleep.* I swallowed the second one. My hands were trembling from emotional exhaustion as I tried to replace the lid and the pill bottle fell into the kitchen sink, scattering the medication everywhere. I turned and walked away, defiantly leaving the mess in the sink due to my anger, and I went to bed.

The next morning my father's shift started at 7:00 a.m., so he left early for work. I was in a deep sleep when I felt someone shaking me. "Wake up, Laurie. What do we do? How many of those damn pills did she take?" Tim asked Joan.

"I don't know how many were left in the bottle, and they are all over the place now. Just get her up and take her into the shower. The water should bring her around," Joan ordered. I was still very groggy, weak, and could not stand on my own. I was not fully conscious, but I could hear everything going on around me. Perhaps by my Spirit Guide's design, I was privy to their entire conversation as I continued struggling to wake up.

Tim and Joan lifted me into the bathtub, laid me down, pulled the shower curtain closed, and turned on the showerhead. I was immediately surrounded by White Light, feeling the comfort of my Spirit World as I listened to Joan and Tim's conversation.

"We need to get out of here. She has figured everything out," Joan said.

"We can't leave before she wakes up. Someone needs to look after TJ," Tim replied.

"Just leave him in the playpen and let's go. He will be fine there," Joan begged. They left the bathroom together.

Suddenly, I was fully awake. My son needed me. I got out of the bathtub, removed my wet pajamas, dressed myself, and walked out into the living room. I did not say a word to either one of them. I was extremely calm and composed, as I picked up TJ from inside the playpen and began hugging him and kissing his cheeks.

Responsibility for another soul is a privilege. You have been entrusted with this beautiful soul who loves you, and your Angel is here with you now to guide you. Fear not, for you are not alone.

"The moving company called and our furniture has arrived. I am going to the bank to take the $2,000 out, and then I am heading over to pay them. I will be back in a few hours," Tim said.

"Will you drop me off at Holly's on your way?" Joan asked.

That was the end of any conversation as they walked out the door together. I sensed they were in a panic to get away from me in order to avoid answering any questions, which in all honesty, I had no intention of asking. I already knew everything that I needed to know. I made lunch for TJ, dressed him, and then put him in his stroller. We walked around the trailer park for an hour enjoying the fresh air. As I came in the door from our walk, the telephone was ringing. When I answered, it was my father calling. I told him Tim had gone to the bank, and he had dropped Joan off at Holly's place. "I will call back in a few hours to talk to her. I am going to work a double shift today, so I won't be home until midnight," he said.

By 6:00 p.m. Tim had not returned nor had I heard from him. He had been gone for seven hours. I fed TJ supper, bathed him, dressed him in his sleeper, and put him in his playpen in front of the television to watch *Sesame Street*. My father called back at 7:00 p.m. and asked to talk to Joan. "She is not here. In fact, Tim has not come back either. I think they have run off together, Dad. Why won't you believe me?"

"I will call you back," was his reply and the line went dead.

I cuddled with TJ on the couch for another hour, desperately trying to stay composed as the tears trickled down my cheeks. I was realizing that there were different kinds of heartbreak. One was the slow realization of heartbreak that comes with time; the one that happens slowly and eases you into coming to terms with the reality of the situation. I had learned that heartbreak as a child. Then there was the stabbing in the chest kind of heartbreak; the one that you did not see coming and drops you to your knees. It is a heartbreak that is immediate and intensely unbelievable and unbearable, like blunt force trauma. *Where are they? Have they really run off together? This can't be happening. Please tell me it is all a bad dream.*

A soul does not know when it is too late until it is too late.

It was not a bad dream, and it was happening whether I wanted it to or not. Joan did not show up at Holly's that day. When my father called and asked to speak with her, Holly told him that she had not heard from Joan in weeks.

TJ was finally settled for the night when my father called back. "I hate to say this, but I think you might be right," he said. I did not want to be right. The thought of being right was overwhelming.

"How do we find them, Dad? Can I report my car stolen?" I asked.

"Unfortunately not. It is a marital asset owned by both of you. However I can put in a 'request to locate' because you have concerns of foul play. Maybe Tim was mugged coming out of the bank and the car was stolen," he said.

"Do it," I replied.

By the time my father arrived home at midnight, my car had been found. It was parked at the Toronto International Airport. There was no denying it now. Tim had run again, and this time he was not alone. *I can't believe he has done this to me again. Was this the nagging feeling I had inside of me back in Vancouver? Why didn't I listen?* Now I was left with the burning question of where the two of them had run off to. My worst nightmare was materializing, and I was barely hanging on.

No matter what happens from this point, your Creator will never leave you to face it alone. Understanding why this happened is going to change everything.

My brother, Steve, had joined the military when he graduated from high school, and he and Grace were now living in Ottawa. Having recently returned from a six-month tour in the Middle East, he had been home in Windsor on disembarkation leave for the past two weeks. It was Steve's first night back at work in Ottawa when my father called him to let him know that Tim and Joan had run off together. Once the shock and disbelief wore off, Steve went to his boss and asked for a week of compassionate leave to deal with a family emergency. When Steve returned to Windsor the next morning, he and my father drove together to the Toronto Airport to bring my car back home. I had not been to work in the past few days. My emotions were raw and unpredictable, and I was in no condition to deal with the public. After they left for Toronto, I phoned my boss and told him that I would not be coming back to work, apologizing for the short notice.

The moving company called again about payment, and I assured them I would be in as soon as possible. First thing the next morning, I went to the bank. Tim had made a withdrawal two days earlier for $5,000, leaving a $15 balance in the account. I returned to my car and sat in the parking lot crying. *How could he do this to me and his son? It is bad enough he is gone, but to leave us with $15 to our name is humiliating. How could* *he be so selfish? The least he could have done was leave the money for the moving company.* Once I composed myself enough to drive, I headed back home. When I told my father and brother what had happened, they were as shocked as I was.

"This just keeps getting better and better. Never mind. We will handle it," Steve said. "You make lunch for TJ."

My brother stopped at his in-laws. They graciously wrote him a cheque for $2,000 which he cashed and took to the moving company to settle the account. My father told them to place the contents in storage and paid for the first two months of storage fees. When they returned home, I promised Steve that I would pay Grace's parents back. I did not know when that would happen, but I promised it would.

The reality had finally hit my father as he broke down. His marriage was over and so was mine. We poured ourselves a drink and sat down to talk. "I am so sorry that I did not believe you," my father said. "I am shocked she has done this. After twenty years of marriage, you think you know someone and then they do something like this. I don't get it."

I got it. This was personal. This was planned and orchestrated by Joan in order to attack me directly. I could feel it in my gut. Tim was just a means to an end. She did not want him nor did she love him. Her goal was to seduce him and destroy my marriage. She had succeeded. I had warned Tim before he left Vancouver to be careful with Joan, but he chose not to listen. He was caught in the black widow's web of lies and deceit, and he was just as much at fault as she was. He made the decision to get involved with her. I decided not to express my feelings out loud. I knew eventually the truth would come out. Joan would take pleasure in letting her feelings be known. It was only a matter of time.

Two days later, Tim's mother, Fran, phoned my father. She was living in Lac La Ronge, Saskatchewan on an Aboriginal Reserve and had taken Tim and Joan in when they called her from the Toronto Airport. They had just returned from spending five days in the Bahamas, using the $5000 cash he withdrew from our bank account, coupled with my father's credit card, for flights, hotels, clothing, drinks, and food. "Please don't hate me, Jim, for taking them in. He is my son, and they had nowhere else to go. I just thought you should know where they are."

33

Fran's phone call confirmed where they had run off to, and there was no question as to where they were now. Everything that I had planned for and all the money I had saved for a new start was gone towards a vacation for Tim and Joan. I pictured them on the beach - in the beautiful paradise setting, drinking, partying, and oblivious to the damage they had left behind for me and my father. To say I was bitter and resentful was an understatement. *How dare they! I despise them both, so much so, that they deserve each other.*

Be cautious. What is in your heart in human form is what you will become.

Is hating someone like drinking poison yourself and then waiting for the other person to die, when in reality, you are the one that is dying by being consumed in hate?

To add insult to injury for my father, Joan had the nerve to call the next day and ask him to send her clothes to her. "Why did you do this, Joan? If you were not happy in this marriage, you could have chosen any other man to leave me for. Why Laurie's husband?"

"I had to compete with her my whole life for your attention. I promised myself that one day when she got married, I would take her husband away from her, just like she took mine away from me for twenty years," she replied.

"I don't even know how to respond to that. You are sick, Joan. There was no competition. I loved her as my daughter and you as my wife, and I had enough love for both of you. You really need help."

My brother was shocked when my father conveyed their conversation to us. "Let's have a bonfire," Steve said. "Burn the bitch's clothes. I would." Although I am sure he was tempted, my father sent Joan her clothing a few days later.

Soon after my father got off the phone with Joan, the bank called. I had missed a payment on the car after I closed the bank account in British Columbia, and they had traced me to my Windsor account with my $15 balance. "I have no way of paying you. You will have to come and get the car," I said choking on the words. Within a few hours, a tow truck arrived and I tearfully handed over the keys to the driver. Now another piece of my life was gone too. In less than one month, I had no marriage, no job, no money, no car, and no home - along with a two-year-old baby boy who was depending on me to nourish his soul and provide a stable environment for him.

The next day while my father was at work, Steve and I had a heart-to-heart talk. He wanted me to go back to Ottawa with him. "You can't stay here, Laurie. Every time you two look at each other, it will be a constant reminder of what those two idiots did to you both. Ottawa is full of public service jobs, and you will probably find a job within a week. Come back with me," he said. At this point, I was not capable of thinking for myself. I had no idea what to do next or how to cope. The next morning after a tearful goodbye with my father, TJ and I were on our way to Ottawa. To what exactly, was unknown. I was in survival mode and trusting that Spirit had a plan.

Shortly after arriving in Ottawa, I interviewed for a job with Oceans and Fisheries and was hired. The lady currently in the job was retiring, and I would take her place in three weeks. I stopped into the welfare office on my way home and explained my situation, asking for some money to tide me over until I received my first paycheck. They cut me a cheque for $350 from their emergency fund to buy food and diapers.

During supper that night, Steve had news, but was not quite sure how to tell me. "Just say it. Nothing can come as a shock at this point," I said, but I was so wrong. Steve and Grace were being posted to Germany, and I had six weeks to find my own place to live.

I was still desperately trying to cope, living moment by moment. I looked at my son sleeping so peacefully that night and I was in awe at his beautiful face. He looked like a perfect little angel. I knew that he needed me now, more than ever. His father was gone and his mother was an emotional wreck. I had to find a way to pull myself together. *Please, Father, help me. I don't know what to do. I don't want to stay in Ottawa by myself. I feel so alone and I am frightened. Tell me what to do.*

I am here with you, My child. I will help you pick up the pieces. Trust in Me.

The following night during supper, I had a long conversation with Steve and Grace. I told them that I did not want to stay in Ottawa alone and that maybe going back to Windsor was the best solution. I had a support system there.

"I think that would be a bad decision, Laurie," my brother replied. "You have lots of Reserve experience. Why don't you go down to the Recruiting Centre and see what they have to offer? The military could become your new family, and your support system and you would have a career to look after your son. You might be surprised. You don't know if you don't try."

I took his advice and went to the Canadian Forces Recruiting Centre the next day. I was considered a 'skilled applicant' with my prior Reserve service, which meant I would probably bypass having to go to bootcamp and trades training. Chances are, I would be posted directly to a job on enrolment. That news sounded promising, so I made application to join the military on the spot and left the building scheduled for an interview the following week.

I was nervous as I sat waiting for my interview. I needed to put my best foot forward. My future was depending on it. Ten minutes later, there was just me and a Chief Petty Officer in the interview room. For the first fifteen minutes, I started out on a positive note and was doing well answering all his questions. When the topic of my family background came up, I began choking on my words. When he asked which parent the authoritarian in the family was, I burst into tears. I could no longer speak and I was sobbing uncontrollably. He handed me a box of tissue and left the room. A few minutes later, he returned with the Sergeant from the front counter who sat down in the chair beside me. He probably felt it was a good idea to have a witness in the room.

"I seem to have hit a nerve," the Chief began. "Your family appears to be a difficult topic for you. Do you think we can continue talking about them now?" he asked.

I explained that my emotions were still raw from my husband running off with my stepmother, and I apologized for my lack of control earlier. I could see the shock on his face, followed by the empathy, as my words registered.

"Is this just recent?" was his next question.

"Yes, within the last month," I replied.

"That explains a great deal now. I am sorry," he said.

"Please don't close my file because of my outburst. You are my only hope right now to find a new life for me and my son," I pleaded. We continued the interview for the next half hour, and then he thanked me for coming and closed the interview by saying that he would be in touch. I left that day thinking that I would never hear from him again.

The Recruiting Centre called back five days later with an offer of enrolment from National Defence Headquarters. If I chose to accept it, I was being offered a posting to the Canadian Forces Survival Training School (CFSTS) in Edmonton, Alberta, with an enrolment date of June 5. An appointment was made to meet again to sign the final paperwork and take my oath. My prayer to finding a new beginning had been answered without hesitation. *Thank you, Father, for this blessing and thank you for my brother coming to my rescue. Please bless my father now, as he tries to pick up the pieces of his life.*

My father decided to drive to Ottawa for a visit and to say goodbye in person. He brought the paperwork from the storage unit, in order for my furniture to be shipped from Windsor to Edmonton. The next step would be to take a house-hunting trip to find a place to live. I knew I could not live on the economy in Edmonton. I was a Private on a meager salary and without transportation. My brother spoke with his boss, who had a connection in Edmonton. After Steve's boss made a phone call, a message arrived the next day offering me a two-bedroom house on the base as my new residence on arrival. By the Grace of my Creator, everything seemed to be falling into place; every obstacle was being removed as quickly as it appeared.

After supper, I decided to take TJ around the block on his new tricycle that his grandfather had just brought for him. As I was walking, I summoned my Spirit Guide.

Call me Helena.

Everything is happening so fast, Helena. I know every day is a new opportunity, but I am just seeing it as another challenge to my existence, and I am overwhelmed with grief.

You need to let go of Tim. Hand over all your pain and sorrow. Letting go means you trust your Creator to pour out a blessing so great that nothing can compare.

That night when I went to bed, I took her advice, sobbing from the depths of my soul, while begging for His healing for my son's sake. Once again, my Creator did not disappoint.

Spiritual Beings on a Human Experience

Laurie's soul is privy to the knowledge of what has transpired between Joan and Tim as she overhears their conversation from the bathtub. Her soul is being blessed and enlightened with the truth and reality of the situation, while the Holy Spirit protects her heart and mind with White Light. Trauma automatically rewires the brain for protection, but White Light brings immediate peace and clarity. Amidst all the devastation, her son's soul becomes her priority as she fully awakens, composed and able to face her truth with logic, in order to tend to her son.

The Creator sees all and knows all. Laurie's soul's arrival in human form and the lessons she needs to learn in this lifetime have been designed by her with His blessing. Although she is not able to remember the blueprint they designed together, He will attempt to keep her on the chosen path of her journey.

He speaks to the heart of Laurie's recruiter. She is an unsuitable candidate for recruitment - out of the preferred age range, a single parent, financially destitute, and emotionally distraught, yet her recruiter gives her file a glowing review when he forwards it for consideration. Her Creator provides her with a new beginning in a world she is already familiar with. He has been preparing her for her future since she was a young Sea Cadet at sixteen years old. She is also blessed with the military's choice for her first posting, although the blessing has yet to unfold before her eyes. He rewards his child for her belief and trust in Him with a brand-new beginning on her chosen path.

By design, Laurie's soul has been connected to her brother's soul since the age of six - a deep, nurturing bond of understanding due to their chaotic, abusive, and neglectful home environment. Her brother immediately responds to her situation with love and compassion as he tries to help her rebuild her life. He is instrumental in her new beginning, which quickly transpires due to her geographical location with him in Ottawa. Their relationship is meant to withstand the test of time as they part and come back together several times throughout their individual journeys. Their bond is unbreakable - a bond of common experience.

CHAPTER 4

GRACE GIVES US WINGS TO SOAR

How do you start with a new beginning that you did not expect or, perhaps, even want? I was experiencing insurmountable fear, unbearable pain, cruel injustice, and family tragedy - not joy or excitement. I felt like my life force had been spilled away with all the devastation of the past few months and I was struggling. *Please Spirit World, give me the courage to accept this change and the strength to start over again.*

Take heart and trust that the work of self-change is progressing in your life. This is your immediate contact with your own true destiny, which rises like the phoenix from the ashes.

I definitely paid attention to those words. I wanted to be that bird rising up. I wanted to be self-sufficient, and I wanted to be happy again. I wanted my life force back, but most of all, I wanted stability. In a three-month span, I had left Vancouver with the intention of a new beginning in Windsor, I left Windsor with the intention of a new beginning in Ottawa, and now I was leaving Ottawa with the intention of a new beginning in Edmonton. *Have I come full circle? Has the West Coast been my destiny all along? It somehow feels like home.*

It is oddly freeing to walk through your fear and through the worst thing that you could ever image happening to you.

I thanked my brother and his wife for their love and support and for taking us in so unexpectedly. I wished them well on their new adventure to Germany while hugging them both goodbye. I walked down the ramp, boarded the airplane, and settled my son into his seat. We were starting a brand-new life together, just the two of us.

TJ fell asleep shortly after takeoff, so the three-and-a-half-hour flight left me with lots of time to reflect on my life. As the sun appeared through the clouds, I thought of my childhood with Cindy, the unbreakable bond we had, and how happy we always were together. Even as adults, time and distance had not changed a single thing between us. I thought of my high-school friends and the experiences I had shared with them. They were instrumental in fulfilling my need to belong. For a fleeting moment, I thought of my first kiss with Jason and smiled, wondering where life had taken him. I thought of Lloyd. Even after all this time, I missed his smile, his comforting touch, and our nights of insatiable love making. He had removed my fear of human touch and for that alone, I was thankful he had been my first love. I wondered if I ever crept into his thoughts occasionally, like he did into mine. I thought of my mother and the year we had spent together in Montreal getting to know each other. A foundation for us to bond had begun during that year, but I was still conflicted with her abandonment and the childhood I had to endure because of it. Having said that, I was happy to have her in my life again. I thought of my father needing to start his life over after a twenty-year marriage shattered, and my heart went out to him. I knew the pain of starting over firsthand. Maybe his blessing in all of this was to finally be free from a psychotic spouse; leaving him with the ability to open himself up to finding true happiness with a normal person.

As TJ stirred a little, I covered him again. I realized in that moment that everything I had been through with Tim had left me with two blessings. First, and perhaps the biggest blessing of all, was that I had this precious little boy. Secondly, I was finally free of Joan for good and that was worth its weight in gold. Now, I needed to stay strong and embrace this new future that my Creator had so graciously provided.

When we arrived at the Edmonton International Airport, my sponsor was there to meet us. Her name was Rhoda, and she was my new boss. Rhoda was petite in stature, with strawberry blonde hair and a quiet, mature demeanor. She was a few years older than me and married to a military spouse, and they had a four-year-old son named Wayne. Little did

I know at the time, but we would become lifelong friends. Rhoda would be the pivotal person in my life for the next year as I adjusted to a new city and a new career and struggled to be rid of my past.

She drove me by a two-bedroom house in Griesbach, known in military terminology as PMQs (Private Married Quarters), so I could see where I would be living. It was the perfect little wartime house for the two of us. We continued a few kilometers further down the road to Lancaster Park, so she could show me where I would be working. Then she dropped us off at a hotel for the night, saying she would be back to pick us up in the morning.

In 1984, Canadian Forces Base Edmonton consisted of two bases located in the north end of the city. Griesbach began at 97th Street and 137th Avenue. The base was mainly comprised of PMQs and barrack blocks for transient personnel, but it also had a gas station with a corner store, the Junior Ranks Mess, the Canadian Forces Service Prison and Detention Barracks (CFSPDB), and the Canadian Airborne Centre (CABC). CABC was an instructional school to qualify Airborne soldiers in basic parachute, free fall, and jumpmaster courses. The Detention Barracks was a small, twenty-five cell prison run under a very rigid penal system. It was used for punishing and attempting to reform military personnel required to serve any judicial sentence of two years, less a day. I would feel those metal bars close behind me within my first year on the base.

A little further north down 97th Street was another base known as Lancaster Park. At that time, it was an air base and the main base of the two. Off to the left side of the highway, there were more PMQs that housed aircrew and officers. To the right of the highway was the main base, where you had to enter via a Military Police guardhouse. The base logistical support consisted of the Base Headquarters, Base Hospital, Dental Unit, CF Supply Depot, Base Transportation, Base Accommodation, Military Police, and the Air Movements Unit (AMU). Operational Units occupying the base at the time were 435 Hercules Squadron, 440 Search and Rescue Squadron, and 408 Tactical Helicopter Squadron. There were two runways and a traffic control tower for aircraft, with the Canadian Forces Survival Training School (CFSTS) located near the end of one of the runways. CFSTS was going to be my place of employment for the next two years.

On Monday morning, I picked up the keys from Base Accommodation and returned to the PMQ to wait for the movers. I did not have much for them to unload from the truck, so they were gone within two hours. I spent the next few hours unpacking boxes and trying to set up a home with what little we had. I did not have a car, but the grocery store was only a block away. I put TJ in his wagon, and we ventured off to buy some cereal and milk. I paid for the items, stuffed them into my backpack, and I walked back home. TJ was cranky and not feeling well, so I set up his crib after we had a bowl of cereal together. For the next two hours while he napped, I unpacked my kitchen contents through little bursts of tears.

When my son awoke from his nap, he had a fever, his nose was running, and he had developed a horrible cough that sounded like a seal barking. I had some broth and a package of noodles that I had unpacked earlier, so I decided to make some chicken noodle soup. He ate a bowl of soup and seemed better by bedtime. I figured I would wait until the morning to get some medicine for him.

I had two more boxes to unpack, and it was close to midnight when I heard TJ struggling to breathe. I grabbed him in my arms and ran to the front door. I did not have a car or a phone so I was looking for a neighbor who still had their lights on. I ran across the street with TJ in my arms. When the gentleman answered the door, he witnessed my tears and flung the door wide open. "Please sir, can you call an ambulance. I don't have a phone and my son can't breathe." The neighbor rushed me to the hospital in his own car, with his wife in the backseat holding TJ. His wife was a nurse, so she monitored his ability to get air into his lungs and responded appropriately as needed. There was no doubt in my mind that this kind couple saved my son's life that night. TJ was admitted to the hospital upon arrival and set up in an oxygen tent. Diagnosis: croup. Croup causes swelling and narrowing in the voice box, windpipe, and breathing tubes that lead to the lungs, thus, his struggle to breathe. Within twenty-four hours, he had gone from a happy little boy running around to breathing in an oxygen tent. Three days later, it was hard to believe that he was the same little boy that I had brought to the hospital. I was amazed at how quickly he bounced back.

Despite the fact that I had not been to work yet, my new Search and Rescue family rallied around me instantaneously. They took turns driving me to the hospital, picking me up at the end of the day or feeding me a meal. Search and Rescue is an elite trade and highly sought after in the military. The trade is only available to people who are already in the military and is extremely competitive to enter. There are twelve candidates chosen each year from across Canada to undergo the eight-month training program at CFSTS with the result that one or two more would fail throughout the training process. Due to their small numbers, the trade is closely knit. I realized that I had been blessed with a new family of incredibly special people. I was a virtual stranger to the staff at the school, yet I already had a sense of belonging.

For the next few months, I was busy organizing my life and dealing with past issues that kept continually resurfacing. Perhaps a physical life is designed that way. You cannot continue with a productive future until you absolve yourself of the past.

I finally had a phone connected and called my parents to give them my number. When I had left Ottawa, my father decided to call my mother to tell her what had transpired between Tim and me and to let her know that I was struggling financially. "She could really use your help right now, Laura. Unfortunately, Joan has left me in an awful financial mess. Your daughter needs you now more than ever," he said.

When I called to give my mother my phone number and tell her what was going on in my life, she wanted to come for a visit. She had moved from Montreal to Toronto the year before and was now living with a man named Donald, who also had a daughter living in Edmonton. "I will give you some time to get settled, darling, but maybe we could come for a visit in the new year. In the meantime, I am going to send you a cheque for $1000 to help you get settled." I was shocked and thankful as I hung up the phone.

Later that evening, the lady living in the PMQ next door to me came over and introduced herself. She and her husband were being posted to Germany in a few months, and they were selling most of their belongings in lieu of putting them in storage. I ended up buying a queen size waterbed and a lawnmower from them. They threw in an old television for free, to tide me over until I could afford to buy another one. That television took twenty minutes to warm up before you could see a picture, but it was better than nothing at all. She also offered to babysit TJ until I could find a permanent solution.

A week had gone by since my arrival. It was Monday morning and time to go to work. Rhoda picked me up and we drove to work together, chatting on the way. Getting some form of transportation was a priority for me now, and she mentioned that one of the staff at the school was selling his daughter's car. It was an older car and perfect for the time being. The money from my mother could pay for the car and buy my independence from relying on or troubling others. Life was coming together, little by little.

My job at CFSTS was to logistically prepare for the arrival of students. That entailed typing nominal rolls, arranging for meals and accommodation, and typing reports at the end of each course. The school was an extremely busy place. The Search and Rescue (SAR) side of the house was responsible for teaching the eight-month Basic SAR Tech course, together with running several medical refresher courses for the trade, throughout the year.

The survival training side of the house was established to teach ground search, land survival, sea survival, and Artic survival to aircrew. There were several pilots and air navigators on staff for those courses, and they were augmented by the SAR Techs who were available as training requirements permitted. I loved my job and the staff I was working with. I looked forward to going to work every morning.

A few weeks after I had arrived, I ran into more hot water with Scotia Bank. They had traced me to Edmonton and sent a legal letter claiming that I still owed them $4000 for the car they had repossessed in Windsor. Unknowingly, I had signed a chattel mortgage when I took out the car loan, meaning the entire amount of the loan was due. Since they received $5000 for the car at auction and $3000 had already been paid off, I was now on the hook for the other $4000. I was struggling financially as it was and had no way of paying this extra amount. Rhoda offered to help and made an appointment for me to see the Base Financial Officer. He negotiated with the bank to drop the payment to $2000 and suggested they go after Tim for the other $2000 since the car was jointly owned. The Benevolent Fund paid off my debt with Scotia Bank for $2000 on the condition that a legal document be provided removing me from any further obligation to the bank in the future. In return, I was required to pay the Benevolent Fund back with a payment of $100 a month.

Now I was in a situation where I could not afford daycare for my son. I was put in touch with an Edmonton Social Services Worker, who agreed to augment his daycare costs until such time as I could afford to pay the full amount myself. The catch was TJ had to be placed in a licensed daycare, not with a private babysitter. I busied myself getting that set up. Each time my financial situation changed, such as a promotion or a pay increase, I had to provide the paperwork to Social Services, and they would adjust my costs accordingly.

Less than two weeks later, my past reared its ugly head once again. This time, Tim wanted to come for a visit. I was apprehensive and had no desire to see him again. However, I felt it was important for him to be a part of his son's life, so I agreed to the visit. When he arrived at my front door, I was calm and my feelings were indifferent. As he wrapped his arms around me to hug me "hello", my skin began to crawl. His touch, after he had been with Joan, was blood curdling to me and I pulled away quickly.

"What's wrong?" he asked.

"Do you really have to ask? You touching me is repulsive. This visit is about your son, not about me. Our marriage is over, and we should start thinking about getting a divorce," I replied.

"But Joan and I are not together anymore. She buggered off with some other guy a few days after we arrived in Saskatchewan. I really am very sorry for what I did to you. If I could take it back, I would. Can't we just move on from here?" he continued.

"That is exactly what I am doing. I am moving on without you. I will never deny you access to your son, but as for you and me, there is nothing left, so there is no going back. You burned me twice, Tim, by taking off on me, and I will never give you the chance to do it again. I should have been done with you after the first time. You saying you are sorry now has no meaning whatsoever."

Does he really think that by coming here, he is going to be part of our lives again? How very brazen of him. He left me high and dry without a second thought. He might be sorry now and want his family back, but I certainly am not going to live in a loveless marriage for the next sixteen years for TJ's sake. I want to live my life at the same time as I raise my son and be happy doing it.

When you make a choice, something always gets sacrificed. It is the balance of the Universe.

Tim spent a few hours at the park with his son while I made supper. After supper, he bathed him, and they settled together on the couch to read books and watch television. I had agreed to Tim spending the night with the plan that he and TJ could sleep together in my room, and I would sleep on the couch. The next morning, I took my cup of coffee out to the backyard. I felt melancholy and I was not sure why. Before I got a sip of coffee past my lips, TJ and Tim were up. Tim buckled his son into the highchair, gave him a bowl of cereal, poured himself a cup of coffee and sat down at the kitchen table. I came in from outside and sat directly across the table from Tim. He looked different. He was not acting arrogant or self-centered. He had a quiet stillness and his eyes were glassy with tears. In that moment, I could feel his pain.

I don't understand. My anger and pain are gone but now I am feeling sad with his pain. What is going on?

Compassionate empathy is your soul speaking to you. Embrace his soul with yours and release him.

In that moment, it was clear to me what needed to happen instinctively. I emptied my head of my own thoughts and let the words of my soul speak to Tim. These words were not spoken out loud. My soul was speaking to his soul through my thoughts. *I forgive you for your choice to leave your family behind. I forgive you for the pain and turmoil that was caused by that choice. I thank you for the journey together and the precious little soul that resulted from it.* As the last thought left my soul, my sadness immediately lifted.

Tim left shortly after his coffee to go back to Saskatchewan. He disappeared from my thoughts almost immediately, like a puff of smoke in the wind. A week later, I received a cassette tape in the mail. It was a recording Tim had made acknowledging what he had done and apologizing for it. Within the next two sentences, he declared that he was not going to be a "weekend dad". He was not going to come to visit TJ, knowing that I was with another man. If I wanted him to be part of his son's life, it would have to be "all or nothing".

How juvenile and selfish! Am I supposed to live like a nun for the next sixteen years while he goes on with his life so that he does not have to witness me eventually finding happiness with someone else? Being a dick must be hard. No pun intended. What did I ever see in this jerk?

At the end of the recording, I was appalled. He was back in his physical self again. It was all about him and what he wanted. It always had been. My intuition told me to keep that cassette. One day when TJ was old enough to understand, the cassette would explain everything that happened between us, in his father's own words. That was the last that I heard from Tim. I did not reply. There was no need. I had made my position clear during his visit, and I had already let go of the relationship. Being alone felt better than being in a relationship with him. Just in case he should have a change of heart with regards to being a part of his son's life, I sent a Christmas card to his mother every year with a photo. She always knew where to find us and had a telephone number to call anytime.

The lady next door stopped in one Tuesday night. They were a few days away from leaving for Germany, and she was wondering if I wanted her son's waterbed and stereo to put in TJ's room. TJ was not far off from needing another bed. He was quickly outgrowing his crib, so I took her up on her offer. She refused to take any money from me. Her husband moved the bed over and set it up for me that night. My son now had a queen size waterbed in his room. She even threw in the bedding. I put the stereo in my living room on top of the television, delighted that I finally had music back in my life.

In September, I received a phone call from an old friend from HMCS *Hunter*. Anne had been in Edmonton working with the Reserves for the past six months and had heard that I had joined the military and was now in Edmonton as well. On Friday night, she stopped by with her boyfriend, Jeff, and we opened a bottle of wine and began reminiscing. Anne and Jeff were engaged and planning to marry in the spring. It would mean so much to her if TJ and I would attend the wedding. I agreed to at least attend the marriage ceremony.

In October, we had a ground search course arriving at the school for training. The Captain running the course came into the office and asked Rhoda if she was able to let me go from the office for two weeks. One of the scheduled students was unable to attend and had cancelled last minute. He needed another female to take her place. The course entailed a week of classroom training, followed by four days in the field to execute the training learned. Rhoda looked at me. "If you would like to take the course, Laurie, I will watch TJ for you. It is only for four days." I hesitated for two reasons. Rhoda was pregnant with her second child, so her energy level was low and I did not want to burden her. My second reason for hesitating was the thought of leaving my son without his mother.

Is it too soon? This will be the first time that I will be away from him, and I am nervous leaving him. His little life has been so topsy-turvy.

There is no higher calling than to raise a child but have faith that children are resilient.

I agreed to take the course and was glad I did. Spending time with other adults and having some alone time for me was exactly what I needed. My son made out just as well at Rhoda's house. He quickly became friends with her son, Wayne. They were both an 'only child' so having a playmate was exciting for them. I had worried for nothing. My son was definitely resilient.

Two weeks before Christmas I received a card in the mail from the Base Benevolent Fund. Enclosed was a cheque made out for $500 with a note attached, "Please accept this donation as a gift sent to provide Christmas for you and your son. Merry Christmas." I was moved to tears by the generosity. *Thank you once again, Heavenly Father. You always seem to know just what I need when I need it.*

I bought a live Christmas tree from a tree lot, a stand to hold it, a string of lights, and some craft supplies. Every night after supper, my son and me would embark on a craft project together. Our mission: to make ornaments for the tree. We cut out paper angels, made strings of popcorn, put toothpicks into foam balls and spray painted them silver and made stars from pipe cleaners. TJ's personal achievement was an ornament he had made for me by gluing Smarties into a pinecone, except for the chocolate ones, which he was consuming. He was beaming with pride as he hugged me and said, "This is for you, Mommy." We ended up making more pinecones together because they were so colorful. His idea turned out to be the masterpiece of the tree.

I bought my son some new pajamas, a winter coat, some Hot Wheels cars (one in particular that would be the death of me), and some coloring books and crayons. I spent $100 on groceries to restock my cupboards and fridge. I was looking forward to the holidays now instead of dreading its arrival. A package arrived from my father with presents for TJ and a box of Turtles for me. Turtles were my favorite chocolates back then and still are to this day. The tradition of that box of chocolates every Christmas would continue from 1984 until my father's death. My mother sent a card with $200 in it, along with photocopies of airline tickets. She and Donald were coming for a visit from February 10 to 21. I was looking forward to 1985 and what the year would bring. It was definitely off to a good start.

My mother's visit could not have gone any better. We had not seen each other since I left Montreal in 1978, so we had lots to talk about. On Valentine's Day, I came home from work to find a brand-new floor cabinet television. Televisions were furniture back in those days. There was also a new coffee table with a dozen red roses in a vase centered on it. The card read, "To my beautiful daughter. I love you more than you know, Mom." The eleven days flew by. My mother spent countless hours with TJ and several more with me, once he was in bed for the night. A few days before they were due to leave, my mother and Donald went out for a few hours to visit with Donald's daughter. When they returned home, we made ourselves a drink and sat down to chat.

"I hope you don't mind, Laurie," Donald began. "I gave your phone number to my daughter tonight. Sharron is single and your age. She has been living in Alberta for a while now, knows a lot of people, and I think you both would really like each other." *Mind? Why would I mind? She might be the final piece of the puzzle that is missing. I really need a social life away from work.* I told him that I was looking forward to hearing from her and thanked him.

Less than a week later, there was a knock at my front door. "You must be Laurie. Hi, I'm Sharron, Donald's daughter. Can I come in?" I welcomed her inside and we spent a few hours getting to know each other. Sharron was outgoing, confident, and very independent. I sensed from some of our conversation that she had quite the colored past, like me. We clicked immediately. I was particularly impressed with the cute little swagger she had when she walked and her playful vocabulary when she spoke. Sharron and I became inseparable from that night on. Our journey together had begun and would last for decades to come.

In order to close the door to my past, I had one final thing I needed to do. When I filed my income tax in March, I had a $2,400 refund coming. When the refund arrived in the mail, I purchased a thank-you card, placed a $2,000 cheque inside, and mailed it to Grace's parents. They had never met me, yet they were willing to lend a hand to a stranger in a time of need, without any hesitation or expectation of return. I never forgot their act of kindness.

My first nine months in Edmonton had flashed by like the speed of a shooting star. I had the perfect little home. I had a career that was fulfilling. I had my own transportation again. I had a military family. Heck, I even had a new sister. I had discarded my marriage for good, and I had cleaned up the financial wreckage from it. Like the phoenix, I had risen from the ashes, but the Universe evolves on balance. It would not be long before I would fall from Grace. It would be a colossal fall - a fall that would push me to make the decision to abandon my Spirit World entirely.

Spiritual Beings on a Human Experience

The Creator sees far beyond Laurie's pain and suffering and provides her with a new beginning as He promised. He does not condemn her for her poor choices, but instead, frees her from being chained in the deep, dark pit of her past choices.

Grace is a journey with direction, not a destination. Grace provides a time of joyful deliverance for a soul. Laurie's difficult state of mind is clarified with a new life and a new path, and she is blessed with the strength to achieve completion and resolution with her past. Movement to the unknown can involve danger, and yet, timely movement releases what a soul needs to leave behind. It is liberation from unconscious action and liberation from oppression caused by emotional turmoil. Grace soothes the pain of loss and makes the risk of loss worth taking again.

It is time for Laurie's soul to let go of her marriage. Her relationship with Tim was entered into out of a sense of neediness, feeling incomplete, and the fear of being alone. When happiness depends on another soul, the relationship is doomed by a loss of freedom to love out of choice as opposed to need.

Tim and Laurie's souls are in a past life karmic connection meant to shake them up and change them deep inside. Karmic connections can be the most destructive, toxic, and painful experiences for a soul, but with the balance of the Universe, karmic connections also cleanse the soul and help the soul let go of its limiting behaviors so it can grow again. Her Spirit Guide revels in her decision. She has finally decided to stop trying to force a happy ending to a story that was never meant to be. Their relationship has served its purpose of karmic debt, and now she is open for a true spiritual companion to enter.

Laurie has realized from a young age that she possesses the ability to connect to Spirit. Her choice to do so has allowed her to experience energy in a way that many souls do not when they are in human form – to feel the energy of her own soul, as well as the souls of others around her, with extreme intensity.

The physical self comes to life when the energy of the soul enters, and the soul evolves by exchanging energy with other souls throughout the journey. In her own personal journey of self-change, Laurie experiences Tim's soul's energy by his sadness at the breakfast table and responds with her soul's energy to remove the sadness through forgiveness. Their karmic connection has now ended because it has served its purpose. She is unaware that this experience is her introduction to working in the healing arts. Once again, her Creator is preparing her to align with the blueprint she designed.

CHAPTER 5

GRACEFULLY BROKEN BUT BEAUTIFULLY STANDING

Everything that we experience in a physical life is followed by the Law of Karma - a law of action and consequence. The past has resulted in the present, and the present will shape the future. Karmic debt owed *by you* to another soul or debt owed *to you* by another soul will always surface on a physical journey in one form or another. The list is never ending because it encompasses human interactions in general. The karmic connection may be based on finances, inability to love, anger, revenge, deceit, laziness, blaming others for your actions, commitment issues, selfishness, being superficial, or battling addictions - just to mention a few. Repaying karmic debt is designed to help the soul grow, usually is short lived, and normally shows up when a soul has behaved badly in a previous lifetime and rectification is required.

I was feeling good about my life again. My job at CFSTS was more rewarding than ever imaginable. Although my work was demanding and fast-paced, I was quick to learn and willing to take on any additional requests as a challenge to learning my trade. Rhoda was the perfect boss to develop my abilities. With each task she taught me and I accomplished, there was another one to follow. I was always evolving because of her. At the same time, we had bonded on a personal level. She was compassionate, friendly, considerate, and the adult definition of fun in our social settings.

Occasionally, when there were no students in house, the school staff would get together in the student lounge on a Friday afternoon. Once the alcohol fountain began to flow, tall tales emerged, followed by hysterical bouts of laughter and more tales. It was the perfect way to end a week or start off a weekend. One of my fondest memories was Rumtopf - a sweet and very boozy concoction that threw a wicked punch. Between the fruit that had been fermenting in rum for six weeks and the straight rum itself over ice, one glass was enough to fire you up well into the evening. We were all young, and we were playing as hard as we were working.

My son was three years old now. He had survived the terrible twos, but only by the Grace of God. Anyone who has been a single parent can tell you the challenges of dealing with a small child by themselves, and I am sure my Creator had purposely blessed me with an abundance of patience for playing this role single-handedly. All in all, TJ was a good child, but he definitely kept me on my toes. He was strong willed and independent, but he was also easy to appease and affectionate. Maybe in the task of raising children alone you lose your mind a little bit, but you definitely find your soul.

The Air Force was celebrating its 61st Anniversary in March of 1985. To commemorate the occasion, we had all gathered on the tarmac to witness a fly past of three of our Hercules airplanes. It was a sunny afternoon, and I was standing in a crowd of people from 435 Squadron. We could see the three airplanes approaching 1,000 feet above the runway. The first Hercules flew past and began to bank off to the right on a forty-five-degree angle. The second Hercules was directly behind. The idea of the formation was for the second pilot to count so many seconds in order to pass the first airplane and then bank himself. Due to pilot error, the second Hercules banked too soon, causing it to come into direct contact with the belly of the first airplane. Witnessing what had just happened, the third Hercules banked to the left immediately, flying away to safety. There was a massive explosion as the first two airplanes collided and began plummeting to the ground in a giant fireball. Flames leapt hundreds of feet into the air, as the crowd began dispersing to avoid the raining down debris that was falling from the sky.

Edmonton ambulance workers were on strike at the time, but they immediately dropped their picket signs and headed for the base. The base had two fuel storage tanks holding thousands of liters of aviation fuel, and debris from the explosion was landing within feet of those storage tanks. The base was quickly evacuated as fire trucks, ambulances, and rescue personnel scurried to try and bring the fires under control. What had started out as a celebration had instantly turned into a disaster, resulting in ten aircrew losing their lives. That dismal day became known as 'Black Friday' for CFB Edmonton and marked the end of an era for all non-operational formation flying.

When I left the base, I picked up my son from daycare and dropped him off at the babysitter for the night. Through Rhoda, I had found a babysitter with flexible hours. Candy would charge me a $20 babysitting fee for my son to spend a Friday night at her place. There were always lots of children at her house, so he loved going there. It was a fun Friday night out for him too. When I walked in the door of my PMQ, I called Sharron. She was working as an Animal Health Technician at The Spay Clinic and would be on her way home from work shortly. I left her a message on her answering machine to meet me at the Junior Ranks Mess in Griesbach. I did not want to sit home that night. I needed a diversion from my thoughts.

I took my uniform off and climbed into the shower. As the water cascaded over my body, I began praying. *Heavenly Father, I know that the ten souls who left us today are with You. My prayer is for those left behind. Please bring peace and comfort to the families and guard the minds of the rescue personnel from what they will see when recovering the bodies.* By the time I had showered and done my hair and makeup, Sharron was at my door. "I saw your car when I drove by so I thought I would stop here first. I heard what happened on the base. It is all over the radio for people to avoid the north end of the city. Did you see the planes crash?" she asked.

"I was standing right there, and I can't get the vision out of my head, nor the sound," I replied. "That's why I called you and left my message. I really need to go out and have some fun tonight."

When we walked into the Griesbach Junior Ranks Mess, the place was packed with Airborne soldiers. As we stood in line to get our drinks, every eye in the place was fixated on us. We were unfamiliar faces. Once we made our way to the bar, we were greeted by a tall, thin, beautiful, blonde-haired girl named Debbie. "Hi. What can I get you girls?" We ordered two drinks each, taking advantage of happy hour and found a table to sit at. Within twenty minutes, we had several people join us, and the party had begun. The group grew from a handful of us to over thirty people as tables were being pulled together and chairs added on. Every time we got close to the bottom of our glass, we had several more drinks in front of us, compliments of the boys. That night, Sharron and I were introduced to a new family of friends, including a girl named Lynn who would become my roommate within a short span of time.

We noticed our table dwindling down in numbers around 10:00 p.m. that night. When Lynn came back from the washroom, she sat down with us to finish her drink. "Everyone is heading over to the Rosslyn now. Did you guys want to come?" she asked. There was no need to ask us twice. It was either go hard or go home, and we were not going home yet. We downed our drinks and followed Lynn out the door.

The Rosslyn was a neighborhood pub on the corner of 97th Street and 137th Avenue, and it was only one block walking distance from there to my PMQ. When we walked through the door, the pub was small and quaint with a clientele of both military and civilians and a DJ who knew how to keep the dance floor filled. The music was a mixture of eighties tunes, with oldies from the seventies thrown in. If you were not at the Rosslyn by 11:00 p.m., you would probably have to stand in line to enter. Sharron and I continued partying with the Airborne until the bar's overhead lights came on. From the Rosslyn, we went to Boston Pizza for something to eat and finally poured ourselves into my bed around 5:00 a.m. What a night! We had a ball, and there was no doubt that we were going to pay the price the next morning. I definitely did. I had to sleep on my stomach with one leg over the side of the bed, planted on the floor in order to stop the spins due to the motion of the waterbed.

First thing Monday morning, our Captain called Rhoda into his office. My Career Manager had called from Ottawa on Friday. The Captain had been working on an accelerated promotion for me and the message was on its way. I was being promoted from a Private to a Corporal a year earlier than expected. "This Friday coming is Bosses' Night at the Junior Ranks

Mess in Lancaster Park. I think we should get everyone together and celebrate Laurie's promotion," he said.

"Great timing. I will extend the invitation to all the staff. In fact, I heard rumors that male and female strippers are slated for entertainment. Should be a night to remember," Rhoda said as she left his office.

Bosses' Night is a military tradition, usually held once or twice a year, depending on the base. The Junior Ranks Mess is a military drinking establishment for just that, Junior Ranks (Privates, Corporals, and Master Corporals). Being caught in a mess that is not rank suitable is a chargeable offence. However, that rank restriction is lifted for a Bosses' Night. It is a chance for senior ranks to acknowledge the work of their lower ranks by sitting and having a few drinks together. The Lancaster Park Mess was ten times the size of the Griesbach Mess with a massive dance floor, a stage, and two bars. We closed the school at 3:30 p.m. that Friday and made our way over to the Mess. Rhoda had arranged for her husband to pick up TJ from the daycare and take him back to their place for the night. I was free to party again. Another night of fun was on the horizon.

I placed $100 on the bar, another tradition for a person who has been promoted, and told the bartender to keep the drinks flowing to our table. It was happy hour so the money went twice as far, as we all sat drinking and talking. Several SAR Techs from 440 Squadron joined us within the next hour, and before we knew it, we had confiscated most of the upper floor tables. It was the perfect spot with our own washrooms handy and a second bar that was not as busy as the one on the main level. When I came back from a visit to the Ladies Room, I had several shots of tequila on the table in front of my chair. I had never drunk tequila before nor would I again for quite some time. I immediately got a body stone, followed by a head stone. I could not walk and I could not talk. I just sat in my chair grinning from ear to ear as they all laughed at me. I was lost in a vegetative state, minus the drooling of course. I do not remember much of the evening or how I got home, but I certainly paid the price the next day. Tequila and I were not compatible.

Ann and Jeff's wedding was just around the corner. I took TJ to the mall to buy him a new outfit and bought a dress for myself at the same time. When Saturday rolled around, he was excited to get dressed up in a suit. Once he did, he looked so adorable that it brought tears to my eyes. *My little man!* I put some books, a juice box, and some cookies into his backpack. "Okay kiddo, let's go or we are going to be late," I said trying to get his shoes on.

"I need my countach," he said.

"I have no idea what that is, but we don't have time," I replied. He just kept screaming "countach" at the top of his lungs. "TJ, enough please. I will find it for you when we get back home."

Ann had asked me to go to the front of the church to the pews on the left-hand side. She wanted TJ to be able to see everything. Ann was raised in the Roman Catholic faith and Jeff was Jewish, so I assumed the mass would be a short one as we settled into that front pew. I was wrong. After thirty minutes, I was struggling to keep TJ quiet. Now it had been forty-five minutes, and he was bored. He had eaten his cookies, drank his juice, and read his books. After communion, the priest returned to the alter, raised his arms into the air, and claimed, "Let us give thanks to the Lord our God."

Before I even saw it coming, the words were out of his mouth. TJ screamed, "Thank you. Can we go now?" The entire church broke into laughter, including the priest. My son had spoken out loud what everyone else was thinking.

I was preparing the nominal roll for the next SAR Tech medical refresher course one morning, when the SAR Chief came into the office and asked me to book him a flight to Ottawa for that Thursday. "I plan to catch up with an old friend while I am there, so don't book my return flight until Sunday," he said. I prepared the paperwork he needed and booked his flight, leaving the information in his mailbox. When I returned to preparing the nominal roll, I noticed Brad's name. *Could it be? It is the same name. Is it possible that Brad remustered from his trade in the Navy and is now a SAR Tech?* I flashed back to my time in Victoria. My heart was racing. I would know soon enough. He would be showing up for his course in July.

On Monday morning when the mail arrived, Rhoda asked me to log it in and distribute it. Among the correspondence was a message for me to attend a six-week course at CFB Borden in Ontario. It was the next level of my trade training that I needed to complete in order to keep my new rank.

I handed the message to Rhoda, and we began discussing it. She would need to cover my job for the six weeks I would be gone, and I would need to figure out what to do with my son. "My mother would probably take him if I asked her to," I said. "My dilemma is how to get him to Ontario."

At that time, the Canadian Forces had five of its own Boeing 707's that were used for transporting military personnel domestically and internationally, with one of those Boeings available for government VIP transportation at all times. I could book my son on the same flight as I would be taking, but he would be booked as a Priority 5 Passenger, meaning he would only get on the flight if a seat were available. That was too risky to consider because it was too last minute to come up with a Plan B if the flight was fully booked.

"Talk to Barry," Rhoda said. "There are going to be several Hercs (Hercules aircraft) flying to Edmonton from Trenton to bring out troops and equipment for RV 85." Rendezvous (RV for short) was a large Canadian Forces Military Exercise held every two years in Wainwright, Alberta. It involved several countries training soldiers for a high level of readiness, with a mission to be able to deploy anywhere in the world they are needed. "The Hercs return to Trenton empty," Rhoda continued. "Maybe they would be willing to take your son as crew, but you would have to make sure that someone is in Trenton to pick him up."

Our conversation was interrupted when the School Chief came into the office with his paperwork from his trip. "I ran into a friend of yours in Ottawa, and he said to say hello."

A friend of mine? I don't know anyone in Ottawa. I looked at him puzzled. The friend he was talking about was the Chief Warrant Officer from the Recruiting Centre. "For him to remember you, out of the countless faces he sees, speaks volumes. You must have left quite an impression on him," he said.

"Oh Chief, if you only knew," I replied. I am sure I was probably the only applicant that had a hysterical breakdown during a job interview.

Barry, an instructor at CFSTS, was employed as an Air Navigator with 435 Squadron when he was not instructing. I talked to him about my situation with my son, he made a phone call over to the Squadron, and the deal was done. My son was going to Ontario to spend time with his grandmother while I was on my career course.

I talked to my mother that night. She was excited about having her grandson for six weeks. "Donald and I will travel to Trenton to pick him up. It is not that far from Toronto, honey. Just give us the details of when and where once you have everything confirmed."

When the time came for TJ's flight, and we arrived at the AMU, I was unsure how he would react to being put on an aircraft by himself. *Is he going to fuss? Is he going to cry and refuse to go?* Hand in hand, we walked out to the aircraft together. The loadmaster took his luggage along with his backpack and harnessed him into the seat behind the pilot. Then he put a headset on him so he could hear the aircrew talking. They gave each other a "thumbs up" and the rest was history. No resistance. No crying. He was oblivious to the fact that I was even there. He was on an adventure of a lifetime with no fear of being left alone. I thanked the crew for their generosity and gave them a contact name and number for the other end of the trip.

"No problem. Don't worry. He will be fine," the loadmaster replied. "TJ say goodbye to your mom. I need to close the door now." My son shouted goodbye and waved his hand, remaining focused on the pilot and the instrument panel in front of him. He did not even turn back and look at me. I had already learned that my son was resilient. Now, he was fearless too.

My course dates fell over the Easter weekend, so I decided to call my mother to see how she was making out. TJ answered the telephone. "Hi son. It's Mom. What did the Easter Bunny bring you?" I asked.

"He brought me chocolate and chicken pops," he replied. I asked him to put my mother on the phone.

"What are chicken pops?" I asked her.

She laughed. "He is trying to tell you he has the chicken pox, but don't worry. He doesn't seem to be overly bothered by them. I have been bathing him in Calamine Lotion. He really is such a good little boy, and we enjoy having him here. I spoke with your father yesterday. He will be picking TJ up here and driving him to Trenton to meet you when you are finished your course. He wants a little time with the both of you before you go back to Alberta. Hope everything is going well. We love you."

Two weeks later on a Friday, I was on a bus from Borden to Trenton. I had passed my course, and I was looking forward to seeing my son again and getting back to Edmonton to my normal routine. It had been a long six weeks. My father and TJ were waiting for me at the AMU in Trenton when I arrived. TJ let out a blood-curdling scream and ran into my arms. I hugged him for several minutes and then stood up to hug my father. All the while my father and I were hugging, TJ had a death grip on my leg. It was so good to see them both. When I went to the check-in counter, there was only one Priority 5 seat left. There was a woman on the list ahead of my son and she was in line behind me. When asked, she refused to give up her seat for TJ.

"Are there any other flights leaving here over the weekend?" I asked.

"Just one, but it has dangerous cargo on it, so it is not taking any passengers," she replied.

I had no choice but to get on my flight. My eyes welled with tears. "I will take TJ to the Toronto Airport and put him on a commercial flight back to Edmonton," my father said. "I will time the flight for after your arrival so that you can pick him up at the other end." TJ was not having any of it. He was screaming for me and crying as my father picked him up and carried him out of the AMU. My heart was broken as I watched it all unfold. *Poor little guy. He does not understand. Please calm him, Spirit.* Surprisingly, the return home went well for both of us. My son's flight arrived later that evening. We hopped into the car and sang all the way home to our normal lives again. I called my father when we arrived home to thank him for going out of his way to get my son home.

On Saturday night, I decided to call Sharron to catch up with all the news. She had been hospitalized for a week while I had been away and was telling me about a friend she had made while she was sitting in the hospital lounge watching television one day. His name was Brian and he owned a warehouse on the waterfront in downtown Edmonton. The first level of the warehouse was a used appliance business. The second level was just open floor space, and the third level had an apartment where Brian lived. Brian used the second level as a place for local bands to practice. He did not charge them any money to use the space. In return for using his facility, he asked them to play to a crowd of his friends on the occasional Friday night. Sharron and I now had a new friend and new place to party without a closing time.

My first week home, I received a phone call at 2:00 a.m. It was the School Chief. "This is a base recall, Laurie. You are required to report to the AMU, ready to deploy by 3:00 a.m. I realize you are a single parent, so I will mark you down as "unable to reach", but for future recalls you will need to be available," he said hanging up the phone. I talked with Rhoda about it the next morning. "Single parents are allowed to have a house-keeper for this reason," she said. "Check with Base Accommodation as to how to go about it."

On Friday night, I ran into Lynn at the Mess. She told me she was looking for a new place to live, so I ran the idea by her to move in with me. There was no hesitation on her part. I filled out the paperwork for approval and requested to move into a three-bedroom PMQ. Lynn moved into our two-bedroom bungalow that week. We would make do until a bigger PMQ was available.

Life went from calm to crazy within two weeks' time. Lynn loved to party and would drag the Airborne soldiers back to the PMQ when the Rosslyn closed. It was not unusual to wake up in the morning to bodies sprawled across my living room furniture or spread out on the floor with a pillow and a blanket. It was an obstacle course to try and get to the kitchen to put on a pot of coffee. Many of those soldiers were married with children of their own, so they would entertain TJ by wrestling with him or teasing him incessantly. My son loved all the attention and was disap-pointed if he woke up to an empty house. Quite quickly, my PMQ became the party house for transient soldiers on course due to its proximity to the bar and Lynn. We were quiet during the week, but all bets were off come Friday night.

During this time, I began making new civilian girlfriends. I became close with Debbie, the bartender at the Griesbach Mess, who had nick-named me her "little dumpling". Through her, I met her roommate Lea, who was the Mess Manager for the Griesbach Mess. Lea was older than us, quieter, and had a heart of gold. If you were one of Lea's friends, that meant something. Everyone liked her and respected her. Through Lea and Debbie, I met Pattina and Darlene. Pattina had moved to Edmonton from Nova Scotia and was working as a meat cutter for Safeway. Darlene was a nurse who was living with a transport driver named Tesh. Through Darlene and Tesh, I met Mike, another transport driver. We became a tight group of friends who loved to party together or with transient friends. On a Friday night, life was always interesting and fun for us all.

One night, I was at the playground behind my house, pushing TJ on the swings, when one of my neighbors approached me. She was the wife of a SAR Tech who worked at 440 Squadron, and she was upset with one of the instructors at the school. According to her, her husband was on a medical refresher course and was failing because one of the instructors did not like him. I knew all the instructors at the school well, and they were the epitome of professional. For her to accuse this instructor of failing her husband on purpose for personal reasons did not sit well with me.

"If your husband is failing his course, it is because he does not know his stuff. It has nothing to do with the instructor. That's just his excuse," I said. I knew her concern because failing a career course can have severe consequences; however, she was way off base with her accusations.

The next morning, I was called into the Captain's office, along with Rhoda. He went up one side of me and down the other. My neighbor's husband had gone into the School Chief's office to complain that I had been discussing his career with his wife. "Do you know how serious this is, Laurie? You could lose your security clearance over something as simple as this. Do you want to lose your career?" my Captain asked. I was floored, but I also understood the point he was trying to make. After he dismissed me, he continued talking with Rhoda. A few days later, I was told to report to CFSPDB for a tour.

When I walked through the front door of the Detention Barracks, I was met by a Sergeant. "Come with me," he said. The heavy metal bars started rolling and I jumped at the sound as they slammed shut behind me. I was now part of the prison system, and it felt eerie. As we began walking down the corridor, an inmate appeared in the hallway as he walked out of his cell. He stopped, came to attention, and acknowledged the Sergeant with the word "Staff". He continued standing there at attention as we passed by.

A few seconds later, the Sergeant stopped, turned around and ordered the prisoner to "Carry on".

"When you arrive here, you have no privileges. You must earn them. You do not speak unless spoken to. You do not move unless told to do so. You eat exactly what is put on your meal tray. You better hope the cook likes you that day. The meal trays are removed exactly fifteen minutes later. There is no conversation while eating. You shower when we say and for how long we say. You do not receive your mail until you earn that privilege. The same goes for phone calls." He continued with many more rules as I toured the facility.

I spent a half hour with the Sergeant that day, and I do not recall uttering more than two words myself. As I walked out the front door to my freedom, I realized this was somewhere I never wanted to see again. The fear of CFSPDB was firmly imprinted. Mission accomplished.

July had arrived as Brad walked through the school doors. It was him - my sailor from Victoria. He was as handsome as ever as he smiled and nodded. Brad was posted to 442 Squadron in Comox, British Columbia and had driven to Edmonton to attend his medical refresher course. We made plans to go out to dinner together and catch up. He would come by to pick me up at 7:00 p.m. When he pulled into my driveway in his brand-new Corvette, my jaw hit the floor. As he opened the roof and I buckled myself in, I was excited. It was a warm summer evening with a gentle breeze blowing. That gentle breeze quickly amplified into a gale as we picked up speed and the engine roared to the blast of Billy Idol's song "Rebel Yell" on the car stereo. *What a liberating feeling! Forget about eating. I just want to cruise around all night.*

I let Brad decide where to go for supper. I was too busy enjoying the sun on my face and the wind in my hair. When we finally found a place to stop, we spent an hour chatting over dinner. We had five years to catch up on, so there was no shortage of conversation. Brad was still single, but he had a girlfriend who was living in Victoria. He did not miss being a sailor. He loved his new trade as a SAR Tech. I gathered from our conversation that he was happy and content with where he was in life. When he dropped me off that night, I walked away with a smile. It had been a delightful evening.

We still had that little spark, but it was the spark of comfortable friends enjoying time together and teasing each other as to what might have been.

As I lay in my bed that night, I thanked my Spirit World. *All that I am and I hoped to be, I owe it all to you. My son is happy. I am happy. I have family. I have friends. I have a career. I belong.*

Belonging is not about the where. It is about the who, and yes, you belong.

Could life get any better? Of course, it can always get better. The beginning of October, another SAR medical refresher course was starting. As the students entered the school and passed by the office, my eyes connected with the most beautiful eyes I had ever seen and my heart fluttered. I was shaking inside as I turned away. Love had just walked through those doors and I felt it deep in my soul.

Spiritual Beings on a Human Experience

Where a soul is in their current physical journey is the cumulative effect of all their karma from past lives, and what a soul experiences by interacting with other souls is a result of karma. How a soul responds to the experience is a choice that will either create new karma or repay old karmic debt. It is known as the fork in the road and not pre-determined in a blueprint. Laurie's soul has learned many lessons from Tim as she repays her karmic debt. The most significant lesson for her has been how to leave another soul without regret. By choosing to free Tim's soul, in return she frees her own.

A soul cannot replicate what it has lost, but it can put something else in its place. It is a process that continually happens until a soul has what it needs. Laurie's soul has let go of her past - her false identity as a wife. By letting go, she has achieved spiritual growth. That process has allowed her to build a new life with a new identity. Trying times always lead to meaningful times as the soul evolves. Her Spirit World rewards her with the gift of freedom from which many more bountiful gifts flow.

CHAPTER 6

EYES WITHOUT A FACE

It is said that our eyes are the window to the soul, and we cannot stop them from reflecting how we truly feel. They always show our truth, no matter what face we put on because the soul is incapable of lying. Can we understand another soul's emotional state by looking into their eyes? When eyes sparkle or shine, do we need a person to smile to know that they are happy? Do our eyes expose us to others without uttering a single word? Can we transcend our physical limits and see another human's soul by looking into their eyes? I was about to find out.

Mark was a handsome man with chestnut-brown hair. His eyes were a light brown color, speckled with bright green and gold colors near his iris. They were so fascinating to look at. So much so, that the rest of his face automatically disappeared from view. Beauty was in those smoldering eyes, but also in the way that he looked at me. He was completely exposed, penetrating, sincere, and filled with desire, even though we had yet to speak a single word to each other. I wanted to meet those eyes. I wanted to know the soul that owned those eyes.

I spent four days watching those eyes pass by my office several times a day. *Please let him speak to me. I want to meet him.* My eyes were locked on his with the same intensity and burning desire with each look we exchanged. Although I tried, I was incapable of turning away. I knew one thing for sure; neither one of us would have ever won a staring contest with each other.

On Friday, Mark walked into the office to drop off some paperwork given to him by the course instructor. "One of you ladies could probably help me out. Where is the hot spot to go on a Friday night in Edmonton? It has been a long week and some of the boys want to unwind tonight."

"Laurie is our wild child on Friday nights. She knows all the party places," Rhoda replied. Rhoda had spent an evening out partying with us several times before, so she knew firsthand how crazy our Friday nights could get. She used to tell her husband, "Don't wait up for me. I will see you in the morning." Mark and I made plans to meet up at the Griesbach Mess for happy hour and let the night unfold from there.

Sharron, Lynn, Pattina, and I were sitting among several Airborne friends when Mark and his buddies walked in. They grabbed a few drinks from the bar, pulled up a chair around the table, and introduced themselves as they sat down. Mark positioned himself directly across the table from me. As our eyes locked, his energy hit me with the force of a stun gun. I tried to speak, but any and all words eluded me. I blushed and tried looking away, but a second later, I was looking at him again. He smiled and winked at me. *Oh dear God, he has found my trigger. Who is this soul? What is it about his eyes?*

The need for restraint is unquestionable here. He is your Twin Flame.

I had never shared my spirituality with other humans, and I had never heard other humans speak about talking to Spirit. So, I was still trying to figure it out for myself. *What is a twin flame? Is it possible this feeling is pure soul-to-soul love with an adult?* I knew that particular love with my child - unconditional love. Were Mark and I two souls colliding based on our Creator's Divine Plan? Was he the one that I had been searching for all along? Does "happily ever after" really exist? Once again, I was about to find out.

Happy Hour was ending as several trays of shooters appeared on our table. I was not going to partake. It was too early to get wasted and somewhere deep inside I knew this was going to be a night to remember. "Laurie, you jam tart. We are not drinking without you. Grab one and suck her back with us, little lady," Andy coaxed (one of my Airborne friends).

Sharron handed me a shooter and smiled. "It's not tequila, and I'll make sure you get home," she said laughingly.

"I'll help you with her too. We will tag team," Mark said bashfully to Sharron while looking directly at me. We all raised our shooters into the air, waiting for the toast delivery.

"To the bad decisions we make, to the fucked-up lives we lead, and to the choices that make us who we are. Airborne. HUA (heard, understood, acknowledged)"

I tossed my shooter of Sambuca back, feeling the heat as it slid all the way down to my stomach. *Yum! Much better than tequila.* As I licked the black licorice taste off my lips, I could feel Mark's eyes staring at me. I looked up and flashed a grin, followed by several bouts of giggles.

"What's so funny, Laurie? Share with the rest of us," one of the guys shouted.

Sharron responded with, "Nothing is funny. Say hello to Laurie on Sambuca." The room filled with laughter. Another tray of twenty shooters arrived on the table.

"Let's play a game. It works like this. I will start by saying one word. The person next to me needs to repeat my word and add their own word. As soon as you cannot repeat the entire sentences that have been formed correctly, you have to take a shot. I will start," Andy said. The sentences went from clean to dirty very quickly, and before I knew it, I had another two shooters in me. I was on my way to only God knows where.

Several hours later, we left the Mess for the Rosslyn. The Hollies song "Long Cool Woman" was beginning as Pattina and I made our way directly to the dance floor. I did not stop. I did not pass "Go", and I did not need any more liquor. I was on the perfect high of dancing juice as I lost myself in the rhythm of the music. Several songs later, Pattina and I joined everyone else at the table. Sharron had bought me a drink when she walked in and was holding an empty chair for me beside her. Her and Mark were engaged in a conversation, speaking medical terminology that I could not follow, so I sat down in my own world, lost in the music as I watched people's smoke twisting into the air in such an artistic way.

Mark stood up. "I am going to the bar for another drink. Can I get one for you two ladies?"

"I'll have one," Sharron replied. "A rum and coke please, but Laurie is fine. She has barely touched the one I bought her. She has her buzz on and will just want to dance for the next few hours. Trust me when I say that."

When Mark returned from the bar, the DJ had decided to slow things down with Lobo's song "I'd Love You to Want Me". Mark set the drinks on the table and reached for my hand. "Come dance with me, Laurie." You never had to ask me twice to dance. I lived to dance on Friday nights.

When we reached the dancefloor, he placed his left hand firmly onto my hip, locked my right hand into his with a twist of his wrist, and pulled me close into his chest. I folded into his strength and confidence, realizing how perfectly his body fit mine. His aftershave was intoxicating, taking control of all of my senses. I could feel the pounding of his heart and his warm breath on my neck. His whispers were sumptuous in my ear as he began to sing to me. "Baby I'd love you to want me. The way that I want you. The way that it should be. Baby you'd love me to want you. The way that I want to. If you'd only let it be."

I was no longer dancing. I was floating with exploding energy. I could feel all the broken pieces inside of me melding back together again. I had just been introduced to Mark through my soul. Words were not necessary. We were instinctually communicating with our bodies and the flickering flame of our souls. I was shaken by the intensity of the bond I was feeling for him - a complete stranger. *Please don't let go. Not yet!*

No sooner had I finished my thought, when Mark whispered into my ear, "I don't want to let go of you for fear of losing this feeling I have right now. Beautiful mystery lady, please take me home with you tonight." We were thinking the exact same thoughts at the exact same time. I wanted to take him home. I was hoping to take him home. *The connection I feel with him is so deep on every level. What is happening?*

You are experiencing a sacred gift of unconditional love, a restoration of the physical self properly aligning with the Spiritual Self.

Thank you! Thank you! Thank you! Mark and I danced up a storm for the next two hours. That man could move. Dancing came as naturally for him as one walks.

Mark and I left together before the bar closed. The electricity of the attraction between us was becoming unbearable for both of us. After I had paid the babysitter and locked the front door, Mark looked at me with such passion that I had to restrain myself from wanting to climb inside of him and devour him. He began teasing me incessantly with butterfly kisses as he explored my neck, my lips, and my mouth. His lips were sweet, warm, and well worth the wait. He stopped kissing me several times, brushing his thumb along my lower lip while gazing into my eyes. Both consumed by his foreplay, the intimacy took over as we swallowed each other's tonsils with a deep, passionate kiss. I had never been kissed so perfectly. He began exploring my body with the silky touch of each caress. If touch was a language, we instinctively knew how to speak to each other. Even though he was the one doing the touching, I could tell he was reaping the same benefits as I was with each playful stroke. His eye contact, combined with his physical touch, turned into a tempestuous scenario quite quickly as we both lost control. We made love for many hours that night.

Finally exhausted, we both collapsed onto our pillows. "God, I can't believe the way I feel right now. I am physically exhausted, but I still can't get enough of you," he said as he grabbed my hand, holding on tightly.

"I feel exactly the same way," I said, "but we need to get some sleep. It's 5:00 a.m. and my son will be up in a few hours." I kissed his cheek and rolled over onto my side.

Mark cradled himself into my back, placing an arm over my hip and onto my stomach. He pulled my hair back in soft sweeps and gently kissed my neckline. "I don't want to scare you," he whispered, "but I love you. I have since the first time I saw you. Is that even possible? Good Night, Sweet Angel." His words did not frighten me. I loved him too. It was as if I had known him all of my life. I squeezed his hand.

Trust his words. He wears no disguise.

We both drifted off to sleep early that morning in euphoric bliss.

Three hours later, I awoke to the sound of scissors in my ear. TJ was awake and had decided I needed a haircut. I bolted up in bed, waking Mark with the sudden movement. I was surprised by my energy level after such little sleep. I slipped out of bed, made TJ a bowl of cereal, and let him take it into the living room to watch cartoons. Then I started the coffee pot.

When I returned to the bedroom, Mark was already up, dressed, and making the bed. He wrapped his arms around me. "Good morning, Laurie.

Did you have any plans today? I thought maybe we could take your son to the Waterpark at West Edmonton Mall."

"We would love to do that. We haven't been there yet, but let's have a coffee first," I replied jokingly. Obviously, his energy level was as high as mine.

West Edmonton Mall is North America's largest mall with over eight hundred stores, two hotels, nine major attractions, one hundred dining venues, and parking for twenty thousand cars. The Waterpark itself is a five-acre playland with the world's largest indoor wave pool that generates waves over two meters high. We stopped at a swimwear store next to the Waterpark where Mark bought himself and my son some new swimming trunks.

"I love this bathing suit for you," he said. "Please try it on for me." It was a black, one-piece suit that was low cut down the front to my naval and high cut up the sides to my waist. When I exited the dressing room, his response made me blush. "Damn girl, you have the most gorgeous body I have ever seen and those legs. God, those legs never end."

"I don't need a new bathing suit. I brought one with me," I said. "I just tried it on because you asked me to." Mark paid for the bathing suit without telling me while I was getting dressed again and then we headed into the Waterpark for a day of adventure.

We had so much fun together, and he was incredible with my son as they struggled through the waves, shrieking, and laughing. I was experiencing a true family in every sense of the word. It was comfortable, familiar, and effortless. The interaction between him and my son was genuine, and it was obvious that Mark loved children. We stopped at McDonald's on the way home at TJ's request. What three-year-old child doesn't love McDonalds? When we arrived home, Mark settled himself on the couch and began reading TJ a few stories from the books he had brought to him. He was animated while reading, and TJ was basking in the attention as he cuddled into his side.

Within a half hour, TJ was sound asleep. Mark carried him into his bed and tucked him in. "He is out like a light. What a great kid!" he said as he returned to the living room. "Thank you for such an amazing day today," I said hugging him.

I made us a drink, and we sat down at the kitchen table. "Laurie, I need to talk to you about something before you hear it through the rumor mill. I am married. Well, technically I am married," he began.

"But you are not wearing a ring and what does technically mean?" I asked.

"My marriage ended six months ago. My wife is involved with one of my co-workers and is planning to move to the East Coast with him when he is posted to CFB Greenwood in the spring. My marriage is unsalvageable, and we have been sleeping in separate bedrooms for months. Our battle now is over our six-year-old daughter. I can't imagine my life without her, and now I can't imagine my life without you either."

I could see the sorrow in his eyes, and I wanted to make all his demons go away. The moment felt perfect to tell him my truth, to tell him about my marriage to Tim. When I finished, he stood up and pulled me to my feet, wrapping his love around me. I could feel the White Light swirling around us both as we held each other for several minutes.

"Please say something," he said as he pulled away and began looking into my eyes.

"Thank you for being honest with me. I believe you, and it does not change a single thing between us. In fact, I respect you for letting me hear it directly from you." That moment cemented our bond, and that night, we were impassioned lovers wrestling for hours once again.

Sunday morning I made breakfast for the three of us. After eating, TJ wanted Mark to help him find his "countach".

"Please help him, Mark. He has been driving me crazy with that, and I have no idea what he is talking about."

"It's a sports car, Laurie, made by Lamborghini," Mark replied. Since I did not know what it was, I began to wonder how my son had learned that word. Maybe his grandfather had taught him during their phone conversations. By the time I finished the dishes, the countach mystery had been solved once and for all, and my son was happy to have found his Hot Wheels car again.

By 4:00 p.m. I began feeling melancholy. The weekend was over and Mark had called a taxi. "I hate to leave you, but I really need to get back to the barracks. I have laundry to do, and I need to study." I must have been wearing my disappointment in the expression on my face because he looked at me and said, "Do you know you have such a pretty little pout? Come here, Angel." I walked over to him. "I will be back," he said. "I promise." He hugged me and kissed me goodbye and then bent down to give TJ a hug as he ran to say goodbye to him. "See you tomorrow morning. Have a good night," he said, blowing me another kiss as he walked out the door.

I called Sharron after Mark left, and we talked for over an hour as I told her all about my weekend. Halloween was two weeks away, and she wanted to make some costumes. I was already in the process of making a dinosaur costume for my son, and I needed help to sew the three-foot tail into the body suit. "Why don't you come over tomorrow night after work? You can help me finish TJ's costume, have supper here, and we will plan what we want for costumes for ourselves."

"Sounds good" she replied. "Oh and by the way, Brian is having a Halloween Bash at the warehouse. See you tomorrow night."

As Mark passed by the office Monday morning, he smiled at me and winked. I was on such a high, and I did not think that the day could get any better until Barry walked into the office. "I have to go flying for a few hours this morning, and I was wondering if Laurie wanted to go with me," he said to Rhoda.

"I am a week ahead in my workload, Rhoda."

"By all means," she replied. "Have fun, you two."

I was beaming with excitement as I boarded the Hercules. Barry told me to sit in the flight engineer's seat behind the pilot until the loadmaster was ready for me. We spent the first half hour doing a maneuver called a "touch and go". The Hercules would approach the runway, touch for a brief second, and then take off again. That was followed by a "LAPES drop", a tactical military delivery method used to deposit supplies on the ground when landing is not an option. The Hercules approaches the area in a manner similar to landing, the tailgate is opened, and a drogue parachute is released that begins tailing behind the airplane. The force of that parachute pulls the extraction parachutes out into the airstream. All those parachutes release the floor locks, pulling a pallet of supplies across the ramp and out of the aircraft. The pilot then takes off again, raising the landing gear (that was only lowered as a safety precaution), closing the tailgate, and the procedure is complete. Mission accomplished without ever touching the ground.

We were back at the office by noon, and I was on a high from the morning's experience. "Let's go for lunch," Rhoda said. "You can tell me all about your morning."

Shortly after arriving home after work, there was a knock on my door with a flower delivery. Mark had sent a dozen long stem red roses with a card that read: "To my new beginning, Love Mark."

Sharron and I finished my son's costume that night. When we tried it on him, he was excited and began running around the house, knocking everything over with his tail. "Stop, son," I yelled. "We need to take this off now. This costume is not house friendly." Sharron and I were giggling as I quickly undressed him.

"I think we should make costumes as Indian Brides," Sharron suggested. For the next week, we sewed a white satin body garment that snapped together in the crotch. Then we made a white satin skirt with long flaps to the floor, falling down the front and the back of the body suit from the waistline. We made headdresses with bright red and black feathers and strung beads together for our neckline and our arms. Sharron was so creative and the costumes looked stunning when they were finished. When I took my costume into work to show Rhoda, she decided on the spot that she wanted to come out and party with us on Halloween night. We made plans to meet up at my place around 8:00 p.m. after taking the kids trick or treating.

Mark and I bumped into each other Thursday morning in the student lounge. I was getting a coffee refill for Rhoda and me when he brushed up against me. I started shaking as his energy consumed me. "Can I come to your place after work on Friday?" he whispered.

"I'll be waiting for you," I replied. By the time I returned to the office, we only had half a cup of coffee each because I was shaking so bad. *Note to self: Do not get coffee when students are on a break.*

Friday night, Mark showed up at 4:30 p.m. at my door. My son squealed with excitement when he saw him standing in the doorway and ran to him. We decided to stay in that night and order pizza for supper. After supper, we all walked to the gas bar on the base, picked up snacks and movies, and walked back to the PMQ to settle in for the night. TJ snuggled between the two of us on the couch until he could no longer keep his eyes open. Once he was settled into bed, Mark and I watched another movie, cuddling together. I was sad at the thought of him having to leave in three weeks. *Don't go there. You still have time with him. Be in the moment and make the best of it.* Mark was posted at CFB Trenton in Ontario, and it was inevitable that if we decided to continue the relationship, it would be a long-distance one.

When we awoke the next morning, Mark asked to take me to the Edmonton Space Science Centre on a date. He had heard about a laser show that was playing at 10:00 p.m. that night to the music of Elton John. "Let me call Candy to see if she can babysit," I said. The experience was one that I have never forgotten to this day. We were seated in comfortable lounging chairs in a circle, with several tiers of chairs below us. The lights dimmed, the chairs reclined, and the dome opened revealing a perfectly clear, starry sky. The music starting playing and the acoustics were like being at a concert. As the laser show began, we lay there listening to the music, while simultaneously watching the various colors of the laser lights moving so poetically across the sky. I was moved to tears when Elton John's song "Funeral for a Friend/Love Lies Bleeding" began playing as Mark placed his hand over the top of mine and our energies surged together. That song would have far greater meaning than I ever anticipated!

Halloween night, I paraded my son through the neighborhood. He was so excited as he ran from house to house, knocking little children down with the swing of his tail as he was running. When we arrived at the house of one of the SAR Techs from 440 Squadron, Pete called his wife to the door. "This kid has more tail than I get in a year," he said. She smacked him in the arm, telling him to behave around the children. After my son could no longer carry any more treats, we drove to Candy's place. I hugged him and kissed him goodbye, telling him I would see him tomorrow at noon. He was out of sight in a flash and engaging with the other children. Candy was having a Halloween party, and it was mayhem with all the noise.

Shortly after I arrived home, the gang showed up at my door. We opened a bottle of champagne as Sharron, Lynn, Rhoda, and I started getting into our costumes. Lynn dressed up in a tuxedo, with a top hat, black nylon stockings, and spiked high heels. Rhoda dressed up as Shirley Temple, with an adorable pink and white frilled dress, white frilly ankle socks, black Mary Jane shoes, and a huge sucker as her prop. We finished our champagne and headed out the door to the Lancaster Park Mess, where Mark and his friends were waiting for us. When Mark stood up to greet me, he whispered into my ear, "Don't let any other guy marry you tonight my beautiful bride. That privilege is reserved for me."

Wow! Did I just hear right? Did he say in a roundabout way that he wants to marry me? Guess I should start looking at getting divorced. We danced and drank until midnight at the Mess, with the plan to go downtown to the warehouse from there.

Brian was a kind soul who had lots of friends and an open-door policy to his home for everyone he knew. The second level of the warehouse was packed with people in costumes, standing around drinking or dancing to the music of the band that was playing that night. "Wow," Mark said. "What a cool place to party. I had no idea." Anyone we ever took to the warehouse always had the same reaction.

By 3:00 a.m., Rhoda and Sharron were hungry and wanted to leave to get something to eat. "Come upstairs with me," Brian said. He proceeded to make fried rice for the two of them - rice that Rhoda swore was the best fried rice she had ever eaten. We continued partying until 5:00 a.m. before we finally decided to leave. Sharron went back to her place with one of Mark's friends, we dropped Rhoda off at home, and Mark and I went back to my PMQ.

Before leaving to go out that night, I had thrown my bedsheets into the washer and had forgot to put them in the dryer. When I walked into the bedroom from the bathroom, the waterbed mattress was covered in baby oil and Mark was lying there buck-naked beckoning me to come join him. I do not know if it was the slipperiness of the baby oil on the mattress or if we were just too wasted, but having sex that night was next to impossible. We kept slipping and sliding away from each other in hysterical laughter every time we touched, although we did give it an honest attempt several times trying to be serious. Finally giving up, I grabbed two pillows and the comforter from the floor, and we settled for the night on the baby oil mattress.

A few hours later as I opened my eyes, I looked over at Mark and began laughing. "My, you are so pretty when you wake up," he commented.

"Have you looked at yourself?" I asked continuing to laugh. He was wearing half of my makeup smeared all over his face, and he was covered in body glitter. His hair was spiked in forty-five directions on one side and flattened right down on the other, and I was a mirror image of him. In fact, we both looked like characters from a horror movie.

"I think we need a shower. Come join me," he said as he tried to help me out of bed several times through many bouts of laughter. We stayed in the shower until the hot water ran out, consumed with each other's bodies once again, as we tried to wash away all our drunken tomfoolery from the night before. Once we were dressed, I put a pot of coffee on while Mark began cleaning up the bed. He bagged the bedding, and we took it to the laundromat after our coffee. From there, we met up with Sharron and Paul for breakfast at Humpty's Restaurant.

The rest of the weekend was quiet. We stopped at the grocery store to pick up some steaks for supper and then picked up TJ at the babysitter. "Can we watch more movies?" my son asked when he got in the car.

"We sure can if it is okay with your mom," Mark replied. The more time I spent with Mark, the more I loved him, if that was even possible. This was the family I had daydreamed about as a little girl. *How am I going to say goodbye to him? What is life going to be like when he is gone? Is a future even possible or are we just kidding ourselves?*

That night as we lay holding each other, we lost ourselves in pillow talk. He was feeling the same apprehension as our time together was narrowing down. We had one weekend left before our fairy tale existence would shock us both back to reality. "Can you get a babysitter for your son next Saturday night? I have something special planned," Mark asked.

"Shouldn't be a problem. What do you have in mind?" I asked.

"It's a surprise, and you will need to pack an overnight bag. I want to make our last night together an unforgettable one." Every moment I had spent with him so far was unforgettable. I could not even imagine what he had planned now.

When Saturday afternoon arrived, our destination was West Edmonton Mall. We walked down Bourbon Street in the mall, passing several restaurants until we decided to stop at a seafood place. The meal was delectable, and the man I was sharing it with was suave and sensual. From the restaurant, he took me to the Fantasyland Hotel where he had booked us into the Polynesian Theme Room. When he opened the door to the room, it took my breath away. There was a huge, four-person Jacuzzi in the room that was surrounded with volcanic rock. When you turned the taps on to fill the tub, the water poured out from the top of the volcano, flowed down the rock walls, and landed in the tub. One entire wall had a picturesque view of the ocean. There was a queen-sized bed nestled in a warrior catamaran boat against that wall, and several palm trees surrounded the bed. It was paradise.

"One day, I am going to take my beautiful angel to an exotic destination in person, but this will have to do for now," Mark said. He had thought of everything that night. We even had champagne and chocolate-covered strawberries delivered by room service as we enjoyed the Jacuzzi. We shared laughter and tears. Perhaps due to the emotional setting surrounding us. We talked about the future. We made love with all the emotion and romance that it's associated with, and we were fully present in each and every moment. We were deep, and we were vulnerable with each other. I had never been able to express my deepest thoughts with anyone else prior to meeting him, but he removed all that fear. The night had definitely turned into one that I still remember fondly to this day.

The following Thursday, Mark walked past the office for the final time. My heart was aching as I tried to contain my tears, watching him walk out the door. He returned to Trenton, calling me a few times every week, but I was struggling. I was realizing for the first time that a twin flame relationship was not without pain. Our connection ran so deep that I was frustrated with his absence. His presence balanced me out, made me feel whole, and I could be myself with him. *A relationship with anyone else is never going to compare to the incredible bond we share. How am I going to get through this?*

Shared energy will keep you linked regardless of physical space.

I did not understand that message in the moment, but I was going to find out very quickly exactly what sharing energy meant.

My mother called a few days after Mark had left. "What's wrong, honey?" she asked. "You don't sound like yourself."

I was not myself. I was empty and I was lonely. My nights were spent crying myself to sleep. I longed for his eyes and his energy. "Nothing, Mom. What's up?" I asked.

"Donald and I were talking, and we would like you and TJ and Sharron to come to Toronto for Christmas. I will send airline tickets for everyone."

Suddenly, I perked up by her offer. Trenton was only two hours away. Maybe if luck would have it, I would get to see Mark again. My next phone call with Mark, I mentioned that I would be in Toronto for Christmas. "Please make sure you come to see me," he said. That was all I needed to hear.

During one of our phone calls, Mark told me that he was going to Bermuda to renew his scuba diving certification. A week or so later, I received a small package in the mail containing a 14-karat gold broach of two birds, accompanied by a letter he had written; a letter so deep that I have kept it for thirty-four years.

Bermuda - Nov 85 - My Dearest Angel

Sweet Lord Jesus, how I miss you. Honey, I love you so much. You have entered my heart, soul, and body like no other person alive has up to this point of my life. You have totally changed my outlook on this lovely experience we Homo sapiens call life. I am so glad we met. I can't believe we have transcended all earthly boundaries together. You have no concept of what you have done to my soul, and you have totally resurrected my spirit. You are like an aphrodisiac to me, and I can't believe my good fortune in meeting you, my Angel. God, you make me feel 16 again. If you could only see yourself through my eyes.

I am sending you this broach from Bermuda as a token of the high esteem in which I hold you. I hope you can relate to it like I do. The Bermuda Longtail is a native bird to the island and symbolizes love and freedom, the feelings I experience when I am with you. I love you more than words can say, and I miss you terribly. I feel empty without you. See you in December.

Love, Mark

Our trip to Toronto started out wonderfully. We had Christmas at my mother's, and she spoiled us. She wrote me a cheque for $2000 that she placed in a card, knowing I was looking for a new car. We took the train to Windsor and stayed overnight with my father and had Christmas with him. When we returned to Toronto, I called Mark and we made plans to meet up on the 29th in Trenton. Mark and I were still on the phone when I asked my mom if she would mind watching my son for the day while Sharron and I took a train to Trenton to visit a friend. She was more than accommodating, but she was sober at the time.

Mark picked us up at the train station in Belleville, and we drove back to Trenton to his PMQ. When I walked in the door, there was no indication anywhere that Christmas had even taken place in his home. No tree, no presents, no people - just the three of us sitting at the kitchen table having coffee like any other normal day. Mark seemed different. His eyes had lost their beauty; his stare was dark and cold, and he was avoiding any eye contact with me. Through conversation, we learned that his wife had decided to spend Christmas on the East Coast and had taken their daughter with her. Once she arrived, she called Mark to say that they were not coming back. When he finally decided to look at me, I could personally feel all the turmoil inside of him. He was broken, bruised, and struggling without his daughter. There was a tiny flicker of a flame in his soul and that was close to being extinguished. I felt helpless and destroyed as I connected to his energy - his feelings, not mine. Returning to Toronto, I prayed all the way back on the train for our Creator to save him from himself and his despair.

When we walked back into my mother's apartment that night, she had been drinking all day and was angry. That anger was seething as she lashed out at me. "What am I to you? A piece of shit?" she began with slurred words. "Your father is so perfect, and I am just a bank account to you. Is that it?" she asked.

I tried not to engage with her in that drunken state, but she would not let things be. "You think all I want is your money?" I replied. I took the cheque from my purse and ripped it up, throwing it on to the coffee table. "Our relationship is not about money at all." I had hoped that would send the right message to her, but to no avail.

Donald tried several times to calm her down, but she was on a tear. She vamped up even more, finally throwing us out of the apartment at 2:00 a.m. with less than $20 between the two of us, and three more days before we were due to fly home. "What are we going to do?" I asked Sharron, while trying to warm TJ from the cold December air. My poor son. He had been yanked out of a nice warm bed and was now standing on the frigid streets of Toronto with nowhere to go. In that moment, I regretted the decision to rip up the cheque my mother had given me. Sharron found a phone booth and called her mother who lived in Richmond Hill. Her mother welcomed us into her home and paid for the taxi when it arrived at her door. This had turned into a horrible Christmas, and all I wanted to do was get back to Edmonton as soon as possible.

Several weeks passed as I settled into my routine again. I had not heard from Mark in over a week, and I was starting to worry. When I arrived home from work one night, I could not get Mark out of my mind. I thought of him often, but this was different. I felt like I had the weight of the world on my shoulders. I felt despair. I felt panicked, and I wanted to cry. I tried to distract myself from the sinking feeling in the pit of my stomach. I made supper for TJ, gave him his bath, turned the television on, and brought him his coloring book and crayons. I did the supper dishes, read TJ his bedtime story, put him to bed, and went to have my shower.

That is when the emotion that had been bottling up for the past four hours let go. My heartache had nowhere to hide at that point. My feelings were raw as I burst into uncontrollable sobbing, gasping for air with each breath I took. My heart felt so heavy - an indescribable aching that would not be silenced. *What is happening to me? I literally feel like I am going to die. The emotional pain is excruciating.*

While twin flame love can be euphoric, it inevitably involves a time of crisis.

What are you trying to tell me? Has something happened to Mark?
No answer.

The next morning, Rhoda walked into the office with her cup of coffee. "I just came from the student lounge and the instructors are all talking about Mark. He died last night, Laurie." I do not know if I stopped believing in God in that moment or if He was just too far away for me to reach. I felt abandoned and the anger inside of me was about to separate me, fracture me, and suffocate me from my Spirit World.

Spiritual Beings on a Human Experience

Twin Flames are mirrors of one another, often recognizing the need to be with each other as soon as they meet. They intuitively know what the other is doing, thinking, or feeling and easily communicate without speaking out loud. They have the same thoughts or emotions at the same time even if they are in different physical places, so it is safe and natural to be authentic with a twin flame. There is also a strong need between the two souls to understand the hidden parts of each other, the vulnerabilities, and the weaknesses, and that need strengthens courage to reveal hidden emotions or unhealed wounds. The relationship is extremely intense and usually involves a crisis stage, where one flame cannot handle facing issues that frighten them about the relationship.

Laurie and Mark are experiencing Authentic Power as they meet on the dancefloor. Their personalities align with their souls for both of them during this initial contact. External Power is superficial and only serves to feed the ego. Through Authentic Power, they learn the difference between sleeping with someone and sleeping with someone that you love unconditionally. Their focus and intention with each other becomes genuine love, with compassion and respect. The union is timely for both souls. This rare emotional, physical, mental, and spiritual connection is a sacred occurrence that happens to less than one percent of souls on a physical experience. A twin flame connection to each other's spiritual energy is so powerful that it will be life changing for both of them.

Laurie has yet to realize the spiritual gifts her Creator has provided for her through this union. She has experienced authentic love with an adult soul for the first time and now knows what a healthy relationship should feel like. She has found courage to reveal her inner most self to another human without judgment. She has learned that she can trust the words spoken by another soul, something she has been incapable of until this point, and her spiritual energy has been heightened by her Creator in preparation for a future path in her blueprint.

CHAPTER 7

HEAVEN'S ANGEL, DEVIL'S DAUGHTER

Have you ever experienced pain? Have you ever experienced loss? How about trauma? Of course you have, because everyone on a human experience has. It is part of our journey to evolve the soul. Perhaps how we endure those experiences, how we process them in our mind, and how we choose to cope says everything about who we are as a soul. Are we willing to face our pain and own it, or are we more comfortable in anger or denial? Do we let go of our loss and celebrate the experience and what we learned from it, or do we live in regret? Are we willing to face our trauma head on with faith or do we suffer a crisis of faith?

My history had left me with three relationships that had ended - each filled with either pain, or loss, or trauma, and I was not prepared for any of the outcomes. With Lloyd, I was inexperienced and infatuated and not without pain as I walked away from that relationship. With Tim, I was impetuous and a pushover and not without loss as that marriage ended. With Mark, I was bereaved by losing my twin flame and the thought of what might have been. Now I was left with the trauma of facing his death and not knowing "why".

Mark died last night? (question) Mark died last night. (statement) Oh God, Mark died last night! (reality) His death had finally registered after several seconds of repeating the words to myself.

"What happened?" I asked Rhoda trying desperately not to cry.

"A farmer heard a shotgun blast around 9:00 p.m. last night, and when he went to investigate, he found Mark in his field," Rhoda replied. "He died instantly."

I turned and headed for the washroom. I was a mess and did not want any of my co-workers to see me. After crying over the initial shock of the news, I washed my face, returned to my desk, and buried myself in my work. It was extremely difficult to stay composed for the day, but I managed by putting my professional face on. Through many years of practice, I had become a master at concealing my feelings when I needed to, especially in front of other people.

When I got home that night, I put on my mommy face. After my son was in bed for the night, I let go of all the survival personas that had helped me make it through the day and began thinking through my tears. I was with Mark when he died last night. I was showering in that fateful moment when he pulled the trigger. I felt like I wanted to die. I felt the excruciating emotional pain. Even worse, I had felt all his turmoil for the four hours before he actually pulled the trigger. Everything made sense now as to my emotional state the night before, but at the same time, nothing made sense.

Why Mark? Why? Why didn't you call me? How could you leave me like this without so much as goodbye? What pushed you over the edge? Was it me? Did I play a part in your decision? How could you do this to us? How could you do this to your daughter? What happened that made you feel so desperate and so lost that you couldn't reach out? There were so many unanswered questions, but the reality was that he was dead and never coming back in this lifetime. Little did I know it, but some of those questions would be answered shortly in very unexpected ways.

Heading for my bedroom, I grabbed a bottle of wine from the fridge and a box of Kleenex. I propped myself up on my pillows and lit the candle sitting on my night table. My bedroom was nothing more than a reminder of Mark now as I sat sobbing for hours. I emptied the box of Kleenex and the bottle of wine. Exhausted from crying, I tried to fall asleep, but sleep was stonewalled. The bottle of wine I had consumed began playing tricks with my mind as the walls of my room commenced wallpapering themselves with memories of him - his eyes, his face, his smile, his laughter, our dates. I could see him everywhere I looked, so I shut my eyes, sobbing from the depths of my soul.

I am so sorry, my beautiful angel. Please don't cry. I wish I could take it back, but I can't.

I immediately opened my eyes, witnessing his silhouette of energy twisting in circles beside my bed. As I reached for him, he disappeared. *"Please come back,"* I begged. *"Without you, I am only half alive."* If I had a choice in that moment, I wanted to live in his world instead of living without him in mine. My Spirit Guide quickly intervened.

Stand in your darkness and trust your heart will mend. Authentic love never dies.

Every night for the next week, I would sit in the darkness of my lonely room waiting for him to re-appear. His memory lingered so hauntingly, but he never returned. That only angered me. *Spirit, why are you punishing me with such brutality? You have broken my heart yet again! Why did you take Mark away from me? No! Why did you even give him to me in the first place? You always give me love and then you take it away.*

His choice to leave was his own by an exit point in his blueprint.

I don't even know what that means. God, I don't know how to live without him. I can't live without him. Please bring me home too.

Your pain is the intensity of losing your twin flame. You MUST find your way forward. Find comfort in knowing your paths will cross again.

How is that supposed to bring me comfort now? You know what? I AM DONE WITH ALL OF YOU. You need to stop talking to me. Just leave me alone.

I did not want to hear from my Spirit World anymore. I was wounded and looking for a place to hide. I was not ready to face my reality. Each time Spirit attempted to speak to me, I sent them away. I had made up my mind that I was going to live my physical life in my own way, on my own terms, and without any help from them. I was consumed by the darkness of my grief and had made the choice to defiantly walk away from the Light.

For many months, I continued to struggle to find my way forward without my Spirit World. I was now in a very dark place with the anger of my life seething inside of me. I was angry by day and begging to die by night. My child was the one constant thing in my life that kept me going.

His father had already chosen not to be a part of his life and his mother choosing to do the same thing had the potential to destroy his soul. I knew the pain firsthand of not being wanted, and I never wanted to do that to my son, so he slowly became my reason to keep going. I did not share my feelings with friends or family. I kept everything inside, pretending that life was normal and I was fine, but my actions would soon give me away to those who loved me.

As I lay in bed one night in a semi-conscious state, a white stallion appeared in a mist. Riding the stallion was the most handsome man I had ever seen with long, flowing hair and wings that spread for miles. As handsome as he was, I felt nervous and jittery inside. My gut instinct was telling me to beware as he began to speak.

Him: I am not your enemy. I am the alternative.
        Isn't that what you are looking for, an alternative?
        The way down only hurts for a second and then you will forget.

Me: I know who you are now, and I know who I am. My faith has
        been shattered and I have lost my way, but I am still a child of
        my Creator - the Alpha, the Omega. I still belong to Him.

Him: I don't see your Creator here with you right now.
        Where is He in your time of need?

Me: I sent him away, and I am doing the same with you.
        Go away and leave me alone.

He is not your friend. He is not anybody's friend. He comes from a place so dark you can't even imagine and his only goal is to destroy. Stay in the White Light, My child.

Please go away! Everyone, please go away!

During a human existence, is everything we experience given to us directly from our Creator and does everything have two meanings in order for our existence to balance? Is the Devil nothing more than a choice from God? Is he a test of our faith or does the Devil really exist? I wondered if perhaps he had appeared as the result of my loss of faith and he really did exist. Is faith about living without having to evaluate or understand and just believing in a higher power?

Lynn and I were eating dinner the next night, when she told me she had a friend who needed a place to stay for a few weeks. Lynn was very seldom home, so a new face around sounded welcoming. Lynn's friend's name was Linda. She had been renting a room from a psychic lady and her son, but she was no longer comfortable in their environment. After meeting her in person, I agreed, without any hesitation, to have Linda move in. She had a vibrant personality, always happy and laughing. During our first conversation, she had a sexual undertone that I picked up on right away. Her mind was consumed with dirty thoughts or funny thoughts, and she was quite vocal about both with me. Linda was a soul who was out there living her life on her own terms and happy just being herself with a "take me or leave me" attitude. Within a week of staying with me, Linda was coming home with bags of lingerie from La Senza or toys from the adult sex shop and showing me all her new purchases with excitement. When she saw something that she thought I might like, she would buy it for me. I loved Linda's generosity and her crazy character. She was refreshing in the very dark world I had plunged myself into.

The Psychic Fair was coming to Edmonton, and the girls were talking about getting together that Saturday to check it out. "If you want to go see a psychic, I can send you to the one who I lived with. Why wait for the weekend?" Linda said.

Two nights later, I was sitting in front of a lady named Dianne. Of the four of us who had booked appointments with her, I was the last reading. She laid some cards across the table and paralyzed me when she opened her mouth. "Why do you keep thinking about dying? The Universe is always listening to your thoughts. You need to stop that. Eventually you will get your wish and then what? Death is final for you and your son, and it will leave you with terrible karma that you will have to repay to his soul. Are you listening to me?"

"Yes," I replied.

"There is a man standing here with me. He says his name is Mark. Do you know who I am talking about?"

"Yes," I replied as my eyes welled up with tears.

She continued. "Oh dear God, he died a horribly violent death by his own hand. He is really sorry he did it - especially after being shown what might have been in the future had he endured the hardship. Crisis in a soul's life is a crossroad and the end of life as you originally know it. It is a threshold for something much bigger than you can ever imagine. Something new is being born in a crisis, and it requires us to let the old die."

As she continued the reading for the next half hour, I felt as if I was talking to my Spirit Guide. "Where are you getting this information from?" I asked when she finished the reading.

"A Russian lady named Helena mostly," she replied. You could have knocked me over with a feather.

Before leaving, Dianne asked me for my phone number so I wrote it down for her. On the way home, the girls were talking about their readings as I sat quietly in the backseat looking out the window, trying to process all that had been said to me that night. Several thoughts were flooding my mind. *Had Linda appeared in my life for a reason? Was I supposed to meet Linda to learn about a soul who was independent from the opinion of other souls? Was I supposed to meet Dianne through her? How did Dianne know all that personal stuff about me? Was Mark really there with her like she said?* It was one thing for me to talk to Spirit in my own solitude. It was another when I was being exposed by a stranger. The whole experience left me feeling very unsettled.

I tried to put Dianne's reading out of my mind and figure out how to get on with my life. However, I did heed her advice and stopped thinking about wanting to die. Perhaps I was past that point in my grief. I tried surrounding myself with friends and partying, but that was not working either. Something deep inside was now driving me to manipulate my external world to fill that void, to numb my pain.

When a part of a soul's personality is out of control, the result is usually an addiction.

My physical need for control and power in my life again had morphed into an addiction - a sex addiction. My compulsive behavior became out of control in no time and remained that way for many, many months as I tried to come to terms with Mark's death. I did not see it for what it was at the time, nor did I care to listen to my soul or Spirit World. My behavior was serving its purpose and I was not about to hang myself with a celibacy rope.

Mark had always made me feel beautiful, both inside and out, and now I was beginning to realize that he was right about the outer beauty by the attention I was receiving from men around me. I had my mother's dark hair and eyes and my father's height and smile. I was aware that men were giving me a second look and I liked the sexual energy being exchanged between us. I was discovering that I had power to seduce men by returning that look, and it was exciting. I felt alive again.

When an Airborne course arrived on base, I was in a routine now of going to the bars on a Friday night and fishing in the dark to find my next lover. I definitely had power - power between the sheets. That chosen soldier would continue to hook up with me every weekend until their course was finished, and they returned to their home base. Nine times out of ten, they were married, but that did not stop me. I felt safe. They could not lie to me, make promises they could not keep, or hurt me. It was what it was - a good time, not a long time. I was no longer a victim of love. Often times, I was the aggressor, and when they were the aggressor, I was definitely a willing participant. I was no longer vulnerable and I was fulfilling my need for control of my life again. Each time I would experience temptation calling me with regards to a married man, I chose to ignore my soul speaking to me. This new behavior was working for me, and I was not about to change it, not one little bit.

Shortly after Mark died, I received a card in the mail from my mother, apologizing for her behavior in December, along with a cheque for $2000. I phoned her to acknowledge the card and thanked her. During our conversation, I told her what had happened to Mark, choking several times on my words as I tried to tell her the news.

"I am so sorry, honey. Are you okay?" she asked.

"I will be eventually," I replied. That night, I appreciated our phone conversation more than words could express. My mother was feeling her daughter's pain.

In March, Rhoda and I closed the office for a week and took a Military Boeing to Comox, British Columbia. CFB Comox was the home of 442 Squadron, a SAR Squadron heavily active in response to distress calls from Victoria, the Yukon, and ships out on the Pacific Ocean. It was also home to CFSTS' sea survival courses due to its geographical location on the ocean. At the request of one of the school's instructors, Rhoda and I had decided to take the course together. It would be fun to get out of the office for a week, and the distraction was perfect timing for me. Little did we know what wild adventures lay ahead.

We spent Monday morning in the classroom, and the afternoon was my introduction to parasailing. So far, not so bad. Tuesday morning we donned our parachutes once again and boarded a ship to execute a procedure known as a 'drop and drag'. Student by student, we were hooked onto a cable that was attached to a crane at the rear of the ship, and we were hoisted into the air. There was a safety boat tailing behind the ship to help us through any emergencies. This course was designed to simulate pilots needing to eject from an aircraft, emphasize the importance of releasing themselves from their parachutes when landing in the water, and teach them how to survive until rescued. There is no better teaching tool than real-life exposure to a situation.

On a wave of the safety boat's flag, the cable was released and I dropped from several feet in the air, splashing down into the water below. The procedure I should have followed once I hit the water was to open my arms and legs to stabilize my body on top of the water, while simultaneously releasing myself from my parachute harness. Simple enough, but not for me! The ship is continually towing you through the water until you release yourself from the parachute harness, simulating the potential for a parachute to get caught in an undertow. Getting out of your parachute quickly can be a matter of life and death.

I shrieked when the cable let go, swallowing a huge mouthful of saltwater as I landed in the ocean. I was gasping for air and my stomach was heaving as I began rolling around in the water, totally disoriented. I could hear the megaphone from the safety boat: "Spread your legs open, Laurie."

My initial thought was, "I am drowning and all these idiots can think about is sex. Not funny guys!" But after hearing it several more times, I opened my legs and stabilized myself on the surface of the water. Still panicked and wanting to be free from being towed as quickly as possible, I hit a lever on the harness (the wrong one) and flipped onto my stomach. Now I was being dragged face down through the water. I only had two levers to push in a sequence, and I had managed to push the wrong one first. Go figure.

Finally free from the parachute harness, I climbed into my one-man raft. After violently vomiting, I leaned forward to get the seasickness pills from a side pocket on the raft, only to hear "Psssshhhh." I leaned back quickly. Good grief. Now I had a hole in my raft and needed to get to that pocket to find a patch, as well as the Gravol. I eventually managed to swallow a pill and patch my raft, but it was an exceptionally long day and night as I sat bobbing around at the ocean's mercy. Each student had been dropped into the water in such a way that we were totally alone. We could not see each other and our only contact was with the rescue boat when it came by every few hours to check on us. After the sun set in the sky, I was cold and lonely with way too much time to think. My mind never stopped at the best of times but having nowhere to go and nothing else to do, I was driving myself crazy with constant thought. I was never so happy in the wee hours of the early morning, as one by one, we were plucked from the ocean and I from my dismal thoughts of what a mess my life had been.

The third day, we had a break from the water and went back to the classroom to learn procedures for survival in a ten-man raft. We were left in the ocean once again, and after only four hours in that ten-man raft, I wanted to be in a one-man raft again. Rhoda and I were told not to get involved in any of the survival procedures, such as setting up a solar still for fresh water. It was more important for the pilots to learn the training because one day their life might depend on it. As spectators, we watched in disbelief as these young pilots argued with each other and could not get organized. We had to stay battened down for the first four hours and the water was rough. We were nothing more than a spinning top and some students were beginning to get seasick. By the time we were rescued from that raft, Rhoda and I both needed a drink, something really strong.

The course was finally finished and not a moment too soon. Unable to get a seat on the Boeing returning to Edmonton because it was fully booked, we stayed in Comox for another day, flying home Saturday as crew on an Aurora. It was the one and only time throughout my entire career that I would fly on that specialized aircraft, and it was an amazing, unforgettable experience; one that I cannot describe to my readers for national security reasons.

Shortly after I arrived home, I received a phone call from Dianne asking me to go for coffee. Instead, I decided to invite her to my place. She spent six hours at my house that night, answering many of my questions about Mark. It was midnight, I was tired, and I needed to work in the morning. The next day when I told my girlfriends about the visit, they seemed concerned. She had not reached out to any of them, just me. The next time I saw Dianne, I asked her outright why she had called me and not one of the other girls. Her response was, "I go where the Creator tells me to and I do not question His intent. You may think that you are disconnected from Spirit, but they are always with you, keeping you in line with your blueprint." *Was Dianne sent to help me find my way back?* I was certainly not ready to return yet. I was still angry inside and that anger was crying out for salvation with every man I slept with.

My father was planning a trip to the West Coast and filled me in on his intentions one night when he called. "I would like to come to Edmonton in May. From your place, I was thinking we could drive to Expo 86 in Vancouver. We can stop in Calgary and visit with your brother Jimmy. Then, we can stop in Trail and Vernon, British Columbia, so you can meet your aunts and uncles from my side of the family, and we will finish the trip in Vancouver. I will call Rick to see if he wants to meet up with us. What do you think? Can you get some time off work?" My father would be at my place in less than three weeks.

By the time my father arrived from Ontario, I had bought another car from one of Sharron's friends. It was a 1978 candy-apple-red Monte Carlo, and it was a boat in comparison to my old car. It definitely took time to get used to driving an eight-cylinder and not having a lead foot. That new car was going to be the perfect vehicle for our road trip, allowing my son a full playground in the backseat to keep him occupied. Laws with regards to seatbelts were still quite relaxed in those days. We stopped in Calgary overnight, and I had the chance to meet my new nephew who was a year old. Jimmy and Jaimie barbequed steaks for us, and we had such an enjoyable visit. Who doesn't like cocktails and a steak dinner with loved ones?

The Rocky Mountains in British Columbia enhance some of Western Canada's most breathtaking scenery. The sheer size of the mountain range, the crystal-clear waters of the lakes, and the ice caps off in the distance is Mother Nature at her best. The drive through the Okanagan Valley was just as breathtaking; a drive filled with fruit orchards, vineyards, and glacier deposits. Our first stop in British Columbia was to visit my father's older sister Mary. Aunt Mary had a heart of gold and all the patience in the world as she cared for her husband through his dementia. She reminded me of my Aunt Liz. They were two sisters filled with love and empathy for other people.

Uncle Dave was a character who loved to wander around on the breathtaking property they owned. After being introduced, I told my father I was going to sit at the picnic table and have a cigarette. Uncle Dave trailed behind me while my father and his sister went into the house. "Can I have one of those?" Uncle Dave asked as we sat down. I proceeded to give him a cigarette and lit it for him.

No sooner had I done so, when my Aunt Mary came to the back door to see if I wanted something to drink. She came barreling out of the house and grabbed the cigarette from my Uncle Dave's mouth. "Did you give him a cigarette, Laurie?" she asked.

"Yes" I replied. "He asked me for one."

"He does not smoke," she said. Oops! "David, David, David," she giggled, shaking her head as she walked back into the house.

After visiting for several hours, we stopped at my cousin Roger's place (Mary and Dave's son). Roger had a career playing professional football with the Edmonton Eskimos and the Toronto Argonauts before retiring. He was now married with a baby on the way and was teaching physical education to the local high-school students. My father and his nephew sat reminiscing about the old days for a few hours before we carried on.

Our last stop was at my father's older brother's home. Uncle Bill and Aunt Steff were so happy to see us and rolled out the welcome mat with a scrumptious meal and several hours of entertaining conversation. My father and his brother Bill could have passed for twins; the identical likeness was uncanny. It had been a privilege to meet each and every one of my father's family that day.

Continuing our drive to Vancouver, I began thinking about my Aunt Liz and figured this was the perfect opportunity to talk to my father about her. "Dad, do you ever regret not going to see Aunt Liz before she died?" I asked. "You were both so close and she wanted you to come to the hospital. She wanted to make peace with you."

He sat quiet for a minute, focusing on the road, but I could feel his remorse and his shame by the look on his face. *Why do we allow other souls to dictate our actions when our hearts and minds know better?* "I will live with that regret until the day I die. If I could go back and do it over again, I would do things differently. I should have just gone and seen my sister without telling Joan," he replied. *Why is hindsight always clearer after the fact, and why is there so much uncertainty when faced with being decisive in an exact moment? Is it because our emotions cloud our view or because we doubt ourselves? Is it because we allow others to influence us or make the decision for us?*

If a decision is made out of love, it will always be one you can live with.

I sat recalling my visit with my cousin, Debra, when we were nineteen years old and her telling me that her father had insisted that she and her sister, Maryanne, move out of the house after Aunt Liz died. His reasoning was that he was not comfortable having females living under his roof without a mother. They were seventeen and sixteen years old at the time and grieving the loss of their mother. I had always envied Debra's perfect life. To think that her father could rationalize such behavior was hard to comprehend. *Why are humans so cruel at times and why are we so worried about what other people will think?*

Through many more miles of highway, I thought of Joan and how many lives had been affected by her psychosis. My mother's family. My father's family. Our immediate family. *Does evil really have that much power over other souls or does the emotion of fear profoundly affect the way the brain processes the experience? Is fear a greater evil than the evil itself or is fear there to guide us into making the right decision?*

Fear feeds evil. Whenever you choose to resist evil, it loses power.

My brother Rick and his wife Catherine had gone their separate ways shortly after their daughter Megan was born. He had taken his release from the military at the end of his five-year contract and was now working as a prison guard at the Matsqui Institution, a federal medium-security prison facility in Abbotsford, British Columbia. Rick hopped on the SkyTrain and met us at Expo 86 the next morning, and Catherine and Megan joined us as well. We had a full day enjoying all the exhibits and spending time together.

Our return trip to Edmonton went much faster than the trip out to Vancouver as we drove straight home without stopping. For my father's last night in Edmonton, we enjoyed perogies for supper at my son's request. "Bubba taught you well," he said. "That meal alone was worth this trip." He spent a few hours watching a movie with TJ while I cleaned up the kitchen and then we decided to go to the Rosslyn for a nightcap. He wanted to see my favorite watering hole.

The bar was quiet for a weeknight, with just a handful of patrons. When the DJ began playing the song "Run Around Sue" my father pulled me to my feet with liquid adrenaline running through his veins. We began to "jive" with all its fun and energy, kicking and swinging in perfect unison. Our movements flowed with a dazzling grace. I had no idea that my father was such a good dancer. Perhaps, I had inherited my passion for dance through him.

All in all, it had been a great vacation and I cried after dropping my father off at the airport the next day. I was going to miss him. We had finally found our way back to each other again, without interference from any other soul. Our trip had been healing for both of us.

When I returned to the office on Monday morning, I was invited to go flying with the school's chopper pilot from 408 Squadron. He needed to log some flying hours, and I had never been in a CH135 Twin Huey tactical helicopter. It was more than a little scary being able to see the ground below my feet as we were flying, but it was thrilling once the initial fear dissipated. I had the wrong career. I should have been a pilot based on the euphoric high I got whenever I went flying with the instructors. To this day, if I watch the first four minutes of the movie *Top Gun* where the aircraft are taking off and landing on the flight deck of a destroyer to the music of Kenny Loggins' "Danger Zone", it is hard to contain my excitement. It makes me wonder if I was a pilot in another lifetime.

At the end of the day on Monday, the Commanding Officer gathered all the staff together for a meeting. "The next week is going to be quiet with a lull in training. I think this is a good time for all of the staff to get together at Jarvis Lake and do some training together - some team work so to speak," he said. "We will finish off the training with a Mess Dinner; dress will be civilian attire with a tie. Make sure you bring a tie with you." The meeting adjourned and the next two days were busy as the training staff prepared the curriculum, the supply staff loaded up the MLVW (Medium Logistics Vehicle Wheeled) with equipment, and Rhoda and I arranged for rations while continuing to prepare for the next course arriving the following week. Finally we were ready. Let the adventure begin!

Rhoda and I drove to Jarvis Lake together in her Bronco, blasting tunes from Dwight Yoakam's debut album *Guitars, Cadillacs, Etc., Etc.* and singing at the top of our lungs. When we arrived at the camp, it was a beautiful setting beside a river in the foothills of the Rocky Mountains. We removed our kit from the Bronco and set ourselves up in one of the para cabins (a half-built log structure covered with a parachute). The camp employed a civilian year-round whose job was to maintain the camp and teach "bush craft" when students were on site. Jack was a fountain of knowledge, immediately showing us how to start our water immersion heater.

There was also a civilian cook on site who would make meals for the staff whenever they were at the camp to instruct. Students were not provided with meals because they were learning to survive off the land. In extreme situations, they were given a survival candy (that equated to 1,000 calories) to help them keep going. We unloaded groceries and equipment and then gathered together for a nightcap in the kitchen to discuss the following day's activities.

After coffee and toast the next morning, we began loading the zodiac boats into the water of the Wild Hay River. Rhoda and I climbed into one of the boats, accompanied by Pretty Boy Bob, one of the SAR Instructors. I did not know how that man could look at himself in the mirror every morning and not feel himself up. Saying he was drop-dead gorgeous does injustice to the expression. Bob was the raft guide on the front of our zodiac. Rhoda was paddling from the right side, and I was paddling from the left. Watching for boulders in the water, Bob would yell out commands to us, "Back left. Forward right. Strong right. Easy left," as we navigated the winding river. That split second that he took his eyes off the water to shut off the alarm on his watch, we heard, "Strong back both! Strong back both!" No sooner had he barked the last command when we hit a boulder, swinging the boat to the left, and turning it backwards as Bob flew through the air off the front of the boat like a cartoon character. There were a few of us who took some spills into the river's foamy peaks that day. He was not the only one.

After supper we went into the town of Hinton for a few drinks, stopping at the Timberland Hotel. Rhoda and I spent most of the night two-stepping with the local cowboys while the boys drank pitcher after pitcher of draught beer. Not ready to go to bed yet, we continued partying when we returned to camp. Bob slipped away quietly, sneaking off to bed, and when Rhoda and I noticed he was gone, we went looking for him. We found him in his bunk and kept coaxing him to get up. One of the supply guys came through the door on his way to bed and said, "I will help you get him up," as he proceeded to yank Bob's blanket off of him. His sleeping attire left his face quite red and ours too. We saw a whole lot more of Bob than we had bargained for, and he was not a happy camper. Maybe it was time to go to bed ourselves. As we began walking towards the para cabins, we heard shouting from the top of the ACCO trailer behind us. It was the supply guy with Bob's blanket wrapped around him and let me tell you, "A blanket was all he was wearing," as he slipped and fell from the roof, landing on a mound of dirt below. The Commanding Officer, having had enough of all our high jinks, sent us all to bed.

Most of us regretted the decision to party so hard the night before as we set out for a hike up Mount Morrow the next morning. Normally, the hike to the summit takes about two hours and is challenging, but the night before had taken its toll on a few of us, resulting in blood, sweat, and vomit. We made it to the top by noon, had lunch, and took photos of the most spectacular views. After signing the registry, we headed back down the mountain. Our next stop was the Miette Hot Springs, the hottest hot springs in the Canadian Rockies. For the next two hours, we basked in her brine, letting her soak up all of our aches and pains.

At 7:00 p.m., we made our way to the ACCO trailer to attend the Mess Dinner, and there is no such thing as being fashionably late for such an occasion. The table was beautifully set as we stood behind our chairs waiting for the Commanding Officer to tell us to sit. Because the dinner is formal, you cannot smoke or go to the washroom without permission and conversation is kept to a minimum. A Mess Dinner demands social grace; a grace that went right out the window as the speeches began after our meal. Copious amounts of alcohol had been consumed throughout dinner, and the speeches were heading down hill quickly as all topics became fair game. The evening drew to a close in the early morning hours as we all stumbled back to our sleeping quarters. It had been an incredible few days with some very special people; people that I still hold dearly in my heart to this day.

When we returned to the school on Monday, there was a posting message waiting for me. My job at CFSTS was ending in August, and my new job for the next three years would be working at the Recruiting Centre (CFRC) in downtown Edmonton. I was heavy hearted at the thought. I was going to miss the school and the camaraderie. These people had become a family to me and the thought of not seeing them on a daily basis was a depressing thought. Rhoda had been an incredible boss, but additionally, she had been a wonderful friend and someone I could always depend on.

I had discovered a respect for the Search and Rescue trade as I learned all the qualifications that were required of them on a daily basis to do their job; qualifications such as parachuting, mountaineering, swimming, hiking, and scuba diving, not to mention the paramedic side of things. They wore their red berets proudly and now I knew *why*. They were a team of highly qualified rescue specialists that I had had the privilege of knowing and working with for the past two years.

I was also going to miss the thrill of flying with the aircrew instructors. An unbelievably special chapter of my life was ending. Another loss coming so soon after Mark was about to send me spiraling even deeper into my addiction.

Spiritual Beings on a Human Experience

Exit points in blueprints give a soul an option to stay in physical form or return to the spiritual realm if the soul finds that life has become too unbearable. An exit is written into a blueprint during a specific time of crisis for the soul, and Laurie has now passed two exit points on her journey. The first is her near-drowning experience in Florida when she was sixteen years old, written in as an option to free her soul from her child-hood experiences. The second exit point for her soul is the death of her twin flame, which she has now chosen to forego in order to be with her child. Laurie's soul has designed a total of five exit points into her blueprint for this lifetime, and because leaving affects many souls, exits are carefully planned in a blueprint with the Creator's blessing.

Grief is the greatest badge of love to another soul. As Mark witnesses Laurie's struggle to recover from the loss, as well as the struggle of other souls that were touched by his life, his soul is learning that he has not found peace in his choice to exit. Suicide is a free will choice and not without consequences even though it can be a designed exit point. The soul who chooses to leave in this manner is responsible for karma to every other single soul that they have touched in a significant way.

When a soul disengages from Spirit, so will Spirit disengage from the soul and stop intervening in respect of a choice, but Spirit will still con-tinue to work behind the scenes to keep a soul on its chosen path. The voice of Spirit can quickly get drowned out by the sounds of anger. When Laurie's soul is no longer listening due to her anger, her Creator continues to speak blessings and encouragement to her through other souls. Often times that encouragement appears through someone who IS listening. Dianne has become Laurie's connection back to the Spirit World without her fully realizing it yet.

Evil presents itself to Laurie as her childhood fantasy, her Knight in Shining Armor coming to rescue her during her despair. As the Devil tries to win over her soul for the second time, her Angel is guarding her heart and mind with the same forceful power.

Authentic power is the alignment of the personality with the soul, but True Power is learning to love yourself. Laurie is still looking for another soul to validate her. Her pursuit of External Power, rather than turning inward to fill her emptiness, has resulted in a sex addiction. Addiction is usually born from a terrible strain of life events and serves a purpose to the soul at the time. Laurie is using this addiction to feel more powerful, more worthy, and more lovable. She believes this behavior is making her feel better about herself - that it is filling an emotional craving and an inner emptiness, but she will learn the consequences of her actions soon enough. Once a soul has an addiction, the addiction can only be conquered through choice. She is free to choose her addiction, but she is not free from the consequences of that choice.

Temptation is a gift from the Universe. It allows a soul to recognize and heal a part of itself that is unhealthy before the soul creates negative consequences. It is designed to make a soul stop and think. Below Laurie's temptation with married men is pain. By challenging the pain, she will become more aligned with her soul and grow spiritually. She has a choice between that spiritual growth or remaining in the unending cycle of the same consequences. Her Spirit World waits patiently for her to figure it out. If she does not, they will be there to help her pick up the pieces of her soul when she self-destructs and align her once again with her chosen path.

CHAPTER 8

SPIRALING OUT OF CONTROL

Are we co-dependent by nature in order to survive? Does our happiness depend on a thriving relationship with another soul? Do we need a hand to hold through the darkness, and how dark should the darkness get before we realize that we need to reach for the light, with or without that hand to hold?

I was still struggling with the loss of Mark, and my son was not being helpful through my grief. He missed Mark too and was constantly asking for him, especially if he was frustrated with me. Tonight was no different. "I don't want you. I want Mark. Make him come back," he began.

"He won't be coming back, son. He is far away now," I replied hugging him.

"Is that why you cry?" he asked.

"Yes, Mommy really misses him too. How about we go into the kitchen and make your snack together," I said. I was trying to distract him from a conversation that I really did not want to have. I began wondering what a five-year-old mind could understand about death. Then I wondered if Spirit was speaking to him like they had spoken to me when I was his age. *Can he hear them too and does he know that Mark is dead?*

My mother called to tell me that she had moved from Toronto back home to Tecumseh, Ontario. She and Donald had bought a mobile home in the same park where my father was living. "I was talking with your father the other day over a few cocktails, and we were wondering if we could have TJ for the summer? You can even send him now if you want."

Maybe that was not such a bad idea, so I agreed. I had not been acting rational lately, and it might be good for both of us to be apart for a short while. I phoned my father to give him my son's flight information, and he assured me he would be at the Toronto Airport to pick him up. Two days later, TJ was flying solo once again on a commercial aircraft as an "unaccompanied minor".

Base Accommodation called advising me that they had a three-bedroom townhouse available for me to move into, and I could pick up the keys at my convenience. Lynn and I decided to move things over slowly that week by using our cars. The entire kitchen was set up in the new place, our clothes were hanging in the closets, and several boxes of personal items were moved. By Friday, all that was left in the old PMQ was the heavy furniture. Lynn rallied her Airborne friends and two people she knew with trucks. Within two hours, including a run to the liquor store, we had moved into the new place and the housewarming party had begun. I was on a mission to get the beds set up and filled with water before I began partying.

"I will help you, Laurie," Rob said. "There is one condition though. I really want a home cooked meal. I am sick of mess hall food."

"Done," I replied.

When I walked into the living room the next morning, it looked like a Wendy's war zone. There were french-fries scattered everywhere, spilled drinks, pickles and onions strewn across my coffee table, and Rob had passed out face down on the floor, planted into his cheeseburger. When he lifted his head, we all began laughing as we witnessed the hamburger patty stuck to his cheek, glued on with ketchup, mustard, and cheese. Several people left when they awoke, while others remained to help with the cleanup. That night I cooked roast beef, mashed potatoes, carrots, gravy, and homemade buns, as eight of us sat down to dinner.

Another Boss's Night was rolling around again as Sharron and I made plans to meet up at the Lancaster Park Mess on Friday night. By the time she arrived, I was well on my way to feeling good. I was partying with my girlfriends and some Airborne friends who were in town on their free fall course. It did not take long for Sharron to catch up with us as she pounded back a few doubles. On my return from a trip to the bar, I walked past a table of SAR Techs from 440 Squadron sitting with some of the school's instructors. "Hi, Laurie," Doug called out. "Come over and say hello."

There was an empty chair at the end of the table so I sat down and began chatting. The chair I was sitting in belonged to the SAR Tech who had reported me to the School Chief for talking out of line to his wife. When he returned from the washroom, he grabbed the back of my chair and dumped me out of it onto the floor. Then he poured my drink on top of me. Everyone started laughing, but I failed to see the humor. Without saying a word, I stood up and walked away.

Sharron had seen what had happened and followed me into the washroom. I began crying as I tried to wipe off my clothing. "He is a jerk. You should have just smacked him one good. I would have," she said. Sharron was a tough, no-nonsense girl who was not afraid to defend herself, unlike me. "You really need to toughen up girl," was her last comment to me as we exited the washroom.

On our way back to our table, Doug stopped us halfway. He put his arm around me. "Laurie, Pete is an asshole. Pay no attention to him. Come to the bar with me and let me buy you another drink."

"Leave me alone," I replied pushing him away. He placed his hands on my shoulders, trying to pull me closer and console me. I was not having any of it as the anger inside of me began surfacing. I placed my forearms on his chest and began pushing away as he continued to try and pull me in.

"She said to leave her alone," Sharron shouted getting everyone's attention.

He finally let go, but not before he was grabbed from behind by one of my Airborne friends. In a matter of seconds, the brawl was on between the SAR Techs and the Airborne as Sharron and I tried to get out of the line of fire. There were not enough bouncers working that night to control the number of people fighting. The lights in the Mess came on and an announcement followed. "The Mess is now closed, and the Military Police have been called. Anyone still in the building when they arrive is going to jail for the night." The building emptied very quickly, and we made plans in the parking lot to go to the Rosslyn. It was 10:00 p.m. by now, and I had been drinking gin since 4:00 p.m.; a drink that was bought for me in error, but one that I was rather enjoying as I continued to consume it for the first time.

When we walked into the Rosslyn, I heard "Don't say hello, stupid," as I walked past a table where one of Mike's friends was sitting. Jim was no stranger to me. He and Mike had been roommates at one time, and Jim and I had gone out a few times before my senses returned in a moment of clarity.

"Hello, stupid," I replied.

That angered Jim as he became quite vocal. "Sorry. Do not talk to Laurie tonight. She is with the Airborne. Well go fuck the Airborne, you little slut," he shouted at me confrontationally. My heart began pounding and I was shaking as rage pulsed through my veins and gripped my ability to think clearly. *How dare he speak to me like that!* The Gates of Hell swung wide open as that rage surfaced and I closed my fist, driving him right between the eyes. The punch hit him with such force that his chair flipped over backwards, leaving him lying on the floor with his feet dangling in the air. Jim quickly rolled over and stood up.

"I will kill you, you little bitch!" he threatened as he attempted to lunge for me across the table, but I was surrounded by Sharron and five Airborne friends.

"You and what fucking Army is going to lay a hand on her? You started it, asshole. You want to fight someone? Come on big man, let's take it outside right now," one of my friends bellowed.

"It's cool man," Jim replied shrugging his shoulders while regaining his composure. No sooner had Jim sorted out his chair and sat down again when I felt the back of my shirt at the neckline being lifted. It was the bouncer. "Time to go home for tonight, Laurie. You threw the first punch."

"Party is at Laurie's," they all shouted following me as the bouncer showed me to the door.

When I awoke the next morning, my hand was swollen and bruised. It hurt to move it. As I walked into the living room, Sharron stirred from under the blanket on the couch and then sat up. "What the hell happened last night?" I asked her.

"You clocked Jim right between the eyes, but he deserved it. I never liked that guy. He is just a little mouthpiece who never knows when to shut up." She proceeded to give me a blow-by-blow description of what took place and finished by praising me for standing up for myself. I did not feel proud. I was horrified by the turn of events. I had never hit another soul in my life, and God knows there were many souls who deserved it. That kind of behavior was totally out of character for me. I was always a happy drunk. "The boys and I had your back. Jim was out for blood after you hit him, but he reeled himself in pretty quick," she continued. As I washed my face that morning, I began wondering if my frustration and anger were now leading me down a road of aggression.

"Sharron, what is wrong with me?" I asked as we sat down at the kitchen table with our coffee. "I feel so angry inside all the time lately."

"You have been through a lot," she replied.

"Do you think it was the gin? Is that what made me so aggressive?" I asked.

"Could be, but I tend to think it is more your grief over Mark. He was so devoted to you, and there was never any doubt in my mind how much he loved you by the way he treated you and how he spoke about you to me. No wonder you feel so lost without him. I noticed the change in you after he left to go back to Trenton. Things will get better, Laurie. I promise. I have been in those dark places myself."

What Sharron was about to share with me, I could have never seen coming in a million years. She began to fill me in on her childhood. She was the Cinderella of her family - the child of less worth and the family workhorse. Her father started sexually abusing her at twelve years old. By the time she was fifteen, she was pregnant. As a result of incestuous genetics, her child was born with spinal bifida and ended up becoming a ward of the court when she could no longer care for him. Suddenly, the pain of my childhood seemed trivial to hers as my heart went out to her. I could not even imagine what that must have been like for her. It explained so much about her personality now; her independence from her family, her aggressiveness when backed into a corner, and her contentment to be alone and self-sufficient. She was a survivor. Even more disturbing to me now was the fact that my mother was living with an incestuous pedophile and a child rapist. This story was only beginning. The dirty little secret was about to unfold over the next few years, and the secret would affect quite a few people by 1989, with me being smack dab right in the middle of it all.

The following weekend, Sharron had a pool tournament she was attending out of town. Sharron was a strong billiards player, and her home was filled with trophies of her accomplishments. Pattina and I decided to have supper together on Thursday night. While dining, she mentioned that a few of the girls were heading to Cold Lake on Saturday and asked if I wanted to join them. Cold Lake is a city in North Eastern Alberta and was home to Canada's Western F18 Fighter Squadron at that time.

"What's going on there?" I asked.

"It's Exercise Maple Flag, and they are having a 'meet and greet' on Saturday night. You know how much Debbie likes her pilots. Should be a lot of fun," she said.

The mission of Maple Flag is to bring Allied Air Forces together in a combat role against a hostile aggressor. Approximately five thousand pilots and support crews participate in this annual event from countries worldwide, and if your desire is to meet a pilot, Maple Flag is the place to be. A man in a flight suit is a man after my heart, so I was not about to say 'no' to a night of eye candy. Lea and Debbie were planning to stay in Cold Lake for the night, but Pattina had to work the next morning. So I took my car as well, and we all headed for Cold Lake late Saturday afternoon.

You could hardly move in the room as we walked into the Officer's Mess. There were wall-to-wall pilots; everywhere a person glanced were handsome men in their flight suits. After several hours of drinking, I noticed a man standing by the bar who had been undressing me with his beautiful blue eyes for the past half hour. When I approached the bar to buy another drink, he struck up a conversation with me by paying for my drink. He was from Australia and his accent was captivating to listen to.

After twenty minutes of conversation he asked, "Would you like to see my cockpit?"

"I assume you are talking about your fighter jet," I replied.

"Of course," he said as he took my hand and led me down a narrow hallway towards the hangar. I was excited at the thought of having my picture taken in the cockpit of an Australian fighter jet. Before we reached the hangar, he pushed me through a bathroom door and into a stall. *Oh dear God. He is going to rape me. Relax, Laurie, relax. You cannot overpower him!* He unzipped his flight suit, exposed himself and placed his hand under my skirt, literally ripping my thong from my body. His manhood was made for cattle, not humans, as he turned me around and slammed me up against the wall. Holding his forearm against the back of my neck, he entered me from behind. He was rough and aggressive and fear had paralyzed me from any movement or sound.

When he finished relieving himself, he zipped up and left the stall without a word. My stomach emptied into the toilet immediately from the shock. I sat on the toilet crying for several minutes as I tried to compose myself and control the bleeding from the damage he had done. I took handfuls of paper towel, wadding it up under cold water to make a compress and held it against my body. I picked up my underwear from the floor and threw them in the garbage. I took out another pair of grannie panties from my purse, made a sanitary pad from toilet paper, and left the washroom to find Pattina. Not a single person had entered the washroom the entire time. He knew exactly what he was doing when he took me there. We had been totally isolated from the rest of the party.

When I returned to the Officer's Mess, my rapist was nowhere to be found. It was after eleven when I found Pattina and told her I was not feeling well and wanted to go home. "I have had enough myself," she said as we made our way to the car. When we finally returned home, I had to sit in a bathtub for hours to ease my pain and swelling. One would think that this horrific experience would have snapped me back to reality, but I could not see the addiction for what it was. I saw the rape as an isolated incident, the result of a bad choice on my part.

By Monday morning, I needed to see a doctor. It was obvious to a medical professional that I had been raped, but I refused to disclose any information to her. I was ashamed and just wanted her to make the physical pain go away. So I told her that the sex was consensual, and we got carried away in the moment. I am sure that she did not believe me, but she let the subject go and wrote me a prescription. I never spoke of the incident to anyone. Perhaps it was the shame that I felt. Or perhaps, it was the fear of judgment by others - judgment that might lead to rejection. Either way, I had made the decision to take that secret to the grave.

I was partying at the Rosslyn the following Friday night when I was approached by Fred, an Airborne instructor at CABC. I knew who Fred was. He had tried to hit on me several times in the past few months, but I also knew he had a girlfriend - a tough cookie that I had no desire to tangle with. "Come here, Laurie," he said wrapping his arm around my waist. "I want to ask you something." He proceeded to tell me that the instructors from CABC were flying to Yuma, Arizona in two weeks to do a few desert jumps. "The Herc is leaving on Friday night and coming back on Sunday. Come with me for the weekend. I will pay for your hotel room, and I will get your name added to the flight manifest. There is great shopping in Yuma," he said.

"Let me think about it," I replied as I pulled away from him and returned to the dance floor.

Debbie called me a few days later. "Did Fred ask you to go to Yuma with him, Laurie?" she asked.

"Yes, why? How did you know?" I asked.

"Allison (Fred's girlfriend) was in the Junior Ranks Mess tonight, and I overheard the conversation she was having with some of the guys from behind the bar. Please don't go. He is setting you up to gang rape you and leave you stranded in Arizona. Fred has no intention of putting you on the return manifest to get back home," she said. There was a lull in the conversation. I think I was in shock at what I was hearing.

"Why would he do such a thing?" I finally asked her.

"I really don't know. I am just letting you know what I overheard."

"Thanks, Debbie, you are a good friend," I said as I hung up the phone.

The following Friday, Fred asked me for my decision, and I immediately declined to go with him. My excuse was that I had company coming in from out of town. "Besides, I barely know you and I know you have a girl-friend. How does SHE feel about all of this?" I asked. He replied with, "Ali is not my girlfriend although she likes to think she is."

"Whatever," I said as I stood up to walk away. That is when he grabbed me by the wrist. "You need to take your hands off me right now," I shouted at him sternly. Mike, one of my Airborne friends that I had grown up with in Windsor walked over.

"Fred, let go of her. Come and have a shooter with me, Laurie," he said as he placed his hand in the small of my back and guided me to the bar. "Fred is bad news, darling. You need to stay as far away from him as you can. He is a pompous ass who is full of himself. There are rumors at CABC that he has an agenda with you because you have rejected him. Nobody says 'no' to Fred. So as your friend, I am telling you to be careful. Cheers!" he said raising his shot glass into the air. I already knew Fred's agenda through my earlier conversation with Debbie, so I promised Mike that I would keep my distance as we tossed back our shooters. My experience in Cold Lake was still very fresh in my mind, and I had no desire to go back down that road again.

As I continued drinking, I began wondering if there was a part of the human psyche where good and bad or right and wrong get lost. Do we always know better subconsciously and just make a choice to exercise our own free will based on our emotions in the moment? I had never done anything to Fred. Why would he purposely set out to hurt and injure me? I was a complete stranger to him, more or less. Was rejecting him reason enough for him to plan and execute such a cruel retaliation? Or was he an evil soul with no conscience, just like Joan?

I had not lied to Fred about company coming to visit. Cindy was going through her divorce and wanted to come to Edmonton for a week. She was messed up (over her ex refusing to give her the children) and needed a diversion from the chaos she was going through. There are lots of things that we feel bad about in life and things that we wish we had done differently. There is no avoiding that, but the one thing that a soul never feels bad about is following the heart when it comes to family. I was always happy to see Cindy no matter what her state of mind was and enthusiastically agreed to pick her up at the airport. When your own life is a mess, it is hard to be much help to anyone else, and who was I to judge her state of mind when my own was off the rails. Maybe all we needed was each other in order to heal.

We spent countless hours talking about what was going on in both our lives. Although our struggles as children were different, we both had struggles, and the lack of nurturing parental guidance had left us both floundering as damaged adults.

The week flew by, but not without fun as well. We spent time at West Edmonton Mall shopping and taking in all the tourist attractions. We sat on a bench outside of a recording studio and watched through the glass window as people made recordings of their favorite songs. I was amazed by the talent as well as the lack thereof, as we entertained ourselves for half an hour while sipping an Orange Julius.

We went to the Griesbach Mess and the Rosslyn on Friday night and partied with my friends. Being unfamiliar with a military environment, Cindy found my Airborne friends to be crude and aggressive. The Airborne Regiment is a rapid reaction force of highly skilled soldiers, the quick responders in protecting our national security, a rogue regiment. They are definitely a different breed of soldier; the kind you need protecting your country. I had been accepted into their inner circle and their loyalty and protection was unfaltering. They were friends that I did not expect to be polite or politically correct. It would have made them appear odd given the very nature of what they did for a living. Perhaps they appear crude and aggressive to all civilians until you get to know them. Cindy was the first one to ever mention it.

Cindy was leaving to go home on Sunday so we decided to spend a quiet Saturday night with Dianne. Before Dianne's arrival, I warned Cindy that she was a spiritual psychic who was different from most people. She speaks her mind in the moment and is often unaware of the impact she has on others with what she blurts out. I was used to her by now, but tonight she was going to have my heart hammering against my chest with a captivating fear too.

Dianne arrived at my place around 6:00 p.m., and we gathered at the kitchen table. After an hour or so of idle chitchat, Cindy asked Dianne if she would tell her who her real father was. "Are you sure you really want to know?" Dianne asked.

"I have always suspected who he was, and I think that he is the family's dirty little secret," she replied. "He is dead now if it is who I believe it is. What is the harm in knowing?"

Dianne asked me to bring her a white candle. She anointed the candle with an oil she had in her purse and said a prayer while lighting it. She asked Cindy to sit directly across the table from her, so Cindy and I switched chairs. "I want you to look through the flame of the candle directly into my face. I am going to leave and whoever wants to speak to you will come through my body."

As we sat watching, Dianne straightened up in her chair and closed her eyes. Almost immediately, her face changed as she opened her eyes and began speaking French. She was angry. Meme had arrived and was not happy with Cindy. "Laisser seul" (Leave it alone) were the words shouted at Cindy, mixed in with other words of aggression. Cindy and I looked at each other.

"I need to know," she said to me as she returned to looking through the flame, telling Meme that she wanted to speak to Nort.

The candle flame began flickering wildly. Dianne's face changed again and a man came through as her voice deepened. "I am your father, but you have always known that" were the next words out of Dianne's mouth. Suddenly my house became a house of anger. Bedroom doors began slamming and windows were rattling. Terror washed over me as the hairs on the back of my neck stood straight up.

"Dianne, please come back," I shouted. *What is it about family secrets? Nobody talks about them, but everybody knows about them, except the people who should.*

When Dianne returned to her body, she asked Cindy if she had received her answer. "Do you speak French?" I asked Dianne.

"No, why?" she asked. We sat discussing what had happened for hours. Cindy and I were both still afraid of what we had witnessed, and I never wanted Dianne to do that again. Neither one of us slept well that night. As we talked about it again the next morning, I was still unsettled by what I had witnessed. My comfort level with Dianne had changed, and I was afraid of her again. Cindy flew back to Ontario later that afternoon and called when she had arrived home safely, thanking me once again for the hospitality. Thirty-three years have passed and to this day, we still speak about Cindy's last night in Alberta with Dianne.

Linda had found her own place before we moved to the three-bedroom townhouse, but she spent more time at my place than her own. My home had a revolving door, so you never knew who was going to be there when you arrived. There was always lots of activity and fun to be had. I had purchased an oversized sectional couch for the living room that slept several people very comfortably, and Linda often crashed at my place for the weekend. I loved having her around because we both had the same wicked sense of humor. She stopped by one night and offered to help me set up TJ's new bedroom before his return home. We made up his bed with new linens, unpacked all the boxes, and hung pictures on the walls. I missed my son and I was looking forward to seeing him. Three more weeks and my life would be complete again.

To start my day Monday morning, I turned on some music and began French braiding my hair, putting on my makeup, and dressing for work. I was starting my new job at the Recruiting Centre (CFRC) today, and I was feeling the stress and anxiety of the unknown. The lady living next door to me was already working at CFRC, so we made plans to carpool together. Kate had come over and introduced herself when I moved in. Her husband was retired from the military and a stay-at-home father, who occupied his time by looking after six-year-old twin girls. The age difference between Kate and her husband was very apparent, but it seemed to work for them. Kate spent many Friday nights partying with us while her husband stayed home with the twins and was content to do so.

My first week at CFRC went well, but it was a busy place with a learning curve and I was often exhausted when I got home. Friday around 4:00 p.m. Debbie called me to give me a heads-up that two of my previous lovers had just arrived back in town. They had been in the Mess earlier for a few drinks. "They are both here for their jump masters course. What are you going to do? Who is going to be the lucky guy?" she asked giggling.

"I am going to avoid both of them," was my response. Easier said than done. Perhaps the Universe was on a mission to show me the error of my ways before I ended up in a place that would be impossible to come back from.

Before I left to go out that night, I had every intention of coming back home alone. I was nervous about meeting up with both of them again, so I proceeded to drink heavily with the boys, including tequila shooters. When I awoke Saturday morning, I was in a three-way script with two previous lovers, one on each side of me and no recollection of the night. I was in pain as I tried to get out of a waterbed that was challenging my every attempt to free myself. I had no idea what had gone on in my bed or how we had ended up there together. *I need to stop drinking tequila. I always seem to black out when I overdo it.* I turned the shower on and attempted to wash the filth from my body as tears rolled down my cheeks. *I am such a mess! I really need to get a grip. I need to stop drinking so heavily, and I need to stop jumping into bed with all these men before something really terrible happens.* While I was in the shower, my ex-lovers left that morning without a single word being exchanged between us.

Navigating life on my own terms had resulted in an awful mess that I was struggling to figure out. My travels had taken me down a road that had left me morally and ethically wounded. My soul felt destroyed by the shame of my actions and I longed for conversation with my Spirit World again. *Father, I am reaching out for your healing hands even though I do not deserve them. I know now that you are the light where my darkness ends. I am so sorry. Please come back and forgive me. The more I look for validation using seduction and fantasy, the more physical pain I feel. I need you to help me understand. I need to get my act together before my son comes home so that I can be the mother that he needs me to be. I know I don't deserve your Grace, but please come back into my life! I am so lost without you.*

Suddenly my Creator began speaking as I cowered at the brightness of the White Light and fell to my knees. I could not look up. The brightness was blinding.

I have not come here to condemn you, My child. Your pain is coming from your own heart, a heart that needs time to digest what your mind already knows. Put your thoughts on paper. Words have power when written in pain and sorrow, and they are healing to your soul.

I wept tears of joy from His grace, and I began to put my feelings on paper that day. As I continued writing for several weeks, the words took shape as highly rhythmical and expressive literary works. I was finally starting to see my behavior for what it really was. By telling myself that I was in control and no soul was ever going to hurt me again, I was in essence hurting myself with outrageous behavior and the delusion that I could live my life without love from another soul or the Spirit World. Let me be clear. It took me many months to figure it out through deep conversations with Sharron and Linda, by putting my thoughts and feelings on paper, and by reconnecting with my Spirit World. It was a process. As the months passed, my soul was slowly becoming a cornerstone of a building in progress once again.

I had a shift in roommates the following week. Lynn decided to move to CFB Petawawa in Ontario and Linda had already found her own place weeks earlier, so it was back to my son and me. I needed another roommate as soon as possible for military reasons. When I ran into Pattina a few days later, we started talking about Lynn's decision to move to Petawawa, and by the end of the conversation, Pattina had decided to move in with me. I was back on track again.

Life in my new home settled down after Lynn's departure, coupled with my son's return. TJ was happy in his new environment and happy to have his mother back in his life again. He had lots of stories about his time away - swimming in the park pool, having breakfast and watching cartoons with Grandpa Jim, eating shrimp cocktail with his Grandma and Aunt Anne, playing with his cousins from the United States, and riding tractors with Grandpa Don. He was a happy little boy as we snuggled together on the couch watching *Ferris Bueller's Day Off* and eating pizza. He was starting grade one in a few days, and I had enrolled him in a gymnastics program with a local community group. He was forever climbing up on the furniture and tumbling off, sometimes on purpose, other times not so much. Gymnastics might just be the perfect solution.

Once a soul has recognized a dysfunctional behavior, are we out of the woods? Can we just flip a switch and the behavior disappears? Or does successful change only come in stages with awareness and repetition of a new behavior or a different coping skill? More importantly, if we are aware there is a problem and we have made a conscious commitment to take action to fix it, is it inevitable that we are bound to relapse by triggers of the old behavior? Even though I had reconnected with my Creator and Spirit World, had a wonderful support group of friends around me, and I was finally beginning to understand why I had been acting the way I had been acting, I was definitely not out of the woods yet. My addiction would remain a struggle whenever I was presented with a crisis, and I adopted it off and on as my means of coping and survival for the next twenty years.

"Why?" you might ask. Because my life was not about to settle down in any way, shape, or form anytime soon.

Spiritual Beings on a Human Experience

God is love and all aspects of him speaking to a soul are rooted in love. Children can and do hear from Him because every soul is welcomed to have a relationship with Him. Hearing is especially easier for young children because they remain connected to where they arrived from for several years. As time passes, it is by choice that souls stop listening because they stop believing. Laurie has learned that her Creator is accessible to her from a young age. He speaks to her in many different ways, such as nature, music, dreams, and visions. He comes with messages of truth and words of knowledge specifically designed for her when she needs them most. Laurie's son is hearing his Creator speak to him but recognizes it as his own thought in his busy physical world. Spirit is waiting for her to share her experiences with her son and others, to speak her truth, but she still withdraws as she continues to try and figure out who she is. Fear of judgment continually holds her back.

All the feelings a soul experiences are designed as information to help a soul to grow. Movement towards a feeling is essential for clarity and to avoid self-abandonment. Judging yourself or turning to addictions to numb the feelings fills a soul with fear and false beliefs. Laurie has abandoned her loving self through her pain of Mark's death and replaced the pain with the false belief that she is not worthy of love. Coupled with a fear that the future will only hold more pain, loss, and suffering, she is attempting to numb herself and continue her life without feeling. She needs to put her energy into a relationship with herself, for only then will she realize she is someone worthy of love, respect, and compassion. She will know it when she learns to give it to herself.

During her rape, Laurie is unaware that her Angel is blessing her soul by returning her to the Spirit Realm. Those few moments of removal are designed to spare her mind and heart from the intensity of her harsh reality.

She will not be spared the physical result of her actions. She is responsible for the choice and the consequence. An Angel will always continue to protect a soul until that soul discovers that its choices are no longer serving a purpose.

Laurie's anger and aggressive behavior is rooted in pain, but without pain, the soul is not capable of transforming. With pain comes the necessity to get on with the challenge of self-change. She must learn to submit and retreat from her anger. She must feel her pain in order to become who she truly is. By returning to her Spirit World, she has made the first step towards healing and self-change. She is welcomed back immediately and provided with the wisdom she needs to achieve her healing.

When Laurie reaches out to her Creator with shame and remorse for her behavior, along with a renewed clarity and the desire to dispel her darkness, He appears with blinding White Light of understanding and forgiveness. In this moment, by His light of love and compassion, she is experiencing the death of a way of being that is no longer valid to the Self she needs to become. She is witnessing the magnitude and glory of her Creator's restorative power.

CHAPTER 9

SEARCHING FOR SALVATION

Knock! Knock! Knock! "Hey Dianne, come on in. Let me turn the music down. Sorry! I have had a thought in my head for two days now, and I was trying to chase it away with some music," I said as I turned the stereo down to an acceptable level.

"What's the thought? What is bugging you?" she asked.

"I have been thinking about the whole blueprint thing and karma. I must have been pretty bad in my last lifetime - abusing children, callous about love, just to mention a few things. Look at my life so far this time. It has been one catastrophe after another," I replied.

"That's not how I see it," she said. "A blueprint is balanced as well as life itself. Do you want to break some of it down together?"

"Over coffee with Baileys?" I asked.

"Is there any other way?" was her response.

"First of all, your life HAS been a series of catastrophes as you put it, but you designed it that way. Maybe you wanted to get through your lessons quicker by choosing a high number of more difficult challenges. Maybe you decided to try and get through three lifetimes in one. How has that worked out for you? Did you bite off a little more than you could chew?" she asked chuckling.

"It certainly feels that way sometimes," I replied.

Dianne continued, "If you hear nothing more today, hear this. You have never abused children in any of your former lifetimes, so you were not sent back as an abused child to repay that karma. You volunteered to help another soul on their journey. Hear me! You volunteered to be Joan's child. She was supposed to come back in this lifetime and NOT abuse her children. She failed miserably at that, but that's her crap to deal with. Make no mistake: Joan will have to face her actions once she gets to the other side. Your childhood had nothing to do with you or previous lifetimes. It had everything to do with Joan. As for your father's choice to not protect you and your brothers, he is accountable to the Creator for standing by and doing nothing and then becoming an abuser himself."

We sat talking for many hours that afternoon. She told me it was time to close my chapter with Tim and start divorce proceedings. "You have a second marriage close at hand, and you need to put your affairs in order." We talked about normal things as well - everyday life, my new job, my son, my mother, and Cindy's visit. I decided to make a spaghetti sauce in the crockpot while we were chatting and invited her to stay for supper. I liked Dianne when she was acting normal and not rattling my house with visiting spirits. I also liked how much I had been learning about my Spirit World and about myself as a soul on a journey. She was filling in some of the pieces to the puzzle about how a human experience was supposed to work, but I was quickly realizing that the process was extremely compli-cated, with many twists and turns along the road. Every time I learned something, I was left with more questions. Today was not any different. *If we make a blueprint with our Creator before we arrive in physical form, why are we not privileged to any of that information? Or are we?*

My son broke up the conversation as he barreled through the front door on a sugar high. Brian (my friend from the warehouse) had taken him to Chuck E. Cheese, a local children's entertainment facility for the afternoon. "Good luck getting him to eat any supper tonight. He has been eating pizza and candy for the past three hours," he said.

"Well, thank you for taking him there today. I appreciate it. What about you, Brian? Are you full too or would you like to have some spaghetti with us?" I asked.

"I'd love to," he replied.

We sat down to supper while TJ was in the living room watching *Ferris Bueller's Day Off*. For some reason, he loved that movie. It was all he ever wanted to watch. My company decided to leave shortly after supper. I thanked Brian once again for spending the afternoon with my son. On her way out the door, Dianne asked if I could invite a few of my girlfriends over for some readings to help her out financially. I agreed as we made plans for her to visit the following Saturday.

Like Dianne suggested, the following week I decided it was time to pursue getting a divorce. What was I waiting for? Obviously, the marriage was over. As I made a few phone calls, I quickly realized that I did not have money for a lawyer, so I decided to phone a paralegal company. For $240, the firm would draw up the petition for divorce and file it with the court; however, the fee did not include legal representation in the courtroom.

By May of 1987, I was in a courtroom, seated for the afternoon session. I had been scheduled as the last case of the day on the docket but arrived early because I wanted to understand the formal procedure by watching the cases before mine. I was on my own and I had no idea what I was doing. At 3:30 p.m., I was the only person left seated in the courtroom. When I heard my name, I stood up.

Judge: You must be my last case of the day, young lady.
Step up to the bench.

Me: Yes, your Honor.

Judge: You are petitioning this court for a divorce today on the grounds of irreconcilable differences and mental cruelty. Where is your council?

Me: I am representing myself, your Honor.

Judge: Explain in your own words why you want this divorce.

Me: My husband had an affair with my stepmother and the two of them ran off together. When I saw my husband again, he gave me an ultimatum of all or nothing. I had to either take him back or he was not going to have anything to do with either one of us. I have not seen or heard from him in over two years now, your Honor.

Judge: Why have you not petitioned this court for child maintenance?

Me: I have a military career that is supporting the two of us. I just want to move on with my life and not have to deal with long drawn-out court battles to try and get blood from a stone.

Judge: I see the defendant has been served and has chosen not to appear or to send legal representation today. His absence tells me you are speaking the truth. I hereby grant your divorce, but I am attaching a "Reservation of Maintenance and Alimony" to this file. Should you become incapacitated in any way because of your career, he will have no option but to support you both. Court adjourned.

That went better than I had expected. I was relieved, but I was sad as I left the courtroom that day. Relieved that I could finally close that chapter of my life for good, but sad for my son and the father he was never going to know. TJ would be nine years old before he would hear from his father for the first time and that call would end up doing more harm than good to his precious soul.

I definitely felt a little sad that night. Does the old self need to die in order for the soul to start over again? As I worked my way through the sadness of what might have been, I felt like I had just walked out of the fog, as if the old Laurie had never existed. I was a brand-new me with infinite potential towards a new future, but do the gates to your memories or past ever really close?

Dianne arrived around noon the following Saturday. I made her comfortable at the kitchen table to do her readings while the rest of us congregated in the living room. The bar opened early that day as we poured ourselves drinks and sat around chatting. Throughout the course of the afternoon, a petite redhead named Caroline showed up at my door for a reading. She was well known to my friends from the Griesbach Mess, but this was the first time I was meeting her. Caroline left directly after her reading instead of visiting with us, so my encounter with her that day was brief. When just a handful of us were left, Dianne joined us in the living room and I made her a drink. "The little redhead that I just read is going to be an integral part of your journey for many years to come," Dianne said while taking a sip of her drink. I could not envision it. I did not even know

Caroline, but Dianne was not wrong. Caroline would become a part of my journey within the next two years - a journey that has kept us connected to this day.

One night as I sat on the back step watching the sun set in the sky, I began thinking about that dreadful encounter with my two ex-lovers. In that moment, I made the decision to lock the door to my candy store. I continued partying with my friends, but with the decision to drink less, avoid tequila all together, and sleep alone. I had no longer been engaging in destructive behavior when it came to men, but tonight I was about to find out whether my soul had learned anything from the past eight months.

When we walked into the Rosslyn, Pattina and Sharron made a break straight for the dancefloor. I was right behind. The Outfield's song "Your Love" was playing as we wormed our way into the crowd. Losing myself in the music, I began singing. "I just want to use your love tonight. I don't want to lose your love tonight." In that precise moment, a strikingly handsome man walked out of the shadows like a dream, surrounded by a mist of green and white light. This was my first experience with being able to see energy around a person. *Are you sending me a message?*

Let him be the best friend you have ever had.

He pulled a chair away from the bar that surrounded the dance floor and sat down. He was handsome, with salt and pepper hair, the broadest shoulders I had ever seen, and a handlebar mustache that most men would envy. Our eyes met, and we smiled at one another.

My friends and I continued dancing through several more songs before leaving the dance floor. Sharron and I made our way to the bar to buy a drink, and Pattina went to the Ladies Room. While sipping our drinks, the handsome stranger I had been smiling at, walked up to us, and introduced himself as "Dave". He was a medic, known to the Airborne Regiment in Petawawa as "Doc" and was in Edmonton on a basic jump course for the next six weeks. Pattina interrupted the conversation several minutes later saying she had a headache because the music was too loud. "I am going back to the PMQ with some of the guys to party. Don't worry," she said. "My name is not Lynn. The party will be tame."

Pattina left with her entourage of Airborne friends following. The next words out of Dave's mouth floored me. It really is a small world. "I just finished a Pathfinder course last month, and at the end of the course, the boys were sitting around a campfire having a few beers. The course was done, but it had been grueling. So, one by one, we began to tell tales of happier times in our lives in order to lift the mood. One of the guys shared his favorite memory of taking a jump course in Edmonton and partying at Lynn and Laurie's. Quite a few other guys lifted their beers into the air saying, "Here! Here!" Are you that same Laurie?" Dave asked.

"That would be her," Sharron replied before I could answer for myself.

"Then why are we still standing here?" he asked. We finished our drinks and left the bar.

When you let your guard down, are you more likely to go down a dangerous path? Is it possible to ignore the potential for love when you are craving love subconsciously and is your state of mind only as sick as the secrets of your past that you have not made peace with? Would Dave be any different from all the others? I really wanted to find out. After all, Dianne had said I had another marriage coming in the near future, but I was definitely going to proceed with caution.

When the three of us arrived back at the PMQ, my living room was filled with people partying, including Linda and Kate from next door. We joined in, playing drinking games until the wee hours of the morning. Sharron and Linda slept over that night, crashing with me in my bed. Kate wandered home when Pattina went to bed. A few of the guys stumbled back to the barracks while the rest passed out on my couch and floor, Dave being one of them. When we came downstairs in the morning, we had McDonald's coffees and breakfast sandwiches waiting for us. *God, I love my friends!* Suddenly a reality hit me. None of the boys had cars. They must have taken my car to McDonalds without asking. "I should be mad at you guys," I said, "but you are off the hook because you brought back coffee." Shortly after breakfast, everyone went their own way for the day. Pattina had to work, Sharron had a pool tournament that night, and I needed to take my son to his gymnastics class at 2:00 p.m.

I opted for a quiet night at home Saturday night. On the way home from gymnastics, I stopped to pick up some Kentucky Fried Chicken ("Frucky Fried" as my son used to say). Then we went to the corner store to rent a few movies. I let TJ choose his own movie. I had overdosed on *Ferris*

Bueller's Day off. What was I thinking when I bought him that movie? He decided on *Back to School* with Rodney Dangerfield, and I rented *Platoon* for myself to watch later that evening.

We were a half hour into my son's movie when there was a knock at my door. As I opened it, I was surprised to see Dave standing there. "I was bored over at the barracks and thought I would walk over and see what you were up to," he said. Dave joined us in the living room, but I think TJ spent more time studying his mustache than watching the rest of his movie. Linda called wanting to know if I needed anything. She was on her way over. "Can you grab some milk for me, please? I forgot to get some when I was out earlier, and I want to bake some chocolate chip cookies for TJ before he goes to bed."

When the movie was over, Dave and Linda began playing Snakes and Ladders with TJ while I went into the kitchen to bake cookies. I smiled to myself as I listened to all the hooting, hollering, and laughter coming from the living room. *I am so blessed with the most amazing souls anyone could ever wish for. Thank you, Spirit!* After playing several games, having a bath, eating half a dozen cookies, and indulging in a bedtime story, my son had finally crashed for the night from a full day of activity. Dave and Linda went to the liquor store while I was putting TJ to bed, and when I came down the stairs, I had a Bloody Mary waiting for me on the coffee table. Three other Airborne friends stopped by with cases of beer, and by 9:30 p.m. we were engrossed in the movie *Platoon.*

A half hour into the movie, Pattina came home from work and stopped in the living room doorway to say hello. "I am going to take a quick shower, change my clothes, and head over to the Rosslyn for a few drinks. If anyone wants to go with me, I will be ready in twenty minutes," she said. I went into the kitchen to make myself another drink when Dave appeared.

"Are you going to the Rosslyn tonight?" he asked.

"No, I just want to stay home. You go ahead if you want to," I replied.

"I would rather stay here with you, if that's okay?" he asked.

"By all means. You are more than welcome. I know what living in a barracks is like," I said. "Been there, done that." Twenty minutes later, everyone left with Pattina except for Dave, Linda, and me. When the movie was over, the three of us sat chatting for another hour before Linda decided to go home for the night.

Dave and I sat talking a while longer. I found out that he was married, but that he and his wife had an open relationship. *What the heck does that mean?* He proceeded to tell me that they had been together since high school and the best way to describe the relationship was "best friends with benefits". They stepped outside of the marriage on each other whenever they wanted and without judgment from the other person. There were no hidden secrets or deceit between them. "I can give you my phone number right now, and you can call me anytime you want to. If my wife picks up the phone and you ask for me, she will hand the phone to me. No questions asked. I do the same for her. We have a bond together that works for both of us." *Well, all righty then! I need time to digest this. What is the point to being married is my question? You could just as easily be roommates. There has to be more to this story.*

"I am exhausted and I really need to go to bed," I said. "You are welcome to crash here on the couch if you want or have a few more drinks on your own. I am sure another party will begin shortly when Pattina comes home from the bar." I brought Dave a blanket and pillow, checked in on my son sleeping, and then went to my bedroom for the night.

At 2:00 a.m. I felt someone shaking me. "Laurie, can I crawl in with you, please? I can't get any sleep downstairs, and I don't want to party anymore." I am not sure if I answered Dave or just made a halfhearted attempt with a mumbling sound. I do remember feeling his body heat as he snuggled into my back and I drifted back to sleep again.

The next morning as I appeared in the kitchen doorway, TJ came running into my arms holding a spatula. "Look, Mommy, me and Dave are making pancakes just for you," he said hugging me. "Mine has smiley faces."

"That is awesome, son. I hope you are going to do the dishes after too," I said winking at Dave.

"I am not a girl," he said as he returned to the grill, so proud of his cooking accomplishments. Dave and I both laughed. *Hmmm! I will have to work on changing his line of thinking, or he will never find a wife.*

Every spare moment for the next week, Dave and I spent countless hours together. I enjoyed his company. By the time the third week had rolled around, my hormones were in a state of perpetual anticipation. I was ready for the next step with him and that weekend, I went past the point of no return. I could not stop myself as my trembling fingers went to all those forbidden places. We were not having sex. We were making love, something I had not experienced since Mark's death. The emotional vulnerability and the sexual compatibility were instant. I was confident and secure as I headed for the love zone one more time. The connection felt right. *It might not be forever, but it is real. I have missed real, and I will miss him when he leaves.*

When two people are on a journey, there may be miles where they fall silent, but that does not mean that they should not be traveling together. Have faith.

It was Dave's last week in town and Christmas was only ten days away, so we decided to spend an evening at the mall getting some shopping done. It was perfect having another adult to shop with. I would encourage TJ to play in the toy section of stores so I could get a feel for what he wanted. Once I knew, Dave would distract him with a trip to get a drink or hamburger, while I purchased the gifts and put them in the trunk of the car without my son knowing. We left the mall that day with a trunk full of presents and a very tired little boy.

"I need to make one more stop, please, Dave. I want to pick up a Christmas tree from the gas station on the way home," I said.

"Do you have something to tie it to the roof?" he asked.

"Of course, you are talking to a military girl," I said smiling. He was impressed as we tied the tree to the roof of the car with ratchet straps. Once we arrived home, Dave emptied the trunk and set up the Christmas tree while I got my son settled into bed.

Dave stopped by three days later to say goodbye. "These are for you and your son," he said handing me a bag filled with wrapped gifts. "Merry Christmas, Laurie. Thank you for making my time here so great, and remember, you can call me anytime you want to. I should be back for my free fall course in the spring, so I hope we can see each other again then. Take care and thanks for everything. Lynn and Laurie's place is the best place on earth," he said as he kissed me goodbye and walked out the door.

I was feeling melancholy when Linda stopped by on Friday night. "Where is TJ?" she asked.

"He is spending the night at Candy's for a birthday party," I replied.

"Call Sharron and let's go party. Tell her to meet us at the Griesbach Mess," she said.

"It is not going to be the same. Everybody has gone home for the holidays. Let's just stay here," I suggested.

"Nope. We are going out. We are just going to change it up a little and party with new people. I've got it. Let's go to Esmerelda's and drool over the cowboys. Giddy up," she said pretending to ride a horse across my living room. When I called Sharron, there was no answer. She was probably out with her boyfriend or doing last-minute Christmas shopping.

Linda dragged me out to Esmerelda's that night, and I was happy that she did. We met some phenomenal dance partners that we two-stepped with for hours. We line-danced, we drank, and we partied with some really fun people. Finally arriving back home around 2:00 a.m., I cracked open a bottle of Sambuca for a nightcap or two, not that we needed anymore liquor. We plunked ourselves on the couch, filling our shot glasses. "Thank you for convincing me to go out, Linda. I had so much fun," I said. We rambled on about the people we had met that night.

Then the subject changed to Dave. "I have to ask you something about his mustache," she began. I cringed. "Was it a cookie duster or a womb broom?" she asked.

"Linda!!! Let's change the subject, please. You are a real little minx," I teased.

"Okay, I have been looking at that bare Christmas tree for three days now. When are you going to decorate it, before or after Christmas?" she asked changing the subject as I had requested.

"I don't have any decorations. I meant to buy some and forgot. I will do it tomorrow," I replied.

"Well Laurie-Loo, Linda-Loo is here to save the day," she said as she left the room and returned with two of my dresser drawers. After we had polished off a quarter of a bottle of inspiration, we began decorating my tree with lingerie - garter belts, thigh-high stockings, white crotchless pearl thongs, lace teddies, sheer ruffled bras, and G-strings - just to mention a few unmentionables. We were pretty impressed with ourselves until we woke up the next morning and had sobered up. "Good Lord, I need to take this stuff down before my son sees it," I said walking into the living room. I was glad it was just her and I, and no one else, who had witnessed our grand scheme of tree decorating.

"I am going home, and I'll be back with some coffee and decorations," Linda said. "I have boxes full of ornaments in my closet." Linda had an uncanny way of bringing out the mischievous side of me - the crazy, untamed side. I loved her for that. We would laugh about that tree for many years to come, as well as continuing to use our adopted nicknames of "Laurie-Loo" and "Linda-Loo".

Sharron called and I informed her of our plans to decorate the tree. "I am heading over to Candy's to pick up TJ, and Linda has gone home to get her decorations. When will you be here?" I asked her.

"I am going to jump in the shower, grab the turkey from the fridge, and I'll be on my way. Do you need me to stop and pick up some rum and eggnog for later tonight?" she asked.

"Sounds good. I have champagne and orange juice for the morning. See you soon," I said and hung up.

It had become a tradition for Sharron and me to spend Christmas Eve and Christmas Day together, and this year, Linda was going to join us. The three amigas! *Are friends the family that we get to choose?* Each of our lives were filled with adventure, often becoming insanely complicated, but we were bound by enormous affection for each other, without jealousy, resentment, or competition. *Is there any way that a man can ever understand you like a woman can?*

Christmas tunes and a bottle of rum made tree decorating a blast. After my son was in bed, we began feverishly wrapping presents and getting ready for the morning. My mother and father had each mailed a box of gifts, and Dave had also left gifts that I brought up from the basement. In the past, Christmas had never been a time of excitement or elation for me. As a child, I had the fear of being excluded as punishment. As a young adult, I had the fear of going without for financial reasons, but that had all changed. I was surrounded by love now. Love of my child, love of a sister, and love of a friend. All three were genuine relationships of unconditional love. I felt very blessed. As we crawled into bed after midnight, we sighed with relief. We were finally ready for the morning.

The Christmas tree was lit and twinkling, coffee was brewing, and the sausage rolls and quiche were baking in the oven. Presents with colorful paper and ribbons lie scattered beneath the tree. Snow danced through the air, tumbling to its blanket below as I looked out the living room window. *Merry Christmas, Spirit World.* The sound of my son's sheer excitement as he ran towards the living room brought such joy to my heart as I turned to greet him. "Merry Christmas, Mommy," he said wrapping his arms around my neck. "Merry Christmas, son."

The turkey was stuffed and roasting in the oven. We made ourselves some mimosas and sat down to relax before continuing with the rest of the food preparation. TJ was busy playing with his new toys when Dave called early that afternoon. I thanked him for the blue jeans and sweater he had bought me and the Hot Wheels racetrack he had bought for my son. It was good to hear from him. I had no idea where our journey was taking us, but I was content with where it was in the moment. There were several more calls throughout the day from my mother, my father, and Dianne.

Finally sitting down to Christmas dinner, I said a prayer to myself. *Thank you, Heavenly Father, for the meal You have provided today and for the souls I am sharing it with. I feel truly blessed. And thank you for not abandoning me through my pain or allowing me to abandon myself. I am back and I am so grateful.*

Over dinner conversation, we decided that we wanted to go out for New Year's Eve. I hesitated at first because New Year's Eve tends to be a couple's evening, but Linda and Sharron were insistent. We could get a bunch of the girls together to party at the Lancaster Park Mess and have just as much fun as anyone else, coupled or not.

We went to the Mall that week to buy fancy dresses and we made appointments to have our hair and makeup done. Finally ready to go and looking like a million dollars, we cracked open a bottle of champagne, emptying the bottle before we left. I dropped my son off at Kate's for the night to play with the twins. We were on our way out to a night of celebration and fun.

I was the first one through the main door to the Lancaster Park Mess. I was leading the charge, and I was excited as I headed for the long staircase. As soon as my foot hit the first step, my spiked high heel got caught up in frayed carpeting. Down I tumbled, hitting the first landing with so much momentum that I continued tumbling down to the second and third landing as well. Sprawled out on the floor at the bottom of the three-tiered staircase, my friends came rushing to my aid. They picked me up, dusted me off, and we went to find a table. I was not going to let a silly fall interfere with my New Year's Eve celebration. I already had a buzz from the champagne, and I did not appear to have injured myself. *Party on with your bad self. You are fine, girl.*

The next morning, I opened my eyes and began surveying the room. I was alone. Good start! I was still fully dressed and laying on top of my bedding. Bonus! I got out of bed and made my way to the washroom. Time for a reality check now. I had holes in the knees of my pantyhose, huge runs from those holes running up and down my legs, and my knees and elbows were scraped up and starting to scab over. As I looked in the mirror, I noticed rug burn on my nose and my chin. I was troubled by the thought that I had started the evening looking like a red carpet million-dollar lady and finished it looking like I had crawled out of a dumpster. It was time for some serious New Year's Resolutions.

Spiritual Beings on a Human Experience

Souls are privileged to their blueprints through conversation with Spirit, intuition, a gut feeling, or being in the present moment undistracted while listening to the soul. Three components will hold a soul back from following their blueprint - fear, feeling unworthy, and core beliefs. Fear of the unknown, feelings of unworthiness from rejection, and core beliefs instilled from childhood can all keep a soul from its true purpose, but a Spirit Guide is always nudging a soul back to its chosen path, back to its blueprint. A soul feels excited when they are on their life path and drained of energy when they are not.

One of the main reasons for difficulties in a physical life is to drive a soul closer to their Creator. Understanding yourself as a soul allows you to master the mind and control moods, emotions, and restlessness. Behaving from the soul allows you to understand and feel empathy towards others. Being tested is the Universe's way of providing a soul with the greatest of blessings, and difficulties are designed as an indicator that the soul is ready to evolve to the next level.

The knowledge of the soul has authentic significance to a relationship with the Creator, whereas the knowledge of the mind leads to the soul's evolution with either negative or positive results. The spiritual and the physical are intertwined like a horse and its rider. The physical ego's fear and insecurity causes it to attempt to control the uncontrollable, while the spirit will simply allow life to unfold naturally and trust the process. Laurie's behavior since her twin flame's death has been ego driven and self-destructive. Her fear feels very real, but the true Self can never be hurt or threatened. Obstacles are nothing more than opportunities in disguise.

Meeting a soul from a past life indicates there is a challenge that needs to be accomplished together in the present life. It represents a shared history that is being played out to either accomplish unfinished business together or learn a lesson from one another. Dave and Laurie have known each other in a past life. He has a fear of stepping out of his comfort zone. For her, it is a fear of being unworthy of love. They are both looking for true love, and the choice is theirs to make as their paths cross. Through individual blueprints and the Creator's blessing, both souls have chosen this pivotal moment in their lives to meet up with each other.

Laurie is blessed with the ability to see Dave's aura when she first meets him, which she describes as a green and white mist surrounding him. Auras are a vibrational level of energy displayed in colors. Every living thing has an aura because all living things are comprised of energy. Auras represent the Divine Self or soul and its state of spiritual and physical health. The heart chakra, which is green in color, is indicative of compassion, trust, giving, receiving, nurturing, and the desire to serve people. Dave's soul walks in the White Light with the path of a healer, displayed in his chosen profession of medicine.

CHAPTER 10

TRUE HUMILITY LIFTS YOU HIGH

Bad is a term we use to describe something unwanted, but does our higher self always agree that what we are experiencing is bad? Perhaps, the bad is teaching us what we came here to learn so, in essence, does that make it good? When we think something is good and our higher self does not agree, is it because we are experiencing an illusion without all the facts? What if what we think is good is really bad and what we think is bad is really good? Is there a way to tell the difference? Perhaps intuition allows a soul to know whether what they are thinking or doing is or is not for their highest good.

The year was 1988, and I was pondering a New Year Resolution as I looked back on the previous year. The last year had been about searching for salvation, desperately trying to overcome, letting go of all the mistakes I had made, and trying to forgive myself. My internal dialogue was always one of feeling like I never measured up to what was expected of me. *My life has been one stupid mistake after another, one bad choice after another. What is wrong with me, Helena?*

The Creator is proud of you, mistakes, and all. He wants you to pursue your dreams, but not by rejecting the person he made you to be. Be proud of who you are. You are His child.

Faith in myself had slowly been returning – not with a strong, power-ful rush, but through bouts of humility. My shameful behavior had been forgiven by my Creator, and even though I did not feel deserving of such a blessing, I embraced His forgiveness whole heartedly. If He could forgive me, certainly I could forgive myself and do better.

I made the decision to spend the next year focused on my son and my friends and to stop my quest for the love of a man. If I were meant to be loved, love would find me all by itself. In that exact moment of soul searching, I realized that I was already surrounded by love from many different souls on my journey – my son, my friends, my family. Maybe it was finally time to learn to love myself. Obviously, they saw someone who was lovable, flaws and all.

The Recruiting Centre was a busy place as the days, weeks, and months flew by. Kate and I worked well together, and we had become close through conversation as we traveled back and forth to work. She approached my desk one day in a competitive spirit. She was processing officer files and I was processing trade files. "Let's have a competition. Whoever has the most enrolments in the next month is the winner, and the loser has to get a tattoo," she said. Kate had several tattoos, but it was not something I had even considered.

"I don't know if I want a tattoo," I replied.

"If you lose, you can choose what you want and where you want it. No pressure," she said. We agreed and I lost the bet by one enrolment.

When the weekend arrived, we were at the tattoo parlor. "A bet is a bet," she said. I began looking for something really small and wanted it tattooed in a place that was well hidden. I settled for an inch-high devil that I had tattooed on my right upper thigh. Painful does not sufficiently describe what I went through, and an hour later I was overjoyed to get off that table. To this day, I have never wanted another tattoo nor have I had another one done.

In April, a military directive came down from Ottawa stating that Edmonton was going to open up a Recruiting Detachment in Yellowknife. A Captain and a Petty Officer would be arriving in Edmonton for a week of training and to oversee a functioning Recruiting Centre, followed by a trip to Yellowknife to set up the new Detachment. The Yellowknife Recruiting Detachment was to be opened and operational in time for a scheduled airshow in May. The Commanding Officer approached Kate and

I requesting that one of us be available to travel to Yellowknife with the new team and help them.

"Decide amongst yourselves," he said walking away. Three weeks later, I was on my way to Yellowknife. Kate and Pattina had agreed to spell each other off looking after TJ. Kate had spent two years posted to Yellowknife and had no desire to go back. I was on board for a change of scenery and some adventure. After all, it was only for a week.

Yellowknife is the capital city of the Northwest Territories and, in the 1980s, it was the center for government services. The landscape was rocky with many scattered small lakes and an abundance of spruce and birch trees. Eighty percent of the population was English speaking, three percent French, and the other seventeen percent were Indigenous languages.

The temperature was -11 when the Hercules landed on the runway and we began offloading supplies into a truck that was waiting for us on the tarmac. From there, we stopped at the building that would become the new CFRC and moved all the boxes inside, ending the day by checking into the local hotel. We agreed to meet up in the hotel lounge for dinner at 6:00 p.m. I was fifteen minutes late when I arrived because I wanted to shower and get into some clean civilian clothing. They had already ordered their meal and were relaxing while enjoying a beer. I looked at the menu and settled on ordering a bison burger. I had never eaten bison, and when it arrived, I was impressed by the taste. After supper, we climbed into a taxi and drove to the liquor store, deciding to drink in our rooms for the rest of the week after we saw our bill for dinner.

Bison and Arctic Char became my go-to meals for the week. Arctic Char is a cold-water fish, similar in nature to salmon and has been a staple to the Inuit of Canada for hundreds of years. It has a very mild fishy taste, very few bones, and is delightful to the palette. I returned home with a case of Arctic Char that had been processed similar to cans of tuna one would purchase at a supermarket. My trip to the Northwest Territories and enduring its cold temperatures had been worth it just for that case of tasty fish.

One of my fondest memories of Yellowknife was the "Northern Lights". I had seen them in Edmonton during large magnetic storms, but not to the same degree. Also referred to as the "Aurora Borealis" or "Polar Lights", they are the most spectacular natural light display on the Earth's surface. I saw my Creator in all that splendor as I enjoyed the view from my balcony one night while sipping a cocktail.

Five days later we were boarding the Hercules destined for Edmonton. I was homeward bound. The CFRC in Yellowknife was organized and ready for its doors to open and none too soon. It was Friday and I was anxious to meet up with all my friends and see my son again. When I stopped in at Kate's PMQ, TJ did not want to come home. He was having fun with the girls, so Kate and I made plans to go out while her husband babysat for one more night. The Petty Officer I had been with in Yellowknife decided to join us at the Rosslyn that night and we partied into the wee hours of the morning. I was back in my comfort zone again.

Sunday, I received a phone call from Dave. He was returning to Edmonton for his free fall course in a week. "Have you found a new boyfriend yet?" he teased.

"No, and I have not been looking for one either. I have been too busy," I replied. Dave and I picked up where we had left off five months earlier, as if no time had passed at all.

Edmonton holds over fifty festivals annually. One of my fondest memories with Dave and TJ was taking my son to the International Children's Festival, a festival designed to introduce children to a bigger, more exciting world through curiosity and creativity. *Maybe my son will travel in space or design the next Lamborghini. His imagination is limitless when he plays. I definitely do not want him to wear Army boots like his mother. He is too much of a free spirit.* Before I could blink, Dave's course was finished, and he was on his way back to Petawawa.

My brother Steve had returned from Germany and was now posted to Vancouver, British Columbia. I could tell from our phone conversation that he was struggling. His two daughters, Angela and Jennifer, who were born in Germany, were now living in Windsor, Ontario with their mother. Between child support and spousal support, he was barely surviving on the Vancouver economy. Grace (his wife) had decided to leave Germany a month earlier than Steve. She wanted to spend the time in Windsor visiting her parents, a month that would allow her parents some quality time to get to know the two girls. The plan was to meet up with Steve in Vancouver once he arrived there. Instead, Grace decided to stay in Windsor permanently and blindsided Steve with divorce papers that he was not expecting. I could tell from our conversation that he was angry and still trying to come to terms with where his life was. I invited him to come to Edmonton for a visit. Maybe a change of scenery would help. It always seemed to work for me.

Steve caught a military flight and spent a few days with me. Our conversations were deep as he vented his frustrations over his marriage ending. Not being with his two daughters was a struggle for him. Here we were in our mid-twenties with a failed marriage each. "Do you think we chose the wrong partners to marry or do you think we are both messed up from our childhood and no one can live with us?" I asked him. Only time would answer those questions for both of us.

It was a weekend and we were all in party mode. Steve was enjoying himself with my girlfriends who were all fawning over him, especially Linda. There was definitely a sexual chemistry between those two. When he left, he thanked me for a great few days. "This was just what I needed," he said as he hugged me goodbye. I was happy with my life because of his help, and I had never forgotten how quickly he rescued me without any hesitation. I owed him and it felt good to be able to return the favor, although it paled in comparison.

The summer was busy with endless amounts of activity. Sharron and I were playing baseball in a city league. After a trip to the Okanagan, we spent a weekend canning peaches and cherries. We went out to dinner with Brian, enjoying authentic German food. We went to Sunday brunch with the girls once a month, enjoying eggs benedict and mimosas. We went to home lingerie parties, adding to our already massive collections. We went to Klondike Days, dressing up in costumes dating back to the Gold Rush days in the 1800s. My son's thrill was the rides, games, and food of the Midway, especially the freshly fried donuts and the gooey candy apples. In between all of that activity, we still found time to party with our friends.

As autumn set in, Sharron and I began contemplating Halloween costumes again. The previous year, TJ had worn a bumblebee costume that I had made for him, and Sharron and I had gone out as "Hochtaler Girls". Hochtaler Wine was popular at that time, and we dressed like the girl on the commercial. We wore a black top hat, a white tuxedo shirt, a black long-tailed jacket with a black cumber bund and tie, a black bathing suit bottom over black stockings, and black high-heeled stilettos. And yes, we carried a bottle of Hochtaler wine as our prop. The salesman at the tuxedo rental shop was a little perplexed that we did not want any pants with our rentals, but we just giggled as we walked out of the store with only half a rental. Halloween was always so much fun with Sharron. This year would be no different.

I decided to make TJ an Indian chief costume and began feverishly sewing from a pattern with material I had purchased the week before. The headdress took up most of my time, finishing his warrior look with beading and feathers and a war painted face. He looked amazing as I tried the entire costume on him.

With two more weeks to go, Sharron suggested we go out that year as "sex kittens". "What's your vision?" I asked.

"Picture this," she began. "A white turtleneck with a black studded dog collar on our necks. Black cuffs over both wrists with white buttons. Black stockings with a short, sleeveless black jumper. A black, furry tail attached to elastic around our waist that pulls out of the back of the jumper through a hole. White leg warmers around our ankles with our black stilettos. A hairband with cat ears. Teased hair and painted faces in black and white makeup. Oh and long black fingernails. What do you think?" she asked.

"Let's go for it," I replied. We picked up material for the jumpers and cuffs and all the required accessories to complete the look.

Our costumes were a hit and people were constantly pulling on our tails. Each time someone did, we would turn with a loud "meow" while clawing their arm with our fingernails. If someone were close to us, whispering in our ear, we would purr. We spoke very few words that night. We were in character. I came across that costume in a trunk not too long ago and took a trip down memory lane before putting it back.

By the middle of November, Dave had returned for his jump masters course. In the past year, we seemed to have found a comfortable place with each other, one of mutual respect and fun, but that was all about to change. Rhoda had invited me to join the staff of CFSTS for their Christmas party when she heard that the Recruiting Centre was not having a party of their own. I asked Dave to be my date for that evening, which he gladly accepted, and Linda agreed to be our designated driver. The destination was a barn outside of the city in no man's land and drinking and driving was not an option.

The night started off really well. The music the band was playing had us all up on the dance floor, everyone except for a handful of people, including Dave. When someone asked me to dance, I would look at Dave and he would give me his nod of approval. I was trying to be respectful, but I also loved to dance. I was between a rock and a hard place so I turned down a few requests trying to spend more time with him. Dave was not a dancer so he continued to sit and drink while Linda, and I made a few more trips to the dance floor with different partners. Around 10:30 p.m., I returned to my chair that was situated directly across the table from Dave. As I began to sit, he threw his drink into my face and called me a "bitch". Speechless with anger, I went to the washroom to clean myself up. I was embarrassed at the thought of all my friends witnessing what had just happened. Then anger overpowered me again as I asked Linda to go get my purse.

"We are leaving right now," I said. "He can find his own damned way home."

As we sat in the car waiting for it to warm up, Linda kept trying to bring me to my senses. "I feel really bad leaving him here, Laurie. We brought him, and we should take him home. He is drunk and he probably just got jealous. You have been drinking too, and you are not thinking clearly. Let me go back in and get him."

Look at him with your heart and not your eyes.

I listened to my Spirit Guide as I agreed to take Dave back to Edmonton, but I insisted that he was being dropped off at the barracks. I wanted nothing more to do with him.

After leaving Dave at the barracks, Linda and I stopped in at the Rosslyn. She left the bar before I did and when I walked into the PMQ two hours later, Linda and Dave were sitting on the couch talking. Sobered up a little by now, Dave had wandered back to my place to apologize, thinking that I had gone directly home after dropping him off. I did not want to see him. I did not want to hear his apology. I considered throwing him out but decided to leave things be and go to bed instead. Things might look different in the morning. I walked up the stairs and closed my bedroom door with nothing more than a "good night" to both of them.

I had drifted off to sleep when I felt someone rubbing my back. It was not uncommon for Linda and me to do that, so I thought nothing of it in the moment until I heard a male voice. "I am so sorry, Laurie. I just went crazy and I'm not sure why. I love you and I want to show you how much. Make love to me," Dave said.

Is he kidding right now? Does he really think that sex is going to fix everything?

"Let me introduce you to the Laurie that you have not met yet. You know, the one that you called a bitch. Sex is not happening tonight, Dave. You say that you love me, but I am finding that really hard to believe. You need to leave. We will talk tomorrow," I replied. I was wounded and not ready to forgive and forget. He got out of bed, dressed himself, and left the bedroom.

The next morning, Linda had coffee brewing when I came down the stairs. "We need to have a chat," she said. I grabbed a cup of coffee and sat down on the couch. "You have no idea how beautiful you are or what you do to men," she began. "I see it all the time. Practically every guy you meet wants to marry you, and I am not lying because many have told me so. Hell, I would marry you in a heartbeat myself," she said with a very straight face. "What I have to tell you is going to really hurt you and that is the last thing I want to do. I debated not saying anything, but I think you need to know. Dave is not here this morning because I threw him out last night. He tried to have sex with me after you told him to go away."

I appreciated Linda's honesty and loyalty as I struggled to come to terms with the truth. Maybe I was at a crossroads with Dave, and I needed to get out of the intersection before I got run over.

Forgive him. He has done all the wrong things for all the right reasons.

That makes no sense to me. He hurt me and because I was not ready to forgive him, he tried to punish me by sleeping with my best friend.

Forgive him because he loves you.

I can't right now.

Eventually, I made the choice to let go of my anger towards Dave and forge ahead. Our stark reality was hitting me right between the eyes. He was married, whether happily or not, and he had another life in another province. I was thankful for what we had shared and the love that I had felt for him, but perhaps our connection had served its purpose and it was time to let go. *Is love nothing more than a lie that both comforts us and destroys us at the same time?* In my mind, whatever we had established in the past year was over. We were left with nothing more than memories of yesterday, but our blueprints would say otherwise.

Spiritual Beings on a Human Experience

A physical life is extremely complicated. Each soul is on its own unique journey and it becomes complicated by the aligning of the soul with the personality, as well as the interaction with other souls and their personalities.

Laurie left her childhood humbled by life, and it became deep-rooted in her personality, a blessing provided by her Creator as a reward for enduring her childhood. That humility gets lost in the anger of her personality as the two battle each other for control. Other souls are attracted to her soft, humble spirit, yet bewildered by the change in her when her anger surfaces. Until she learns how to sit with her anger, understand it, and express it constructively, she will continue to bury it, becoming a seething volcano always on the brink of erupting.

Dave and Laurie's paths will continue to cross by design. Their journey together has not served its purpose yet. Dave displays a possessive jealousy with her when he feels threatened by other souls who are interrupting a relationship that he values. In that moment, jealousy replaces his love for her.

Laurie's anger has always been a spiritual gift designed to open her heart and allow her soul to transform that anger into an understanding of her true self-worth. Instead, she sees it as an ungodly expression of aggression that she does not understand and continually buries it. If she does not learn to express her anger, the result will be a passive-aggressive personality through no choice of her own. Anger replaces her love for Dave; she feels the betrayal deeply as she makes her choice not to forgive him.

The words "humility" and "human" interact as a soul accepts its place among many other souls, no more or less important than themselves. Humility is the basis of true love. Once Laurie understands her self-worth, she will find true love again. Her Spirit Guide and Angel continue to encourage her to release her anger and learn to love herself unconditionally, mistakes and all. A mistake is nothing more than a learning process to a soul and is expected as part of the journey.

CHAPTER 11

PRECIOUS LOVE

Sometimes things can appear random because our Creator allows us to make choices, but does He have the ability to make choices on our behalf by overriding our choices? Had He made the choice to introduce Dave into my life at a specific moment in time, and if so, why that moment? Perhaps, it was because I had prayed for a new beginning and I wanted to know that I mattered. Even though Dave and I had designed each other into our blueprints, had the Creator decided on the exact timing? Was every single moment on a physical journey all about HIS timing?

Even though I had made the choice to walk away from Dave, Divine Intervention was not going to allow that to happen. I was nagged by the feeling that things had been left unresolved, and as the weeks passed, I was remorseful for the way things had ended so abruptly. I had allowed one night to erase a year of fond memories. I wanted to forgive him. I was ready to forgive him. If nothing more, it would allow us both to move on with closure.

The New Year brought new beginnings. When Dave called in January, our conversation was deep from the heart. His apology was sincere, and he was remorseful for his behavior. *Does time heal all wounds when the anger subsides and we take time to reflect?* "I know I am asking a lot by wanting you to forgive me for being such an ass, and I know I don't deserve it, but I am sorry, Laurie. I truly am," he said. I believed him so we agreed to remain a part of each other's lives through telephone conversations for the time being. That nagging feeling I had been experiencing lifted as soon as

I hung up the telephone. Dave and I stayed in touch, but usually the phone calls were initiated by him. His life was busy with the Airborne Regiment and more often than not, he was away from home. If long periods of time lapsed where we had not spoken, I did not see it as anything more than him being extremely busy. I was busy myself.

Three quarters of all military occupations opened up to women in 1989, immersing the CFRC into constant activity. We were on a recruiting blitz as the civilian population was bombarded with television advertisements announcing equal opportunities for women. The months flew by as we processed female applicants for their dream jobs - pilots, mechanics, combat arms soldiers, just to mention a few. I was at the forefront of military gender integration and equality, but it was not going to be without its challenges, as I would discover soon enough.

In April, I received a posting message from my Career Manager in Ottawa. I had been selected for a one-year French course in St. Hubert, Quebec. Promotions were being stifled for military members who were not bilingual, especially in support trades. I saw the opportunity as a blessing. Where else can a person attend school full time while simultaneously receiving a full salary? Just as quickly, I was conflicted with the thought of having to leave everyone behind in Edmonton and venture out all alone to start over again. In the back of my mind, I had always known that the day would come, but now that it was here, it was a very frightening thought.

When I called Dave to let him know that I was being posted, his wife answered the phone. "Dave is not here. Is this Laurie?" she asked.

"Yes, it is," I replied.

"Dave and I have decided to try and put our marriage back together. Woman to woman, I am asking you to please step back and stop calling." I agreed to her request, but it was not without pain and confusion. For a few weeks, I struggled with the fact that he had not told me the news himself and wondered if I would ever hear from him again. There was only one right choice to make in that moment. My choice was to respect their decision and walk away. I was never one for injecting myself into any situation where I was not welcomed or wanted.

What is happening with him is timely to your process.

I did not call Dave again, and he did not call me. We had said goodbye to each other without uttering a single word, but our paths were due to cross again in 1999, a meeting where the entire truth would be revealed.

When a military member is posted, the first step involved in the moving process is to take a house-hunting trip (HHT) to secure accommodation at the new location. It is the most cost-effective way to facilitate a door-to-door move. I needed to be settled in Quebec for August 1, so I chose to take my HHT the last week of June. My son was thrilled to be staying at Kate's for the week while I was gone. When I told my mother about the posting, she gave me a phone number to her best girlfriend in Montreal, a lady named Ginger. "You remember Ginger, don't you?" she asked. "Call her and say hello when you arrive. I am sure she would love to hear from you again," she suggested.

I rented a car at the Montreal Airport and drove to a motel that I had booked a few blocks away from the base. Before settling in for the night, I called Ginger, and we made plans to meet for lunch the next day. When I awoke the next morning, my first thought was to head for the lobby to get a coffee and a newspaper. As I was walking, I passed a motel room door that was wide open and I looked in without even a second thought. It was probably a chambermaid making up the room. I was in shock as I stopped dead in my tracks. I was witnessing a man dressed in black leather chaps, a black vest, and a lone ranger mask. His genitals were fully exposed and he was kneeling on the bed, with a magazine spread open in front of him, masturbating. He turned to look at me watching him and never missed a beat. *Good Lord buddy, close the door!* Still in a state of shock, I forced myself to continue walking to the lobby and remained there drinking my coffee for the next twenty minutes. I did not want to walk past that room again before he was finished with his task at hand. Pun intended.

As I sat drinking my coffee and trying to erase this unexpected vision from my mind, my thoughts went into overdrive. I had never witnessed such a public display of sexual gratification. What was his intention leaving the door wide open? Was he hoping someone would come along and help him out? Did he need that shock factor of a passerby's reaction for the ultimate release? Then I shifted gears and began wondering what my Creator's view on masturbation was. Had He made our arms long enough to reach on purpose? Was masturbation simply a healthy way of meeting a soul's physical needs if they were on their journey alone?

When Ginger arrived that morning, I told her what I had witnessed. "Pack up your things and check out. I am taking you home with me and I am not taking 'no' for an answer. I think you booked yourself into the 'no tell motel'", she said. We both laughed. Ginger owned a four-bedroom home in Laval and lived alone. We spent the next few days commuting from her place in search of somewhere for my son and I to live. Ginger had lived in Montreal all of her life. She was fluently bilingual, understood the culture, and was a huge help with the language barrier. By the fourth day of searching, I finally decided to lease a two-bedroom basement suite located on a side street around the corner from the base. Ginger's home would become my home away from home on weekends, and she would become a surrogate mother for the next year of my life.

On the flight back to Edmonton, I was absorbed in thoughts of my father and where life had taken him in the past five years. He had moved on slowly with his life after Joan, eventually selling the mobile home they had once shared together. He was now living with a lady named Collette on Windermere Road. Collette was an avid bingo player at the Tivoli Bingo Hall where my father often worked off-duty, and they had known each other as casual acquaintances for many years. They began dating and eventually moved in together, marrying several months shortly thereafter. Collette had three children of her own and a grandchild on the way. Together, they reminded me of young love with all its innocence, infatuation, and intense emotion. I was thrilled for the both of them.

When my father found out that my intention was to drive from Edmonton to Montreal, he paid for a CAA Membership for me. No doubt for his own peace of mind. I was thirty years old and felt invincible, but his decision to do this made me feel safe and loved. As I planned my trip, I knew that it would take me four days to drive to Windsor and my furniture was not arriving in Montreal until ten days from the date of pickup. That would leave me four days to visit in Windsor before I would need to continue my trip to Montreal. The wheels were in motion. My life was changing drastically, and in two weeks, the life I had known for the past five years would cease to exist.

I was stepping away from Edmonton at the top of my game emotionally, and I was ready to look ahead, but not without saying goodbye first. The last five years of my life could not have been any better – the friendships, the experiences, the love. It was the first time where I had been living life in all its magnitude, with all its mistakes and all its exhilaration. I had lived with intention and passion, with the fire of a lioness. I had also lived with devastation and addiction, with the tenacity of a tiger.

Embrace your new path. The old is not lost.

I had come to terms with the move to Montreal. Maybe I was counting my blessings that I was still alive, uninjured, and had a functioning liver. Yes, it was definitely time to leave the amusement park, my happiest place on earth, my adrenaline junkie's paradise and grow up.

I was no stranger to people leaving me, and I had done some leaving myself in the past, but this time things felt different. I was not leaving with anguish or running away in fear. I was leaving with sadness and nostalgia. I had changed because of all the special people that had come into my life. Each person had helped me feel worthy of love in their own unique way and that feeling was mine to take with me and keep.

The last five years in my military career had taught me confidence, self-worth, and how to be self-sufficient. It had been challenging and fulfilling, and I had learned how to be dependable and professional. I had experienced teamwork to achieve specific goals, and I had learned accountability for my successes and failures. No matter what the future held, I was confident in my capability to look after my son and myself and be happy while doing so.

Both my mother and father were retired now. They were excited about my move closer to home and seeing me again, but they were also worried about the pending trip. In 1989, technology for cell phones, GPS systems, and the Internet were in the infancy stages of availability. I was venturing out on a cross-country trip, through Canada and the United States, as a woman alone with a child and with the potential for many things to go wrong. I promised my father that I would call each night to let him know where I had stopped for the night, and I promised my mother that I would call each morning to let her know my travel plans for the day. They both expected my collect calls and truthfully, those calls gave me comfort just to hear their voices.

Wrapped up in looking at my road maps and charting out each day's drive, I made the decision to start driving around 5:00 a.m. each morning and stop for the night by 4:00 p.m. at the latest. It would allow my son some physical time in the evenings away from the car ride. It was a pretty clever plan and it worked like a charm. I would wake my son early each morning and put him in a sleeping bag in the backseat of the car. He would continue sleeping until nine or ten o'clock and then we would stop for breakfast once he was awake. I had filled the backseat floor with activity books, markers, and sticker books that kept him occupied for several hours after breakfast. He also had his He-man figures and his Hot Wheels cars. TJ had an amazing imagination and was incredibly good at entertaining himself. By the time he wanted to get out of the car, we were where we needed to be in terms of the kilometers that I had planned to travel that day. I would find a motel with an outdoor swimming pool and let him swim for several hours to tire him out. We would have some supper together and then settle down for the night. He was content with a full belly and tired after his swim so he usually just lay beside me on the bed watching television until he fell asleep.

The first day of the trip, I made plans to travel from Edmonton to Brandon, Manitoba. The four or five hours that I had each morning while my son slept was my thinking, laughing, and crying time. Every relationship we have with another soul affects us differently, and if we dissect those relationships, we are often left with a more profound spiritual connection to our own purpose. As I set out on my new journey, it was next to impossible not to revisit so many of the relationships I was leaving behind. I had miles and miles to do nothing but think.

I loved my stepsister, Sharron, for all the good times and fun that she had brought to my life, but also for the extraordinary deep memories we had created together. We were practically best friends from the first day we met. I could always go to her for solid advice. Our darkest secrets and our most intimate thoughts were met with compassion and understanding by each other. She had been a true sister to me in every sense of the word. She had commiserated and celebrated with me, supporting me in some of my life's biggest moments. I loved her and I trusted her with my heart. Instinctively I knew that she would be an ally for life.

Our spiritual connection had left me with the ability to be honest and open with her as well as myself, especially after Mark died. Mark had planted the notion of being truthful, but she had taken it to a different level. I was no longer held captive by fear of my truth because when I was with her, I could always find words to reveal the truth in my heart without any judgment. Now I needed to adopt the same attitude with other souls, but I was nowhere near there yet. As I drove away, my heart went out to her because it is always harder to be left behind than to be the one leaving. *Goodbye for now, my dear soul sister. Life is not going to be the same without you.*

In order to avoid the flood of tears preparing to assault me, I stopped to pick up a coffee. As I began driving again, my thoughts went to Linda. To me, she represented built-in entertainment on so many levels. Everyone should have one crazy, off-the-wall friend to journey with. I would be lucky enough to meet several more through the years ahead. Whether Linda and I were relaxing on the couch watching a movie or in a group of people partying, she was always full of life and energy. You could not be around Linda and not be happy. In fact, I cannot recall ever seeing her depressed or angry. Linda seldom drank, but she did not need to. Her crazy character fit right in with the rest of us. When she did drink with us, we usually ended up doing something outrageous together and then laughing about the silliness the next day. Linda had always been larger than life to me.

In our spiritual connection, Linda was the one who was responsible for dismantling many of my emotional barriers; for introducing me to the concept that what other people thought of me was of little consequence. She was living her life that way and she was happy. Maybe I could get there someday myself. *Goodbye for now, dear friend. Hope we meet up again soon.* That was about to happen sooner than I expected.

TJ popped his head up from his pillow. "Mommy, I really have to pee," he began, "and I am hungry."

"Can you hold for another ten minutes? The first place I find to pull over, we will stop," I replied. Several more kilometers down the road, I found a gas station with a restaurant. After a half hour stop that included a bathroom break, a fuel refill, some food, lots of snacks, and another coffee, we were back in the car and Windsor bound once more. I listened to TJ read me a story and then he was content to quietly color for a while.

My son was now seven years old, and I began wondering how this move was going to affect him. He was in the same position as I was. He was starting over in a new province, at a new school, and had to make new friends. Through our history together, we had developed a marvelous relationship with communication being one of our biggest strengths. I had always encouraged him to talk to me about anything and everything from the time he was young. I made it a point to listen, acknowledge his feelings, and follow through with open-ended questions until I had all the information I needed. What my son was thinking or feeling was important to me, maybe because no one had ever cared about my feelings or thoughts as a child. *Why is it so simple to talk to him, a child? Why can't I be relaxed with adults like that?*

One moment that is recognized and seized will transform your life forever.

I kept that thought. I was about to discover communication in all its vastness, both verbal and nonverbal. With Spirit in the forefront of my thoughts, my mind quickly reverted to Dianne.

Dianne had been my connection back to my Spirit World, and I was beyond grateful that she had been a part of my life. How many people are lucky enough to have a psychic as a friend, as a spiritual adviser? I did not see her as an abomination, as something evil. She walked in the White Light, and I was instinctively drawn to the Light. In the beginning her capabilities often frightened me, but after four years of spending time with her, we had adopted a normal, everyday relationship. Her shock factor had worn off. Coupled with the fact that three quarters of the time we were just two souls on a physical journey together, our relationship had become as natural as any other.

I thought back to her words during our last conversation. "You have come full circle and a new journey is beginning. Remember to always stay in the White Light. When you feel depressed or you are overwhelmed with life, imagine yourself as a steel peg ground in Mother Earth. She will absorb all your negativity as the White Light feeds you positivity from above. You designed your life. Embrace your struggles and learn from them."

"By the way, your second husband is extremely close. You will be married before the end of the year," she said as she hugged me goodbye. *Goodbye for now my unique friend. May our journey together continue by the Grace of our Creator.*

We stopped in Brandon, Manitoba for the night, and TJ swam for the first two hours. Finally waterlogged, we went back to the hotel room and ordered a plate of loaded nachos with chicken, a raw vegetable plate with dip, a chocolate milk, and a tea from room service. I loved my child's eating habits at this age. He always had a healthy appetite, was rarely picky, and often preferred adult foods like shrimp cocktail or Caesar salad to hotdogs or Kraft dinner. Tomorrow we were heading for Duluth, Minnesota with the plan to stop in Grand Forks, North Dakota for a breakfast/lunch break. Within five minutes of lying down on the bed to watch television, we were both sound asleep.

I was awake and restless, so our second day of travel began at 4:30 a.m. I was only an hour and a half away from the Canada/United States border and another three hours from there to our mid-way stop of the day. The timing was turning out perfectly. TJ should be waking up right around the time we would land in Grand Forks, North Dakota. As I crossed the border early that morning, I had a chance to view the International Peace Garden, a garden representative of a 1932 pledge by the United States and Canada to never go to war with one another. Once I had crossed the border, I had a front row seat to a perfect sunrise, surrounded by lush, green, rolling hills with an escarpment of rocky rises dotting the landscape here and there.

Nature always had a special place in my heart and being right there in the moment, memories of Jarvis Lake and Comox came flooding back, as well as fond memories of Rhoda, as I continued to drive. I had easily integrated into a military environment because of where I was and who I was with. In the beginning, I knew that there were times that I annoyed Rhoda, but I was a work in progress, a baby bird that had just been knocked out of the nest, trying to find my wings. I was learning every step of the way and simultaneously stumbling over the speed bumps of life. Rhoda remained patient and nonjudgmental, encouraging and helping me find my way. I had my car and my freedom very quickly because of her. I had an accelerated promotion that eased my financial burden because of her. We worked well together, socializing in exactly the same manner. It was not unusual to walk into the office and find us having a cup of coffee while smoking a cigarette and laughing at some outrageous story we were sharing.

Rhoda was responsible for laying the foundation for my military accomplishments that were yet to materialize. She had been the perfect boss, my friend, and my mentor. *So long, dear friend. Thank you for my introduction to self-confidence. I will always remember you fondly whether we are side by side or miles apart.*

My son was awake as we pulled into the parking lot of a Big Boy Restaurant. He was in his glory when we walked into the restaurant and he saw the breakfast buffet. "If you leave hungry, it will be your own fault," I said as he headed for the buffet with his plate in hand. Three plates later, after consuming French toast, pancakes, bacon, sausage, scrambled eggs, and fresh fruit, he finally pushed away from the table. *Please do not let him get carsick now.* When we returned to the car, I placed a small suitcase on the front seat, sat him on it, and buckled him in. Imagine. You could never get away with that today or him sleeping in the backseat of the car either. Times have definitely changed. We chatted about the move to Quebec. We played "I Spy with My Little Eye". We played "Punch buggy" until I was tired of getting my arm punched. We listened to music and sang together. Before I knew it, we had arrived in Duluth, Minnesota and we were stopping for the night.

On my way to Mackinaw City in Michigan the following morning, my thoughts led me to Pattina. She had been a wonderful roommate. We both loved a clean place, so once a week we would embark on a major clean with the tunes cranked. One can get a lot of dusting or vacuuming done when one is dancing. She brought home groceries and cooked, but the best part of our relationship was that Pattina was like a psychiatrist with a sense of humor. She had a knack for always doing the right thing for the right reasons – a true moral compass. We would be so absorbed in a serious conversation and then look at each other and burst out laughing. Perhaps she was my comic relief as well, a messenger to let me know not to take life so seriously. No matter how hard we tried to get back to being serious, we never could, so over time, we just gave up. I was definitely going to miss her unique laugh. She was a giving and affectionate soul who overlooked my flaws and imperfections and loved me just the same. *Goodbye for now, my priceless therapist. Keep laughing that contagious laugh. I will miss you.*

As I continued driving, I was heading directly into a meteorological phenomenon. The sun was shining with the odd cloud floating in the sky, but within seconds, I was directly in the middle of a sun shower. *How beautiful! I have heard this is a sign of good luck.*

Luck is nothing more than fortune by design, ordained by the Creator in His time.

I was feeling the loss of intense emotional bonds as I passed through the sun shower. Was nature trying to apprise me of the fact that my previous journey was coming to an end and I needed to let go? Did I need to descend into the darkness of the rainstorm and then rejoice in the sunshine of a new beginning?

Memory lane took me back to the Griesbach Mess next. I could visualize Debbie's smiling face from behind the bar and I could hear her saying, "Hello, my little dumpling." Debbie was funny, especially if she had too much scotch in her. My mind quickly flashed back to one of our drunken nights when she insisted on having a baked potato from Wendy's as we were walking back to my place from the bar at 2:00 a.m. The restaurant was closed. The drive thru was still open, but we had no car. When we walked up to the takeout window, they refused to serve us 'without wheels'. *Not a problem. I have got you, girlfriend. If you want a potato, a potato you shall have.*

I found a shopping cart and she agreed to get into it but getting her in there was more of a challenge than we had anticipated. I came close to peeing my pants with all the laughter. Finally successful, I pushed her up to the Wendy's drive-thru window to order her potato, and they served her. When they handed her the potato, she dropped the container onto the ground, the lid flipped open and her potato landed in the dirt and gravel. I picked it up, dusted the dirt off of it, put the lid back on, and wheeled her to the edge of the parking lot. When we arrived at my PMQ, she ate her potato before passing out on my couch. The next morning she was in a hurry to get home and brush her teeth. "I don't know what happened last night, but my mouth is all gritty like I was eating dirt." *Really? I cannot imagine why.* I never did tell her the truth until many months later. *This is your little dumpling signing off. Goodbye, my amiga. Thank you for always having my back.*

My friendship with Lea was effortless and natural. I admired her kindness and how she treated people with respect. She was also honorable at keeping secrets. It was impossible to get information out of Lea if something was told to her in confidence. She had an abundance of friends, and I wondered if it was one of her Sagittarian traits. Most people with that zodiac sign are social creatures by nature. Everyone loved Lea and it was not hard to see why. *So long my sag bag friend (my nickname for her). I am one of your biggest fans!*

My son and I decided to forego stopping for lunch. We grabbed snack food after I refueled, and we were on the road again within fifteen minutes. TJ was starting to get excited about seeing his Grandmother and began busying himself in the backseat making a card for her. We would be in Mackinaw City within the next three hours. "Son, what would you like to do for our last night on the road?" I asked.

"Swim please," he replied. *I am surprised he has not grown gills the way that child loves to swim all the time.* Had I been alone, I probably would have pushed right through to Detroit, but there was no urgency. I wanted to make the trip fun for my son and I was enjoying some quality time with him.

The last leg of my journey home was the hardest. It was time to say a final farewell to Mark. The tears began as soon as he entered my mind, and it was a blessing that TJ was sleeping in the backseat and would never see those tears.

Embrace this healing moment.

I took a deep breath. *Thank you for loving me with every fiber of your being. No other soul will ever be able to replace the special love we shared. In this exact moment, my tears are a painful reminder to me of what might have been, but it took me a long time to start living again, so I do not want to go back to those thoughts. I have found peace and healing, but it was an extremely hard struggle to get here.*

Understand that he had no intention of ending his life. His focus was to end his pain.

Thank you for that bit of wisdom, Helena. I paused to reflect on her words before I continued. *I forgive you, Mark, for my moments of self-blame, confusion, and despair. I also forgive you for this tragic outcome because of your intrusive thoughts and impulses to end your pain. May you rest in the peace and love of your Creator until we meet again. Goodbye for now my one and only precious love.*

Needing a break from the flood of thoughts and emotions I had just put myself through, I turned on the radio to lighten my mood. Gino Vanelli's song "I Just Wanna Stop" began with all its intensity. The words were speaking directly to my soul as Lloyd entered my mind. I had not thought about him in ages. Why now?

"When I think about those nights in Montreal, I get the sweetest thoughts of you and me…" I just wanna stop and tell you what I feel about you, babe… I just wanna stop for your love."

Over the years, I had discovered that Spirit used the lyrics in music to speak to me, but I was too exhausted emotionally to try and decipher the intention of that song in the moment. Lloyd was the furthest thing from my mind until that song began playing. As I crossed the Windsor/Detroit border through the tunnel, TJ looked up from the book he was reading and asked, "How far is Grandma's house now, Mom?"

"Very soon," I replied. My physical destination was twenty minutes away. My emotional destination was closer than ever.

Spiritual Beings on a Human Experience

The Creator's timing is never early or late. It is right on time. Every event in history has been His timing. Human nature brings impatience to His timing, but He knows exactly where every soul is, by either putting the soul there, or allowing the soul to be there. Laurie's life has unfolded with His perfect timing because of her trust in Him.

Divine intervention, also known as providence, is the care and guidance of the Creator. Humans refer to it as "coincidence", but nothing happens that God does not create, cause, or allow. Luck is also the Creator's fortune by design.

Souls present themselves to other souls on a journey as a teaching tool to evolve the soul. A soul can be learning something themselves or teaching something to another soul. By dissecting a relationship, spiritual lessons are bountiful. Without dissection, life lessons will continually repeat for as long as they are needed. Laurie's Spirit Guide is delighted by the insights she achieved on her journey home to Windsor. Her challenge is to practice her knowledge in real time until it becomes part of her being.

Laurie and her son automatically communicate using energy from their souls – a magnetic attraction, a unique energy of pure, unconditional love that is manifested by their bond as mother and son and available because of her connection to Spirit. This energy is invisible and independent from human communication such as listening or hugging. Laurie has become empathetic based on her life experiences. She is connecting to the essence of her son's heart through that empathy.

CHAPTER 12

TRUTH AND ILLUSION

Does the past continue to haunt a soul until we share our truth, until we own our mistakes and apologize to other souls, until we accept their truth and forgive them? If the soul is only capable of telling the truth, why is it not the same for humans? Is it because humans have free will? Is it the balance of the Universe at play? Or maybe a combination of both? Perhaps the fine line between a lie and the truth is so murky that a grey area appears when we mislead or omit telling our truth. Is telling the truth or a lie only black and white?

I was starting to notice that my past had a way of presenting itself at the most unexpected times. Right now was no exception. Why had Spirit brought Lloyd back into my thoughts with that song while I was driving? Was I supposed to stop and see him again and tell him how I really felt? His phone number was unlisted and I had lost it, so I could not call him even if I wanted to. Many years had passed. I had no idea whether he was single or married or if he was still living in Windsor. Was the intention for us to meet again designed into my blueprint? The thought had crossed my mind, but the odds were stacked against me to even find him. For that reason, I let go of the thought of meeting up with him again. However, the Universe had a different plan.

Back home in Windsor, my first night was quiet. I was tired from four days of traveling and was enjoying an after-dinner drink with my mother when the doorbell rang. It was Nona and her boyfriend. Although we had kept in touch over the years, the last time I had seen Nona was before I left for British Columbia in the early 1980s. "Surprise," my mother shrieked. "Nona called me two days ago looking for your phone number. Seeing her in person is so much better, don't you think?" my mother asked strutting as proudly as a peacock back to the kitchen table. The kitchen party had begun as we all sat down together.

Several cocktails later, Nona asked me if I had talked to Lloyd lately. I had not. "I ran into him a few months ago, and he gave me his phone number. I can give it to you if you want it, but it is unlisted so you did not get it from me," Nona said laughing. I wanted his number, but at the same time, I did not. "Take it," my mother said handing Nona a paper and pen. "You don't have to call if you do not want to, but if you change your mind tomorrow, you will be happy to have the number."

Nona and her boyfriend left around midnight. My mother and I continued to sit at the kitchen table drinking. We took several strolls down memory lane as we laughed about the old days in Montreal – like the time I walked into a cement streetlight pole and knocked myself out cold because I had been looking at a dress in a shop window instead of watching where I was going. We were enjoying the memories when Donald walked into the kitchen and began rubbing my shoulders.

"Stop it," I said pushing his hands away. "Please don't touch me." He looked surprised, but then put his hands right back onto my shoulders again. I exploded. "I am not your daughter. Keep your filthy hands off of me!" I said sliding off my chair to get away from him. He went back to the bedroom, but the cat was out of the bag. My mother wanted to know why I had snapped at him like that and why I said what I did.

"Explain yourself," she demanded. *How far do I go? Do I tell her everything I know? Why did he have to touch me again when I asked him not to? This is not my story to tell.* I knew my mother well enough to know that she was not going to let my comments go so I tried to ease her into the story. "Did Donald tell you that Sharron has a son?" I asked.

"Yes," she replied.

"Did he tell you that her son is *his* child, that Grandpa is actually Daddy?" I asked.

"What! (silence) Oh, I don't believe you. I suppose Sharron told you that," she replied.

"I know this is coming as a shock, Mom. I am really sorry that I said anything at all, but I believe Sharron. What would she hope to gain by making up something like this? Donald started raping her at twelve years old. I don't want him touching me physically – no backrubs, no hugs, no nothing. He creeps me out," I said wishing I could take the whole conversation back.

"Sharron is a liar, and she is never welcome in my home again," was my mother's final comment as she took her last gulp of vodka and staggered off to bed. I followed closely behind.

As I sat on the front porch enjoying nature and my first cup of coffee the following morning, my mother came out of the house with her coffee and sat down in a chair beside me. "Your father just called and he wants to take you to lunch. Just you and him. He will be here around noon," she said. So far, there was no conversation about the night before. Maybe she did not remember any of it. I could only hope. Truthfully, my mother had a memory like an elephant even when she was drinking, so the likelihood of her forgetting our conversation was next to impossible. For now, she was choosing not to acknowledge it, and I was happy to let sleeping dogs lie.

I was surprised when my father arrived to pick me up and did not want to take his grandson with us. He spent a half hour wrestling and tickling TJ. After making plans to take him for breakfast the next day and after one final hug, we both turned and walked out the door together. My intuition was telling me that something was terribly wrong.

Halfway through the meal, my father blurted out the reason for the mystery lunch. "I have cancer, honey, and I know I am not going to survive it." I could not believe what I was hearing as the rest of the conversation echoed through my ears in the distance. Words were being spoken, but they were not registering in my brain. I was in shock and still trying to grasp the reality of his first sentence as I continued to look at him. He was only fifty-six years old. I tried to control the tears that began spilling, but my heart was breaking with the news. When he placed his hand on top of mine, I was jolted back to the present moment and the echoing in my ears stopped.

"I need you to know that I am so very proud of the beautiful young lady you have become, in spite of me." He paused, choking on the last four words with emotion. After composing himself, he continued. "I am just as impressed by my grandson. He is such a happy little boy who adores the ground you walk on. The love you both have for each other is obvious and unquestionable. We should have had that same love, but because of my fear and weakness, I missed out. I hope you can find it in your heart to forgive me for robbing you of the love and safety that you deserved." He proceeded to remove a beautifully wrapped gift box from his pocket. "I was going to give you this for Christmas, but I am afraid I might not be here. Take it now and open it on Christmas Day," he said handing me the jewelry-sized box.

When we returned to my mother's place, I sat quietly. I was still trying to process my father's news and wanted solitude to do so. "I am going to have a shower," I said making my way to the bathroom. Showering had become part of a spiritual ritual for me, a ritual to wash away my sins or remove my burdens. It was a safe place to express my emotions without affecting anyone else. As soon as I stepped into the shower, the floodgates of my heart opened as my father's words replayed in my mind with enormous intensity. *Please don't take him home, Helena. Not yet. Please bless me with just a little more time so our journey together can end in love and peace.*

When something heartbreaking occurs, something magical always follows. Trust the balance of the Universe.

I found comfort in my Spirit Guide's words about my father as my train of thought reverted to Lloyd. I had held him close in my dreams the night before, haunted by his smile as I drifted off to sleep. As I continued showering, I wanted to run to Lloyd. I wanted to see him again. I wanted to ease the pain of my father's news.

Seek your truth with Lloyd. There is healing in all truth.

My parents had walked across the street to take my son to the outdoor swimming pool. I was alone in the house when I finished showering. I sat in the rocking chair with Lloyd's phone number in my hand and began rocking. I was contemplating taking a leap of faith. After several minutes, I dialed the phone number and Lloyd answered. "Hi, this is a blast from your past. It's Laurie. I am passing through town and would love to see you," I said. I was hoping that he would not hang up on me. There was silence for a few seconds, a deafening silence, but then his reception was welcoming as he gave me his address, and we made plans to meet at his place around 4:00 p.m. that day.

Since leaving Edmonton, an emptiness had found me again - a deep loneliness that was crying out to be soothed. So I refused to look in the rear-view mirror as I drove straight to my past. I had already learned that Lloyd and I were fundamentally incompatible when we were younger. Was it presumptuous of me to trust that the Universe would bring us back together after ten years, back to a different and more mature relationship? Were both of our souls in a different place now with a new beginning on the horizon? The thought excited me which begged the question: Is there a difference between loving someone for who they are as a soul and loving someone because we long for them to meet the expectations of our own soul?

Continuing the drive to Lloyd's apartment, I reflected on my relationship with Mark. Through a moment of clarity I realized that once you have authentic love, you are now opened to truly feeling life. Although that can be very scary in all its largeness, it can be just as rewarding. I thought about my marriage with Tim, and I wondered if telling someone that you love them before they say they love you first, posed a threat? Those three words seemed to cause all sorts of reactions from other souls, my own included. If a soul is feeling needy, does it grasp for someone who once told them that they loved them, hoping for a rekindling of that love when in all actuality, it is anything but? *Am I trying to take a relationship from the past and make it into what I want it to be instead of just letting the visit with him be what it is meant to be?* In my mind, his invitation had endless possibilities and they were all positive.

While stopped at a red light, my mind refused to quiet itself as I continued to bombard myself with "what ifs". *What about lust? Lloyd and I have always been good at that. Is lust technically a clean love that you can step in and out of? Can you swim in that lust in the moment and then climb right back out of it and be fine? Is lust nothing more than a physical connection and love about an emotional one; two totally separate entities? Helena, please bring me a spiritual connection with him tonight. Please.*

Be yourself, not what you think someone else wants you to be. Know that your heart will always look for a happy ending with him.

"*I am trying to be myself. Cross my heart,*" I replied, but sometimes the unknown can throw everything off balance, begging an answer to two questions. *The more often we go through something with a soul, does it enable us to better handle the results when the same pattern continually repeats itself and we know what to expect?* I chewed on that thought for several minutes followed by a second profound thought. *Is it a recipe for disaster for my soul to deal with the fallout of our two souls reconnecting when they were best kept apart?*

I sensed that I had my Spirit Guide's blessing to reconnect with Lloyd. I was being pushed to follow through with him, in lieu of being warned not to. For some reason yet unknown to me, it was important for me to meet Lloyd in person once again. I let go of the notion to turn around at the last minute. With my heart pounding as I entered Lloyd's apartment, I realized that I had gone to a dangerous place, one that I had not envisioned during my endless daydreaming of possibilities on the drive over. Yet there I was, at his mercy with no certainty of anything. To complicate the situation, Little Laurie had surfaced and I was seventeen years old all over again. We engaged in superficial conversation while enjoying a drink, but I knew from the way that he was looking at me, we were heading for the bedroom. I wanted him to ask me to stay for the night. I wanted him to want to spend time with me and get to know 'the me' I had become. I wanted him to want to give our relationship another try. I was a woman now, not a teenager anymore. I had been married and had a child and a career. Instead, we fell into our same old pattern of lust. We swam in the moment, and when we exited the water, I could feel the dread. It was a knot that had me all tied up inside and would not let go. I was struggling to overcome my inescapable truth with him.

What happened next was not surprising. It was the logical thing that Little Laurie did when she was hurt and confused. I ran. I needed to get out of there. I was trying to save myself, but there was no denying the gut-wrenching pain I was feeling as I climbed into my car.

Ask yourself why you did not tell him how you felt.

I do not need to ask myself that question. I already know the answer deep in my soul. I am afraid of what his truth might be - that our bond is nothing more to him than lust.

There is power in truth no matter what the outcome.

Maybe there was power in the truth, but I had decided to play it safe and not share the secrets of my soul, perhaps to my own detriment. Knowing what could have been seemed better than knowing what was *never* going to be. I was tired of feeling wounded and rejected by the men in my life.

On the drive home, I felt an orchestra of angels surrounding me as Cheap Trick's song "The Flame" began playing on the car stereo. I sang those words so fiercely to Lloyd through my tears. "I've been hit by lightning. Just can't stand up from falling apart. Can't see through this veil across my heart over you. You'll always be the one…Whenever you need someone, to lay your heart and head upon. Remember after the fire, after all the rain, I will be the flame."

My truth was always in the tears I cried. As the song ended and the angels dissipated, my pain was gone and logic returned. Maybe seeing him again had played out the way it was meant to. I comforted myself with that thought. *Is the past just that, the past, and it should be left in the past? Is the key to life about going forward no matter what and making the best of what life has to offer?* I had learned that I had no control over what another soul said or did. My power was in choosing how I was going to react to it. Was it really fair to expect Lloyd to be honest with me when I was not being honest with him? Maybe he *was* being honest with me. Was a relationship with him always going to be nothing more than the two of us playing a game? I was still not ready to face the truth and let go of him until I heard my Spirit Guide's words.

Forgive yourself for not speaking your truth and then let go of the hope that the past could have been different in the future. Timely retreat is among the skills of a Spiritual Warrior.

I pulled up in front of my mother's trailer, shifted the car into park, and stepped out into the cool night air with a brand-new purpose. I was determined to find a new beginning in Montreal and leave Lloyd in the past once and for all. I hated the fact that I was still running away from him at thirty years old. Was he always going to be in my heart because he was my first love? Probably. Was I always going to want a happy ending with him like my Spirit Guide had revealed? Perhaps, or I could take back my power. Right then and there, I made the decision to walk away from Lloyd without knowing what might have been or not been. The time had come to say goodbye to him.

I am saddened by the end of our journey together, Lloyd. I know now that you will never be able to give my soul what it needs, through no fault of your own. Either love is or it is not. Tonight, your truth spoke louder than any words ever could and although it was painful to go through, your truth helped me to face my truth. I will always carry you in my heart for the milestones you helped me to achieve, and I will always remember you with fondness. God speed your love to me if it is meant to be. As the last words left my lips, letting go had finally brought me peace as all the "what ifs" evaporated into the sunset.

TJ jumped into my arms as I walked through the front door. "I missed you so much, Mommy," he said with an endearing hug. Holding him in that moment spoke to my soul. His love was the most important love in my life and the only love that mattered. My mother, Donald, and Aunt Anne were seated at the kitchen table enjoying a drink and some conversation together. I hugged my aunt and then made myself a drink. "How did your visit with Lloyd go?" my mother asked.

"Lloyd who?" was my response.

Spiritual Beings on a Human Experience

Souls arrive in the physical realm with all the information they need to navigate a lifetime, but they rarely choose to tap into that knowledge. Every experience is designed to help a soul become who they need to be. Being in one place physically while being in another mentally will rob a soul of experiencing the life they have designed for themselves. By acknowledging the truth about Lloyd to herself, Laurie is ready to embark on a new journey. Her soul has been freed from past pain, joy, and love with him. Her truth will allow her soul to reappear on a more advanced level.

By design, Lloyd experiences Laurie's love in the way that she looks at him – a look firmly embedded in his mind. He has yet to realize that her look is one of love from deep within her soul, viewing it instead as passion through his eyes of lust. They will continue on separate paths as each soul seeks to evolve independently from the other. A journey with him is still not appropriate to the person she needs to become as they continue to be seduced by the momentum of old ways.

Every soul enters a physical life with a life theme. Laurie's theme in this lifetime is to experience and move beyond 'rejection' by other souls while keeping her own soul intact. She has experienced rejection from the moment her soul arrived. Laurie will begin to accomplish her path to understanding rejection when she learns that another soul's rejection is inconsequential to her own soul's worth. Until she is willing to remove all fear of rejection, be confident in who she is, and speak her truth to all souls, she will continue her journey struggling with rejection by other souls.

The Universe is one of balance. To compliment Laurie's life theme of rejection, she is given the Spiritual Gift of "resilience" towards other souls' opinions of her.

In the past ten years, Laurie's soul has experienced authentic love from her child and an adult (Mark). She has experienced speaking her truth to souls she trusts. She has discovered her self-worth through her friendships. She is lovable for exactly who she is, imperfections, mistakes, and all. Her career has instilled self-confidence and a desire for achievement. Her Spirit World is delighted by all of her progress. One of her biggest accomplishments is her awareness and choice to listen for the infinite wisdom her soul provides when she is questioning life.

CHAPTER 13

UNTIL DEATH DO US PART

At my mother's request to leave my son with her, I spent the month of August by myself in Montreal. In hindsight, her plan was the perfect plan. My son loved spending time with his grandparents, and I did not need to worry about finding a babysitter for him as I focused on going to school full time. Alone in the evenings, I had the time to slowly unpack boxes and get organized before introducing my son into his new world. My mother always enjoyed any time she spent with her grandson, and I was grateful for the relationship they were building. Grandmothers have a unique way of learning how to see the world through a child's eyes and my son adored her. She never ran out of hugs or cookies for him. Perhaps through her relationship with him, she was trying to make up for the lost childhood with me.

When I arrived at the French Language School, I was greeted by a familiar face from Edmonton. "Are you Laurie?" Caroline finally asked after studying me from across the room for several minutes.

"Yes," I said continuing, "hi Caroline. I remember you now. You came over to my house for a psychic reading with my girlfriend Dianne."

"That's it," she replied happy to finally place my face. Our journey together had begun in a different place and a different time, just as Dianne had predicted.

Caroline was a breath of fresh air as we reminisced about the Junior Ranks Mess in Griesbach, the common friends we shared, and all the crazy partying. Caroline had beautiful, long, wavy, red hair that fell over a voluptuous body, but her true beauty was in her personality. She had a vast amount of knowledge on a variety of subjects, a walking encyclopedia so to speak, but she was also a quick study, intelligent, and witty. Her mind, combined with her sense of humor, often resulted in laughter from others around her.

During classroom breaks, students usually assembled outside to enjoy the fresh air, have a cigarette, or wake up from sitting sedentarily at a desk. Cliques were established as we instinctively gathered in social circles by rank. The course was a mixture of all ranks, all trades, and classifications, and a lot of different personalities due to age differences. We were told that we were all students without rank for the next year; however, rank is hardwired into military members and hard to ignore.

In order to determine individual levels of proficiency, the first week of the course was spent with every student going through a battery of tests in reading, writing, and speaking French. Six classrooms were then established with six to eight students per class. I was glad when Caroline ended up in my classroom. The intention of smaller class sizes was to allow students to get comfortable with each other and with speaking French without a large audience. From the time the teacher entered the classroom, speaking English was forbidden. As we stumbled over words, threw English in where we lacked the French equivalent, or used the French words we knew incorrectly when trying to answer questions, there was always copious amounts of laughter coming from our classroom, including the professor.

During one of our breaks on the second week of the course, I was introduced to an Air Defence Artillery Gunner named Steve, along with three other Gunners from his Regiment. He was shy and quiet, a lone wolf standing off in the distance observing the actions of the pack. I would often catch him studying me but thought nothing of it. We would swap a glance and a smile, but very few words were exchanged between us.

As Steve stood beside me in our social circle one day, I could feel the closeness of his energy. It was calming and pure and it felt good. *I have never experienced pure energy before. What does that mean, Helena?*

Pure is not what you expect or want, but what you need.

I loved talking to my Spirit Guide and was thankful when she chose to answer me (which was not always the case), but nine times out of ten,

I struggled to understand the intent of her messages. I had no idea what 'needing pure' meant and would not discover the true meaning of that message until many years later when it would make perfect sense.

By the third week, Steve and I found ourselves walking to the parking lot at the same time and struck up a casual conversation. He asked what I was doing for the evening. "I am still trying to get settled into my apartment before my son arrives next week," I replied.

"I could come over and help you if you want. I have a toolbox in the trunk of my car," he said. I had my own toolbox but took him up on his offer anyway. I could use the company as well as the extra pair of hands. We spent the rest of the week making my apartment feel like home and celebrated by going to the movies on Saturday night. My treat for all his help. I was enjoying our time together. His energy was positive, and I intuitively felt safe, happy, and relaxed around him.

Labor Day weekend arrived and I headed off to Ginger's house that Friday after school. My mother and my son were taking the train from Windsor to Montreal and everyone would be at the house when I arrived in Laval. The anticipation had been building all day and I was losing patience with the traffic. "Allons-y!" (Let's go everyone!) Montreal driving consisted of gridlocks or driving Mach Ten with your hair on fire. There was no in-between.

I spent the entire weekend at Ginger's place. Being with her and my mother took me back to 1976 in Montreal all over again, minus the crazy bar hopping. We played board games, polished off a few bottles of vodka, enjoyed a prime rib dinner, laughed about the good old days and boyfriends past, and enjoyed silly conversation. It had been the perfect weekend as TJ and I said goodbye to my mother and Ginger on Monday afternoon and headed back to St. Hubert. While grabbing our luggage from the trunk of the car, several neighborhood boys ran over. "Veux-tu jouer avec nous?" (Do you want to play with us?) they asked. "Go play, son. Have fun, but don't leave the street. Supper will be ready in an hour," I said. He was off playing with new friends without the slightest hesitation or the slightest fear of the language barrier.

Several weeks later when we returned to afternoon classes, the Course Administrator appeared at our classroom door, asking to speak to the teacher and me in the hallway. "Laurie, your son's principal just called, and they need you to go over to the school right away. You are excused for the day," she said. She refused to give me any more information than that. When I pulled into the school parking lot, there was an ambulance parked at the front door entrance. The principal was waiting in the lobby and I could see the paramedics with a gurney halfway down the hallway to my right. My heart was pounding and I felt sick to my stomach as I raced to meet them. When I approached the gurney, my son was awake, but distant. He seemed disoriented. "What happened?" I asked.

"Is your son epileptic?" one of the paramedics asked.

"No," I replied.

The principal joined the conversation. "Laurie, your son toppled from his desk onto the floor and began convulsing. The teacher buzzed me on the intercom to call 911, sent the other children to the gymnasium, and stayed with your son until the paramedics arrived."

After strapping my son onto the gurney and covering him with a blanket, the paramedic asked me for his health care card while saying, "From the teacher's description, it sounds like your son had a grand mal seizure. Since he is not epileptic, we are going to transport him to the hospital for a diagnosis. We will meet you there."

I sat for several hours in the waiting room before the doctor came to speak with me. I was alone and I could not quiet my mind. *Please, Helena, let him be okay. He is my whole world and the reason I exist. If it is bad news, please give me the strength to face what is coming. I can get through anything if you are with me.*

You cannot outperform your own level of self-confidence. When you are in deep water, become a diver. I am right beside you.

"I have good news, and I have bad news. Your son has epilepsy. That is the bad news. However, the epilepsy is generalized in his brain and not attacking any one particular area. That is the good news. Given his age and the fact the misfiring in his brain is generalized, chances are he will outgrow it before the age of twelve. I will give you a prescription to control the seizures, and then you can take him home," the doctor said as he walked with me to my son's bedside.

Home for the evening now and after settling my son into bed, I made myself a cup of tea and sat down to sort through my plethora of emotions. I was in an aggressive emotional battle with guilt - a suffocating, heavy feeling in my chest as the tears began to flow. *Is this all my fault? Has this move put too much stress on him? Did I turn his entire world upside down and now he is sick because of me? This poor child has lived in four provinces, and he is only seven years old. What kind of a mother does this to her child?* The knock on my front door was relieving as I wiped my tears and made my way to the living room. It was Steve stopping by to check on me after Caroline had told him that I had been called away from class. He joined me for a cup of tea and I felt much better after our conversation. He had reassured me that I was blaming myself for something that I had no control over, while also reassuring me that the prognosis for my son's recovery was incredibly good news. He had been the voice of reason that I so desperately needed in that moment.

On our afternoon break the next day, Steve mentioned that one of the guys in his class knew someone who wanted to give away eight-week-old kittens. "Do you want to pick up your son after school together and we can go look at them? What child doesn't love a pet?" he said. *An Animal Spirit! That's brilliant, Steve.* We arrived back at the apartment several hours later with a tiny, playful male kitten that my son named "Tigger". When TJ returned to class the next morning, the teacher handed him an envelope to bring home. Inside the envelope were "get well cards" that the other students had crafted for him. I sat and read each one with him.

Autumn was quickly closing in. Green leaves were being cast aside with the most vibrant hues of red, orange, and yellow as they tumbled from the trees to carpet the grass and streets. I loved the fall season. To me, it was nature's way of saying, "Come dance with me." Distracted by looking out the window, I forced myself to return to studying. Seconds later, my mind wandered to thoughts of Steve. *Good grief! I can't seem to stay focused tonight.*

Make way for a new life about to unfold.

To best describe Steve through my eyes, I saw him as tall, lean, and athletic - an avid weightlifter and runner. Quiet by nature, he was notice-ably confident and mature for a twenty-year-old, but it was the gentleness of his actions that was speaking the loudest to my heart. I had enjoyed the time that I had spent with him in the past two months. He was definitely boyfriend material, but he was being posted to Germany when the French course was finished. Long distance relationships had been a colossal failure for me in the past, so I conveniently placed him in the 'friend' category.

Still submerged in thought, my doorbell rang. When I opened the door, Steve was standing there. I was surprised when he handed me a dozen red roses for no reason at all, but there was definitely a reason. "Laurie, will you marry me?" came spilling from his lips without any hesitation. I certainly did not see that coming. I was blindsided by the question and speechless to find an answer. To this day, I have never forgot the way that he looked at me when he asked me to marry him. His strength and sincerity in his quest for love was right there in the moment, staring back at me.

Finally gathering my thoughts, I invited him in. "Can we talk about this before I answer you, please?" I said as I began putting the flowers into a vase. "I really need you to answer a question for me. Why do you want to marry me and please don't answer with 'because you love me'? If that is the reason, please tell me *why* you love me," I asked. I thought he would struggle with the question, but he responded almost immediately.

"I look at the love between you and your son," he said with an affection-ate, sweet essence in his eyes, "and I would be the luckiest man alive to know a love like that. I love your heart and your compassion, but I also love your sense of humor and your zest for life. I always feel so alive and happy when I am around you. You are the full package of what I expect love to look like." *Wow! That was deep. How old are you again? You are so much more than a number. I can feel you deep within my soul.*

Old souls instinctively search for inner wholeness.

We continued talking about how the marriage would affect his future. He would probably lose his posting to Germany. Service spouses with dependent children were rarely posted out of the country. He was walking into being a parent to a seven-year-old little boy and he was barely twenty-one himself. He stood to give up a great deal by taking on so much. After a lengthy conversation, Steve had not changed his mind. In fact, he had already considered the points I was bringing to his attention. "I know this seems fast," he said, "but I want to give our Career Managers time to co-locate us." He had a very valid point. I had two more thoughts that I needed to consider before I would be ready to give him my answer.

"I think you should spend the night," I said as I led him by the hand to the bedroom. We had never been intimate and since it is an important part of a relationship, we both needed to know if we were compatible.

I began memorizing every detail of the experience that night. He was different with a beautiful side of slowness and with a tender quietness. He was unlike any soul I had ever met. He was in the center of every moment and feeling the deep connection as our bodies touched. I was falling in love with his stillness, with his calm, and with his emotional intensity. But I was also looking at him with excitement, wonder, and fascination as I had so fondly done with nature as a child.

Finally settled into a blissful sleep together, I was startled awake by the telephone ringing. I answered to hear, "Kick that guy lying beside you out of bed and have phone sex with me." I knew that voice. I knew it well. "I can't do that. I have to go," I replied as I hung up the phone on Lloyd.

"Is everything alright?" Steve asked.

"Just a wrong number," I replied. *A very wrong number.*

As I tried to fall back to sleep, I wondered if Lloyd calling was a test from the Universe. Was I at a crossroad in life? *If I follow the path to the left, is it my new beginning to truly finding love and happiness with Steve? If I follow the path to the right, am I headed for more disappointment and hurt with Lloyd?* I had already given my love to Lloyd, and he had discarded it, sending me back to Montreal without a second thought. Taking the path to the left made perfect sense.

The alarm went off at 6:00 a.m. the next morning to Def Leppard's song "Pour Some Sugar on Me", a song that always made me think of Lloyd. *Enough, Helena, please. Stop bombarding me with Lloyd. I said goodbye and I meant it. I want to go forward not backwards this time.* That would be the last time I would talk to Lloyd or think about him for many years to come. I had finally said goodbye and meant it, making it very real.

Steve showered at my place that morning and kissed me goodbye on his way out the door. He was heading back to the barracks to get into his uniform and have breakfast at the Mess Hall. "I will have an answer for you tonight," I said kissing him goodbye. I still wanted to talk to my son.

He had been through so much change and now another major change was coming his way.

As TJ poured cereal into his bowl that morning, I opened the conversation. "Steve and I have been talking about getting married. How do you feel about that, son?" I asked.

"I am so happy for you, Mommy. I like Steve," he said as he poured milk onto his cereal. "Is he going to come live with us?" he asked.

"Would you like that?" I asked.

"Yup. Maybe he can teach me to play soccer," he said. That conversation had gone well. My son always amazed me with his level of compassion. His first reaction was to be happy for me.

That morning I walked into the classroom a little earlier than usual to find Caroline already at her desk. "How was your night?" she asked, referring to why I had been called away from class.

"Steve asked me to marry him," I replied.

She stopped what she was doing, stood up from her desk, and grabbed my arm. "Take a walk with me," she said dragging me out into the hallway. A million questions and a million and a half answers later, she hugged me and congratulated me. We made plans for her to come by the apartment on Saturday and take TJ out for the afternoon. She wanted to give Steve and I some time alone to make wedding plans.

After I accepted Steve's proposal, we had a meeting with the School's Office Administrator to advise her of our intentions. The next day, she asked us to stop by the office during one of our classroom breaks. "I have spoken with both of your Career Managers. Laurie, your Career Manager's intention is to employ you in St. Hubert after your course. There is no money in her budget to move you again," she said. I hung my head in disappointment. She continued while turning her eyes towards Steve. "When I spoke with your Career Manager, he told me that this marriage would preclude your posting to Germany, unless your wife is willing to take her release from the military. However, he is willing to pay for both of your moves to Chatham, New Brunswick. Both Career Managers require a copy of your marriage certificate before the new year."

Due to time constraints, we made plans for a small intimate wedding with family that would take place in Windsor. My only desire was to have a church wedding, to be in the presence of my Creator this time, and to have my father walk me down the aisle. When I called my mother and father to give them the news, they both offered to make the arrangements for us and handle all the details. All that we needed to do was get the marriage license and our wedding bands. Their offer was euphonious given the intensity of my studies and my inability to get any time off. I made them both promise to keep things simple.

For my family, the news of the wedding was shocking, but it was even more so for Steve's family. He was marrying someone they had never met, someone he had only known for three months, someone nine years older than himself, and someone with a seven-year-old child. Nonetheless, his mother and father agreed to travel to Windsor to attend the wedding, along with his brother Shane, who had accepted Steve's request to be his Best Man.

With the wedding date set for December 23, I phoned Sharron to give her the news and asked her to be my Maid of Honor. We had promised each other that if the day ever came where either one of us was getting married, we would be there for each other. She called me back a few days later with the details of her flight. She would be arriving in Windsor on December 21, and I promised to be at the airport to pick her up. In the meantime, she would search for a black, three-quarter length cocktail dress to wear.

December 20 rolled around with lightning speed as Steve, my son, and I loaded up the car and began the twelve-hour drive from Montreal to Windsor. The next few days were going to be a whirlwind of activity, so I made a point to enjoy the drive and spend quiet time with both of them. My son and I were staying with my mother. Steve was staying with my Aunt Anne who lived a half a block down the road. Steve's parents planned to arrive in Windsor on December 22 and had booked two hotel rooms, one for themselves and one for Steve and his brother.

The morning of December 21, my mother carried my wedding dress out from her bedroom and asked me to try it on. It was perfect - a long sleeved, three-quarter length, beige dress that was beaded on the top with chiffon pleating on the bottom. I was pleased and excited as it brought tears of joy to my eyes. It fit perfectly and was exactly what I had envisioned. Simple and elegant.

My father arrived at the trailer that afternoon. "We need to leave for the airport in the next ten minutes," he said.

"I am just about ready," I replied.

Donald was on his way out the door to pick up Ginger at the train station, and we were on our way to the airport to pick up Sharron. As my father and I drove together, I asked him how he was feeling. The twenty-five pounds he had shed in the last four months was undeniable and he looked fatigued. "I am fine, honey. The last thing that you need to be doing is worrying about me right now. You have enough on your plate," he said. I was worried, but I was also grateful. *Thank you, Helena, from the bottom of my heart for giving me this special time with my father, for keeping him here long enough to walk me down the aisle. He is being strong for me right now, but I want to be there for him too. We still have so much to say to each other. Please bless us both with just a little more time.*

I was so excited as I watched Sharron walking on the tarmac from the plane to the terminal. I hugged her and thanked her for making the trip on such short notice. "Are you kidding me? I wouldn't have missed this for anything," she replied. "I am so happy for you."

The three of us drove back to the trailer oblivious to the devastation that was about to unfold. Donald was back from the train station and Ginger, Cindy, my aunt, and my mother were sitting at the kitchen table enjoying a glass of wine. When we walked through the front door and my mother saw Sharron, she immediately became enraged. "Get out of my house right now," she screamed.

Sharron exited quickly, as did my father and I. Donald was not far behind us. In that moment, I knew that my mother had not forgotten about our conversation shown by her display of aggression towards Sharron. "You need to tell Laura the truth," Sharron said to her father. "It is time to own it, Dad." I started crying as my father and I stepped back to allow Sharron and her father to talk.

Fifteen minutes had gone by before the four of us walked back inside the trailer. "Laura, I need to tell you something. Sharron is not lying about her son. He is mine. I never told you the truth because I was too ashamed," Donald said.

Please Helena, let my mother handle his truth with grace. No such luck. My mother had been drinking and there was no reasoning with her. "Get out and take your filthy daughter with you. I want nothing to do with either one of you. As for the wedding, don't either of you dare show up."

The four of us walked back out the door. "Both of you need to come with me," my father said to Sharron and Donald. "You can stay with Collette and me while we let the dust settle and figure this all out."

After they left, I went back inside to talk to my mother. "Please, Mom, don't do this. It is not the time," I begged. "Sharron is innocent in all of this, and she has flown across Canada to be in my wedding."

Her response was headstrong. "If they go to your wedding, I will not be there," she said. I decided to leave it alone. Maybe she would have a change of heart by the morning. In the meantime, Cindy and her mother left to look for a dress for Cindy after she offered to step into Sharron's role as Maid of Honor.

The drama was not finished. In fact, it was far from over. The next morning when Steve and I stopped to see my father, I was informed that Collette would not be going to the wedding either. She was going to stay home with Sharron and her father. Now my father, a sick dying man, was going to my wedding by himself, without his wife who should be by his side.

By the time we left my father's house, Steve needed to meet up with his family at the hotel. "I am so sorry that you are going through all this drama, sweetheart. After I have supper with my family, I will stop by for an hour tonight to check in on you. I love you. Tomorrow the craziness will all be over. Stay strong," he said as he hugged and kissed me goodbye.

My mother had been drinking all day and was in a surly mood when I returned. I sent my son for his shower and then read a story with him once he was in his pajamas. He was the calm in my life that I so desperately needed. Besides, I had not had any quality time with him since we arrived.

Steve returned later that evening and cracked open a beer, but once again, it was the calm before the storm. My mother asked Steve to join her in the bedroom for a private conversation. I thought nothing of it at the time as I continued to sip my wine with Cindy, Ginger, and my aunt.

Two minutes later, Steve walked out into the living room with a definite purpose to his walk. "I have to go," he said. "I will see you tomorrow."

"Wait!" I shouted, placing my wine glass on the coffee table. I grabbed my shoes and followed him out the door. When I looked at him, his cheek was twitching, a tell-tale sign that he was angry. "What happened?" I asked.

"Your mother slapped me across the face," he replied. We went for a walk around the block to discuss what had happened in the bedroom.

Being as our wedding was so close to Christmas, plans had been made to spend Christmas Eve with my father and Collette, Christmas Day with my mother, and then travel to Stroud, Ontario on Boxing Day to have Christmas with Steve's family. His family had agreed to wait the extra day so we could all have our first Christmas together. My mother was insisting that we spend Boxing Day with my Aunt Marcie in the United States before leaving, a part of my mother's family tradition.

"I am sorry to disappoint you, but we cannot change our plans now. My parents are expecting us on the 26th and my mother is preparing a turkey dinner for our arrival. Maybe next year," was Steve's reply to my mother's request. Annoyed by his response, she called him an "arrogant son-of-a-bitch" and slapped him across the face.

"I am so sorry for my mother's behavior," I said. "I would not blame you right now if you decided to bolt on this wedding." We stopped walking when he pulled me close to him and wrapped his arms around me. "I love you, Laurie, and it will take an Army to keep me away from that church tomorrow. I will be standing at the alter waiting for you. That's my solemn promise to you. A little family drama will never change my love for you. Just wait until you meet my family." His words were definitely reassuring as we said goodnight and he went back to the hotel to join his family.

When I walked back into the living room, my mother was infuriated by her conversation with Steve earlier. "If you marry him tomorrow, I will never speak to you again," she said. I decided not to respond. She was impossible to deal with when she was under the influence of alcohol - opinionated, stubborn, and relentless. Cindy and I went back with my aunt to her place. Maybe Ginger could talk some sense into my mother, one-on-one. Isn't that what best friends do?

My wedding day finally arrived with more fighting from the moment I opened my eyes. I could not take it anymore. "I am done with all of this bullshit. I am getting married at 5:00 p.m. today and whoever is there is there, and whoever is not is not," I said storming into the bedroom and slamming the door. Silence was usually my go-to strategy when dealing with conflict, perhaps the passive child within me. Anger was always choked down fearing the response of others until I hit the point where I could no longer swallow it. That was when emotional or impulsive aggression surfaced as I spoke my mind with certainty and then retreated immediately. This behavior had become a pattern for me as an adult and was not a very becoming behavior, nor one that I recognized as dysfunctional until many years later when my son would point it out.

I showered and began curling my hair when my mother walked into the bathroom. I turned away from the sink and hugged her. "Mom, I really hope you decide to come to the wedding today. I am your only daughter, and I don't plan on ever getting married again. You worked so hard to put this day together for me, and I want you to be part of it. Take a shower and let me do your hair, please." She agreed. I finished curling my hair and left the bathroom so my mother could get ready.

Cindy was back from the florist and the flower arrangements were beautiful. My bouquet was made up of three long stemmed red roses nestled into evergreen boughs and tied together with bright red ribbon. Steve had a red rose as his boutonniere. Cindy's bouquet was the same design only with white carnations and white ribbon. There were white carnations for my mother, my father, my son, and Steve's brother. My father arrived around 3:00 p.m. that day to help TJ get into his tuxedo. I finished putting on my makeup and slipped into my dress. I walked out to the living room and my eyes teared over as I looked at my little man all dressed up. He looked so grown up. Ginger had finished helping my mother get ready, and she looked so pretty in her green dress with her white pearl necklace. Finally, we were ready to go. Aunt Marcie, Uncle Jim, and their two sons had arrived from the United States as we were taking pictures.

"It's time," my father said. "We need to get the last of the flowers to Steve and Shane at the church."

When we arrived at the church, Cindy and I remained in the front lobby while my father took TJ with him to find Steve and Shane. Steve's father made a point to introduce himself as he walked into the church. "Welcome to the family, Laurie. I am Harry, Steve's father," he said while shaking my hand. Everyone had arrived, everyone except Donald, Sharron, and Collette. When the music began, TJ was the first one to head down the aisle carrying a satin pillow with our wedding rings tied onto it. He stopped in front of Shane, handed him the pillow, and then went to sit with my mother. Cindy followed my son down the aisle, turning to wait for me at the altar.

When the "Wedding March" began, I placed my hand around my father's forearm and we stepped into the doorway.

This is your moment to embrace your father's soul.

Suddenly, I was Daddy's little girl again. I could feel his pain as I made soul-to-soul contact. However, I was in more pain than his cancer. There would be no more going to Dairy Queen for ice cream, no more family vacations together, no more Turtle chocolates for Christmas, no more phone calls, and no more hugs. My childhood pain that once burned like fire inside of me was reducing itself to an icy numbness as my heart embraced him. The only thing I could hear was my own heartbeat. I was struggling to stay composed as we took that first step together. The tears of sadness began to flow as I thought about my father dying. I cried the entire way down the aisle. By the time my father handed me over to Steve at the altar and shook his hand, I was inconsolable. I was gasping for air as Steve continually squeezed my hand.

"Is everything okay?" the priest whispered. "We can take time if you need it."

Instantly, I felt the calm return. "My tears are not about marrying this wonderful man I love. These tears are about my father dying of cancer. Please go ahead. I am so sorry," I whispered back to the priest. I was not going to feel any different about marrying Steve in a few hours, a few days, or a few months. I loved his energy and his soul.

"I, Laurie, take you, Steve, as my lawful husband, to have and to hold from this day forward, for better, for worse, for richer, for poorer, in sickness and in health, until death do us part." I was choking on those last five words and I had no idea why.

Spiritual Beings on a Human Experience

Old souls are at a self-awareness level where drama or material pursuit is of little interest to them. It is the final stage of the reincarnation journey, where an old soul sees the bigger picture and the greater truth. They are free from the programing of society and content to live in the present moment. Relationships are often long lasting and loving with a focus on more sensuality than sex.

Steve is an old soul who has learned many of life's lessons and is content to be alone. He recognizes Laurie's soul as one of deep spirituality that aligns with his beliefs in his search for love; thus, the reason for his strong and intense connection to her so quickly. He has solid faith in his judgment to marry her.

Steve possesses the skills of an empath and Laurie witnesses those empathic skills by his compassion for her son and herself. She values the stillness of his presence and his deep thought. His soul will help Laurie return to stillness and live in the present. She is already aware that he has been written into her blueprint as she embraces his marriage proposal without fear.

The union of these two souls has been blessed by the Creator. A lifetime journey together has been established, but a decision Steve will make at 32 years old will determine whether he remains in the physical realm or returns to Spirit.

CHAPTER 14

DEATH ON HIS DOORSTEP

Does life really come full circle? With all its turns and twists are we sup-posed to see both sides of another soul equally, the good and the bad? Perhaps, it is designed that way in order for us to sincerely understand them as a soul. Or perhaps, it is designed that way in order for us to avoid or release emotional baggage caused by other souls. Does coming full circle make us stronger in the end?

After signing the official paperwork and while walking back to the altar, I could see Collette and Sharron stand up and leave from a pew at the back of the church. They had both watched me get married and were now sneaking away before my mother could find out they had been there. Donald had refused to come in. He was waiting for them outside in the get-away car. I was excited when I saw them both. Maybe a change of heart was going to allow everyone to celebrate the day with us. No such luck! Sharron, Donald, and Collette had made the choice to respect my mother's wishes not to attend the wedding reception. However, she could not stop them from entering a public place to witness our marriage.

The plan after the church ceremony was to gather for a reception at the St. Joachim Hotel. A corner of the bar had been sectioned off and nicely decorated for a small wedding party. The head table had four place set-tings for me, Steve, Cindy, and Shane. On a forty-five-degree angle to my left was my mother, Aunt Anne, Aunt Marcie, Uncle Jim, Ginger, Nona, and her boyfriend. To my right was my father, Collette's daughter (sent in Collette's place), and Steve's mother and father. The tables were covered in white linens with a wedding cake placed in the center of the head table. There were candles with small flower arrangements placed sporadically as well. It was tasteful and much more than I had anticipated. I thought we were just going to a bar to have a celebratory dinner - food ordered from the menu and accompanied by a few drinks.

The meal was delicious with shrimp cocktail, Caesar salad, and a choice of either prime rib with Yorkshire pudding or stuffed chicken breast. After dinner, my son and his two cousins from the United States, Michael and Brian, left the dinner table to sit at the bar. Surrounded by a handful of regular patrons who frequented the bar, it was adorable to see the three of them sitting on bar stools like grown-ups. Steve had left the table to talk to the band as they were setting up, when TJ appeared in front of me pulling on the tie to his tuxedo. "Mommy, I feel funny," he said. My first reaction was the thought of an epileptic seizure coming on. I walked around from behind the head table and loosened his tie.

"What's wrong, son?" I asked bending on one knee to his level.

"I feel like I am going to throw up," he replied as his eyes began rolling.

My father grabbed him quickly as they headed for the men's washroom. A few minutes later, I saw my father carrying TJ in his arms out the front door of the hotel. Cindy and I went to see what was going on.

"Laurie, your son is drunk. I can smell rum on his breath. I brought him outside, and he began shivering from the cold air so he will be okay. There is no need to take him to the hospital," my father said.

"I will take him home and put him to bed," Cindy said. Bless her heart! She always had my back. She had stepped into Sharron's role without one moment of hesitation, and now, she was coming to my son's rescue.

"Would the bride and groom please come to the dance floor for your first dance." As I heard those words, I could see Steve standing on the dance floor looking around for me, totally unaware of everything that had been transpiring with TJ. After kissing my son goodbye and thanking Cindy, I scurried over to the dance floor. The band congratulated us, and then began playing their rendition of "Angel Eyes" by the Jeff Healey Band. The moment Steve took me into his arms, I could feel butterflies as he began dancing circles around my heart. I nestled into his chest, singing to the lyrics: "How did I ever win your love? What did I do? What did I say? To turn your angel eyes my way?"

As a surprise, Steve had booked us into the honeymoon suite at the Delta Hotel without telling me or anyone else where we were going. It was a luxurious, tranquil, and romantic experience, one that I definitely needed after all of the chaos prior to the wedding. The surreal, white ambiance of the suite was calming as I entered, and I was blissfully happy that I had just married the perfect partner to savor the evening with.

My son was very hung over the next morning. How many people can say that their seven-year-old son got drunk at their wedding? Probably, less than a handful! Maybe I should rephrase that. How many children can say they experienced being drunk and hung over at seven years old? To this day, I do not know what happened. I assumed the bartender would never have served him alcohol knowingly. Maybe another patron's drink was put in front of him by mistake. Thinking it was pop, when in actuality it was rum and coke, he guzzled it down and the rest was history.

After consuming a delicious breakfast dropped off by room service, we began packing to leave the honeymoon suite. It was Christmas Eve day, and we needed to pick up my son. My father and Collette were expecting us around 2:00 p.m. When we arrived, Collette had a full house, at least twenty-five people or more. She had prepared a Ukrainian feast with cabbage rolls, perogies, salads, lunchmeats, fresh bread, and several platters of delightful, homemade sweets. The food was laid out smorgasbord style in food warming trays. People could help themselves whenever they wanted throughout the afternoon and evening. As well, she had set up card tables in the basement for the meal and also for a euchre tournament to be held later that night. Euchre was my father's favorite card game, one that he was extremely good at.

When I opened my father's gift, the jewelry-sized box that he had given me in July, it brought tears to my eyes. He had retired from the Windsor Police Department a year earlier and had his police badge engraved into a piece of gold that was hanging from a chain. On the back of the pendant was his badge number and the words "Love Dad". To me, that necklace represented the happier times in his life, away from his miserable existence at home. My father loved his job, was exceptionally good at it, and was genuinely respected by his colleagues and the public alike. I was thrilled that he was still alive as I wrapped my arms around him to thank him in person. *Thank You, Heavenly Father, for this amazing blessing! The voices of a million angels could not express my gratitude right now.*

That day, Sharron and I had a heart-to-heart conversation as I apologized once again for how terribly wrong everything had gone. "Please don't apologize, Laurie. I understand. None of this is your fault," she said, but I felt it was my fault. If I had not said anything to my mother, none of this would have happened, and my mother and Donald would still be together and Sharron would have been at my wedding. I was so traumatized by the turn of events that I buried the memory for decades in order to ease the pain. Another less forgiving soul would have written off our relationship, but Sharron shrugged it off. She was no stranger to my mother's behavior, and she was also the epitome of forgiveness.

It was time for the Euchre Tournament. Sharron and I decided to partner up, and we won the tournament that night in a final round against my father and his partner. The prize was a Texas Mickey of Crown Royal, which she insisted I take home with me, along with her wedding gift. She had purchased a bottle of sparkling wine from Spain that had a personalized label attached congratulating us on the marriage. I still have that bottle to this day, and it has never been opened. As we said goodbye the next morning, I promised to stop in again before we left on December 26.

My mother was on her best behavior when we showed up at the trailer. Perhaps, for TJ's sake. It was Christmas and her grandson was so excited as he raced through the front door and gave her a big hug. He was the one who had set the tone for our reception that day. I was still fearful of her words that if I married Steve, she would never speak to me again. I did not know what to expect. My mother engaged in conversation with TJ and me but turned a cold shoulder to Steve. It was obvious that she was tolerating him and that all was not forgiven. I was still at a loss as to why she was so angry with him. After all, she was the one who slapped him. If anybody should be mad, it should be Steve.

As Steve packed the car the next morning, my mother and I finally had the conversation I had been hoping to avoid. I was putting on my shoes and asked her how much we owed her for the bar tab from the wedding.

"Nothing, Merry Christmas," she replied. Then without a moment's hesitation, she added, "I hope that marrying him was worth our relationship." I did not know how to respond. *Certainly, she can't mean what she is saying. Is she really going to write off our relationship because we are not going to Aunt Marcie's for Boxing Day brunch? What happened in that bedroom with Steve? Does she really hate him that much? Please say it is not so.*

The day comes in every daughter's life when she needs to see her mother not as a mother but as another woman with a heart that has been broken by her past. This is that day.

Life never stopped surprising me, and this moment was no exception. My view of life was that it was never hopeless. It was just not easy. I hugged my mother goodbye that day, unaware how determined she would be to hold true to her word. I believed that she would eventually come around. If not for me, at least for her grandson. With a final goodbye to Ginger, Aunt Anne, and Cindy, I climbed into the front seat of the car.

On our way out of town, we stopped at my father's place for one last goodbye. My time with him was precious and I wanted every minute I could get. Besides, I really wanted to see Sharron one more time before she flew back to Alberta. I held onto each individual hug with the two of them until it was embedded deep in my soul.

From Windsor, the trip to Steve's parents' place took four and a half hours. We arrived around 2:30 p.m. The smell of turkey cooking was welcoming as we entered the house. Steve introduced me to his siblings I had not met yet - his brother, Scott, and his sister, Kim. Steve was the oldest of the boys. Kim was the oldest of the family and was married with a one-year-old little boy named Jeffrey. I felt awkward at first, but then quickly relaxed. We were all in the same boat of trying to get to know each other and the reception was warm. I appreciated all the effort they had made to travel to Windsor for the wedding, especially so close to Christmas, and I also appreciated the fact that they had delayed Christmas waiting for our arrival. Both were loving gestures in my eyes.

As I sat listening and watching Steve's family interact with each other, I learned a lot about the dysfunction in his family. *Perhaps all families are dysfunctional to some degree, some more than others.* His father ran a catering business that was based out of Mississauga. His mother was a stay-at-home mom who busied herself with her children. Harry (Steve's father) was an alcoholic when Steve was growing up but had been sober for the last four years. Being sober had its own challenges for Harry. He was verbally aggressive with his wife and life frustrated him at the best of times. Steve's siblings were not close with him or each other. Everyone appeared to be living in their own world while tolerating the world around them.

We spent a few days with Steve's family before returning to St. Hubert. When we arrived home, we unpacked the car and then made a quick trip to the grocery store to restock the refrigerator. It felt good to be home, just the three of us. After the last week of chaos, I was enjoying the quiet. I spent the next few days making phone calls. The call to Dianne (my psychic girl-friend) was entertaining as she giggled at the news. "I don't know why no one ever listens to me. Everyone thinks I am a batty, old broad," she said.

"Well your prediction seemed a little farfetched at the time," I replied. We spent an hour catching up on the news and then I phoned Linda. She had been posted to CFB Valcartier in Quebec. "I am only two and a half hours away from you now. I want to come and meet your husband. I want to know the man who finally won your heart after the dozen marriage pro-posals you turned down," she said. We made plans to see each other again at Ginger's place for a weekend in February. I made several more phone calls before the New Year to fill everyone in on the news.

The beginning of January, I received a phone call from my father telling me that my oldest brother, Bob, was in the hospital in a coma. It was not something I ever expected to hear. Bob had always been invincible to me, totally in control of any situation, and a force to be reckoned with. At least that is how I remembered him from my childhood. "What happened?" I asked.

"He was beat with a baseball bat in a parking lot behind a bar," was my father's response. He did not have exact detail, only that it had something to do with a girl who had run away from her pimp in Nova Scotia and was now working for Bob. Rumor was that this girl's pimp arrived in Calgary with the intention of bringing his worker bee back home with him, and when Bob refused, he had sealed his fate. Bob came out of his coma a week later, but not without suffering brain damage. My brother, Jimmy, took him into his home to care for him, but the writing was on the wall. On

January 27, at the age of 34, Bob died from a brain hemorrhage while he was in the shower.

When I heard the news of his death, I was in a battle between my Spirit and my Flesh and now my soul was in an arena where these two armies had collided. Bob and I had never had a meaningful brother/sister relationship. In fact, I could count on one hand the number of conversations we had in our lifetime together. I had no pity for him. He was self-centered, arrogant, hostile, and rude to most people. He had spent his whole life beating up people who annoyed him. How fitting that his ending was about someone beating him to death.

Your flesh is speaking. Now embrace him with your spirit.

Heavenly Father, please have mercy on Bob's soul as he makes his journey home. Bob, I forgive you for believing that I was your enemy. I really only wanted to be your friend. I also forgive you for your anger and aggression that physically and emotionally injured me as a child. Thank you for not killing me or maiming me for life and for teaching my soul resilience.

Your soul had to endure the horror of what happens when helpless people cannot defend themselves. For that reason I have created mercy for those who don't deserve it. His soul will review his physical life through My eyes, and he will know the error of his ways. The debt to other souls he affected will be inevitable.

Are you saying I have to be with him and Joan again in another lifetime? No answer.

I made the choice *not* to go to Bob's funeral. It felt hypocritical to mourn over someone I barely knew and someone who had terrorized me as a child, but the biggest fear that was paralyzing me about going to that funeral was seeing Joan again. I knew she would be there to say goodbye to her favorite son. I was nowhere near ready to see her again or to forgive her for that matter.

In February, I was promoted to the rank of Master Corporal (MCpl). Steve was beaming with pride as the Commanding Officer removed my old rank and replaced my shoulder chevrons with the new rank. All his fellow Gunners were teasing him about who wore the pants in the family and that teasing became more evident the following week when we were required to qualify on our weapons at the range.

The day before leaving for the range, we had a weapon familiarization class. It is part of the protocol to be able to strip our weapon and put it back together, as well as knowing how to clear stoppages once we are on the firing range. I had two left hands that day as I chased my weapon parts around the classroom. Springs were flying and parts were dropping onto the floor. "I want someone on her at all times on that range tomorrow," the instructor said to one of the other instructors in the room.

During supper that night, Steve asked me if I was nervous about going to the range. "Not at all," I replied. I had no logical explanation for my clumsiness with my weapon that day. Perhaps my Creator had a sense of humor. I always seemed to be the comic relief during stressful military situations.

The following morning, we boarded the buses. On arrival at the range, twenty students were given their weapons while the other twenty retreated to the butts where the targets were. From a lying position on the ground, we were given our magazines, and several rounds of ammunition. I was at Target Number 13. Steve was at Target Number 2. On command, I loaded the magazine with my first five rounds to site my weapon. With each shot fired, the pointer from the butts was coming up on the target indicating a bull's eye.

"I think you are fine," the instructor said as he walked away. After sixty rounds in total from the lying, sitting, and kneeling positions, the command was given to "down weapons" as we broke for lunch. The twenty students from the butts emerged to join us.

"Who was firing at Target Number 13?" one of the guys asked.

"That was Steve's wife," someone replied.

"Hey Steve, some words of advice. Don't piss her off because she won't miss your sorry ass as you are running away," someone commented.

"I would let her wear the pants in the family if it were me," another said.

Linda was at the apartment waiting for us when we pulled into the driveway from school on Friday night. We changed out of our uniforms, packed a few things, and drove to Laval to spend the weekend with Ginger. It was the first time I had seen Ginger since the wedding. We cracked open a bottle of vodka, threw some steaks on the barbeque, and made a tossed salad. After supper, Ginger brought out the pictures she had taken at the wedding. We did not have a photographer so we were seeing pictures from the wedding for the first time. As we passed the pictures amongst ourselves, Linda was experiencing the day with us at the same time. Most of our conversation that night was about the wedding and everything that had taken place - the good, the bad, and the ugly.

Saturday consisted of rain and more rain so to keep ourselves entertained, we had a Monopoly marathon for eight hours with my son. The last three hours were the most entertaining after several drinks. Perhaps that is why my son ended up owning every property and bankrupting us all. Linda and I took TJ downstairs to get him settled for the night and then we sat talking for a few minutes in the family room.

"You look so happy, Laurie, and I can see why. The way Steve looks at you speaks volumes of his love for you. It's like his head is in the clouds, but his feet are still on the ground. He is so mature. So tell me, how does he make you feel?" she asked.

"Falling in love was the furthest thing from my mind. He is my strength. I find myself always making excuses for a reason to touch him. He makes me feel safe and comfortable, and he loves me for exactly who I am. I dote on his energy. It feels so good," I replied.

For the first time in my life, I found myself wanting a man instead of needing one. *Is it possible that I actually do need him in order to know that I do not need him?* Linda continued, "And, how is Mama Cougar keeping up with her Young Buck?"

"This conversation is over, Linda. I am going back upstairs. If you are that curious, find a Young Buck of your own. I highly recommend it," I said turning towards the staircase, while winking back at her.

Spiritual Beings on a Human Experience

Coming full circle gives a soul a chance to master what has been accomplished during a learning cycle by putting the knowledge into practice. Like a caterpillar transforming into a butterfly, the Creator has provided Laurie with a relationship that seemingly came out of nowhere but will radically impact her life. Their relationship is manifesting in His season and for His reason.

Laurie's spiritual destination is to live her adult life being true to who she is, rather than living a life of childhood wounds and patterns that continually reappear, or living her life based on another soul's idealization of who she should be.

Laurie's mother has placed conditions on their relationship. She is used to getting her own way and feels challenged and angered by Steve's refusal to accommodate her wishes. Her mother's decision is not Laurie's battle to fight. Spirit rejoices in the fact that she decides to accept her mother's choice, with the hope that time will reunite them once again as mother and daughter.

Death is not the end of life, but rather a return home by the severing of a "silver cord" connecting a physical body and a soul. Every soul has the capacity to love and forgive another soul with the right intent of releasing the soul for a journey home. Laurie is learning through her brother's death that healing is about forgiveness and carries impact for both souls.

CHAPTER 15

SHARED SENSE OF PURPOSE

The human brain is brilliant and devious. It will block out what it cannot handle or what it does not want to know. It is called "denial".

The Easter Weekend was just around the corner. We made plans to return to Windsor, so I could visit with my father. I spoke to him on the telephone every week, but I had been struggling with an urgency to see him again in person.

When I walked through the front door to the house and saw my father lying in a hospital bed in the living room while Collette tended to him, I immediately turned around and went back to the front porch step to sit. Collette had been changing my father's pajama top as he sat on the edge of the bed with his back to me. He was seriously underweight, skeletal to be precise. His ribs were protruding through his back. I burst into tears when Steve sat down on the step beside me and put his arm around me. "Why did you bolt like that, sweetheart? What's wrong?" he asked.

"I can't do this, babe. I don't want to remember him like this. He is not my father anymore. He is a skeleton filled with cancer," I replied.

"Trust me. Your father is still inside that skeleton. He needs to see you. He needs to know that you are here. You will never forgive yourself if you walk away now. Hold my hand and we will go back in the house together," he said pulling me to my feet.

"Where is TJ?" I asked. In my own personal mayhem, I had lost track of where my son was. "Collette's daughter took him to the basement to play. Stop stalling now. You can do this, Laurie. Let's go back inside," Steve coaxed. He squeezed my hand as he opened the front door.

My father was propped into a semi-sitting position with several pillows and smiled at me as soon as we walked in. I loved his smile. I was going to miss that smile. "There's my girl. Come and give me a hug," he said while reaching out with his arms.

"Hello, Daddy," I said as I wrapped my arms around him. We hugged in silence for a long time. Steve said hello and then excused himself to go check on TJ and bring in the luggage from the car. I knew as he walked away that he was leaving in order to give me some quality time with my father.

For the next few minutes, our conversation was lighthearted as we talked about my French course. Perhaps, it was a blessing. I was still in shock and trying to regroup. His health had deteriorated so much since Christmas. The cancer had spread rapidly through his abdomen, resulting in him needing to have a colostomy. He had a morphine drip for the pain that was tended to several times a day by a home visit from a hospice nurse. He was struggling to eat and when he did, he would immediately vomit the two bites he had swallowed. He was frail and he looked like he was eighty years old. My father had been right when we had lunch together in July. He was not going to survive this.

The morphine drip left my father with very few lucid moments. I spent most of that day thinking about death as I watched him sleep. I felt blessed that his death was not going to be a sudden death that leaves so much left unsaid. He was sick and dying from a disease, so I still had time to say goodbye, to help him pass with peace. But at the same time, my heart ached for him and the quality of life he had been left with. Although we had very few conversations that weekend, I would see my father one more time before his death. That meeting would give us both the serenity we needed to say goodbye with forgiveness and love in our hearts.

Two days after returning to St. Hubert, Dianne called. "How is your father?" she asked.

"Not good," I replied. We talked for a few minutes about my experience seeing him again.

"You know your father is going to die. He has chosen this time as his exit point. He told you so. He does not want a physical life anymore. He is consumed with guilt over your childhood," Dianne said. Although I heard her words, I was grappling with accepting his death. I did not want him to leave. I wanted him to be healthy again and grow old with his children and his grandchildren.

"Just being alive is not the same as living. Do you want him to continue to live so that you can still have him? Do you want him to continue to suffer so that you do not have to know the pain of letting go? Don't beg him to stay. Give him your blessing to leave and then say goodbye from your heart," Dianne said, assuring me that in doing so, it would bring peace to both of our souls. "I wish that souls understood that asking a soul to remain in the physical world to ease their own emotional pain is very selfish and results in bad karma." Those were her last words before we continued with a normal conversation.

As I began preparing supper, my Spirit Guide appeared in my thoughts. **Consider not only what will benefit you, but what will benefit him. Refusal to see clearly will cause pain to him and damage to yourself.**

It was unquestionably clear in that moment that I needed to heed this advice and let my father go home with my blessing. I had been told twice within a span of a few hours, alleviating any room for confusion or misunderstanding.

While washing the supper dishes, I thought about Collette and decided to sit down and write her a heartfelt letter. In the letter, I thanked her for being such an incredible caregiver to my father. I paused on that thought to reflect. *She is always by his side, day and night. My heart is at peace knowing that he will not die alone. He will be surrounded by her love as he takes his last breath. I just know it and I cannot thank her enough.* I returned to writing the letter. I did not tell Collette what Dianne and my Spirit Guide had told me. I did not tell anyone. Instead, I reassured her that no matter what the outcome was, we would always consider her to be family and be there for her. The intention of my letter was to bring her comfort. It did exactly the opposite. Through her grief, she viewed the letter as me burying my father in his grave before the man was dead and that angered her. She tore up the letter. Although she continued to hand the phone to my father when I called every week, her reception was cold when she answered, and she was not forthcoming with any information about his condition. He was always "fine". I had no idea why she was behaving like she was. It would take a phone call from my brother Steve to understand the damage that letter had done.

Students were excited with the news of posting messages arriving from Ottawa, so the news of these postings became the main topic of conversation during our breaks. When Steve's fellow Gunners learned he was going to Chatham, instead of Germany like the original plan, they began teasing him. "Lucky you, Steve. You are going to live in the same area as Allan Legere, the "Monster of the Miramichi". *What are they talking about?*

"He is back in jail again, guys. They caught him last week. Relax!" Steve said. Allan Legere was a convicted rapist, arsonist, and serial killer who escaped custody in 1989 and went on another killing spree of four more people, including a priest, before being caught eight months later. *Hmmm! Maybe I should have taken my release from the military and followed Steve to Germany. Now I am nervous about this whole move, Helena.*

Trust that you are exactly where you need to be.

Effective July 1, Steve was posted to 119 Air Defence Artillery Battery (119 Battery) in Chatham, New Brunswick, and I was posted to 210 Workshop alongside him. The Workshop was a unit that augmented the upkeep and repair for all of 119 Battery's equipment. I was being plunged into the Army's world, into an operational unit expected to deploy on a moment's notice, and into a unit of 43 electrical and mechanical engineering men, as their first female. *Welcome to gender equality, Laurie. Prepare yourself for the bumpy road ahead where no crying is allowed.*

On Mother's Day, I decided to try reaching out to my mother. We had not spoken since the wedding, and I was hoping that she had reconsidered her decision not to speak to me as long as I was married to Steve. Donald answered the phone when I called. It was apparent from that call that Donald and my mother were back together again. I was miffed and angered in the moment. I felt like all the chaos at my wedding was for nothing. My mother refused to take my call that day, so I asked Donald to wish her a "Happy Mother's Day" and to let her know that I was moving to Chatham, New Brunswick in July.

At supper that night, my son handed me a gift bag, along with a homemade card. He was excited as I opened them both. The gift was a bottle of my favorite perfume, "L'Air Du Temps" by Nina Ricci, a gift that he and Steve had bought together during a trip to the mall, but the card was even more precious. Their love was exactly what I needed after my mother's rejection.

My challenge in leaving St. Hubert was leaving Caroline behind. She had become such a good friend, especially to my son. She used to have "fun days" with him when she would pick him up on a Saturday and take him on an adventure for the day - to the zoo, to the park, or to the mall. He was always so excited when he knew she was coming over. Caroline was genuinely happy about my marriage to Steve, but sad that we were leaving for New Brunswick. I was going to miss her, but our journey together would reunite us sooner than we both expected.

Our furniture was packed and loaded into a moving van as we began our road trip to New Brunswick. We had twenty-one days to find a place to live, move in, and be ready to start our new jobs. The French Course had not allowed time for a house-hunting trip, and there were no PMQs on the base available for rent. We needed to find somewhere to live on the local economy. The unknown, along with the time crunch was incredibly stressful.

Two traveling days later and on our arrival in Chatham, Steve reported to 119 Battery. I did not report to my new unit. They were not expecting me until July 21, so I could not see the point. Perhaps that is the difference between an Army mentality and an Air Force one, which I was about to discover very soon. When Steve was introduced to his Divisional Captain, the Captain informed him that he owned a house in Chatham, one that he had bought as an investment and had just finished renovating. The house was empty if we wanted to have a look at it. Steve returned to the car with a set of keys and the address to a home on Wellington Street. I had a million questions to which Steve had no answers. *I wish men thought like women. Why do they never ask questions?*

All Steve said was, "He did not give me any details. He just handed me the keys, told me to have a look, and said he would meet us there within half an hour."

Could we be so lucky? I chatted with my Spirit Guide for the entire ride as we drove excitedly to our potential new home.

The house that fell so quickly into our hands was a landmark home, a Loggie home that had been built in 1879 for a businessman named William Stewart Loggie. The home had remained in the family for 100 years until it was bought by the town of Chatham in 1979 for $50,000. As we toured it, the most appealing part of the house was that every room appeared to have been left with remnants from eras gone by. It had a clawfoot tub in the bathroom, built-in custom cabinetry in the dining room, and a vintage wallpapered room on the second level. The home was spacious with a wood-burning fireplace in the living room, and the kitchen had plenty of cupboards, including a pantry. We were definitely impressed. It was like taking a walk back in time.

As we finally finished touring the upstairs level, Steve's Captain pulled into the driveway. I decided to wander into the backyard, leaving the boys alone to talk. The backyard was fully fenced with mature trees and landscaping, and there was a large deck off the patio door from the kitchen. In the middle of the yard sat an original anchor from a 1940's merchant ship. It was massive in size. A chain ran down the anchor from the top, twisting itself around the anchor to finally rest in the depths of the soil below. The most beautiful bed of wildflowers finished this monumental centerpiece of the yard. I often wondered if the graves of the Loggie family members who had long passed were located below that anchor. For that reason, I refrained from digging up anything in that area. Somehow intuitively, it felt like a sacred spot. Moments later, when I stepped back through the glass sliding doors, the deal had been sealed for me. The Loggie Home became our home that day at a rental cost of $400 a month. It had been handed to us on a silver platter.

After lunch, we returned to the base to begin our in-clearances and advise R&D (Receipt and Dispatch) that we had secured accommodation so they could deliver our furniture. The moving truck would be arriving in four days. So far, we were off to a great start, but we both had no idea what was waiting for us around the corner.

It was the second week of July when my brother, Steve, called. "Hey Sis, I just came back from visiting Dad. He is really close to the end now, so if you want to see him alive again, you need to go soon." I was silent as his words registered. With the upheaval of the move and Collette giving me so little information, I was thankful for my brother's update. "By the way," he continued, "what did you write in the letter to Collette that pissed her off so badly?"

As I explained what I had written, and he explained her reaction, I was dumbfounded by the impact of that letter, but at least her behavior made perfect sense now. When I got off the phone with my brother, I made myself a cup of coffee and took it to the backyard. I felt a strong need to connect to nature. *Helena, please forgive me for upsetting Collette. That was not my intention.*

The Universe supports and empowers your action. Be still and wait on the will of the Heavens.

A large moving van can be a major attraction of curiosity in a small community. After several hours of movers emptying our contents, they had disappeared for a lunch break. As I sat on the front porch step enjoying the sunshine, I was greeted by a lady, who lived across the street, carrying a homemade lasagna. We introduced ourselves as she handed me the supper she had prepared for us. Her name was Angela, and she had a son named Romeo who was the same age as TJ. "Your son is welcome to come over and play for the afternoon while you continue moving in. He must be very bored," she said. TJ was excited about making a new friend and without the slightest hesitation, he followed Angela home.

By the time I needed to start my new job, the boys had become inseparable, so Angela offered to babysit. We enrolled them both in swimming classes for the month of August at an outdoor pool half a block up the road. I was impressed by how easily we seemed to be fitting into this little town of Chatham. Maybe my Spirit Guide had been right. Maybe I was exactly where I needed to be.

I had eased into my new personal beginning effortlessly, but my professional beginning would be an entirely different story. Perhaps the balance of the Universe was at play here - the easy versus the challenging. Saying I was uncomfortable when I reported to 210 Workshop for my first day of work is an understatement. I was a female, wearing an Air Force uniform, and entering an Army environment with nothing but men and way too much testosterone. I felt like a red head in a blonde parade with forty-three spectators hanging on my every word or move. That day was my beginning of being "sized up" and "dressed down" for the next six months as I tried to adjust to an Army environment.

My Warrant Officer was showing me to my desk, when the office door opened and a Warrant Officer from the Vehicle Section barreled in. I had barely sat in my chair when I heard, "I need a 1020D for a PPU on an ADATS, and I need it right now." *Huh? 1020D? PPU? ADATS?* He might as well have been speaking to me in Chinese. I had no clue what he was talking about. The look on my face must have said it all as my Warrant Officer took the paperwork and sent him on his way. "Come with me," he said holding the office door open.

He proceeded to take me on a tour of the workshop - stopping at each section, introducing me to each section supervisor, and explaining each piece of equipment he was showing me. I saw firsthand what an ADATS looked like. That was followed by being shown a Skyguard, Javelin, HLVW, MLVW, and APC. All of this equipment was currently in the workshop for repair. I was like a fish out of water as I flip-flopped from the Vehicle Section to the Weapons Section, to the Radar Section, to the Radio Section, trying to catch my breath and take it all in. By the time the tour had ended, I had learned that a 1020D was a workorder, a PPU was a Primary Power Unit, and an ADATS was an Air Defence Anti-Tank System, a highly mobile unit designed to provide air defense protection for mobile units on the ground. *Heaven help me, please. I am in way over my head here.*

My afternoon was consumed by learning the LOMMIS system on a computer, which was the military's record keeping program for all of its equipment. From the time a piece of equipment is purchased, a history for costs of repairs or maintenance to that equipment is recorded throughout its entire lifespan. "Ottawa requires a less than 2% error rate on all files uploaded each month," my Warrant Officer advised. "Success is in the details." I had a steep learning curve ahead, but I had survived my first day. Like it or not, I was being submerged into the electrical and mechanical world of 119 Battery. It was definitely challenging, but I decided to embrace it and give it my best.

Before leaving the office, I looked up the Military Regulations for Compassionate Leave. I was entitled to one week to visit my father before he died OR one week to attend his funeral, but either choice was at the discretion of my Commanding Officer. Operational military requirements always outweighed any personal requests.

"How was your first day in the Workshop?" Steve asked as we sat down to supper.

"It is very obvious that I am trying to infiltrate a man's world, a very unwelcoming man's world," I replied continuing, "and I do not know how to fit in. I am challenged by the job *and* the people."

He knew exactly what I was talking about. 119 Battery had four female Gunners also trying to fit into a world with a history of a "men-only mentality". We continued talking, eventually changing the subject to my father. The final plan we agreed upon was for me to approach my Commanding Officer the following morning and ask to go to Windsor as soon as possible. I had a feeling that the reception to my request was not going to be welcomed. I was new to the unit and already asking for time off from a man whom I had yet to meet. My destiny with my father was in a stranger's hands. I prayed hard that night for Divine Intervention. My life had always been about my Creator's timing, and I needed it now, more than ever.

My request for Compassionate Leave was approved for the first week of August. Steve drove me to CFB Greenwood to catch a Hercules plane into CFB Trenton. From there, I was taking a train to Windsor. "I know this trip is not going to be easy for you. I wish I could go with you. Your son and I are going to miss you terribly, Laurie, but I know that you will do what you need to do. Remember, you are stronger than you give yourself credit for," Steve said as he hugged me one final time.

Nona offered to pick me up at the train station, while simultaneously offering her home as my refuge while I was there. I did not tell my mother or Collette that I would be in town. My father was in hospice care at the Metropolitan Hospital, and I was hoping, by the Grace of God, to avoid seeing both of them. Early the next morning, I walked into my father's private suite to witness him directing traffic on a morphine-induced high. He was alone as I pulled up a chair beside the bed and sat. He was reliving his police career and smiling. I did not want to interrupt. Several minutes had gone by before he opened his eyes. He looked calm as he collected his thoughts and began speaking. He was right there, present in the moment, and clearheaded.

"Hello honey, I have been waiting for you," he said.

I answered him back with, "I got here as soon as I could, Dad," as I placed my hand on top of his.

He continued, "I have seen them, and they are waiting for me to come home, but I needed to see you one last time."

"Who have you seen, Dad?" I asked.

He started naming all the family members that had passed and were now in Spirit - his sister, his mother, his in-laws, and my brother. My father and I had never had a spiritual conversation *ever*. He had lived his life with a mindset of logic and reason. I was hanging onto every word as he continued speaking. "I can leave now knowing that you have married Steve. He is a good man, and I know that he will look after you. He won't abandon you like I did. There will never be any words to express how tormented I am by the life you lived as a child. If I could live my life over again with the ability to make one change only, it would be that. I would love you and protect you no matter what. Please don't cry, honey." Tears were streaming down my face as I looked into his eyes and felt every word he was speaking deep in my soul. After digesting the words from his heart, it was time to speak from my heart.

"I know that this is goodbye, Dad. I will probably never see you again in this lifetime, but I want you to go home knowing that I forgive you for my childhood. Joan was crazy. None of us got away from her unscathed. Most of us make choices with the best of intentions, but we can also make gigantic mistakes along the way. Tim is my perfect example! Joan was evil, Dad, with devious intent in all her actions. You were not. For that reason alone, you need to forgive yourself. I will always remember you with love in my heart as will many other souls still here. The next time you see everyone in the Spirit World, go to them, Dad. You will be free from your physical body, free of pain and torment. I love you in spite of all our history," I said, leaning over and kissing his forehead. When I straightened back up, he closed his eyes and drifted off to sleep.

I had been blessed with a half hour of uninterrupted soul-to-soul contact with my father. There were no words left unspoken between us. *Thank you, Spirit World. Thank you for everything.* It was 9:00 a.m. when I left the hospital, and I felt an urgency to get back to Chatham as soon as possible. I had accomplished what I had set out to do. I spent one more day visiting with Nona and then was on my way back to New Brunswick three days earlier than expected.

Steve was at the airport to pick me up, and he was alone. TJ was spending the day with Romeo. "I am glad that TJ is not with us for the drive home," Steve said. "There has been a lot going on since you left and we need to talk."

"Such as?" I asked.

He continued, "The day after you left, the Battery and Workshop received a Warning Order for Operation Desert Shield. I decided not to tell you while you were with your father. The United States, along with thirty-five other nations, have waged war against Iraq for their invasion of Kuwait. I am surprised you have not heard about it on CNN."

"I have not seen the news in a week," I replied.

"If we both end up deploying, what do you want to do about TJ? I have talked to my parents, and they are willing to take care of him while we are gone," he said.

I replied with, "I need to go back into my unit tomorrow and see where things stand. Maybe I can get out of deploying." How naive of me!

When I returned to the Workshop earlier than expected, they were surprised to see me. Within an hour, I was called into the office of my Commanding Officer. I was not being deployed with my unit, but not because my Commanding Officer was showing me any preferential treatment by my request. In fact, his words to me were, "If we wanted you to have a family, we would have issued you one." I was not deploying because a message had been received from Ottawa loading me on a combat leaders course at CFB Gagetown, New Brunswick, starting September 4. The course was a ten-week career course that I needed to pass in order to keep my promotion.

For the next week, I struggled with what to do with my son. His grandmother would have been the perfect solution, but she was not speaking to me. Steve's parents barely knew TJ, so although I appreciated the offer, sending my son there was going to be an adjustment for everyone concerned. We had not been in Chatham long enough to know anyone that I trusted to care for him on a twenty-four-hour basis for potentially many months. I was in a quandary as to what was best for him.

I finally made the decision to send my son to Steve's parents for his first semester of school with the plan to hopefully join them for Christmas and bring TJ back home with us afterwards. On August 31, my son was on a plane to Toronto. His flight would be arriving at approximately the same time Harry was finishing work, and he would pick him up. I cried all the way home from the airport after dropping him off. My life seemed to be non-stop, and I felt like I was making decisions on a wing and a prayer, with no time to think. Once I composed myself, I apologized to Steve for crying so much.

"Never apologize for your heart. Your heart makes you who you are, and it is what I love the most about you," was his response.

That same day, while I was saying goodbye to my son, my father died. I was the last person that Collette called with the news. Ten hours after he had passed, I answered the phone to hear: "Your father is dead," followed by a dial tone.

I immediately called my mother in tears only to hear her harsh words in the background. "I knew six hours ago that her father was dead. I don't need her to tell me. I hope she is happy being an orphan now." As I hung up the telephone, my grief became so overwhelming that my chest was tight, and I was gasping for air. Was it even possible to recover from the multiple wounds that had just been inflicted on my soul?

Spiritual Beings on a Human Experience

Denial is designed to be a temporary state of mind. The soul always knows the truth, but denial allows the personality of a human to ignore the truth during a painful experience, threatening information, or emotional conflict. Used as a coping mechanism short term, denial allows the personality to work through the reality of the situation in a healthy manner, but ignored over long periods of time, denial can have devastating, long-term consequences for the soul. Collette is experiencing vulnerability and a loss of control. The thought of losing her husband is too much to bear. When Laurie reaches out to comfort her and offer support through her letter, she is met with the hostility of Collette's denial.

Laurie's old (life with her father) has come to an end. She cannot remain in the old and not suffer. She must concentrate on her own life, live a true present, see the humor, and keep her faith firm. Her inner being is shifting and reforming on a deeper level.

Laurie and her father are sharing a purpose before his death, a purpose to restore both souls. Her Creator has given them the time to speak to each other's deepest needs - to feel an authentic connection, to eliminate past suffering, and to feel love.

Powerful forces of change are at work. The deepest stratum of Laurie's being, the bedrock on which her destiny is founded, is experiencing a death. In this moment, she needs to let go of her father, her mother, and her son - no exceptions, no exclusions. Renewal of her own Spirit is at stake.

CHAPTER 16

NO ESCAPE FROM REALITY

All the preparation for my father's death was inconsequential in that moment. "No! Dear God! No! (pause) No! (pause) No!" I wailed in between the "No's" as my legs collapsed from underneath me. *Heavenly Father, please fill me with Your White Light. I thought I was ready, but my heart is breaking. I can't breathe. My father is gone, my mother has disowned me, my child is 1,300 kilometers away, and I feel so alone right now.* My Creator was my Father of compassion and my God of all comfort. Although I was suffering outwardly, inwardly I could feel that I was being renewed by His presence.

Just as I finished my prayer, Steve walked around the corner and lifted me to my feet. He wrapped his arms around me, hugging me tightly as I wept into his chest. When I finally lifted my face to look at him, he gently wiped away the tears from my cheeks. "Come with me, Laurie," he said leading me to the living room. He sat on the couch and placed a pillow in his lap. "Lie down and put your head here, sweetheart," he said patting the pillow. It was comforting to feel his hand stroking my hair as I began to relax. After several deep breaths, I could finally feel the calm returning.

Suddenly Steve bolted from the couch, twisting my neck in the process as he threw me from his lap. "There is something in this room. I felt it touch my hand. I swear to God!" he said pacing back and forth in front of the fireplace while wringing his hands. Steve never judged me for my belief in Spirit, but he was skeptical. If I talked to him about spiritual things, he would just sit quietly and listen. If he thought I was crazy, he was not saying one way or the other. He always wore a poker face.

"There is only you and me in this room. Now, do you believe in Spirit?" I asked.

"Your friends need to go home and stay there," was his response.

There were many Spirits roaming in our house. I would feel their energy when I walked through them unknowingly. I never felt threatened or afraid. I sensed that they had been occupants of the house at one time, and they would come and go quite often. I had a statue of an angel that I had placed on my wall unit in the living room and, every once in a while, I would find that angel on the fireplace mantel. I would move it back to the wall unit. I finally asked Steve why he kept moving the angel to the fireplace mantel. "I have no idea what you are talking about," he answered. That day, the mantel became the permanent home for my angel statue.

When I woke up the next morning, I received a phone call from Dianne expressing her sympathy for my father's passing. Then she proceeded to tell me that my husband spooks easily. She was the one who had dropped in to visit and touched Steve's hand the night before. She was quite amused by his reaction. I knew that Dianne was not lying to me because she described the scene, right down to the color and design of the wallpaper on our living room walls. "It is called Astral Travel, Laurie. I just instinctively know where I need to travel to and why." Not only did I have Spirits walking around my house and moving things, but now I had encountered a human who could leave her physical body and end up in my living room. *This is just too bizarre to comprehend. Maybe I am going crazy. No wait! Maybe I am already there.*

I spent the weekend preparing for my course in Gagetown, and it was the perfect distraction from everything going on in my life. Steve was a fountain of information as he put my rucksack together with the twenty-seven pieces they had handed me, along with a diagram, when I drew my kit from the Base Supply Section. Then he taught me how to pack it properly. "You need to put garbage bags in both compartments. Trust me, you never want a wet bed or wet clothes when you are in the field. You will be miserable," he said. I would be eternally grateful for that wisdom halfway through the course, after spending four days in the pouring rain while out on an exercise.

Leadership is crucial to a military environment and the training is intense. The Combat Leaders Course (CLC) was designed to be hard hitting and extreme, with emphasis on leadership, map reading, training management, and land navigation, coupled with practical assignments linked to infantry tasks. We were lucky if we could get four hours of sleep a night, and we often skipped meals due to trying to meet the specific timings required of us. But the psychological warfare far outweighed the physical challenges.

This CLC was the pilot course for mixed gender training. I was one of two females on the course, and we were both under a microscope by the instructors, the students, and the Base Commander. Like it or not, I was a soldier now, and I needed to find a way to cope with the tremendous stress of this new environment. Throughout my life, tears had always been my way to relieve stress, but a woman crying in any Army environment would not be accepted. Tears would definitely be viewed as a sign of weakness.

When I arrived in Gagetown, I was given a key to a room in a men's barrack block. This was a whole new experience for me. In the past, if it became necessary to house males and females together in one barrack block, men occupied one floor and women another. Not anymore. Gender equality removed that privacy. Each room slept four people, but because we were the only two females, our room contained two empty beds. There was one washroom on the entire floor to be jointly shared by the forty students. It was comprised of four bathroom stalls, four urinals, and eight sinks. The communal showers lacked privacy and the thought of showering with 38 naked men while we were away from our husbands or having them ogle us while showering was not something either one of us was willing to entertain. For that reason, we decided to shower alone by setting the alarm for a half hour earlier than everyone else in the mornings. For even more privacy, we used the mess hall washrooms during our lunch and supper meals, as there were still male and female washrooms in that area. The men were crude and insulting and acted like Neanderthals most of the time. They referred to us as "split-asses", made fun of us every chance they got, and judged us harshly. Privacy did not exist, except for sleeping.

I was the only MCpl (Master Corporal) on the course, so I was singled out, embarrassed in front of my fellow students, and expected to outperform them because my rank was a grade above theirs. By the second week, I was contemplating quitting. I was overwhelmed. *These little punks have no respect for their elders or rank. I feel like their punching bag.* After incessant pleading by my roommate, I decided to stay for her sake. We were each other's strength. Now I was desperately searching to find a coping strategy if I was going to make it through the next eight weeks.

One morning after a barracks inspection, we returned to the classroom. We had worked all night to prepare for that inspection, only to be told by the staff that the inspection was a disaster and we were all disgusting. Military mind games are common during any type of training. They build a soldier's character, but this particular morning, there were no words needed to describe our disappointment. It was written all over everyone's face as we hung our heads and the instructors left the classroom. One of the students got up from his desk, stood in front of the class holding his head in his hands and said, "What if they are right? What if we are all disgusting?" His mannerisms and that comment broke the tension as everyone began to laugh. When the instructors heard the laughing, they returned to the classroom immediately. "So you all think this is funny, do you? You have five minutes to report to the obstacle course. MOVE!"

It had been raining for the past two days, and the "obstacle course" had become a "mud course". As I was making my way through the "low-wire entanglement", my hair got caught in the barbed wire above. I could not move. Where I had become stuck, there was a divot in the ground that had filled with water and my chest was lying in that freezing cold puddle. Struggling to free my hair and fight the tears, I was miserable as I heard the Sergeant scream, "Move your fucking ass, MCpl! You are holding everyone up." Without the slightest hesitation, I shouted back at him, "I can't. My hair is caught in the barbed wire and my chest is so cold that my nipples are stuck in the mud." The Sergeant turned his back to me and I could tell by the movement of his shoulders that he was laughing. Maybe I had finally found my coping strategy - humor and crudeness.

I was the only student on the course from out-of-town. The other thirty-nine students were posted to CFB Gagetown. So at the beginning of the course, we were given a direct order that there were to be no spouses in the barracks, no exceptions. When the fourth week of the course ended, all students were given permission to go home for the weekend. The barracks emptied very quickly. Before my roommate left, she invited me to spend the weekend at her PMQ, but I declined. I had no issue with being the only one left behind. In fact, I welcomed the peace and quiet.

As I sat cleaning my weapon on Saturday afternoon, Steve showed up in the doorway to my room. On a two-week exercise in Blue Mountain, 119 Battery was preparing for deployment to the Gulf War, and Steve had volunteered to drive to the base to pick up rations. The kitchen staff were still boxing up the food and told him to come back in an hour. To pass the time, he decided to try and find me.

I was delighted to see him. After a hug, we sat at the desk in my room talking for a half hour as I continued to clean my weapon. I told him tales of my frustration and when I finished venting, I asked him, "What do I have to do to fit into this world of men?" His advice was, "You need to become one of the boys. If they talk crude to you, answer them back the same way. Use your wit and humor and whatever you do, don't show any reaction to their swearing or their rude behavior. Once you become one of them, and they no longer perceive you as a threat, they will accept you as part of the team." I could do that. After all, I had a history with the Airborne. Not that I had been submerged in their world, but I was no stranger to men being crude or obnoxious.

As we continued talking, the Corporal living across the hall from me returned to the barracks to pick up something he had forgotten on Friday and saw Steve sitting in my room. Monday morning, he reported me to the Sergeant for having my spouse in the barracks. When I was marched in front of the Commanding Officer, my punishment for disobedience was a $200 fine. My thoughts were wild with anger on return to the classroom. *What a pretentious asshole! He is home screwing his wife for the weekend, and I have a half-hour visit with my husband and I get disciplined. Game on, you fucking jerk!*

We became bitter enemies that Monday morning, and I was out for revenge. Like a peaceful body of water, I was beautiful when I was calm, but like the perfect raging storm, I was dangerous when I was angry.

Compassion is the key to not escalating conflict. Having compassion is a way to disengage.

Compassion? Compassion for him? Why? He should have had compassion for me being left in the barracks alone for the weekend. Your words make no sense to me. I was too angry and choked to listen to Spirit. I was out for my pound of flesh and, surprisingly enough, it would not take me long to get it.

Week five of the course was beginning. I was at the halfway point and more determined than ever to succeed. We were preparing for a five-day exercise in the field in order to put the skills we had been learning in the classroom into practice. This was going to be the true test of leadership - the practical test. Can we organize, execute, and motivate people to do what we ask of them? The odds were stacked against me, and I was not feeling confident.

After breakfast on Wednesday morning, we were driven to the field, with a second vehicle following that contained all the equipment we would need for the five-day exercise. We set up four ten-man tents for the students, one for the instructors, and a final tent as the field hospital. Two medics from the base were dispatched to support the exercise, arriving in a field ambulance two hours later. Hay boxes with hot food arrived from the base kitchen three times a day to feed us. The sole purpose of the exercise was to demonstrate our leadership ability by executing given tasks at a moment's notice and that purpose required fourteen-hour days in order to test forty students.

After lunch we gathered to begin the execution of those tasks. I was the first student chosen to be tested, once again, because of my rank.

Recognize seriousness, clear intent, and concentration.

I was taken aside from the other students by the instructors and given my scenario. "Required materials have been placed sporadically throughout the wooded area. You have ten minutes to prepare for the execution of this task and address the other students," one of the instructors said. "You can choose a Second in Command (2 i/c) before you begin to develop your plan. The clock starts now." I chose a fellow student who I had learned through conversation was a medic by trade. I needed a professional to handle the medical part of my plan. After putting the plan together and addressing his specific role, I began speaking to the other students.

"Listen up everyone. Here is the situation. A hiker has fallen down an embankment and broken his femur on his right leg. He also has several internal injuries. The break is severe, he is losing blood, and he could possibly go into shock and die if left unattended too long. To complicate the scenario, the terrain is steep and unsafe. Our mission is to extract that hiker back to the main road safely where an ambulance will be waiting for him."

"The execution will begin as follows. Everyone needs to scour the surrounding area for anything that can help us get this hiker to safety. You have three minutes to return. Move now!" A few minutes later, we had ropes, pulleys, a stretcher, a first-aid kit, and a field phone.

I gathered everyone again. "Who has a medical background?" A student raised his hand. "You need a safety line immediately. I want you providing medical attention to the hiker until he is ready to be medevacked. You need to apply first aid as required and continue monitoring his vitals until he is released to the care of the ambulance medics. Follow directions from my 2 i/c only. Move now!" That student and my 2i/c left the group.

"Who is good with knots and pulleys?" Another student raised his hand. "Good, I want a pulley system on that stretcher, and I want it secured to a tree trunk at the top of the path. You two people (pointing to two other students) will descend to the hiker's location on my 2 i/c's instruction to prepare him for evacuation. You are to remain secured to a safety line at all times. You and you (identifying two other students) will control the pulley from the pathway and guide the stretcher up safely."

"Who has a communications background here?"

"I do, MCpl," said another student. You need to call to the base camp for an ambulance and give them our field coordinates. The medics need to remain in contact with you at all times until they have the patient in their care."

I continued pointing to individual students and assigning them specific tasks. "You need to wait at the main road for the ambulance and guide them to our location. You four people will take over from the first two once the stretcher arrives on the path with the patient and walk that patient to the waiting ambulance. Anyone else without a specific task will jump in as required on my direction. Is everyone clear with what is required of them? Does anyone have any questions? No? Okay, time is of the essence here. It's 'go time' team! A hiker's life is depending on us."

The extraction had begun, but it was challenged by the terrain. One of the instructors played the role of the hiker and his injuries were made true to life by the use of theatrical makeup. His femur was broken and protruding through his pant leg, surrounded by blood on his pants and blood on the ground below. His skin was pale and bruising was evident in his abdominal area. He played the role well, screaming every time someone touched him. He drifted in and out of consciousness. The other instructors stood over the scenario and made changes as we went along based on what the students were doing. "Your patient has gone into shock" or "his vitals are dropping," they would say. We needed to get him up that embankment as quickly and safely as possible. Killing a patient in any scenario was an automatic failure.

Forty minutes from start to finish, the task was completed, and I was taken aside for a debriefing. My strengths and weaknesses were pointed out, but all in all, the task had been extremely successful and well executed, according to the instructors. All thirty-nine of my fellow students had jumped to the challenge with enthusiasm and professionalism. Maybe they respected the situation. At some point, it would be their turn, and they would require the cooperation of their fellow classmates as I had. Little did I know at the time but going first had been a blessing. The weather would take a drastic turn that evening and continue to rain for the next four days. Fourteen students would end up being transported to the base hospital with severe stomach flues that required rehydration. Morale would hit an all-time low in the last two days of the exercise due to the weather and greater fatigue for the remaining students.

I needed to hear a friendly voice by the end of week eight, so I called Steve. "I have good news," he began. "The Warning Order for deployment to the Gulf has been cancelled for the Battery and the Workshop. Now we can spend Christmas with my parents and bring TJ home with us. I miss you guys. It is lonely in this mansion all by myself. Tigger has become my best friend and that is saying something," he said. I laughed. Steve was a dog person, not a cat person, so I knew exactly what he was implying by that comment. "I am going to look into booking our flights to Ontario for Christmas. Two more weeks, sweetheart. Hang in there. I am so proud of you. I will be in Gagetown to pick you up on November 19. Can't wait. Love you," he said as he hung up the phone. The finish line was closer than ever, and I was proud of myself for making it this far. But it was not over until it was over. I still needed to persevere.

The Corporal who lived across the hall from me was now the Course Senior for the next three days, and he was on a power trip. The role of a Course Senior is to pass on information from the Course Instructors, ensure students get to where they need to be on time, and account for each student's whereabouts. Each night after supper, the entire course would gather in the hallway of the barracks for a fifteen-minute briefing. The Course Senior would pass on what we needed to know for that evening or the following day.

This particular night, my roommate was late making it to the meeting. He singled her out for being late and belittled her in front of everyone. One of the guys blurted out, "Awe. Give her a break. She is late because she is on the rag. Poor little baby!" Everyone began laughing and teasing her. She was so embarrassed. This subject was none of anyone's business and the juvenile behavior by the guys angered me. "Grow the fuck up," I said to the idiot who had announced her situation to the group. Big mistake!

The Course Senior began verbally battling with me in front of everyone. The mudslinging was personal and out of line for the scenario we were in. After he called me an "ass" in front of the other students, I decided to remove myself from the meeting. I stood up, looked at him, and said, "I assume you mean 'fine ass'. Thanks." Everyone started clapping and cheering as I headed for the hallway fire doors with purpose, but someone had locked one of the doors. In my haste to retreat, I hit the locked door with full force and fell over backwards onto the floor. That induced more cheering and laughing. I got up, hobbled through the other door to my room and waited for my roommate to return. After a lengthy discussion that allowed us both to vent to each other, she assured me that she just wanted to forget about the whole incident. For that reason, I decided not to report him for his behavior, but should he decide to report me for walking out of the meeting, I had an entire magazine of ammunition to defend myself. Now, I was more determined than ever to take him down a peg or two.

A few days later, my revenge opportunity presented itself when his wife showed up in the barracks. She was bringing him his freshly washed and pressed uniforms. *How nice!* The following morning, I informed the Sergeant that this Corporal's wife had been in the barracks for the purpose of bringing him his washed and pressed uniforms for the locker inspection that week. Not only was she not supposed to be there, but she was not supposed to be looking after his uniforms for him either. His kit was his responsibility, not hers. The Sergeant was livid and the result was a $500 fine handed out by the Commanding Officer for both infractions. I abandoned my mission of retaliation that day with a smile, knowing that my days were numbered with ever having to see his smug face again. I had finally evened the score.

I completed my CLC with a final standing of second place out of forty students. I missed finishing as the top student by one mark on our final grades. I finally felt empowered to survive in this man's world. The tearful, weak Laurie had disappeared and been replaced by a stronger, more confident soldier. *Hey fellas, word to the wise. Do not count me out yet, just because I am a female in your man's world.*

Spiritual Beings on a Human Experience

Astral projection is a powerful out-of-body experience, where the soul separates from the physical body and travels through the physical plane with a purpose. Every soul has the ability to travel this way. A human's own conscience is their only limitation. Most experiences occur during sleep or hypnosis, but some souls can achieve travel by merely relaxing and meditating. Dianne visits Laurie the night of her father's death to bring her peace and love.

Confidence is a belief in one's self and a willingness to meet life's challenges and succeed. Laurie has been plagued by self-doubt and anxiety for most of her physical life. She is beginning to gain a sense of confidence from her personal and professional accomplishments. To avoid her becoming overconfident, her soul is introduced to the soul across the hall from her who is arrogant and narcissistic with too much confidence. Confidence instills a personal sense of being capable and competent, while overconfidence and narcissism becomes an issue of superiority over other souls.

Compassion is movement away from a soul's own self-interests, with a strong ethical and moral implication towards another soul. It is designed as a basis for a shared humanity. A regard for the good of others should have the same value and importance as a soul's own self-regard. When a soul views another soul's actions with compassion, it de-escalates conflict. Love and compassion are necessities and without them, mankind continually struggles to get along.

CHAPTER 17

PROJECTING CONFIDENCE AND
GAINING CREDIBILITY

The completion of my CLC was life altering, and I began to recognize a shifting pattern in how I viewed my life. In this new Army environment, I was being challenged on a daily basis and learning to tolerate discomfort and work through it. I had taken the first step towards honing my skills as a soldier and was on the path to developing self-efficacy. I was thankful for the experience and the successful accomplishment of this career course. My promotion was now cemented by that achievement. Perhaps, we do not know how strong we are until we have to prove it.

It had been months since I had spent any time with my husband, and I was anxiously awaiting his arrival in Gagetown. We placed all my kit into the trunk of the car and then stood hugging for several minutes. "Let's go home," I said, "and look after that lion in your pocket that is ready to roar."

I had not had any time to think about my father, my mother, or my son during that course. Maybe, it was a blessing provided by my Creator, but I was definitely eager to reconnect with my son. For the next month, we spoke several times a week on the telephone. Each time I hung up, I was filled with excitement at the thought of seeing him again. Is it possible to quantify the love a mother feels for her child? My son was my joy. My son was my strength. My son was my purpose. Through that love, my limit of endurance to the world around me was insurmountable.

The first night on my return home from Gagetown, my Warrant Officer called me. "The Commanding Officer has given you two days of short leave. You do not need to report to work tomorrow. Show up at the unit on Monday morning at 7:00 a.m. wearing your combats and running shoes. We are going on a 10-kilometer run. Enjoy your time off," he said. I decided to put those two days to good use. I registered my son for school in Chatham, went grocery shopping, did some Christmas shopping, and began preparing for our trip to Ontario.

I was no longer feeling the dread of returning to the Workshop, but I was definitely feeling the dread of a 10-kilometer run. "Steve, I need your expertise," I said as we sat down to supper on Sunday night. Once again, his advice was solid as we discussed the pending run. I knew that there was no way I could accomplish that run successfully. The Army's soldiers ran on a continual basis, and they were conditioned to do so. It was like a walk in the park for them. I, on the other hand, would be lucky to achieve three kilometers without puking or wanting to die.

These were Steve's words of wisdom. "The Army always runs in platoon formation. If you fall behind, the platoon has to circle back to pick you up again. The Army leaves no man behind. They will hate you for that. My advice is to run and keep up with them until you pass out. Do not stop to walk and do not fall behind. There is always a MLVW that follows the platoon. When you go down, they will pick you up and put you in the back of the truck. Just give it everything you have, Laurie, and the boys will respect you for the attempt." *Thank you, Spirit, for this amazing man! He is so perfect for me.*

On Monday morning, I was informed that I would be the Rear Marker for the run. I put the traffic vest on and took my place six feet behind the platoon. That decision was based on my female gait being shorter than the men's gait. As we began running, the platoon started singing to set the cadence. I was feeling the beat in my feet with every stomp of my left foot, as the blinding warmth of the sun beamed across my face. *This is not so bad.* As we passed the four-kilometer marker, I could feel a stitch beginning in my side. Breathing was becoming more difficult. My vision was tunneling, and I was seeing stars as I headed towards the dirt on the side of the road. No sooner had my foot hit the soft shoulder when I thundered in with a mammoth thud. I awoke in the back of the MLVW. "Here, Laurie, eat this orange quarter and drink some water. You did better than anyone thought you would. I am curious to know who won the bet as to how far you would run," the medic said while taking my pulse.

When my course report from the CLC arrived at the Workshop the following week, I was called into the office of the unit Master Warrant Officer. "Job well done, Laurie. You are going to fit into this unit just fine. Carry on," he said dismissing me. I was beginning to make my mark and I was beginning to fit in. I was on my way to becoming one of the boys.

Life at 210 Workshop was still challenging. Some souls were more accepting of change than others. I struggled with the Warrant Officer who ran the Vehicle Section, but so did most of his subordinates. He was gruff and rude at the best of times. As he entered my office to pick up his mail, he smelled like he had showered in rum that morning. "You have quite the smile on your face this morning, MCpl. Your husband must have fucked your ass off last night."

Whoa! Well, good morning to you too! I was blessed with quick wit. Probably because my mind was always so active, but rarely did I speak those thoughts out loud. Today was different. Today, I decided to follow Steve's advice. "Obviously, your wife didn't fuck you last night judging by the grouchy look on your face," I replied. My Warrant Officer snickered, stood up from his desk, and left the room, with the Vehicle Section Warrant Officer following right behind.

I had one more encounter with the Vehicle Section Warrant Officer during my first beer call with the unit that Friday. I was uncomfortable and playing with the label on my beer bottle. Eventually, I removed the label only to hear him say, "I suppose you are going to try and tell us all that you are still a virgin, Laurie."

Huh? What? I reflected back to one of my Airborne friends telling me that removing a beer label in one piece is supposed to mean that the girl is a virgin. I replied with, "Well, I am still a virgin, Warrant. I haven't found a man deep enough to take it yet," hoping that would end the conversation. Through everyone's laughter, he stood up and opened the belt to his pants and said, "Well, now you have, honey. Let's go!"

Another MCpl sitting across the table from me shouted, "Sit down, Warrant, I have seen you in the shower. Who are you trying to kid?" Everyone started laughing again.

"I guess this is my cue to leave. See you boys on Monday," I said as I took my last swig of beer and walked to my car. From that point forward, my relationship with the Vehicle Section Warrant Officer became purely business.

The following week, I was sitting outside at a picnic table with three guys while I waited for Steve to walk over from the Battery so we could drive home together. When Steve walked up to the table, I introduced him to the guys. One of them said, "Oh, so this is the guy that hasn't been able to take your virginity."

Really? Are we going there again, guys? "If I put all three of your dicks together, my husband's would still be bigger. Why do you think I married him?" I said walking away with the grin of a cat that had just swallowed a canary. That day ended the dick swinging contest and any further talk about my virginity.

I spent the last few weeks before Christmas trying to make my son's bedroom special for his return. I painted the walls a deep royal-blue color, made curtains for the two large windows, bought new bedding with huge throw pillows, and a television with a stand. As a reward for being away from home for so long and doing well in school, we bought TJ a Nintendo Entertainment System as a Christmas present. Now, he had his own space where he could be with his friends and have his privacy.

Christmas with Steve's family was old fashioned and simple, something I loved. It was about bringing the family together, sharing a meal and laughter, and exchanging a gift. For me that year, Christmas magic filled my heart at the sight of my son. It was a moment of pure joy without a price tag. My gift from Steve, which he had placed under the tree, was a box of Turtles. The tag attached read, "A gift of tradition and love", a true display of his altruistic love.

When we returned from Ontario and my son saw his bedroom with the game system, he was thrilled. "What did you and Steve get each other for Christmas?" he asked.

"We decided to get a puppy" I replied.

"Really? Where is he?" he asked all excited. "We are picking her up tomorrow," Steve answered.

We came home the next day with an eight-week-old, female German shepherd puppy that we named "Cloey". We noticed almost immediately that the puppy was struggling to eat and was lethargic, so we took her to the veterinarian. Our puppy had the parvovirus, and the vet did not give us much hope for her recovery because she was so young. The practical suggestion was to euthanize her, but neither one of us was ready to let her go. There was still a chance of her recovering, so we made the decision to treat her with a vaccine and hope for the best. *Please, Helena, bless this little puppy through her struggles.*

Cloey suffered for the next few days with diarrhea and vomiting. The vet had given us a formula, which I fed to her with an eyedropper, repeating the same procedure with water. Steve set up his Army cot in the front porch entrance, and we took turns sleeping with her through the nights, scrubbing the tiled floor each time she had an accident. Less than ten days after bringing home our precious little bundle of joy, Cloey died.

Father, please forgive me for prolonging Cloey's life for my own selfish reasons. I am ridden with guilt for making one of your creatures suffer.

Although it was not a good decision, it was a loving one filled with hope. Forgive yourself.

We phoned the lady who had sold us the puppy and asked for our $200 back. She refused until we threatened to expose her puppy mill to all the soldiers on the base. The next morning, she stopped by the house and returned our money. Three months later, we had another female German shepherd puppy from a different breeder. My son named this puppy "Chelsey". She was supposed to be a pure breed, but it wasn't long before we figured out she was mixed with something else as she continued to grow.

Coming home late from work one night, Chuck dropped Steve off and came in to say hello. Chuck and Suzanne had become part of our partying group of friends. Chelsey went bounding to the front door in all her puppy fanfare to greet them, flopping all over the floor between the two of them. She was at that awkward stage where she had not fully grown into her body yet. "What mix of breeds is she?" Chuck asked.

"She is a pure-bred German shepherd by Miramichi standards," I replied jokingly.

"Oh, you have not heard, Laurie. Everything here is interbred, including people," Chuck said sarcastically. Maybe he was not wrong about the interbred people part. That could potentially explain the lady who sat in the big oak tree outside my son's bedroom window, wearing neon yellow rubber boots, twirling an umbrella, and singing at the top of her lungs.

The merry-go-round had finally stopped long enough for us to settle into life in New Brunswick as a family. We made friends with three other couples from 119 Battery. On Family Day, Steve took TJ to the base for a ride in an Armored Personnel Carrier (APC). They disguised him with camouflage face paint and taught him to shoot the FNC1 Battle Rifle. He played on the obstacle course where he was running, jumping, crawling, climbing, and balancing over various structures. He was seeing firsthand what we did for a living. After several barbequed hotdogs and bags of potato chips, and too many sodas, he was finally played out and ready to go home.

A year had gone by and I was feeling somewhat confident that I could survive this posting. It was now September and time for the annual Battle Efficiency Test (BET). I had missed it the year before because I was on my CLC. The BET consists of a two by ten march (two days x ten miles each day), scaling a six-foot wall, jumping an eight-foot ditch, and carrying a soldier for 200 meters. The two days require muscle strength and endurance, cardiovascular endurance, and agility. I had my work cut out for me and once again, Steve was my fountain of knowledge and my biggest cheerleader.

The first day, we were dressed in full battle gear that included a fifty-pound rucksack, and an eleven-pound rifle, fixed with a bayonet and magazine. We had two hours and twenty minutes to complete a march of ten miles (sixteen kilometers). I spent most of my time running in order to keep up with the rest of the platoon. I was exhausted and I was not without physical pain when I went home to shower. The water running down my back was burning the blisters caused from my rucksack and my feet looked like hamburger.

The following morning, Steve bandaged my feet with moleskin and rubbed my back with A535, avoiding the blistered areas. When I arrived at the unit, we were missing three soldiers who had been excused from the second day of the BET due to medical conditions. I was still there and proud of myself. We repeated the same march, but without weapons and rucksacks. At the end of the march, I scaled the six-foot wall (after several determined attempts) and managed to jump the eight-foot ditch. Now it was time for the 200-meter carry. As people began pairing up, I stood alone watching. The Sergeant bellowed, "Who wants snatch (vagina) in their face?"

Annoyed by his crude remark, I quickly retaliated. I shouted to everyone standing around, "Approach me with caution. This snatch bites if you get too close."

"I'll take my chances, Sergeant," said a Corporal from the Radar Section. We were roughly the same height and weight so I was happy when he volunteered. He threw me over his shoulder in a fireman's carry and away we went. Once we reached the 200 meters, I had to carry him back. That day, I managed to pass the BET, but it was not without several days of babying my poor body back to a healthy state. *Thank God they only do this once a year!*

Several weeks later, I was in the kitchen baking cookies with my son when the telephone rang. It was Tim. "Hi, Laurie, can I speak to my son?" he asked. I handed the phone to TJ. "It is your father," I said. The conversation did not last more than three minutes, so I asked my son why he had hung up so quickly. His reply was, "He said that he had to go because his two boys were in the bathtub and they were fighting. He has a new family now, Mom, and I don't matter. I am going to my room until supper."

I could tell that my son's feelings were hurt, and I wanted to give him time to process his thoughts. "I am so sorry, son. I am here if you feel like talking," I said as he walked away. My heart went out to him as I began washing the dishes. He had waited seven years to hear from his father only to be hung up on. Tim could have asked TJ to hang on for a minute or told him that he would call him right back, but he did neither. The next phone call to his son would take Tim another eight years to make.

My son and I struggled through several conversations for the next few days as he tried to wrap his mind around his father's phone call. "Why aren't you and my dad together anymore?" he asked.

The time was not appropriate to reveal the truth. He was still too young, so I replied with, "Your father wanted one thing and I wanted something else. I know that it is hard for you to understand right now, but sometimes adults make big mistakes that are hard to recover from." What I really wanted to say was that his father preferred to screw his grandmother so I chose not to be married to him anymore.

Sin will always look attractive for a little while, but it has a significant price attached.

The next day, I was sitting in the living room hemming a pair of pants when TJ approached me. "Mom, I feel funny," he said. I knew immediately by looking in his eyes that he was on the verge of an epileptic seizure. Steve jumped up quickly to move the coffee table and we laid him on the carpet. "Go get a towel, Laurie. I will stay with him." Steve knelt on the floor beside TJ, reassuring him that we were there, and he was going to be alright. When I returned, I laid the towel on the floor beside my son's head. TJ would always vomit after having a seizure and then fall asleep for several hours afterward.

As I watched my son convulsing on the floor, I walked away filled with anger. *Damn you, Tim! Why did you bother to call him at all? It is not like you had a conversation with him. Was the call to satisfy your own curiosity? I wish I had never handed him the phone. Once again, I am left to clean up the mess from your reckless behavior.*

Humans have the power to make choices, and some of the worst choices are made in darkness so that lessons may be learned.

I had no idea what lesson Tim was supposed to be learning, nor did I care at the time. Helena's words would not make sense until Tim's second phone call to his son. TJ had been doing so well on his medication and had been seizure-free for over a year. Our last visit to the doctor had left us hopeful. If he remained seizure-free for another six months, we could try removing him from the medication. Now I wondered if we were back to square one, all because of one phone call and the destruction his father had left behind once again.

My son's tenth birthday was approaching, and we wanted to do something special for him that year. Steve had seen an advertisement in the newspaper for a horse farm that offered children's birthday parties. After making an inquiry by phone and happy with what the farm had to offer, I wrote up nine invitations for TJ to take to school and hand out to his friends. The day before the party, I made a quick trip to the farm to drop off food and decorations.

The parking lot was filled with excited children as we waited for everyone to arrive. Two Clydesdale horses were harnessed to a hay wagon and each child was given a cup of hot chocolate as they found a seat on the bales of hay. The forest was an icy, winter wonderland, surrounded by the quiet of winter nature; there were no birds chirping or squirrels scurrying through the leaves. As the horses' hooves began trotting through the freshly fallen snow, I was embracing the towering evergreen branches, heavily laden with snow, bowing to the earth below. The elegance of the snowflakes dancing in slow motion from the sky above filled my Spirit with tremendous inner peace.

Sometimes it takes something being absent from your life to value its presence again.

Spirit was right. It was time to stop, take a deep breath, and enjoy nature again. I needed to feed my soul.

After thirty minutes of sheer bliss with nature, we arrived at a log cabin in the heart of the woods. It was being warmed by a large fireplace stacked with burning logs, and it felt soothing as we walked in from the cold air of the ride. The cabin was decorated with balloons, streamers, and a "Happy Birthday" banner. There was a pot of hot chocolate and another of apple cider warming on the stove. Hot dogs had been grilled on the barbeque and were warming in the oven. The children ate lunch, played games, enjoyed cake and ice cream, and watched my son open his presents. Three hours later, we climbed into the hay wagon for the thirty-minute ride back. As I looked at all the smiling faces on the children holding their goody bags, there was little doubt that the last four hours had given them an utterly unique experience.

I had taken a chance on life when I married Steve and had progressed far enough in the relationship to feel a measure of safety and happiness. I was living without the need to evaluate or question his love for me. I had been blessed with a man who spoiled me with respect, loyalty, affection, and unconditional love. He was not shy. He was a thinker and an observer. His life's emphasis and value was having true connection with other souls.

In all my past relationships, the future had resulted in devastation, so I was not willing to entertain any thoughts of what was yet to come with Steve. I was happy living in the moment.

You are learning to open yourself to the Will of the Heavens.

Two years had evolved into a life with a loving husband, a challenging but rewarding job, and a son who was finally free from medication and seizures. He had outgrown his epilepsy just as the doctor in Montreal had predicted. *Thank you Spirit for my son's blessing. He is free now to have an unrestricted, normal life by your Grace.*

It was the spring of 1992, when I was surprised by a phone call from Caroline telling me that she was moving to Chatham. Disgruntled in her military career, she had applied for the Force Reduction Plan (FRP) and had been accepted. She was taking an early release from the military, along with the financial benefits package being offered, in order to return to school full time and obtain her Bachelor of Dietetics. For the past year, she had been dating Eric, a Military Strategist, who was now posted to Chatham. I was excited for her and myself.

Caroline's move to Chatham could not have come at a better time for both of us. We spent countless hours discussing life in general and the challenges that we were both facing. Her move to Chatham was seriously being affected by Eric's family's interference, and their relationship was changing. Eric's mother did not approve of Caroline as a prospective mate in life for him, and Eric was not one to go against his family's wishes. My heart went out to her. How sad that he was not willing to live life on his own terms, with his own desires and goals. He was living his life according to what others expected of him. I knew that feeling all too well. Now that I was learning to live life on my own terms, it was extraordinarily liberating.

My challenge was deciding what to do about an Annual Performance Evaluation (PER) that I had just received. There were sixteen soldiers with the rank of MCpl employed in 210 Workshop, and when the Merit Board sat to rank us for promotion, I finished sixteen out of sixteen. I chalked it up to being a female in a man's world, signed it as acknowledging that I had read it, and walked away feeling very disgruntled. The following morning, I was alone in the office when the Sergeant from the Supply Section approached my desk. "You need to redress your PER, Laurie. Every time your Warrant Officer tried to fight for points for you, he was told that no one cared what he had to say. Their exact words were, "She is a female and not one of us. Be quiet!" The Supply Sergeant's final words before he left my office were, "If asked, I will deny ever having this conversation with you. I just thought that you should know."

Through many conversations with Caroline, I learned that her PER was one of the reasons that she had decided to take the FRP. She felt stifled in a man's world too. Maybe it was time for me to make some waves and fight for what was rightfully mine. Acknowledgment of my true performance was not too much to ask. Change needed to start somewhere.

You may not win, but you will never lose. You will always learn something from anything that takes place.

Spiritual Beings on a Human Experience

Self-efficacy is about a soul having confidence to deal with a situation without being overwhelmed. It is a subtle understanding and a centered presence with the soul's energy, a connection to the Divine within.

Laurie's soul has persevered through many obstacles - difficult relationships, hostile environments, fear, setbacks and failures, self-doubt, and rejection. All our stubborn barriers for the soul.

Her most recent shift of her soul is teaching her not to be overwhelmed by life, but to find a measure of happiness, fulfillment, or purpose through self-efficacy. Over time, a strong confidence and belief in herself will manifest as part of her personality.

Many souls wander confused and alone in a material world where darkness and fear can take on a life of its own. Only light can bring true knowledge and clarity. Sitting in darkness and dissecting it, allows the soul to find hope and true purpose. Remaining in darkness will hinder the soul from growth and transformation. Darkness is the balance of the Universe and offering the darkness to the light in prayer is healing.

CHAPTER 18

LIVING IN NAKED AWARENESS

Is living in the present meaningful to a soul? If we let go of dwelling on the past and we are not fantasizing about the future, is the result a mindset of perfect clarity? Does it allow us to view our life with a naked awareness, to find understanding about who we are as a soul, and contentment with exactly where we are on our journey?

For the first time in my life, I was truly living in the present, but maybe it was because my present had taken on a life of its own, leaving no time to reflect back or forward. My focus was being in the moment. Yet simultaneously, I enjoyed the stillness, without tempered impulses, and my mind was tranquil with its thoughts. Perhaps it was a Divine Sanction intended to give my Spirit Guide a break from listening to the constant chatter in my mind. I was facing each new day as it came, surrendering to the here and now and for some unknown reason, life seemed to be taking care of itself without any interference from me. I was genuinely happy.

The sharpness of the last rays of the sun on the horizon filled my spirit as I watched the land begin settling into darkness. I thanked my Spirit World for all the blessings in my life and in a moment of clarity, I realized how flexible and adaptable I had become to whatever role or environment I was being exposed to. Like a chameleon, I was acquiring the skills to change my opinions, ideas, or behavior to fit any situation. As a professional, I had become quick-witted, determined, and persistent to make my mark in an all-male environment. As a wife, I had become loyal, compassionate, and easygoing in my relationship with my husband. As a mother, I was calm, organized, patient and loving. Each role was playing an important part in expressing who I was becoming as a soul.

Your Warrior Nature is revealing itself. Undertake the transformation joyfully.

It was our third year in Chatham, New Brunswick, and changes were on the horizon once again. Steve's Captain dropped by the house one night to let us know that he was being posted and asked if we were interested in purchasing the house for $40,000. "Would you mind giving us the night to think about it?" I asked. My gut instinct was telling me that the timing to purchase a house was not right. After he left, Steve and I sat down to discuss it further. I wanted to explain my gut instinct from a spiritual perspective, but then decided to approach the subject from an intellectual one. "The town of Chatham has a population of 5,000 people - 3,000 of which are military. If we are posted in the next few years, we could be faced with the same issue your Captain has right now. Here is my suggestion. What if I go to Base Housing tomorrow morning and see if there are any empty PMQs available to rent? If there is, then I believe we have our answer," I said.

"Sounds logical to me," Steve replied. There were four empty PMQs, so we declined the offer to buy the house we were presently living in.

Before the move to the base, we decided to gather our friends for one last backyard party. At 8:00 a.m. on Saturday morning, we picked up two dozen fresh lobsters from the fishing vessels returning to the wharf. After dropping me off at home, Steve left for the grocery store to pick up steaks, strawberries, and whipping cream. His final stop was the liquor store to pick up beer and restock the bar. I began washing and wrapping potatoes for baking, washing lettuce, shredding cheese, cooking bacon, and making croutons for a Caesar salad. For dessert, I decided to make homemade strawberry shortcake. The whole time I was busy in the kitchen, TJ was outside entertaining himself with lobster races on the deck. He was totally amused by Chelsey's reaction to the live lobsters scurrying across the deck to get away from her nose. "Son, please stop traumatizing those lobsters. Their meat is going to end up tasting like shoe leather," I said with a chuckle as I walked back into the house.

When Steve returned, he entered the kitchen, placing the groceries on the counter. "What smells so good?" he asked.

"I have an almond cake baking in the oven for strawberry shortcake later tonight," I replied.

"I certainly knew what I was doing when I married you," he said giving me a hug before he left the room. I loved being hugged. The energy from the souls who loved me filled my own soul.

Chuck and Suzanne were the first couple to arrive around noon and quickly began helping us set up the backyard. The guys filled the coolers with beer, cleaned the barbeque, and set up the outdoor cooker for the lobster boil. After washing down the patio table and chairs, they left to pick up ice for the coolers, along with paper plates. Suzanne was busy in the kitchen preparing the garlic butter and washing and slicing strawberries, while I set up two side tables outside, one for the food and the other for a bar. Within an hour, our team effort left us prepared for the arrival of everyone else.

Mike and Patty, and Jack and Lisa, arrived shortly after 2:00 p.m. and it did not take long for the party to kick into high gear as we ate, drank, played horseshoes, and attempted to play lawn darts. Lawn darts are challenging after consuming copious amounts of alcohol, so we nixed that idea pretty quickly when Suzanne hit Chuck in the face with a dart. My son consumed three lobsters by himself and then went off to spend the night at his friend Romeo's house.

The party began winding down in the early hours of Sunday morning. Mike and Patty were the last couple to leave because Steve and Mike were engrossed in a deep conversation over the politics at 119 Battery and their career aspirations. Mike had applied to the RCMP, and Steve was contemplating changing his trade from the Air Defence Artillery to the Military Police.

During brunch the next morning, Steve talked to me further about wanting to change trades, this time in a sober state. He began his reasoning as I listened. Remaining in his current trade had challenges for us as a couple. Postings for him were limited, and it could present a problem for us not being co-located in the future. As well, I would always be subjected to an Army base and Army lifestyle as long as he remained with the Air Defence Artillery. On the other hand, if we both were employed in support trades, it would open up so much more potential for both of our careers.

We could be posted to any environment (air, land, or sea) and on any military base. He finally finished the conversation by saying that he was not happy in his trade anymore. That was all I needed to hear. I wanted him to be happy, so I encouraged him to pursue his dreams. It was my turn to be his biggest cheerleader.

A well-nourished Self willingly nourishes others.

In the midst of the craziness of preparing to move, Chelsey went into heat. I took a pair of my son's underwear, placed a Kotex pad inside, pulled her tail through the pee flap, and pulled them up around her backside. I did not have time to continually wash floors, couches, and bedding from bloodstains. I was too busy packing and cleaning room by room.

I left Chelsey out in the backyard one afternoon while I began packing boxes on the upstairs level. After an hour or so had passed, I headed downstairs to check on her. The scent of a female in heat is powerful, and it had attracted Romeo's family dog from across the street. They owned a purebred 140-pound Rottweiler who had broken loose from his chain and jumped our fence. He was riding Chelsey with fire in his blood, and every time she attempted to get away from him, he snarled and clamped on tighter. I will never forget the look on her face as I appeared at the back door. She looked pitiful and her eyes were pleading, "Help me, please. Get this brute off of me." We had spoken to the vet about having her spayed, but he recommended she have one heat before doing so. Needless to say, my neglect had resulted in a pregnant dog.

The day of the move, there were so many of Steve's friends from the Battery who showed up with trucks that we finished moving in four hours. The biggest obstacle was trying to fit everything from a mansion into a two-bedroom PMQ, the saving grace being the basement. After cleaning our old place and taking one final look through the house before we locked the doors, I was thankful for the time we had spent living in the Loggie home. There are not many souls who can say that they once lived in a home that today is a museum of historical significance.

The next few weeks flew by as I unpacked and began setting up our new home. I dropped TJ off at the Base Theatre to meet up with a girl from school who he had invited to the movies. My son was eleven years old now and quickly becoming a young man. I was saddened by the thought of my little boy growing up. I spent time with Caroline before she moved to Moncton to begin her studies. Her relationship with Eric had run its course, and she was embarking on a new beginning. It was hard to say goodbye again, but I knew our journey together was far from over. I joined the Base Girl's Fast Pitch Team. I spent time at the gym with Steve several times a week. He had become my personal trainer, with a focus on building my upper body strength. Looking back, I was probably in the best shape of my life while I was posted to Chatham.

Chelsey was slowly transforming from a slender, healthy German shepherd into a beachball with legs. She was lethargic and could not get comfortable. My intuition was telling me to get prepared. After supper one night, I asked Steve if he could dismantle the dining room table and stack the table and chairs against one wall. I came home the following night with a Tri Wall Box and set it up in the dining room. I placed a tarp in the bottom, with several old towels and a heating pad. I spoke to the vet about what to expect and none too soon. When I arrived home from work two days later, Chelsey was in the beginning stages of labor.

Timing is everything in life and Chelsey's timing was perfect. It was Friday night - a night that was about to keep us up for six hours delivering puppies. Around 10:00 p.m. Steve lifted Chelsey into his arms and laid her in the Tri Wall Box. I prepared a bucket of warm water with a washcloth and pulled up a chair beside the box. As the first puppy appeared, Chelsey broke open the sac and cut the cord with her teeth. Then, she began licking her baby until it began to squirm, finishing off by pushing the puppy to her teat to feed. After consuming the afterbirth to stimulate her milk production, she laid down her head, resting and waiting for the next contraction to begin. One by one, puppy after puppy appeared. Once they suckled on her teat for a few minutes, I cleaned off each puppy with warm water and placed them in a puppy pile on the heating pad.

Eight puppies later, it was obvious that Chelsey was exhausted and struggling. As we watched the next contraction begin, she refused to lift her head, wildly kicking her back legs. It was up to us now to open the sac, cut the cord, and stimulate the puppy to breathe. When the contractions started again, my focus was on Chelsey while Steve continued to help her birth her babies. I kept stroking her head with the warm cloth, telling her what a good girl she was and encouraging her to keep going. All the while, I was praying for her to survive this labor with every gasp for air she took. Twelve puppies later, the contractions stopped.

Now, we were in a quandary as to how to keep twelve puppies alive. Chelsey did not have enough teats to feed them all, and it would only be a matter of time before she would start to smother the weaker ones instinctively. I called the vet Saturday morning, and he provided us with bottles and formula. His instruction was to supplement each puppy with one ounce of formula every twelve hours.

I was so proud of Chelsey. She had come through the birthing process like a true trooper. I increased her food and water intake to keep her lactating, and I made it a point to walk her at least once a day, fussing over her during our walk. When we arrived back home, she would immediately return to the dining room to be with her puppies. When I lifted her into the Tri Wall Box, the puppies began aggressively jockeying for a position at the dinner table, competing for a teat, and nursing vigorously once they latched on to one. Chelsey appeared overwhelmed in the beginning, but I would remain with her, patting her head until she relaxed and began cleaning them. Within a few hours, she would stand and cry for us to remove her from the box and give her time away from her babies. We followed her lead as to when to put her in the box and when to take her out.

Although supplementing the puppy feedings was time consuming, it was a labor of love. Each morning, I set the alarm for 5:00 a.m. and sleepily walked down the stairs. I would flick on the dining room light with a "Good morning, my little chitlins". They would instantly begin crying out while stumbling or rolling towards my voice. Their eyes were closed for the first week, and it was hilarious to watch them. The scene reminded me of a demolition derby - chaotic with lots of collisions as they tried to reach the edge of the box by paddling their little feet. Once each puppy's belly was full, the silence returned as they nestled into each other and fell back to sleep. During the evening feedings, my son would play with the puppies that had been fed, as I placed them one by one in a box on the kitchen floor. It was the only way I could differentiate between who had been fed and who still needed to be.

As the puppies grew, so did their appetites. By the fourth week, I decided to fill two pie plates with puppy chow and boiling water. Once it had turned into mush and cooled off, the three of us began placing the puppies around the edge of the plates, gently pressing their faces into the food. With the first taste, their tails shot straight up into the air as they excitedly began feeding. Some were more zealous than others, crawling right into the pie plate or over top of each other to reach the middle. They were all covered in puppy chow from their nose to their tail. Like washing a child's face and hands after they consume a meal, each puppy needed a bath after each feeding.

We found homes for all twelve puppies, but it was a sad day when the last one left with its new owner. The Creator sure knew what he was doing when he created babies. I was going to miss the sheer joy those little rascals had brought to our household. *Thank you, Spirit, for this fascinating experience.*

Steve applied for his remuster to the Military Police trade and was accepted. When the message arrived from Ottawa, the Commanding Officer of 119 Battery made a phone call to the Commanding Officer of the Military Police Section. Through a mutual decision, arrangements were made for Steve to get a feel for his new trade by shadowing the Military Police on base as an observer while he waited for his four-and-a-half-month training course at CFB Borden in the new year.

When Steve left for Borden in January, I turned my attention towards writing my redress for my Performance Evaluation Report (PER). I needed a distraction from the loneliness of his absence, and I had been procrastinating putting my thoughts on to paper. Prior to his leaving, I had spent months contemplating how to approach the redress. Now, I was finally ready to begin with what I believed to be a well-thought-out, solid strategy based on my research.

The Annual PER system is designed to provide feedback on a member's professional development, performance, and their potential to succeed at a higher rank level. A numerical score is assigned to each PER, to which the narrative must justify the score. PERs are critical for career management. They are used to determine selection for career progression, such as courses, postings, or promotions and are often the deciding factor in competitive processes. My first PER from 210 Workshop had been written with an average rating and rightly so. I was learning a new job in the Electrical and Mechanical (EME) world of Engineering and that learning curve had been steep given my background.

During the year of this last assessment, I had successfully performed a Warrant Officer EME job for three months during my supervisor's absence. Not only had I functioned at a rank two levels above my own, but also in a field totally unrelated to mine. My performance in my own job on the LOMMIS system had resulted in the Workshop having the lowest error rate across Canada. I had also completed two university courses towards my bachelor's degree through correspondence. Not one of these accomplishments had been written in the narrative of my PER because they would have been in stark contrast to the score that had been assigned to my performance as "average". My strategy to approach the redress was not to have the score changed, but to have the narrative rewritten to reflect my true performance - a performance that had been devalued by a number. I submitted the official redress to my Commanding Officer in March.

While showering before bed one night, a thought of my husband emerged through the burst of steaming water that was covering my body, heightening my sense of well-being. I could smell the scent of his after-shave. I could feel the loving stroke of his hand through my hair. I could feel his beating heart. I could envision the devoted look in his eyes when I caught him observing me from a distance. I had spent the last four months reliving memories of him in order to combat the loneliness, but the finish line was quickly approaching. In two more weeks, I would be reunited with his human touch and the intense, emotional bond of his energy. The anticipation was hard to contain as I continued showering.

When I stepped out of the shower, the telephone was ringing. I wrapped myself in my bathrobe and made a mad dash for the phone. As I answered, I was totally unprepared for the news Steve was about to deliver. "Hi, sweetheart. Sorry to call so late, but I just had a meeting with my Career Manager. It looks like I am going to be posted to Ottawa. He is waiting to hear from your Career Manager before the final decision is made."

I sat for a few seconds letting his words sink in. "I had no idea that you would be posted," I said. His reply was, "Me neither. I just found out that

Military Police are moved to a new base when they graduate to avoid a conflict of interest (retaliation against higher authorities) or preferential treatment (towards friends). Makes sense, I guess, but I was as shocked as you are. How do you feel about going to Ottawa?" he asked.

"I do not care where we go as long as we go together. It has been a long four months without you, and I miss you. I have an idea. I would like to come to Borden for your graduation in two weeks. By then, the decision for your move should be final. If Ottawa is our new destination, we might as well take a house hunting trip (HHT) while we are still in Ontario. Let's talk in a few days," I suggested.

"Sounds good," he replied. "Love you. Sweet dreams."

Two days later, 210 Workshop received my posting message. My Career Manager had accommodated the request for relocation to Ottawa. I was being posted to the National Defence Operations Centre (NDOC) effective June 10, 1993. I was thrilled that we were both moving together, but not so thrilled that we only had five weeks to take a House Hunting Trip (HHT) and make a door-to-door move. *Please, Spirit, bless us with this move and the lack of time to prepare. Thank you for the blessing to be together though. I appreciate it.*

Recognize ambition satisfied, love shared, and rewards received.

With the news of the posting, I decided to reach out to my mother again with the hope that she would finally speak to me. She refused. I hung up the phone feeling frustrated. *She is remarkably stubborn. I figured she would have come around by now. Obviously, her relationship with her grandson is of little importance to her, as well as her relationship with her daughter. All of our time together has been lost in order to spite me for marrying Steve. I just don't get her, Helena.*

Your desired outcome is not appropriate right now. Trust your Creator's timing.

Spiritual Beings on a Human Experience

Living in the present is to know one's true self. It gives meaning to your existence and allows the ego or your false identity to dissolve. When a soul connects to peace, depth, and joy in a present moment, the external world becomes insignificant. When Laurie begins living in the present, she finds mental clarity and inner stability, with no expectations or regrets. Stillness has allowed her to see life from a new perspective.

The intuitive mind is a sacred gift provided to every soul. Intuition (often referred to as gut instinct) is the ability to understand instinctively and without conscious reasoning. It represents the accumulated experiences of the soul. That inner "knowing" voice is designed to bring value and guidance while on a human experience. Laurie's quiet mind is allowing her intuition to surface. Listening to her intuition has prevented her from purchasing a house in Chatham when her destiny is Ottawa.

By ceasing to strive for an outcome, being still, and reconnecting to her spiritual Self, Laurie's Creator has entered into all aspects of her life, nourishing her Spirit. Her own nourished soul is subconsciously turning to nourish others.

Laurie's mother continues to invoke her free will (through stubbornness) not to speak to her daughter. The Creator will speak to her mother's heart in His timing, a timing that will be appropriate to the *needs* of Laurie's soul, not Laurie's *wants*. The separation of their journey together is serving a teaching purpose.

CHAPTER 19

CLOSE YOUR EYES AND BREATHE

The night I received Steve's news of the posting was a sleepless night. My brain was multi-tasking with rushing thoughts from many different directions, resulting in an overcrowded, overwhelmed mind that was far from resting. If I managed to drift off to sleep, I began dreaming only to re-awaken. The next morning, my bed looked like I had been battling a monster all night. Maybe monsters are not just under your bed. Maybe monsters are in your bed too.

When my official posting message arrived at the Workshop, I decided it was time to tell my son that we were moving. I always tried not to burden him with things that might potentially happen or to stress him out thinking about the unknown. He was excited at the thought of moving from a small town to a big city but admitted that he was also a little nervous. "Son, try to think of this move as a new adventure with all kinds of possibilities. Besides, you get to start your summer holidays three weeks before everyone else," I said.

Moving from stability into change is difficult, and a soul can easily become riddled by fear of the unknown. I knew that fear all too well from my past, but through my faith and my own experiences with change, I had learned exactly what my Creator was capable of. Change is not meant to harm us, but instead to advance us with a breakthrough on our journey or to enhance us with a blessing.

Change is opportunity in disguise.

All my plans had been put into motion by the next time Steve called. My train ticket was booked from New Brunswick to Ontario so that I would arrive the day before his graduation. Chuck and Suzanne offered to watch TJ, while I was gone and the next-door neighbor was willing to look after Chelsey and Bear. Even though Bear had been living on the next block behind us, she was one of Chelsey's puppies who found her way home every chance she got. Mama and baby loved to play together. Jason (Bear's owner) always knew exactly where to find her when she disappeared. When she appeared again one night on our doorstep, Jason asked me if I wanted to keep her. His wife was pregnant and did not want her anymore. The Rottweiler traits were dominant in Bear, and his wife was afraid of her. If I did not want to take her, their plan was to drop her off at a shelter. "Please, Mom, can we keep her?" my son asked eagerly. There was no hesitation on my part. One of my little chitlins had come home to roost, and I was thrilled to have her back.

When I boarded the train for Ontario, the conductor looked at my ticket and asked if I would be interested in upgrading the ticket for a sleeper berth. The trip was scheduled to take 23 hours so I paid the $80 difference to have my own private space with a bed and a toilet. I had no idea how much joy that eighty dollars was about to bring me that night.

The conductor knocked on my door at 10:00 p.m. and offered to make up my bed for the evening. *Wow, I have a butler, a very handsome one. How great is this? Can I keep him?* After he left the berth and I locked the door, I felt safe to relax and sleep for the evening. Laying my head on the pillow, I became fixated on taking in every single moment of the experience. I could hear the metallic shriek of the wheels on the tracks, the relentless whining and groaning. I was mesmerized by the rocking motion and the sound of the train whistle crying out over the land. As the trees in the foreground blurred by my window, I had the perfect view of a clear, starry sky. Fighting to retain the euphoric feeling, my eyelids eventually became too heavy and I drifted off into a heavenly sleep.

Harry (Steve's father) was at the train station in Toronto to meet me when I arrived the next day. I spent the evening with Steve's parents, enjoying conversation over a cup of tea. They were excited about our move to Ottawa and looking forward to spending more time with us now that we were not going to be living so far away. They were even more excited about attending Steve's Graduation Ceremony the next day. This was going to be their first time on a military base. When we left Stroud the next morning, Harry asked me to drive so he could take in the experience.

If you have never attended a military parade, the precision of movement is impressive to a spectator. Both of Steve's parents were beaming with pride as they watched their son remove his green beret and replace it with a red one. When Steve was summoned in front of the Parade Commander once again to receive the Top Student Award, I looked over at Harry to witness a tear rolling down his cheek. Although Harry had never told his son how proud he was of him, that pride was evident by his emotion that day.

Saturday morning, Harry and Judy (Steve's mother) drove us to pick up our rental car, and from there, we stopped to have breakfast together before leaving for Ottawa. Six hours later, we arrived at our hotel, settling into a deluxe suite with a Jacuzzi for the night. We were finally alone after four and a half months. As I looked into his eyes, I had to take a deep breath. I was feeling him with my heart, feeling him with every beat, a beat that was in perfect rhythm with my soul.

The next morning, after glancing through the newspaper over coffee, we quickly realized that rent in Ottawa was expensive. One-bedroom apartments began renting at $800 a month, so we switched our mindset into looking at real estate. For the past year, we had been putting Steve's paychecks into our savings account. If we could find something we liked, the down payment was not going to be an issue.

Throughout the process of viewing several homes for the next few days, I made a point to stop in each home, close my eyes, and feel the energy surrounding me. Was I feeling blocked, stagnant, or stuck? Or was I experiencing a harmonious flow of peaceful energy? In the past four years, I had become cognitively aware of the energy surrounding me in any environment, an energy that inevitably always influenced my mindset.

When we walked into the house on Radway Terrace in Orleans, my energy was telling me that this was the perfect home for our family. The backyard was fenced for the dogs, with a swimming pool to battle the hot and humid Ontario summers. There was a wood burning fireplace for frosty winter nights and a garage to park our vehicle out of the elements.

Beyond the material advantages of this house, joy was filling my heart as I entered and exited from each room.

Embrace a home of union and reunion.

We put an offer in that day and within twenty-four hours, we were the proud owners of our first home.

The move from New Brunswick was swift and without complication. When we opened the front door to our new home for the first time, we were met with a welcome basket left on the kitchen counter by the realtor, alongside a welcome note from the previous owners. *How thoughtful! What a welcoming gesture!* It was always the small, subtle things in life that held so much impact for me - a walk in nature holding someone's hand, a trip for an ice-cream cone or someone saying "good morning" with a hug. Simple gestures of kindness or love filled my heart with immense joy.

While we were both busy unpacking, our doorbell rang. It was the neighbor from next door. "Hi. My name is Donna. Welcome to the neighborhood. If there is anything that I can do for you, please do not hesitate to ask," she said. After several exchanges of conversation, Steve told her that he would take her up on the offer with regards to the swimming pool. There is always a wealth of knowledge that can be learned based on another person's experience and a wealth of aggravation that can be avoided from that knowledge. That day was the beginning of a friendship with an incredibly unique lady.

When I walked into the National Defence Headquarters building one week later, I felt as if I was part of a herd of cattle being ushered into the corral. There were several lineups of people swiping Military Identification Cards (ID Cards) while passing through turnstiles. Following the herd as all good cows do, I swiped my ID Card, causing the turnstile to lock and a buzzer to go off. So as not to hold up the rest of the line, I was quickly escorted to a side desk where I was asked to produce my posting message and sign the Visitor Register. If all of this was not intimidating enough, the National Defence Operations Centre (NDOC) would prove to be twice as intimidating. I pressed a buzzer beside a door, watching the camera on the wall swing to place my face in perfect view. A voice through a speaker asked, "Can I help you?"

"I am posted here and reporting for duty," I replied. A six-inch-thick, solid metal door electronically swung open and I stepped inside the cubicle. The door then closed and locked behind me. I placed my posting message and my ID Card through the hole of the Plexiglas window, and I waited for further instruction. Another buzzer sounded as the second door opened. I had just entered the heartbeat of the military.

Four new MCpl positions had been created in NDOC for clerical support to the Desk Officers. I was the only MCpl with time in rank. The other three people were newly promoted. As the Senior MCpl, I was given the task of setting up Standard Operating Procedures (SOPs) for the new positions, as well as designing a shift schedule that would provide 24/7 support, both due by the end of the week. I felt I had been thrust into a delicate situation because we all had the same rank. For that reason, I designed a schedule and then asked the other three to review it and bring any of their ideas forward. Four minds are better than one, and four minds in agreement are half the battle. One person gave up after an hour saying it was impossible, another was fine with what I had done, and the third wanted to make her own schedule. I suggested she take her ideas home, put them on paper, and we would review them the next day. The final decision that was adopted with everyone's consent was my original schedule of twelve-hour shifts comprised of two-day shifts, two-night shifts, and two days off.

That first week, we all worked together in order to get a true feel of what the job required, thereby developing consistency. The job was demanding and highly stressful as we catered to the "in the moment" demands from four Desk Officers (Land, Sea, Air, and Joint Task Force). There were briefings five days a week to high-ranking officials, including four-star Generals and Members of Parliament. Any situation, involving any military member, in any location worldwide was relayed to those high-ranking officials - officials who sat in a balcony above the Operations Center for briefings each morning. During weekends or evenings, any incidents coming into the Operations Center were reported to the appropriate officials at home using secure phone lines, resulting in direction as to how the Desk Officer was to proceed.

The following week, we became one person doing the work of four, when the shift schedule became the new norm. Shift handovers required fifteen-minute briefings to bring the incoming clerk up to speed on what had transpired prior to their shift. The twelve-hour shifts were long and exhausting, and the two days off barely left us refreshed to return to work. Postings to NDOC were designed as two-year postings in order to avoid burnout. I would end up working four years in NDOC to maintain continuity as the people in the other three clerical support positions were posted out, one per year.

Being thrust into a sixty-hour workweek, coupled with Steve also working shifts (usually opposite shifts to mine), left little room for any quality family time. The three of us barely saw each other. My son was in grade seven now and trying to fit in to his new environment, one with established cliques that were difficult to penetrate. Before long, he would find a new friend, a friend that was about to start a downward spiral of our entire family dynamic.

Our first year in Ottawa had been an adjustment, but one that we all seemed to be managing for the most part. We were happy in our new home. TJ had a part-time job delivering weekend flyers to earn spending money. I would volunteer to help him whenever I could by putting the papers together with him or going door-to-door down one side of the street, while he did the other side. The time we spent together was precious time, especially because we had so little of it.

Enjoying a swim one night after work, I thought back to my Spirit Guide's words before leaving Chatham: **Recognize ambitions satisfied, love shared, and rewards received**. Ambition had definitely been satisfied for Steve. When I asked him how he liked his new trade, he replied with, "I love it. I find it exciting, invigorating, and sometimes a little intimidating too. The intimidation keeps me on my toes." Steve naturally possessed many qualities of a good police officer. He had a calm demeanor and emotional maturity. He was modest, non-judgmental, and respectful of others, but his strongest attribute was his integrity.

Although I was a slave to a clock and a prisoner to my job, the shifts I worked were exciting. Every day was different from the last, and I never knew what each new day would bring. I was definitely not bored. I wondered in that moment if my posting to NDOC had been given to me as a reward for enduring three years in an Army environment, one with little to no recognition because of my gender.

It was difficult to find time together as a family, but when we did, the time was usually quality time. It was rare for the three of us to sit down to a meal together, but when our timings were synchronized, the meal was filled with laughter and conversation. All in all, life was good; hectic, but good.

While I was waiting for the bus one day after my shift, Kate (my next-door neighbor from Edmonton) passed by on the sidewalk and stopped to chat. Kate lived in Orleans too and offered to drive me home so we could continue catching up with each other. When we arrived at my place, we exchanged phone numbers and made plans to get together during my next set of days off. For the next two years, Kate and I spent countless hours together sewing or crafting. I was sewing all of my own clothing at that time, as was she, so we often spent a Saturday at the fabric store, enjoying lunch together afterwards. I was happy to have a friend from my past back in my life again.

It was a warm summer morning as I awoke at 5:00 a.m. I made a cup of coffee for Steve, packed his lunch, and kissed him goodbye as he left for work. Since I was already up, I decided to bake some muffins for breakfast. I had a recipe for chocolate muffins that were filled with a sweet cream-cheese center. They reminded me of Ding Dongs as a child and were one of my favorite muffins. By the time I pulled the muffins out of the oven, TJ was up and having his shower. He grabbed two muffins and a juice box on his way out the door to school. "You need to stay home more often, Mom," he said hugging me goodbye.

I loved to connect with nature when I had quiet time, so I made myself a coffee, grabbed a muffin, and went to sit at the patio table on the deck. As I set my cup of coffee on the table, I heard the words, "Good Morning, Laurie." It was Donna having coffee with a friend on her deck. I prepared a plate of muffins for the two of them and handed them over the fence to Donna.

"Enjoy," I said.

"I definitely will. Who doesn't love fresh muffins from the oven? Thank you so much," she replied. I spent the next half hour sipping my coffee and talking to my Spirit World, something I rarely had time to do anymore.

Donna was a single parent to a ten-year-old daughter named Katherine and an eighteen-year-old son named Steven. She also had a full-time career providing clerical support for the Research and Planning Division of the Gloucester Police Force. She was a busy mom with a busy lifestyle, but when we had time to talk, our conversations were always entertaining. All souls have different personalities and different oddities, but we seemed to embrace each other's quirks and laugh about them together. We shared an instant chemistry that kept us laughing through our demanding and crazy lives.

My next set of shifts started on a Sunday. When I arrived at NDOC, it was quiet for the first two hours, but then all hell broke loose. An Armored Personnel Carrier on a peace-keeping mission had rolled over, resulting in four soldiers being seriously injured, and a fifth soldier losing his life. We were a staff of three this particular morning: me, the Desk Officer, and a Switchboard Operator. We had a quick meeting as to what each of us needed to do immediately, and then we swung into action. The message traffic from the Communications Center on the floor below us was arriving constantly through air tube cylinders - most messages requiring immediate action. The switchboard lines were constantly lit up with inquiries from news outlets trying to get the story firsthand or officials trying to reach the Desk Officer because his line was busy. The day was chaotic as Generals came and left, each with their own set of demands. The Public Affairs Officer and Desk Officer prepared a briefing for the Press. The Padre began notifying the deceased soldier's next of kin. On the Padre's direction, I was booking flights and hotels for families to travel abroad and be with their loved ones. I had lost all track of time until Pheme arrived to relieve me from my shift. I quickly brought her up to speed. Not only were we dealing with this tragedy, but also with a suicide on one of our bases and a training accident on another base that had left two soldiers injured and hospitalized. I decided to stay longer as both of us continued to follow directions from the Desk Officer. There was little time to breathe or relax as we went from one task, to the next, to the next. I had been functioning on a coffee, a chocolate bar, and adrenaline for the past sixteen hours.

When 11:00 p.m. rolled around, things had finally settled down enough that I was no longer needed. However, I contemplated if leaving was worthwhile at this point. My next shift was due to start in six hours. The Desk Officer handed me a taxi chit to pay the cab driver for my ride home, and Pheme volunteered to stay longer in the morning. I did not need to return to work until 9:00 a.m. on Monday morning, in lieu of 5:00 a.m.

As I sat in the back of the cab, I thought about Pheme offering to work an extra four hours for me. She offered without a single hesitation and without having to be asked. Pheme was a Newfoundlander with an optimistic view on life. I liked to refer to her as my "no matter what" friend. No matter what you asked of her, she was always willing to accommodate the request. No matter what problem she was faced with, she always sought out a viable solution. No matter what stressful situation she was in, she always managed to find the humor. She was compassionate, friendly, outgoing, fun, and up for anything, no matter what. My journey with Pheme was well on its way to becoming lifelong friends as we began socializing outside of work. She would stop by for a swim or to take TJ to a Senator's Hockey Game. The girl had uncanny luck with winning Raffle Draws at the Junior Ranks Mess, and more often than not, the draw was for two tickets to a Senator's Hockey Game.

When I walked into NDOC at 8:30 the next morning, I told Pheme not to return for her night shift until 8:00 p.m. "You are going to have a busy morning. They have scheduled a briefing for 10:00 a.m. with all the big wigs. If you have a crazy shift and are too tired, call me," she said. That morning, the balcony filled quickly with the Minister of National Defence, the Chief of the Defence Staff, the Canadian Forces Chief Warrant Officer, the Public Affairs Liaison Officer, along with many others. Every seat was occupied.

The briefing was well under way when the Land Desk Officer buzzed me on the intercom, asking me to immediately bring him a fax that would be coming in momentarily. The fax machine engaged while we were speaking. After receiving seven pages, I jumped up from my chair, turned the corner, and headed for the Land Desk Officer, fax in hand. As I passed by the Sea Desk

Officer's desk, he had placed his briefcase on the outside of his desk instead of under it. Still tired from the long hours of the previous day, I tripped over his briefcase, taking a nosedive onto the floor. The sheets of paper in my hand scattered in several directions as the Sea Desk Officer jumped up from his chair and lifted me to my feet. One of my high heel shoes had flipped off my foot and was nowhere to be found. I pulled my skirt back down to its proper position on my body. Embarrassed, I took a theatrical bow to all the high-ranking officials seated in the balcony. *Act Two, find my shoe.* The bow was acknowledged with clapping and laughter as I gathered up the paperwork from the floor and then retreated as quickly as I could.

Geez, Laurie, you really know how to make an entrance. Good luck trying to live this one down. When I rounded the corner back to my desk, the switchboard operator began questioning me. "What is going on in there? Why is everyone clapping and laughing and why are you only wearing one shoe?" I was saved from answering him when his switchboard began lighting up like a Christmas tree.

Twenty minutes later, the Sea Desk Officer approached my desk and apologized for leaving his briefcase in the walkway. "Thank you for the comic relief, MCpl. We all needed it. I think this belongs to you," he said handing me my shoe before walking away.

I had always managed to keep in touch with friends by the occasional phone call, but this new job left me little time - time I rarely had for myself or for my own family. It had been well over six months since I had last talked to Dianne (my psychic girlfriend). The thought of her had just entered my mind when the phone rang. It was Dianne. She was planning on coming to Ottawa for a two-week visit. *I wonder how Steve will feel living with a psychic for two weeks.* Come to think of it, I had never spent more than twenty-four hours with Dianne myself. This was definitely going to be an interesting visit.

Spiritual Beings on a Human Experience

Laurie's soul is slowly advancing from being a prisoner of fear. With less fearful thoughts and emotions, she is witnessing the larger truths of a physical life. She is learning to let go of her fear and welcome change by trusting that her Creator knows all and sees all.

Necessary fear is natural and part of being alive. It is the place where genuine healing and peace take place. Unnecessary or chronic fear results in a soul wearing protective armor that robs them of a true physical experience while stagnating growth.

Every soul has a second language known as intuition. It is a subtle, instinctive feeling that is not derived from conscious reasoning. Laurie has learned to make use of her soul's wisdom from a noticeably young age by connecting to spiritual energy through prayer. Her present path is teaching her to feel energy around her and listen to the feelings she derives from it. She is in the infancy stages for the future path of her blueprint.

Without a solid foundation of family and self, Laurie has learned as a young adult to discover her worth through friendships and relationships. Although she is aware that she can bring her moments of greatest darkness to the light when other souls discard her, she continues to seek to know her true self based on the opinions of other souls. Until she learns to sit with herself, dissect who she truly is, and invest her energy into who she wants to become, she will continue to waste her energy in seeking approval from others. This lesson is imperative to her future.

CHAPTER 20

THREE HEARTS LIVING IN THREE SEPARATE WORLDS

Dianne did not plan to visit for another six months, but I figured I would tell everyone she was coming so they had time to get used to the idea. My son appeared indifferent to the news. I do not think he remembered Dianne from Edmonton. Besides, he was too busy in his own world. Steve, on the other hand, was much more apprehensive. He was a skeptic on the subject of psychics, but soon enough, he would have no choice but to experience her abilities firsthand during her visit. It is hard to pretend to be something that you are not, and I knew Dianne was going to be herself, so I asked her to try and be gentle with her comments to Steve.

Co-parenting is rarely easy and can become even more challenging when one of the parents is a stepparent. Is being the absolute best parent you can be enough? Can we sometimes get so lost in our own world that we end up becoming oblivious to what our children are up to as they discover their newfound independence? Sadly, that is where I was with all the hours I was working.

By the beginning of our second year in Ottawa, my son had buddied up with a problem child. Thomas lived down the street from us and was an only child to military parents, the same as TJ. The first time he came to our house, I was happy my son had found a friend, but Thomas was also raising my hackles.

Pay attention to this dangerous friendship.

Obviously, I did not want my son involved in a toxic relationship but phasing out a friendship can be tricky so I chose not to say anything to my son at the time. I was experiencing a gut feeling that had no merit to it as of yet. I was also realizing my son's need at thirteen years old to separate himself from us and form his own identity. So I kept my thoughts to myself and walked away, hoping my gut instinct was wrong. Only time would tell.

School was out for the summer, and my son had found a group of friends, Thomas included, that spent most of the time riding their bikes, swimming in our pool, playing baseball at the park, or playing street hockey. I always wanted to know where my son was so we had an agreement that he needed to tell me where he was going and when he would be home. We were no longer living in a small town, and I worried about him, especially with the hours I was working. When he headed for the grocery store one afternoon to pick up milk for Thomas' mother, I thought nothing of it and asked him if he wanted some money to get a treat while he was there. He declined. Fifteen minutes later, I received a phone call from the grocery store manager, summoning me to the store.

When I arrived, the store manager met me out front. My son was sitting in his office. "I had every intention of calling the police and charging your son with theft, but I have changed my mind. He was with a group of boys who all ran away when I confronted them about stealing from me. Your son was the only one who stopped, admitted to stealing a bottle of Gatorade, and apologized for doing so. I get the feeling that this is the first time he has stolen something and because of his remorse, you can take him home and punish him as you see fit. However, if I catch him stealing from me again, I will call the police," he said.

I was disappointed with my son's behavior. "Why would you steal a bottle of Gatorade when I offered you money to buy it before you left for the store? This makes no sense to me, son," I said.

"It was just a dare, Mom. It's no big deal," he replied.

"The fact that you decided to steal *is* a big deal. Do you know that if you get a rush from stealing, it can escalate into stealing more often and more expensive things? If the reason is that you gave in to peer pressure, then maybe you need to take a closer look at the friends you have chosen to associate with. Either way, only you know why you did it and how it made you feel. Life is about choices and consequences for those choices. Maybe being grounded for the next week might give you some perspective. There is a lesson to be learned here, and I hope you figure it out before it is too late," I said, but somehow my words seemed to be having little effect.

When we returned home, my son went to his room while I started supper. I quickly became lost in my thoughts. In some ways, I was proud of him. From the time he was young, I had taught him not to lie when confronted by an adult. If he wanted to be taken at his word, he could only accomplish that by always telling the truth. It was the only way I could defend him if he were being falsely accused of something. Then, I wondered if this behavior was normal for his age. I could not compare his childhood to mine. I had not behaved like that at his age, but then again, I had never been given the opportunity either. Maybe he was behaving normally. Maybe, just maybe, he had lucked into not having a criminal record because the store manager was shocked by his truth and remorse. *Thank you, Helena. By the Grace of God, he is not a criminal YET. Please let this be his lesson.* Perhaps, this was wishful thinking on my part.

Less than three weeks later, we arrived home to find my son in the garage with several of his friends. Thomas had a can of hairspray and TJ was holding a lighter to the tip of the can. They were creating a makeshift flamethrower by imitating what they had seen in a music video, unaware that the flame could ignite the hairspray can and cause an explosion. We were both frantic when we witnessed their behavior and raced into the garage. We sent the other boys home, thankful that no one had been injured and the house had not burned down, but my son was in big trouble. Steve's reaction was to lecture him on his choice of friends and their inappropriate behavior. "I think TJ needs to join Sea Cadets, Laurie. He has way too much time on his hands to get into trouble," Steve said after TJ was sent to his room. I had an instant flashback to my childhood. Although Steve was viewing his idea as punishment, I saw it as an opportunity for TJ to make new friends and experience a military lifestyle. If nothing more, he would know whether the military was a potential career for him, so I agreed to the idea.

My son was resistant when we discussed it at supper that night, but I insisted that he needed to make the commitment for one year. If he did not like it, then he could quit. He agreed, although I was sure that he was still reluctant. I left the supper table with the hope that he might change his mind and actually enjoy the experience. It was worth a try.

Before the start of the hockey season, we took TJ to the Ottawa Senators Open House, where he had the opportunity to take pictures with some of his favorite players and have their hockey cards autographed. Randy Cunneyworth (the team's Captain at the time) was quite surprised when my son handed him his rookie card to autograph. "I have not seen this card in ages," he said. I asked my son to give me all the cards he had auto-graphed that day and I took them to a framing shop. They placed the cards in special plastic protectors and then framed them under glass.

Before we knew it, we were leaving for Stroud, Ontario to spend Christmas with Steve's family. Although the trip was only for a few days, due to our working schedules, it was one of my more memorable holidays with his family. A box of Turtles was under the tree (Steve never missed that tradition) along with one other gift - a gift that brought tears to my eyes when I opened it. Steve had a designer denim dress made for me from a small shop in Cookstown, Ontario. The owner of the shop would sketch his ideas onto paper and then sell that idea to make one dress to add to his collection.

This particular dress was designed to a Country and Western theme, with a fringed skirt that flared from the waist and Western accents through-out the bodice. It took me back to a time in Alberta when I would listen to Country and Western music as I prepared a meal, did the ironing, or tackled the house cleaning. Whenever I listened to music from any genre, my chores became fun.

"Do you like it?" Steve asked.

"I can't even find the words," I replied. The dress was stunning and it fit perfectly.

"I measured one of the dresses in your closet, and then gave the designer those measurements, along with your height and weight. I am so impressed with his result. You look so pretty. I have to admit, I had an ulterior motive when we talked about the design of the dress. I was hoping you would teach me how to two-step, and we could make it a date to go dancing together once a month," he said. Unfortunately, we would never find the time to commit to that plan while we were posted to Ottawa.

My son also received an incredibly unique gift that year. Harry had purchased uncut sheets of forty $1.00 bills before the bills were pulled from circulation and replaced by the Loonie. He had bought one sheet for each of his grandchildren and had each sheet protected under glass and framed.

By February, Dianne was on my doorstep. It was so good to see her again, but I was even more amazed by how quickly we picked up right where we had left off, as if no time had passed at all. It did not take long for everyone to enjoy the smell of homemade bread or cinnamon buns baking when we walked through the front door. I had my own personal chef visiting, and I was dreading the day she would leave. Even Steve had no complaints about her being there. They seemed to be getting along great.

Finally I finished working my last night shift and arrived home at 6:00 a.m. to find Dianne sitting at the dining room table having a cup of coffee. "You just missed Steve. He left for work ten minutes ago. He was happy when I sent him out the door with broccoli and cheese biscuits and home-made soup for lunch. Grab a coffee and join me," she said. The following conversation ensued over coffee that morning.

Dianne I have been here for five days now, and I have noticed how scattered your energy has been. You are not yourself. What is going on?

Me My energy is all over the place. I feel like I am running a mental marathon every day, pretending to be happy, while I watch my family fall apart. My son is angry most of the time. Steve is frustrated and not himself. We have been feeding each other with a little crumb of attention thrown here and there, and I am so exhausted trying to hold everything together and be what everyone needs me to be. I am not sure if I am coming or going at the best of times.

Dianne	Let's start with your son. He has been angry in his subconscious mind ever since his father called him. That anger is manifesting itself in his physical behavior now. What is in the soul always finds its way to the physical. Combined with Steve's impatience and aggression towards your son's behavior, the anger is only amplifying inside of him. As for Steve, I have a question for you. Is there any reason why you and Steve did not have a child together?
Me	Not really. It's not something we ever talked about. Why do you ask?
Dianne	His truth is that he really wanted to have a child with you. He never said anything to you because he did not want you to feel pressured into doing something that you did not want to do, just to please him. He was waiting for you to say something and when you did not, he chose not to speak his truth. Sound familiar?
Me	Yup. You are referring to Lloyd now, aren't you?
Dianne	If the shoe fits. The truth will always set any soul free. You, of all people, should have learned that by now. Gosh, humans are thick sometimes. Always so afraid of another soul's reaction to the truth. Steve's frustration is very real. Look at things from his perspective. He is twenty-five years old, married, has a mortgage and a teenage son who is acting out. To add to all this responsibility, he rarely has any time with you. Do you know how I would describe your family right now? You are three hearts living in three separate worlds.
Me	What you just said explains a lot and makes perfect sense. The million-dollar question is how to bring us all back together again as a family.
Dianne	Has Steve talked to you about going on a vacation?

Me   No. Why?

Dianne   He has an inheritance coming, and he will want to spend it taking you on the honeymoon that the two of you never had. It is exactly what you both need. Accept the offer when he makes it, and don't make excuses. It will be the perfect time for the two of you to rebuild your relationship with truth. Your marriage is still fixable. As for your son, he will be fine in the long run. He has to take his journey, in his own way and in his own time. I hate to tell you, but it is going to get worse before it gets better. Sorry to be the bearer of bad news, but hey, don't shoot the messenger. Does this information help you at all?

Me   Of course it does. It explains so much. I have been trying to figure out this mystery without any clues because I am rarely home. Dianne, I hate to end this conversation, but I really need to lie down for a few hours. I am so overtired that I feel sick to my stomach. I set up two readings for you this afternoon, one at 1:00 p.m. and the other at 3:00 p.m.

Dianne   I am going to lie down again myself. Give me a hug and let me give you some peaceful energy to sleep on. See you in a bit.

We spent our last week together making the most of the time that was left. We took a guided tour through Parliament Hill, home to Canada's Federal Government. Dianne was mesmerized by the historic paintings and the architecture of the building. We even attended a live debate during a sitting by the House of Commons, although Dianne was not too happy to have her camera taken away as we proceeded to the balcony. We made a few meals together for the freezer. We enjoyed a roaring fire and hours of conversation like old times. I was truly going to miss my friend.

The day before Dianne was due to fly home, she had a confrontation with Steve, while I was at work. She had witnessed his behavior with TJ and decided not to remain silent. She initiated the conversation by referring to Steve's relationship with his own father. She spoke of things that had transpired during Steve's childhood and told him that he needed to have a hard look at his past because his past reasoning was affecting his present ability to be a good father. She told him that it was imperative that he dissect his past, learn from it, and discard it, or he would never have a meaningful relationship with TJ.

Dianne's comments only angered Steve as I heard about their conversation that night. "I am so glad she is leaving tomorrow. She is a freak of nature. She knows things about me that I have never told anyone, and I don't appreciate her regurgitating my relationship with my father, or anyone else for that matter. She scares me and makes me feel uncomfortable. Please don't ever invite her back here again," he said. Steve chose not to follow Dianne's advice that day and that decision was about to become destructive for all three of us.

I was detained at work one night and phoned my son. "You need to take a bus to Sea Cadets tonight, and I will pick you up at 10:00 p.m.," I said. No sooner had I arrived home, changed out of my uniform, and had a bite to eat, when the telephone rang. It was the Ottawa Police Department calling, and they had my son in an interrogation room. "There must be some mistake. My son is at Sea Cadets," I said dumbfounded.

When the officer handed the phone to my son, I could hear the fear in his voice. "Mom, I'm in big trouble," he said before handing the phone back to the officer.

"We are on our way," I said hanging up and grabbing the car keys. "Steve, we need to go. The Ottawa Police have TJ in custody."

My son had taken the bus alright, but he was not alone. Thomas was with him. Thomas waited outside while my son went inside the building of the Falkland Sea Cadet Corp, signed in for the evening, and then changed into the civilian clothing he had hanging in his locker. When he met back up with Thomas outside, the two of them set out on a spree that would involve police cars, fire trucks, and an ambulance all on the hunt to find them after several 911 calls had been placed.

The drive to the police station was solemn as I listened to Steve berate my son. "You have blinders on when it comes to TJ. Your love for him is clouding the reality of who he really is. Don't you see that? He is self-centered and does not care about anyone but himself. If he had the same love for you, he would not be acting like this knowing how much it upsets you. Take off your rose-colored glasses, Laurie, and see him for who he truly is becoming." Steve's words cut deep into my soul. It was not so much what he was saying. It was the fact that I could feel the intense hatred in his energy as he spoke, and it was breaking my heart as tears began bleeding my pain.

Is it possible to hate and love a person at the same time? Is it true that there is a thin line between love and hate, a line where you have strong feelings of love towards someone, while feeling the same intensity with negative emotions? If a soul is having a battle between love and hate, will the power of love always win out? Steve had developed a love/hate relationship with TJ, and before too long, I was going to find out what a love/hate relationship felt like for myself.

When we arrived at the police station, an officer was there to greet us as we entered the building. He wanted to explain what had taken place and why our son was being held before taking us to see him. We were shocked as the story began unfolding. The boys had been running down one of the main streets of downtown Ottawa and setting fire to the garbage cans on the sidewalk. The first time they encountered a telephone booth, Thomas called 911, screaming for help, telling them that his father was trying to kill him and then hanging up abruptly. In the second call to 911, Thomas told them that his father had stabbed him before he hung up. Emergency services had dispatched police cars, an ambulance, and fire trucks to deal with the chaos of the 911 calls. Then, the officer proceeded to tell us that the use of emergency services for pranks is a prosecutable offence. "Thomas is well known to the police. He is arrogant, fearless, and without remorse for his actions. Lucky for your son, Thomas willingly admitted that he was the one making the 911 calls and setting the fires. Your son is only guilty by association, and for that reason, we are not pressing charges at this time. However, I suggest he find a new friend because the one he has now is leading him to jail time. I will take you to see him now. He is pretty shaken up by all of this, so hopefully he has learned something," the officer said.

The car ride home was less than joyous. "You know, son, twice now you have escaped being charged for delinquent behavior. The third time, you might not be so lucky. You have left me no choice but to forbid you from hanging around with Thomas anymore. If I find out that you two are together, I will ground you until we leave Ottawa. If you think I am kidding, try me. I am done with your attitude and your excuses. This nonsense needs to stop right now. End of conversation." I was always easygoing by nature, but in this situation, there had been a volcano bubbling beneath the surface. I had finally become angered and intolerant of his repetitive behavior, as that volcano spewed with conviction and rigidity. My son immediately recognized the seriousness of my words by my tone. It was evident in his facial expression.

When I went to bed that night, I poured my heart out to my Spirit Guide. *Helena, please help my son see the error of his ways before it ruins his future. He is not a bad child. He is just a child making bad choices. I am so nervous leaving him alone with Steve right now. I do not know what has happened between them, but it is definitely not good. I am afraid for both of them.*

Submit and be still. Their situation is arising from conditions you can do nothing about. Find comfort in knowing that a negative experience is always a teaching moment.

I am not sure if it was the fear of the police, the fear of my threatening words, or my Spirit Guide intervening, but my son appeared to be changing his attitude. Life began slowly returning to normal and not a moment too soon for my sanity.

In May, Steve received his inheritance, just as Dianne had predicted. "What did you want to do with this money?" he asked over coffee one morning.

"Your grandmother left her money to you, not us. It is yours to spend as you wish, although I appreciate you including me in the decision," I replied.

"I have been thinking about it and I really would like to take you on a honeymoon. We could use the week from our Timeshare we purchased last fall and see if we could go somewhere tropical. It shouldn't be hard to go to the Caribbean in July," he said. I knew that his request was important to our marriage, so I accepted the offer and left the details up to him.

Spiritual Beings on a Human Experience

Living a life authentically in front of others, allows a human to become eyewitness to a soul's transformation. As a parent, Laurie has not shared her spirituality with her son, but she is modeling it to him through her daily decisions and her actions, as he struggles to discover his own identity.

Without a strong, connected couple co-parenting together, it is hard for a family to survive. Steve and Laurie have put the needs of their relationship last as they deal with conflicting work schedules and a teenage son. The romantic phase of this marriage had Laurie believing that a stepparent would love her son as much as she does. In the beginning, her son and her husband displayed healthy interaction and bonding, but they have now reached a critical juncture in their relationship. How each soul chooses to be in the relationship will determine their future course.

Anger is an outward manifestation based on an underlying emotion such as fear, hurt, humiliation, rejection, or frustration. Anger is divisive, destructive, and crushing to the spirit of a child when it eliminates love and acceptance. Steve's anger towards Laurie's son is beginning to display itself through criticism and intimidation, with an underlying need for respect and power beginning to surface. His actions should be motivated by the need to teach, protect, and reach out to his stepson, not by a desire to threaten and punish.

Love and hate is the balance of the Universe. Both are necessary to evolve the soul through positive and negative experiences. Hate is a choice, as is love, and the consequences of hate can be soul shattering when the darkness appears. Surrendering the darkness to the light is the only exit from hate.

CHAPTER 21

I WANT AND I NEED

Is it possible to rekindle a relationship or is it just a hopeful fantasy? How do you distinguish the possibility of doing so from wishful thinking? I was leaving on vacation with one goal in mind: to understand my husband's frustration and reconnect with him again. I had spent the last month reminiscing about the love that we once knew. We had been so happy for quite a few years, but the past year had left me feeling guarded and fearful of where the relationship was taking us. Immense love always has the potential for heartbreak, but I was not ready to give up on him yet. Was it conceivable that the way back to each other was only an airplane ride away?

Authentic love is eternal. Personality is the complication.

Donna was looking after Chelsey and Bear for the week, TJ was away at cadet camp in Kingston, Ontario for two weeks, and we were on our way to Sint Maarten in the Caribbean - to revel in the honeymoon that had escaped us for six years. I was on a mission to re-ignite our flame of authentic love, a flame that had been misplaced by our demanding physical life.

Our seats were located at the back of the airplane, the very last row to be exact. It was impossible to recline our chair backs because they were resting up against the washroom wall. To make matters worse, there were two gentlemen seated in front of us who had their chair backs fully extended. They were actually, physically lying in our laps, while smooching with each other. Steve's cheek began twitching so I immediately squeezed his hand to calm him. "I can't believe this. What a way to start our honeymoon! I am so sorry, sweetheart," he said.

"It's okay. Maybe they are on their honeymoon too," I said trying to make light of the situation. *Please Helena, I could really use a blessing right now. We are not off to a good start here.*

Simultaneously, the stewardess appeared in the aisle with the bar cart. Having overheard Steve's comments, she wheeled her cart back to the kitchen and re-appeared with a bottle of champagne and two glasses. "Sir, would you and your wife please grab your carry-on luggage and follow me." She took us up to the first-class section and handed us the bottle of complimentary champagne. "Enjoy your flight and your honeymoon. Congratulations." *Thank you, Helena!*

Maybe it was the euphoric high from the champagne on an empty stomach or maybe it was my soul being re-nourished, but the scenery of the island was speaking to me in each encounter with nature that I was witnessing for the very first time. There were palm trees swaying to and fro in the gentle breeze. Bright yellow and orange colors of the lantana flowers were dressing the island bushes scattered beneath the trees. In the distance, a lush tropical forest trickled down the slopes of the mountainside, resting in the white sand and clear blue water of the beaches. I was lost for several minutes in joy and wonder as I admired my Creator's landscaping. I had officially landed in His tropical paradise.

When I walked into the main lobby of the Divi Little Bay Beach Resort, I was in awe once again by the monumental building architecture designed in the forefront of my Creator's majestic backdrop. The suite was exquisite, but the private patio overlooking the beach and the sea stole the whole show. There was a tall bistro table with two bar stools, potted plants, and two reclining chaise lounge chairs covered with floral cushions. Steve grabbed a beer from the bar fridge as we sat to admire the view. "Why don't you change into your bathing suit, and we'll take a walk on the beach," he suggested. I began unpacking our suitcases that had been dropped in the master bedroom, and when I finished, I put on the bathing suit that Mark had bought for me when we went to the West Edmonton Mall Water Park. I was searching for something to wear as a beach wrap when Steve walked into the room and stopped dead in his tracks.

"Whoa! Wow! You are so beautiful right now. I haven't seen that perfect body of yours in so long. I say we forego the beach for today," he said tossing me onto the king size bed while tickling me. His playful demeanor turned into passion almost immediately. We were in sync with each other for several hours, and I was flying high until the weakness from starvation set in. There is so much that can be said about the stamina of a twenty-seven-year-old man, and not that I was complaining, but feeling my hunger was becoming nauseating.

We had food delivered to the suite and completed the meal with after-dinner cocktails on the patio. An orange haze began casting over the moving sea, reflecting off every wave, as we watched the sun set. One can see such beauty in pictures, but it does not do it any justice until you are experiencing it right in the moment. My heart was so full again. I was reliving our wedding night with all of its intense emotion, as was he. We had definitely found our way back to each other with little to no effort. Perhaps, we had never lost the love. Maybe, it had just been misplaced in the stress of everyday life.

The next day, we spent the morning shopping for groceries, alcohol, and new bathing suits. We also bought tickets for a six-hour trimaran sailing cruise for the following day. By noon, we stopped for a bite to eat and then returned to the resort to enjoy the beach for the rest of the day.

Sipping a coffee with a toasted bagel the following morning, I started to feel the apprehension of the cruise we were scheduled to take that day. I was not a big fan of open water. Maybe, the nervousness was stemming back from memories of my sea survival course. When we arrived at the meeting point at 10:00 a.m., we boarded a dinghy that ushered us to the trimaran that was anchored offshore. Once we set sail, I began focusing on nature to calm my nerves. The sky had an array of white puffy shapes amid the cool blue color. I could taste the salty air as the waves sprayed against the side of the boat. I could hear the music of the wind in the sails. The water was calling to me like a lover and whispering sweet nothings into my ears, as the warmth of the sun welcomed me like an old friend. My fear quickly disappeared as I began savoring each moment.

An hour later, we anchored in a bay to swim and snorkel before lunch. Steve held my hand as we jumped into the clear blue water. I lay there half pumped with adrenaline, while the other half of me was trying to calm down. I put on my goggles and my snorkel and peered into the water below. I was surrounded by a kaleidoscope of flamboyantly colored fish and coral, and I was enjoying the experience until a stringray came into view. I had finally surpassed my level of bravery for the day and immediately began swimming back to the boat.

I awoke the following morning to Steve pulling back the curtains, as he offered me a cup of coffee in bed. "Good morning, my love. I have to make a trip into town, so I have booked you into the spa. I want you to go pamper yourself for a few hours," he said.

"Are you leaving right away?" I asked.

"No, not until noon," he replied. By the time we made love, had a shower, and dressed for the day, noon had arrived.

When Steve returned, he was mysterious about where he had been. "I have arranged for us to have a romantic dinner on the beach tonight at 8:00 p.m. Until then, did you want to go to the poolside or just enjoy the sun from the patio?"

"Let's stay here," I replied. We soaked up the sun for a few hours, enjoyed a few drinks, and then dressed for dinner.

I had no idea what the night would bring nor could I ever have imagined it in my wildest dreams. When we approached the beach, I was choked with emotion by the detail of the setting. I witnessed a white-linen-covered table covered with rose petals and set with fine china. A bottle of champagne was chilling in an ice bucket beside the table. The ambiance was completed by the flames of six torches blowing in the breeze.

Steve had pre-ordered our dinners; mine was lobster and his was steak. After enjoying a glass of champagne, dinner arrived. My rock lobster was succulent, seasoned to perfection, and my mouth was having an orgasm with every delicious bite. "Girl, you are so sensuous right now, I can hardly contain my excitement. Is that lobster really that good?" he asked teasingly. After trying a bite of mine, he ordered another one for us to share. We finished the meal with a decadent piece of chocolate cake, drizzled with a fresh raspberry compote. The night could not have been more perfect, but it was far from over.

After the dinner dishes had been cleared away, he poured us another glass of champagne and then removed two ring boxes from his pocket, sliding one towards me. When I opened it, it contained a man's wedding ring. He asked me to remove the wedding band I was currently wearing while he did the same. He took my ring from the jewelry box he was holding and asked me to do the same with his. We placed the rings on the tip of each other's ring finger and then he asked me to repeat after him: "I love you with my whole heart and with a passion that cannot be expressed by words. Give me your hand today and in return, I promise to give you forever." *Quick, please, someone pinch me.* The wedding bands were identical, the gold twisting together to form a knot in the middle of the ring. They were the perfect symbol of our love. He would hold true to his word to "give me forever". I just had no idea how quickly forever would come.

Three days before we were due to go home, we decided to take one more excursion. This time, twelve people were being taken by boat to an area of the island that was only accessible by water. We arrived on the beach to find a guide and twelve horses waiting for the tour group. We were about to travel by horseback through the tropical forest to a waterfall at the top of a mountain, where we would have lunch and then ride back down.

As we mounted the horses, I noticed mine was a little spirited, but I was not concerned. I had learned how to ride from my sister Sharron and was not nervous on a horse. I asked the guide my horse's name, to which he replied, "Blaze". After fifteen minutes of riding, we came to a point on the climb where the path split in two. Eleven horses chose the path to the left, while Blaze chose the path to the right. When I pulled on the reign with a hard left to get him to change direction, he bucked and reared. He had made up his mind that he was going the way that he wanted to go and being as we were at the edge of a mountain, rearing and bucking had the potential to cost us both our lives. I could hear Steve shouting to the guide and the guide telling him not to worry. "The horse knows the way," he said to Steve. There I was, all alone in the forest, on the edge of a steep mountain path, at my horse's obstinance. Now, I was just along for the ride.

When the group arrived at the waterfall for lunch, I was still out riding around in the forest by myself. When the group finished lunch an hour later, I was still out riding around in the forest by myself. By this point, I was questioning if I would ever see my husband again. *Headline: Woman dies in tropical forest horseback riding while on honeymoon.* Steve became more frantic as the minutes ticked on, and on, and on. He was so worried that he had not gone with the group to eat lunch, opting instead to wait for me where the horses were corralled.

After lunch, everyone returned to the corral and began mounting their horses for the ride back down the mountain. I was still out in the forest, riding around by myself. I could hear the groups' voices through the tree line and when the guide whistled, Blaze decided he was finally ready to join the rest of the group. He began galloping, taking a shortcut through the trees. I leaned forward, resting my head on his mane, to avoid the low hanging tree branches from snagging in my hair and pulling me off the horse. Finally, and not a moment too soon, I was back with the group. When I returned, I immediately switched horses with the guide, at his request. "I am so sorry," he said. "We will reimburse your money when we get back to the boat."

We were content to spend our last two days on the resort, enjoying the beach. The trip had far surpassed any of my expectations, but I still needed to have a serious conversation with Steve. I needed to get to the bottom of his frustration with TJ before we left the island.

While having a few drinks on the patio during our last night on the island, I figured it was time to have our discussion.

| Me | Steve, I want to thank you from the bottom of my heart for this trip. I can't even find the words to describe this experience, other than it has been mesmerizing in every way. The more love we share, the more I have bursting inside of me. Our connection feels like it did when we married each other six years ago. |

| Steve | I feel exactly the same way. Everything feels new and exciting again. We should have done this a long time ago. |

| Me | How did we become so disconnected? Something has been broken in our family for the past year, and I have been afraid to say anything. I just kept hoping things would get better. |

Steve   Your son was a big part of that. Don't take it wrong when I say this because you know I love him, but I am also very jealous of him.

Pay attention to his truth.

Me   Jealous? I am confused.

Steve   We never had a normal courtship of dating and then having a family. It was always the three of us right from the beginning, but ever since we moved to Ottawa, I have found myself envious of the time you spend with him because it takes time away from us. I was missing the way we were in the beginning.

Me   Why didn't you tell me how you were feeling?

Steve   I just kept hoping things would get better. Instead, they got worse. I am frustrated with TJ most of the time now, and I know that he is not a bad kid. Maybe I just don't know how to be a parent to a teenager. My father was always mean to us as teenagers so that is all I know.

Me   I have to ask you a really important question. Do you want to have a baby with me?

Steve   I did in the beginning, but I have changed my mind. In another five years, TJ will leave home to find his way in the world, and then it will be you and me again. I don't want to be raising another child for another eighteen years. Besides, I never wanted you to give up your career, and it has been hard enough on both of us with just one child.

Me   I will still have to work shifts for the next two years, but I will try really hard to make more time for us when we get back home. It was not my intention to make you feel so neglected.

Steve   And I will try to be more patient with your son. I promise!

I was finally in a place to understand what had happened to my family, but now I needed to figure out a plan to fix it. It was not going to be easy. My son had become a teenager, a complex human being struggling to cope with his many feelings; feelings that were causing a constant battle between what he needed and what he wanted, coupled with the feeling that he had no control over anything. I remembered those feelings well from my own childhood.

Maybe being a parent to a teenager was harder for Steve than I had anticipated. Maybe if I became the disciplinarian and took that off his shoulders, the two of them could find their way back to being friends again. Maybe, just maybe!

Spiritual Beings on a Human Experience

The soul is the eternal aspect of oneself and is not bound by the limitations of the physical plane. Authentic love from one soul to another soul will live on eternally, both on the physical plane and the other side. However, the personality is the result of karma and experiences in a present lifetime. Laurie and Steve have rekindled their relationship because they returned to authentic love, soul-to-soul love. They both have been living in their personalities. Steve has lost his way through feelings of jealousy, and Laurie has lost her way by her fear not to seek the truth. She has been struggling for the past year in silence. The Universe supports their truth being revealed to one another.

Laurie's personality wants her family, and Laurie's personality needs her family. She identifies with being a mother and a wife, roles that are deflect-ing from her discovering her own self-worth and from loving herself unconditionally. Her family is validating her need to be loved. She continues to search for acceptance from others instead of realizing her value based on who she is as a soul. The Universe will continue to bless her and encourage her on her journey to self-discovery.

CHAPTER 22

RELYING ON RADICAL TRUST

If we take a detour from our blueprint, are we always led back to where we need to be? Was I finally where I needed to be with Steve again or had I just given him the power to either save our family or destroy it? It was not hard to see that the relationship between the two most important people in my life had changed. My son had become an adolescent with an attitude, and my husband had become resentful towards him. Was it possible for both of them to return to the relationship they had in the past? I was relying on radical trust that the Universe would pull our family back together and get us over life's hurdles in order to become a loving family once again.

The flight home left me time to reflect on the relationship that I had just rebuilt with my husband and to ponder how to fix the relationship between my husband and my son. *Helena, I know that all things are possible through my Creator. My family is everything to me. Please bless us all through this difficult period and help us become stronger than ever.*

The journey is not yours alone to take.

When I stopped at the mailbox on my way home, there were two letters that immediately piqued my interest. The first was from my son. The letter was both heart-wrenching and comical as I read through the several pages he had written - pages describing his experience being away from home for the first time. Getting up at 6:00 a.m. every morning, making his bed, ironing his uniforms himself, and having little down time was a new challenge for him. Some of the happier highlights of his experience included the camaraderie of new friends, playing sports together, and sailing. He ended the letter by saying that going to eat at the Mess Hall was the best part of all. There were so many choices of food, and he could eat as much as he wanted, but a few sentences later, he claimed that he was looking forward to coming home and eating my food again. The letter was priceless, and it warmed my heart. Although he was growing up, he was still my little boy who was missing his mother.

The second letter was a wedding invitation from Pattina (my roommate from Edmonton). She had finally found the man of her dreams, and I was delighted for her. I called her right away so we could catch up. She sounded so excited on the phone, and when I spoke to her about flying to Edmonton to attend the wedding, she insisted that we stay with her, instead of at a hotel. Beyond a shadow of a doubt, I was thrilled about reconnecting with my dear friend from the past and I was looking forward to meeting the man who had managed to capture her heart.

That day, Donna stopped over to drop off the spare house key, and we chatted for half an hour about our trip to the Caribbean and her experience with the two dogs. The day after we left on vacation, the dogs had managed to get into the garbage because I had forgotten to put it out before leaving. As Donna began cleaning up the mess and scolding them, Chelsey slinked away into the dining room. Bear, however, sat watching Donna, baring her teeth with muffled growling.

"I was so nervous. I thought she was going to bite me, so I decided to be quiet and stop scolding her," she said.

I laughed. "Bear always does that when she is in trouble. She wrinkles her nose like she is saying "Ewe" and then sasses back with the suppressed growling. She is harmless," I replied.

I apologized to Donna for having to clean up a mess that could have been avoided, and when I tried to offer her compensation for her trouble, she refused. I was so grateful that she had kept an eye on our place while we were gone and had looked after our two fur babies. To me, Donna was the epitome of what neighbors should be - respectful, friendly, and helpful. Our simple interaction through conversations had slowly become a deeper connection that would become the tie that binds to a lifelong friendship.

When we picked up TJ at the Sea Cadet Unit three days later, he told us that he did not want to return to Sea Cadets in September. "I want to quit,

Mom. I hate parades and drill. I always end up passing out." I was proud of my son for keeping his commitment to give it a try for a year. If nothing more, he was walking away with an experience that had enlightened him as to what the military was all about. As we continued to talk, he told me that he wanted to find a part-time job, and he wanted to play hockey.

TJ had always been athletic, a natural ability passed on to him by his grandfather and his mother. He played basketball in school and most of his extracurricular activities outside of school centered around playing a sport of some kind. In September, I registered him to play hockey in a city league. I took him to a secondhand store for the required equipment, except for his skates, which I bought brand-new. I made him a promise that if he liked hockey, I would replace the secondhand items with new ones the following year. Any parent who has ever had a child play hockey can tell you about the exorbitant expense for equipment, as well as the costly fees for leagues and tournaments.

It was not long before my son found a part-time job working weekends as a dishwasher at Moxie's Restaurant. When he came home with his first paycheck, he was angry. "I worked for two weeks, Mom, and all I made was $2.65. I made more money delivering flyers." When I looked at the stub on the paycheck, they had removed the cost for his uniform ($44) all in one fell swoop, instead of taking it out in increments. I asked him to give me the cheque, and I gave him the cash in return. I kept the paycheck for fifteen years before I had it framed for him. Today, it hangs on the wall of his bar, a humorous part of his history, but it was definitely not funny at the time.

On my first day back to work, there was a note on my desk. The Chief of the Defence Staff (CDS) had requested to meet with me in person. When I appeared at his office door, I was so nervous that I was fidgety, my voice was quivering, and my legs were shaking. "Have a seat, MCpl. I have called you here for several reasons. First, I have your Redress of Grievance that was written with regards to a PER from 210 Workshop in Chatham, New Brunswick. Legal Services and I have gone over the redress. Here is the official letter denying any personal oppression. Although your performance warrants an outstanding assessment, you have failed to consider yourself in competition with your peers. *So what you are saying is that all sixteen people's performance were outstanding. That's a little hard to believe.*

Embrace the learning experience and listen.

Although that is not what you wanted to hear, it is apparent that the PER system is flawed, and for that reason, I made a call to your Career Manager. Under my direction, you have been moved up the merit list for promotion by 100 positions. I did not make the decision lightly and I based it solely on witnessing your performance in NDOC."

"Adding to that, I have received several noteworthy letters of appreciation, originating from the Desk Officers in NDOC, a Duty Chaplain in Edmonton, and the Land Forces Western Area Headquarters staff. All were impressed by your handling of operational situations. To summarize the letters, you are viewed as calm, friendly, professional, and extremely successful in accomplishing any task assigned to you in a timely and efficient manner, often acting without direction. I have passed these letters on to my Deputy and recommended that your name be put forward for the Deputy Chief of the Defence Staff Certificate of Achievement. You are an outstanding individual and a credit to the Canadian Forces. Thank you for your dedication and hard work, MCpl."

As I was leaving the CDS' office I heard, "Is that you, Laurie?" When I turned to look at where the voice had come from, I recognized one of the SAR Techs from CFSTS. He was now the Canadian Forces Chief Warrant Officer. He stood up from behind his desk and greeted me with a hug. I laughed and commented, "Are you allowed to be so friendly with us common folk?" He was now in a powerful position in his career. We sat down in his office and chatted for several minutes before I returned to NDOC. It had been a morning of very unexpected surprises.

Life in NDOC was far from calm for the next few weeks. In 1993, all the positive accomplishments in Somalia by the Airborne Regiment had been overshadowed by the torture and murder of a Somalian teenager at the hands of our soldiers. The military had spent two years trying to restore the once proud reputation of Canada's toughest fighting soldiers, when a videotape surfaced adding a deeply disturbing new dimension to the Regiment. It was filled with racial slurs from soldiers that were once former members of a white supremacist group.

Four days later, the first video was followed by a second video that had been released directly to the media. The video contained a brutal hazing ritual with drunken Airborne soldiers being forced by comrades to eat feces and urine-soaked bread. A black soldier was being led around on a dog leash, with the words "I love the KKK" written on the back of his t-shirt. There were several simulated sex acts and disgusting displays of choking and vomiting. The video was so graphic, parts of it had to be blacked out from public view. I could only watch the first two minutes of the video before I needed to turn away. It was so disgraceful, demeaning, and nauseating.

The second video was now sparking public outrage as the Prime Minister threatened to disband the Airborne Regiment. The military quickly engaged in damage control over the two leaked videos, but that week was the beginning of a downward spiral, one that would result in the Airborne Regiment being disbanded due to their violent and racist culture. The Prime Minister made the formal announcement by declaring, "For the morale of the rest of the troops and the prestige of Canada, we had no choice but to act." Canada had just removed its only infantry regiment that could rapidly deploy into any combat mission. That day was an emotional day for me as I witnessed many of my friends fall from grace in the court of public opinion.

The killing of the Somalian teenager had resulted in nine soldiers facing charges from second-degree murder to negligence of duty. Four soldiers were acquitted, one was jailed for ninety days, two were reprimanded, one's trial was adjourned until a later date, and one young Private was held in cells in Ottawa on charges of manslaughter. Private Kyle Brown would become the fall guy, convicted of manslaughter and sentenced to serve five years in prison.

During his stay in cells, Kyle and Steve became quite close through conversation. When Steve was in the guardhouse alone on night shifts, he would open the cell door, allowing Kyle to come out to watch television or enjoy a pizza with him. Before Kyle left for the Detention Barracks to serve the first two years of his prison sentence, he handed Steve a drawing he had made of Airborne troops on exercise. He signed and dated it, thanking Steve for treating him with dignity and respect. I still have that drawing and I highly recommend reading Kyle Brown's book titled *Scapegoat - How the Army Betrayed Kyle Brown*. It is a very enlightening read.

During a set of days off when we were both home together, Steve had arranged for a financial planner to come to the house. Given the nature of both of our careers, he felt that it was important for each of us to be able to resume life without financial worry should something happen to either one of us. We purchased life insurance policies and survivor income benefits that day. Steve's forethought was about to become my saving grace a lot sooner than either of us had anticipated.

The day of Pattina's marriage was quickly approaching as we headed for Stroud, Ontario to drop off TJ and the dogs at Steve's parents for three days. We arrived in Edmonton the day before her wedding, and the weekend was a whirlwind of activity. That Friday night, the girls decided to meet up at the Crown and Anchor neighborhood pub. It was the first time I had seen some of my old gang since leaving Edmonton. Debbie (the bartender from the Junior Ranks Mess in Griesbach) was now working as a graphic designer and living in Calgary, Alberta. Lea (the Mess Manager) had moved to Nanton, Alberta to care for her elderly parents. Darlene and Tesh had been posted to Winnipeg, Manitoba a year after I left. Most of the old gang had moved on to different careers and places. A pivotal point in history was now just that, a point in history, to live on in memory only.

When Debbie walked into the Pub, we immediately picked up right where we had left off. The years had been kind to her. She was still as beautiful as ever. In fact, I would have recognized her anywhere. We drank, laughed, danced, and carried on like the old days. Fabio (Pattina's husband to be) was less than impressed when we returned to the apartment quite late and quite intoxicated, so they began quarreling. Steve and I retreated to the spare bedroom for the night to give them privacy. I asked him what he thought of Fabio since they had spent the evening together drinking beer. His response was, "I can't put my finger on it exactly, but something doesn't seem right. I get the sense that he is hiding something." I chuckled and told him that it must be the cop in him, but he was the only one who had accurately sensed what was coming.

Pattina and Fabio married each other the following day, and we flew back to Toronto on Sunday. Within less than a year, Pattina's marriage was over. Steve had been right. Fabio had definitely been hiding something. He had been hiding the fact that he was already married to a woman in Winnipeg, and when she threatened to tell Pattina the truth, Fabio came clean to Pattina. She was devastated to learn that she had married a bigamist, a man who was still legally married to someone else. She had the marriage annulled and walked away without pressing charges against him.

Pattina spent several years cleaning up the collateral damage from their relationship, both emotionally and financially, while Fabio made the choice to walk out of her life and carry on with another life. That was my friend Pattina in a nutshell! Always taking the moral high road and acting responsibly. That quality was what I admired most about her.

My son was enjoying playing hockey, and he was good at it. His sheer size was intimidating to other players so he was often left unchecked to score goals. By his second year, the team had voted him in as their Assistant Captain. He was working part-time, going to school, playing hockey, and staying out of trouble. He no longer appeared to be an angry teenager. Instead, he was busy living the happy life that he had created for himself. I was relieved by the calm that had returned to our lives. Although all three of us had hectic schedules, we were getting along and making the most of the time we could find to interact as a family. I was grateful for the change, but it would prove to be nothing more than the calm before the storm. My husband and my son had adopted an indifferent attitude towards each other, tolerating the relationship, in order to keep the peace. It would only be a matter of time before their true feelings would surface and destroy all three of our relationships in the process.

It was December 22 when we arrived in Stroud for the holidays. Steve had made plans to celebrate our seventh wedding anniversary at the 360 Restaurant at the top of the CN Tower on the night of December 23. When we found time alone that night, he handed me $500 in cash and insisted that I go shopping the following morning to find an elegant evening gown to wear to dinner. After trying on several gowns, I had finally found the one - a simple spaghetti-strapped, backless, red satin gown. When the store clerk approached me with a short, stand collar, white winter fur jacket to finish the look, the outfit was complete. I felt confident that my chosen outfit would complement his tuxedo, and I was happy that I had managed to purchase both pieces for less than $200 in the first store.

Dressed to the nines the following night, a limousine arrived at the house to drive us to Toronto. Once we were seated in the backseat, Steve opened the bottle of champagne that was chilling and poured us each a glass. Then he tapped on the window, queuing the driver for the second surprise. As I took my first sip of champagne, John Berry's song "Your Love Amazes Me" began playing.

> "I've seen a sunset that would make you cry and colors
> of a rainbow reaching across the sky. The moon in all its
> phases, but your love amazes me… Forever faithfully,
> your love amazes me."

I reached in my clutch purse for a tissue to dab my eyes and stop my makeup from running. "Why are you crying, sweetheart?" he asked.

"Your heart moves me to tears. Thank you so much for your undying love," I replied. The descriptive words of nature in his chosen song had spoken directly to my soul.

When the elevator door opened at the top of the CN Tower, we were greeted and escorted to a table that provided a panoramic view of the city lights against a night backdrop. When I sat in my chair, the front legs of the chair were broken. Before the chair could be pushed up to the table, I tipped forward and fell to my knees on the floor, reaching for the sides of the table to try and break my fall. The entire table tilted towards me, dumping the dishes and glasses of ice water onto my dress. The spaghetti straps on my dress tore away and the top of my dress fell to my waist. The shock and horror on Steve's face required no words, as he kept gesturing for me to pull up the front of my dress and cover my exposed breasts. I was completely overwhelmed and embarrassed.

Witnessing what had transpired, a female bartender came running out from behind the bar and led me to the washroom, apologizing the entire way. After drying my dress under the hand dryer and pinning my dress straps back into place, I gathered what dignity I had left and exited the washroom to find my husband. *Why me, Helena? Out of all the tables I could have been seated at, I had to get the one with the broken chair. I suppose that you are all laughing up there right now. Enjoy the chuckle. I am so embarrassed.* That night, our dinner and drinks were complimentary as the restaurant tried to compensate for the broken chair and the embarrassment that had followed. Poor Steve! His romantic date for the evening had turned into a walking calamity of charm and elegance. Maybe he loved me as much as he did because he never knew what to expect. Or maybe he loved me for the entertainment factor that I always had an uncanny way of providing at my own expense.

It was 1997, my last year in NDOC, and I was due to be posted that summer. My boss approached my desk in the new year and asked how I felt about a posting to JTF (Joint Task Force). I knew its mandate was to protect Canada's national interests, combat terrorism, perform hostage rescue, and deter any threats to Canadians at home and abroad. "The JTF Desk Officer has requested you be considered for a posting to the unit as their Operations Clerk." I was flattered, but I knew little specifics about the job. I used to refer to the JTF Desk Officer as "Secret Squirrel" because everything he did was so covert. My boss assured me that if I were interested, I would undergo an interview by phone before any final decisions were made. My initial thought was "why not". Nothing ventured, nothing gained.

A week later, I received a phone call from a Sergeant at the JTF Special Operations Force. This new job would require me to sell my home in Orleans and move closer to the job. I would be on-call 24/7 with a half-hour notice to move anywhere worldwide. I would not be allowed to tell anyone where I was going or when I would be returning. In fact, I would not be allowed to have contact with anyone, including family, while on deployment. *Wow! This really is Secret Squirrel stuff.* He continued, "Once you become part of the unit, you will finish your entire career with us."

I stopped him after his last comment. Although the job was enticing, it was not something suitable for my situation. I had a family and I was not comfortable disappearing for months at a time with absolutely no contact, as well as my family having no idea where I was. Had I been single and without a child, I would have jumped at the opportunity, but my family was my priority over my career. I thanked him for the consideration and he thanked me for being honest and upfront. "From what I have heard about you MCpl, you not coming to work for JTF is *our* loss. Your name was highly recommended for the job and the Commanding Officer will be disappointed by your decision when I tell him. Thank you for your time. Have a good day."

The end of March, my posting message arrived in NDOC. I was heading for CFB Borden, Ontario as an instructor for the Canadian Forces School of Administration and Logistics (CFSAL). Steve was being posted with me and he was happy about living a half hour away from his family. We were off on our next adventure together.

My last day of work at NDOC, I received the DCDS Certificate of Achievement recognizing my outstanding achievements in the world of operations. The experience had been rewarding, but I was more than ready to return to a less demanding job and turn my focus towards my family again.

Spiritual Beings on a Human Experience

Steve's emotion of jealousy is stemming from a belief system that is out of line with the truth, a belief system of selfishness. He is comparing Laurie's love for him with that of her son. The attention and love that Steve's inner child is seeking is being given to someone else, and Steve is feeling neglected and resentful. Laurie's journey with her son has nothing to do with Steve. Each journey is unique to each individual. The week Steve spends alone with Laurie has allowed his soul to begin a transformative healing process. Should he choose to admire and praise the good in his son, he will feel the jealousy loosen from his heart.

Although Laurie's desire is to have her family back again as one cohesive unit, that result is dependent upon three souls having the same frame of mind. Her prayers are heard, but the future of her family is undetermined at this point.

Steve and Kyle's friendship is serving a purpose to Kyle's soul. The military's unjust decision should not define him going forward. By Steve displaying a friendship towards him, Kyle will walk away from the experience with dignity and respect instead of shame. His destiny is to discover his passion for drawing, a natural talent designed into his blueprint by his Creator.

CHAPTER 23

THE RIGHT ROAD IS
NOT ALWAYS STRAIGHT

Canadian Forces Base Borden (CFB Borden) is located approximately 100 kilometers North of Toronto. It is Canada's largest training base and the home of eleven training schools for support trades - schools that teach over 20,000 personnel every year. The base has a permanent population of roughly 3,200 military personnel and 1,500 civilians.

CFB Borden sits on 21,000 acres of land. The history of the base is scattered throughout several acres with displays of decommissioned vehicles from WW1, WW2, armored vehicles, trucks, and aircraft. There is a military museum, the Terra Movie Theatre, a youth center for teens from 15-18 years old, a McDonalds restaurant, and a Bleachers Sports Bar - just to mention a few amenities. I was excited about this move. I viewed it as a new beginning for all three of us.

When a military member is posted, they must report to their new base on a designated posting date, regardless of whether their current residence sells or not. Being a homeowner, especially when both spouses have a military career, is one of the most stressful situations of being posted. Neither one of us had the option to stay behind until the house sold. I was praying and pleading that we would not need to carry the cost of an unsold house, while having the expense of another residence in Borden at the same time.

Our home on Radway Terrace went on the market as soon as we received our posting messages and within two weeks of the listing, we had an offer.

Our first viewing resulted in the house selling to a military couple being posted to Ottawa from Gagetown, New Brunswick. *Thank you, Helena, for such a quick blessing. Our biggest obstacle and financial burden has been removed by your Grace. I am so sorry for being such a pest about it.*

When Donna pulled in her driveway and saw the SOLD sign, she stopped by with tears in her eyes. "I guess I will be getting new neighbors again. Am I that bad a next-door neighbor? I really hate to see you go," she said. I was going to miss her too, but I assured her that I would stay in touch. Something deep inside was telling me that our journey was far from over, and I was not wrong. Within the next three years, Donna would become one of my safe places to fall apart without judgment.

Instead of buying another home, we decided to live on the base when we found out that there were several empty PMQs available. My gut instinct was telling me that the timing of buying another house was not right. Once again, that instinct would prove to be invaluable.

On our arrival in Borden, Base Accommodation handed us two sets of keys to view a PMQ on the north side of the base and another on the south side. The north side PMQ was a two-bedroom bungalow on Cleve Loop. When we walked through the front door, I started to tremble. I stopped in the entrance and closed my eyes. The energy I began feeling was alarming, as my heart filled with a sorrowful mercy. When we approached the laundry room, my neck began to hurt and I was having trouble catching my breath. Walking into the kitchen was even more distressing. My chest began throbbing with a burning pain, and I was now struggling to breathe. By the time we reached the bathroom, I immediately turned and bolted out the front door. I stood on the front lawn, gasping for air. *Helena, please help me. I am dying. I can't breathe!*

Surround yourself in White Light and let Mother Earth absorb the energy that is not yours to hold.

I followed her instruction. Within a few seconds, the heavy feeling in my chest lifted and I began breathing normally once again.

Steve followed me out of the house. "What is wrong, Laurie? Are you okay?" he asked.

I was far from okay. "I can't live in this house, Steve. I know that you probably think I am crazy right now, but something really terrible has happened here. I can feel the energy. It is still in the house and it is haunting. Please baby, let's go look at the other PMQ." Steve hugged me reassuringly to stop me from shaking and went back to lock the front door. But I could tell from the look on his face when he met me in the car, he was more than a little perplexed by my behavior. I was perplexed myself.

The PMQ on the south side was a three-bedroom duplex. It was much larger than the first PMQ and the energy inside was tranquil - maybe because it had been empty and under renovation for over a year. After viewing the entire house, we decided to make the duplex on Maple Drive our new residence. Steve liked the layout of the PMQ, but he was more enthusiastic about the location. The South Side Base Gym was only two blocks away and the Military Police Guardhouse was just around the corner. He could walk to work and I could use the car to drive to my new job.

On his first day of work, Steve arrived at his new unit and asked his Sergeant if something had happened in the PMQ on Cleve Loop. The Sergeant looked puzzled by the question and asked, "How do you know about Cleve Loop?"

Steve replied, "I don't know anything. This is going to sound weird, but my wife freaked out when we were viewing it the other day, and she refused to live there. Her reaction has piqued my curiosity, that's all."

The Sergeant began his reply reluctantly. "It gives me shivers to even think about it. A couple of months ago, we were dispatched to that residence when the occupant failed to show up for work. When no one answered the door, we had to get a spare key from Base Accommodation and let ourselves in. Initially, we thought that we had walked into a murder scene. There was a rope attached to a broken rafter lying on the laundry room floor. The kitchen walls and ceiling were covered in blood spatter, and a butcher knife lay covered in blood on the floor. We found the male occupant of the house deceased in the bathtub."

He continued. "After further investigation and an autopsy, we learned that this guy's wife had left him for a woman. In his shock and grief, he attempted suicide by trying to hang himself from the laundry room rafter. When the rafter broke, he went to the kitchen, grabbed a butcher knife, and began stabbing himself in the chest. The blood spatter on the ceiling and walls was the result of him pulling the knife out from his chest and then plunging it back in again. After several self-inflicted wounds, he was still alive. He dropped the knife on the kitchen floor, went to the bathroom, filled the bathtub with water, and climbed in. Eventually, he bled out in the water, lost consciousness, and drowned. Is your wife psychic or something?" In order to avoid the need to respond, Steve quickly diverted his attention to someone entering the room and introduced himself. Perhaps he was not sure how to answer that question.

When I called Dianne to give her my change of address and phone number, I told her about my experience on Cleve Loop and what the Military Police had told Steve. Her reply was, "He is still earthbound. Did you know that you have the ability to help him move on? It is important for you to learn how to do this. Trust me! You are going to need it." After I hung up, I chalked up the phone call to one of those weird conversations with Dianne that I could not understand.

I was in for a rude awakening when I reported to CFSAL for my first day of work. The school's Chief Warrant Officer had removed me from the billet I had been posted into as an instructor and moved me into another billet as the Clerk for Supply Training Company. I was disgruntled and made a point to ask him "why". Politely, of course. "I need a strong clerk in that Company while they undergo a major overhaul of the supply system. I will re-visit the instructor position next year," was his answer.

Temperance and courtesy is required.

I know. I know. You are telling me to roll with it. I am listening, but I am more than a little disappointed right now.

Trust your process.

When I reported to Supply Training Company, I had my own office, which I was more than content with, especially given my current mindset. I could sulk by myself and not have to pretend to be happy around anyone else. I spent the next two days undergoing a handover with the current Company Clerk, who was now moving into what was supposed to be "my instructor position". In some ways, I found his news reassuring. Maybe the same scenario would play out for me within a year, but the uncomfortable feeling I was experiencing in that thought was telling me different. I was sensing that I was about to approach a critical curve in the road ahead before too long.

Settling into our new lives was effortless for the first few months. Steve and I took pleasure in our new jobs, and TJ had made a new friend named Brandon during the summer. Brandon would be the first friend of many friends to come. My son was extremely social by nature, with an uncanny sense of humor when he was not angry at Steve. I knew that he was at a stage in life where he wanted to spend less time with his parents and more time with his friends. He was impulsive, with strong emotions that could drive his decisions in life either way. For that reason, I decided to make it my mission to get closer to him in order to understand what he was thinking and feeling.

While assembling a new barbeque in the backyard one day, I offered to help Steve by reading the instructions to him in order to save him time. That offer only annoyed him because men do not follow instructions. So I returned to the kitchen to season the meat for dinner and put the potato salad together. When Steve told me the barbeque was ready, I could see five parts still sitting on the side tray. "They are just spare parts," he said when I questioned him. *Um…I have never heard of spare parts to a barbeque or any other item requiring assembly, but I really don't want to argue with you.*

TJ appeared at the back door with the telephone in his hand. "Steve, Grandma is on the phone." Steve told me to light the barbeque, start cooking the meat, and he would be right back. When I hit the igniter button, the escaping gas exploded into a giant fireball, setting my hair on fire. TJ began screaming, "Mom's on fire! Mom's on fire, Steve!" The neighbor in the duplex next door was coming out of her house with a basket of wet laundry to hang on the clothesline at the same time as I was attempting to light the barbeque. She quickly rushed over, throwing a wet tea towel over my head. I had finally met my new neighbors, Bo and Lisa. Other than singed hair and no eyebrows, my face was saved from being burned. Steve and Bo fixed the barbeque (by following the instructions), while Lisa put burn salve on my neck and right ear. Things could have turned out so differently. *Thank you, Helena!* Not only had I avoided being severely burned, but I was also thankful that day to learn that I was living next door to a registered nurse and a dental technician.

We quickly became friends with Bo and Lisa, often partying together in the backyard. Bo was involved in the hockey community, so it did not take long for TJ to begin playing Bantam-level hockey for the Essa Eagles through Bo's connections. When hockey tournaments were taking place on the weekend with military members from other bases, Bo would take TJ along with him and pay him $100 for the day to be a scorekeeper. Bo was exactly what TJ needed in his life, a male figure who took an interest in him.

When TJ came home with his mid-term report card, I was proud of him. He had turned the "Cs" and "Ds" from grade nine in Ottawa into "As" and "Bs" in Borden. I expressed my delight by praising him. Steve looked at the report card and the words out of his mouth angered me, "I don't know why you are making a fuss over these marks. He is an "A" student but refuses to apply himself. He will never accomplish anything in life with his lazy attitude. Everything he does will always be half-assed." Steve's irate energy field raised the hairs on the back of my neck as he was speaking. His antipathy for my son was in full view and undeniable.

When I spoke to Steve later that night, expressing my concerns over his relationship with TJ, I was not getting through to him. My heart was breaking as he dismissed me and told me to "get a grip on my son before he becomes a loser in life". I resolved myself to the fact that I could no longer hold out hope that things could get better between them. History was repeating itself and soon enough, it would escalate to a level that would be impossible to come back from.

I took joy in becoming a "hockey mom". My evenings were spent attending hockey games and one weekend a month was spent driving my son to tournaments. I enjoyed cheering him on from the stands, but even more so, I wallowed in our conversations together in the car. It became our special time to talk and laugh about anything and everything. I had missed out on so much of his life while we were in Ottawa. Instead of being part of the family and attending TJ's hockey games with me, Steve always made an excuse that he had something else to do. It was obvious that he wanted no part in TJ's life other than to discipline him or belittle him, so I stopped asking.

At the same time that I was bonding with my son again, I was also trying to figure out Steve's frame of mind. I had noticed that when we invited his family over for Thanksgiving dinner, the relationship between Steve and his father had become strained. When I tried to have a conversation with him about it, he refused to tell me what had happened. Whenever I mentioned his father's name, Steve's cheek began to twitch. Whatever had taken place between them had resulted in a seething anger below the surface, one that was now being directed towards TJ.

After spending five months in my job, I had finally reached a comfortable relationship with my co-workers. My conversations were becoming more personal and humorous, especially with the instructors. I clicked immediately with a Hazmat Instructor named Eileen. We shared a distaste for five-kilometer runs with the students, so she became my partner to run with behind the platoon. The pace was slower as students struggled to keep up, allowing us to become each other's sounding board about life in general. By the sixth month, a Sergeant named Susan moved into my office. We bonded quickly and our friendship would become my saving grace when my whole world spontaneously combusted. Perhaps the Creator knowingly places special people in our life for a reason.

During Supply Training Company's run one morning, I noticed a car for sale parked by the Tank Park. I made a mental note of the phone number on the windshield and called it when I returned to the office. The car was an old jalopy that a man was selling for $800. I thought it would be the perfect car to teach my son how to drive. If he ended up putting it in the ditch or hitting a tree, it would not matter. When I brought it home, TJ was less than impressed.

"Seriously, Mom. It has different colored doors on it. Would you ride around in it?" he asked.

"Do you want to learn to drive or not? If not, I will drive it myself. You need to get over yourself. Our surname is not Rockefeller," I replied. Looking back, it probably was embarrassing for him to be seen in the car, but he swallowed his pride. We spent many hours driving around the base as he learned to become comfortable behind the wheel, but it was usually after dark so he could save face with his friends.

One Friday afternoon, Eileen stopped in the office to pick up her mail and chat with Susan. "The Chippendales are in Barrie this weekend. We should get together for a girl's night. Do you want to join us, Laurie?" Susan asked looking over at me.

"I would love to. Count me in," I replied. The thought took me back to Bosses' Nights in Edmonton and the fun we had being entertained by male strippers. My life had been somewhat stressful at home, and I missed the good old days of having fun and having friends. We made plans to meet at Susan's place for a few drinks before heading into Barrie.

The Chippendales are exotic male dancers, each with their own themed costume and choreographed dance moves. They remove everything by the end of their performance, and the women in the audience behave shamefully, but that is half the fun. The dancers definitely deliver the "tease" in the word "striptease". There is no doubt in my mind that many boyfriends and husbands have the time of their life when women return home after a night with the Chippendales. One of the strippers took a liking to Susan, recognizing her beauty and her shyness. He began gyrating his way onto her lap, and then stirred her drink with his ten-inch swizzle stick. She was not impressed that he had ruined her drink and became quite vocal before he left the table. After the show, he returned to our table with a round of drinks to replace the one he had decided to stir during his performance, and then he sat down to chat with Susan. We stayed another two hours, dancing and drinking before we called it a night. The next morning, Steve encouraged me to go out with my friends more often.

The following week, while having lunch at Bleachers, I ran into Pheme, my co-worker from NDOC in Ottawa. She was in Borden on a career course after being promoted to the rank of Sergeant. As we chatted for a few minutes and exchanged phone numbers, I learned that she was now posted to Halifax, Nova Scotia. I asked her to give me a phone call once she returned home so we could catch up on all the news. Little did I know at the time but running into her again was no coincidence.

It was November 3, a day impossible to forget, even to this day. Nothing could have prepared me for what I was about to see when I opened the back door. My heart began beating out a battle cry when I witnessed my son against the wall with one of Steve's hands around his throat and the other hand drawn back in a fist ready to strike a blow.

Spiritual Beings on a Human Experience

Laurie's intuition has sharpened, and she is beginning to feel the energy of a new skill called clairvoyance. She is in the infancy stage of receiving and attempting to interpret the energy that surrounds her. This gift is the awakening of her sixth sense and is preparing her for a spiritual journey towards becoming an energy healer. Her Creator is rewarding her faithfulness with His inheritance.

Everything living, as well as souls who have returned to the other side, are in a constant state of radiating and receiving energy. During Laurie's experience on Cleve Loop, her Spirit Guide has taught her how to dispose of unwanted negative energy by firmly planting her feet on Mother Earth and divinely protecting herself with White Light. The energy she feels from the soul who has passed is a result of him remaining earthbound. Earthbound souls can refuse to cross over for many reasons. They may be lost, unable to find the light, or they have a message they need to relay before continuing to the other side. In his state of confusion, due to suffering a traumatic death, this soul is still unaware that his physical body has died. He is surrounded by other souls eager to help him, but he must cross over in his own timing. Until then, he remains in a realm known as the Healing Heavens, often referred to in the physical dimension as "being in limbo".

Laurie's road in life will not always be straight. By her own design before arriving, she has set in motion many twists and turns throughout her lifetime. Whether it is for her protection or to experience a life lesson, all her twists and turns are serving a purpose. Being grounded by living in the present, trusting her intuition, and listening to Spirit, she is learning to adapt to life without questioning or needing a reason. She will continue to feel the emotions of her personality, while she is learning to be content and trust her spiritual process. Synchronously, she is experiencing living moments in both worlds with a greater understanding.

CHAPTER 24

CAUGHT IN THE CHASM
OF LOVE AND HATE

I froze with shock at witnessing Steve's hand around my son's throat, but like a boxer being pummeled against the ropes of a boxing ring, a killer instinct flared inside of me to protect my child at any cost. I charged between the two of them, shrieking, "Steve! Don't you dare! Let go of him right now! Son, go visit one of your friends for a few hours." As I stood in silence watching my son leave, my Spirit Guide began speaking.

This is a trying time as well as a meaningful one. Control your emotions, be clear with him, and let the winds of Heaven dance between you.

I took a deep breath and turned to face Steve. "This is the perfect time to say exactly what is on my mind and please listen without interrupting me. I have been quiet for far too long. For the first five years of our marriage, I loved you for the way that you made me feel like your equal. I loved you for the way you made me feel strong and respected in a way that I didn't even know was possible. You made me believe in you, in myself, and in our life together. I wanted forever with you. I wasn't feeling love. I had become love."

He stood quietly, as I paused, took another gulp of courage, and continued. "For the past three years, I have been struggling to figure out who you are when I am not looking. There have been times when I have questioned our entire relationship. How can you say that you love me and then hate the very part of me that is an extension of my love? Your actions with my child have wounded me so deeply, and I don't know if I can forgive you or ever trust you again. I still love you despite my anger right now, but I want you to move out. I cannot allow you to hurt my child in anger and until you figure out where your anger is coming from, the two of you need to be separated. You are the adult in this relationship. There is no excuse for your behavior no matter what he did. Maybe if we spend some time apart, it will give us both a new perspective." Steve packed a duffle bag and walked out the door without speaking a single word.

I needed time to reflect and to discover how I was truly feeling amidst the shock and the anger of the situation. Was it even possible to forgive him, and if I did, what would that mean for a future relationship? Could my love for him ever be the same again? Had the trust been destroyed to the point of no return? I was compelled to discover my personal truth in solitude and without any pressure.

It was not long before I descended into a deep pit of darkness. I loved Steve and I hated Steve. Although I tried, I could not erase eight years of history. The memories of our good times haunted me. He had played such an important role in the person I had become because of his love. At the same time, I despised his actions of hostility and aggression towards my son. What if I had not come home when I did? Would Steve have seriously hurt him? How did we get to this place? Our family had become one of intense hatred, a hatred that was about to spill over between myself and my son as well.

After Steve left, I slept in an empty bed at night and I walked alone during the day.

Accept what is and have faith in what will be.

What will be? Tell me, Helena. Will he ever be able to love my son the way he should? Can a stepparent love a child the same way a biological parent does? Joan certainly couldn't.

You are powerless to do anything but surrender and be still.

The flashbacks of my childhood were consuming in that moment. *If losing Steve means protecting my child, then I guess I am powerless.*

The following week, I decided to go home for lunch and, in the process of making myself a sandwich, Steve appeared in the doorway carrying several boxes. He had been staying with his parents, but he was now moving into a

PMQ on the north side of the base. His demeanor was sheepish as I silently watched him begin packing some of his things. Maybe he wanted me to ask him to stay. Maybe he wanted me to tell him that I still loved him, and we could work it out. Maybe he wanted me to tell him that I had acted in haste. I could not find any words for fear of his response. I wanted him to speak first, but he did not. The silence I was experiencing was paralyzing as I just sat watching my world pack up and prepare to walk out of my life.

Before walking out the door, he stopped and looked at me. His cheek was twitching and the sheepishness had turned to anger. "I hope you and your son will be happy together. It is what he has always wanted - you all to himself. For what it is worth, I hope I will find the capacity to love you again one day, but right now, I despise the both of you."

His anger is in defense to avoid facing his truth.

The reality of everything hit me like a ton a bricks after the back door closed. I was fighting back the tears, trying to stay composed so I could return to work, but the pain was unbearable as I began sobbing. Finally able to control the tears enough to speak, I phoned my boss and asked for the afternoon off to deal with a personal situation. "See you on Monday morning," she replied.

A few hours later, my son came in the door from school and went straight to the fridge without so much as a "hello".

"There is nothing in this house to eat," he said. After he had gone upstairs to his room, I sat down to make a grocery list when the telephone rang. It was TJ's father. *Can this day get any worse? I wish I had never given his mother our new address and phone number.* "I hope you will actually have a conversation with him this time," I said to Tim before calling my son to the phone.

When TJ got off the telephone with his father, he was angry. "What the hell, Mom? He says he is coming to Peterborough to visit his brother, and he wants to meet me in person. Why? I haven't heard from the guy my entire life. No birthday cards! No Christmas presents! Nothing! He probably has never paid a dime to support me. He just left and made another family without looking back. Now that I am grown up, he wants to be my father. Well, it's too late. He is a stranger to me. I could probably walk right past him on the street and not even know. I want to know why he left us. I am not a kid anymore, so tell me the truth this time." The time had come to hand him his father's cassette, the one Tim had mailed to me in 1985. His son was finally mature enough and ready to hear the truth in his father's own words.

After listening to the cassette, he returned to the kitchen angrier than ever. "This is so fucked up! My father and my grandmother! What a loser! I hate him so much right now. You know what, Mom, first you choose that asshole and then Steve. What is wrong with you? Do you know how much you have fucked up my life because of your choices in men? I hate you right now too! I can't even stay in the same house with you. I'm leaving." I desperately tried to console myself. *He does not mean that. Please, tell me that my son does not hate me. Please…* No answer.

After my son walked out, I could not see the dawn for the darkness, and I could not see the joy of life for the pain. I did not reach out to my Spirit World. I did not reach out to anyone. I was isolated in my own personal hell of feeling that I was truly unlovable. Even my own son hated me now. I was nothing more than a colossal failure as both a wife and a mother.

For the second time in my life, I was without hope as I descended into the darkness. My demons were hunting me down and taunting me to die, as the words from my childhood repeated in my mind like a worn-out recording.

You don't care who you hurt just as long as you get what you want.

You are such a heartless bitch.

You are so useless. You can't even accomplish the simplest of things.

I pity the man who marries you. You are a pathetic excuse of a person.

Are you even capable of raising a child? What were you thinking getting pregnant?

I was in a room totally alone, believing all the worst parts about myself, and there was no way out. If words spoken in anger wound the soul, then my soul felt destroyed. As a lifetime of wounds resurfaced, it took me no time at all to convince myself that everyone would be better off without me.

I walked upstairs to the bathroom and looked in the mirror, seeing nothing more than a deplorable human being looking back at me. I filled a glass with water and reached for a bottle of sleeping pills from the medicine cabinet. I did not hesitate. My only escape was to abandon my body.

The pain of who I really had become was too much to bear as I swallowed the pills by the handful.

In the midst of taking the last gulp of water, the bathroom filled with blinding White Light as my Angel appeared. I dropped to my knees and began violently vomiting into the toilet - vomiting pill, after pill, after pill.

God will always send a shepherd when you are lost, and you have lost your way. Your faith has prepared you to meet your Creator, but today is not that day. Listen to the still, small voice in your spirit telling you what your truth is. You are not what others tell you. Their opinion is of no consequence when expressed in anger or with malice.

I felt peaceful as the Light disappeared and my stomach settled down. I took a shower and went to bed at 7:00 p.m. that night, physically exhausted from crying and vomiting.

The following morning, I was back in my physical world, back in a sea of desperation. My son had not come home, and I awoke with a drowning feeling, like I was swimming against a riptide and drifting further away from any help on the shoreline. As much as I struggled to find my life-saver, everything inside of me felt empty and every emotion was intensely painful. *No one understands me, and no one ever will. I feel so lost. Maybe I am unlovable and should spend the rest of my life alone. Perhaps, that is my truth!*

You were not created to live in loneliness. There is a Divine connection waiting for every soul.

I had no desire to get out of bed until the phone rang. It was Steve wanting to come by the house and take some of our furniture to his new place. He showed up twenty minutes later with a friend. "Take whatever you want," I said. Material things in my life had always had little value, unless there was sentiment attached to them. He wanted to take the couch to sleep on and the coffee table to eat off. "I will leave the bedroom set, the dining room table and chairs, along with the television for you. I am going to take the desk and the computer too if that's okay," he said. We had purchased a 1926 executive desk at an auction in Ottawa for $200. We stripped the paint from it for months to expose the solid oak wood beneath and the intricate carvings on the doors. It had been a labor of love restoring that desk together as a family. I choked as I watched that memory leave with him. Once the truck was loaded, he came back inside and grabbed Bear's leash. "I would like to take Bear with me too. You can keep Chelsey. I will be back later today for a few kitchen things," he said. After he left, I spent the next hour packing up boxes with dishes, pots and pans, and utensils for him. When I finished, I threw myself into a cleaning spree in an attempt to keep busy and avoid the pain.

On Sunday, my son called. "Can I come home, Mom?" "Of course you can. I never asked you to leave. As long as I am your mother, the door will always be open," I replied. When he arrived home, I was putting my shoes on to take Chelsey for a walk. He apologized for his earlier behavior and gave me a hug. "The things I said the other night were really cruel, Mom. You know I love you, right?"

"I do. Why don't you come with me for a walk and we can talk?"

We talked about his father and the conclusion he had reached *not* to meet him. I told him not to make that decision based on his fear of hurting my feelings. I remembered wanting to know my mother when I was his age, and, if it was important for him to get to know his father, I was fine with it. We talked about Steve and how he had been bullying him verbally for the past year when I was out of sight. That news came as a shock to me, and I told him that Steve's behavior was about something else, and not him. I felt it in my gut. I asked him why Steve had him by the throat and his response was, "He asked me a question and didn't like the way I answered him. He called me a "cocky little bastard" and then grabbed me and slammed me up against the wall. It was hard to breathe, Mom."

As we continued to walk, I felt so much empathy for my son and the life he had been given because of adults making poor choices. I carried that guilt deep in my psyche. Although his words had been spewed in anger the night he left, he was not wrong about hating me in the moment. I knew his truth only too well from my own relationship with my father and his choice in a mate. I explained to him that I had not made choices regarding the men in my life with malintent to hurt him, or myself, for that matter.

You did then what you knew how to do.

I had done the best I could at the time, and I was terribly sorry that he got wounded in the process. As we headed back up the driveway, my final words to him were, "One day when you get older and make your own mistakes, you will remember this conversation because you will understand it for the first time. Everyone makes mistakes in life; some mistakes vaster than others."

When he walked into the living room, he was shocked to find the room empty, but he was even more disgruntled over the computer being gone. "I take it Steve was here," he scoffed.

"Don't worry, son. I will replace everything. Be patient."

Christmas was one week away and I was dreading the holidays. Steve was not speaking to me, and my son was gone with his friends every chance he got. I was struggling financially, to the point where there was little food in the house, and there was definitely no money for a Christmas tree or presents. I was reliving my life in Vancouver with Tim all over again.

My son decided to spend Christmas day with his friend Jonathan. Jonathan lived a very tumultuous home life. His father was emotionally and physically abrasive with him. I had witnessed it firsthand when Jonathan was visiting our house one day. His father showed up at my door looking for him. When I opened the door, he barged inside my house pushing me aside, while screaming for Jonathan to get his ass home. When Jonathan appeared at the top of the stairs, he physically grabbed him. In his attempt to drag his son down the stairs, Jonathan was reaching for anything to grasp in order to pull away from his father's grip. The shelving unit in my laundry room was toppled over as everything fell from the shelves, including a twenty-pound bag of flour.

His father was so angry that he did not even stop in that moment. There was no apology. There was no snapping back to reality. He was consumed with anger and did not care who or what was in his way. He pulled Jonathan out the door and slammed it behind them. Everything had happened in less than a minute, and I was still in shock as I began cleaning up the mess. When my son appeared in the doorway to help, I told him that Jonathan was always welcome in our home anytime night or day. I knew that kind of abuse only too well. If nothing more, Jonathan needed a safe haven and I was willing to provide it. "His father will never get past my door again without the Military Police being called, son."

Jonathan and my son spent Christmas Day serving dinner to the homeless. My intended meal was going to be a piece of toast with peanut butter, until my son returned with a turkey dinner for me from the shelter. The fact that he had thought about me touched me, as I hugged him and told him I would somehow make everything up to him.

My 1999 New Year resolution was to find a part-time job. Although I had a plan to try and pick up the pieces of my life, I was far from being capable of making sound decisions. I was traveling on a dark and lonely road, and my sex addiction was about to return with a vengeance.

Spiritual Beings on a Human Experience

Repressed truth becomes polluted truth if it festers inside the personality and becomes distorted. Anger is designed as a teaching moment to uncover true thoughts and feelings. If a soul stops and seeks what it believes in the moment of anger, the opportunity will expose the misaligned beliefs that manifested the anger. In his anger, Steve views his son as an obstacle to getting what he genuinely wants: love and acceptance. The misaligned belief and the truth is that his anger has been surfacing with regards to his relationship with his father and not with his son. His anger in truth is directed towards his own painful childhood.

From the Creator's perspective, children need a balance of love, discipline, and guidance. Steve's intention to parent has left TJ feeling hurt, neglected, and abused. Coupled with the abandonment by his biological father and the need to control his environment and neutralize his feelings, he has created a cauldron of anger that is covering up deep wounds. The truth of this young soul's anger are feelings of insecurity, loneliness, and disapproval by the male figures in his life.

The soul knows the path of a current incarnation. It has already walked many previous journeys, has a concrete memory of living a spiritual life on the other side, and refutes a watered-down version of life on earth known as the "Ego". Ego will sabotage any spiritual progress, but when a soul travels in union with its Creator, it is fulfilling its divine purpose as a human being, amidst all the mistakes.

Laurie is experiencing soul exhaustion as she continues to view her self-worth by the opinion of others. The rejection by her husband and her son has resulted in her subconsciously reliving a profound sense of loss, emptiness, and separation from who she truly is. Her overwhelming pain is not coming from the present alone, but also from the spirit memory of far greater losses combined. Her Angel intervenes quickly to restore Laurie's soul by making her physically sick while speaking her truth to her. Laurie has just circumvented the third exit point in her blueprint.

CHAPTER 25

GOD BLESS THE BEAST IN ME

The New Year was coming, the perfect time for new beginnings. Was I finally ready to take a risk, a leap of faith across this impossible chasm of love and hate? I had considered it, but I was still wounded and angered by Steve's silence. When Steve had moved out, he had emotionally and psychologically separated from me and all communication between us had become non-existent, but today was going to be anything but a day of his silence.

It was the last day of December when I came home from grocery shopping to find Steve's key to the house sitting on the kitchen counter, along with a note. It was obvious he had made his own New Year's resolution as I began reading the note:

> "Laurie, it has been almost two months since you asked
> me to leave, and I don't see you trying to make our
> marriage work. If anything, you have done nothing
> but ignore me. Obviously, you and your son are happy
> without me, so I am leaving the house key and getting on
> with my life. I suggest you do the same. Steve."

I don't know if I was tired of crying over him or if I just had no more tears left to cry. I stood in shock as I interpreted his note as the end of our marriage. Maybe I was misguided in my thinking, but I did not feel it was up to me to make the first move to fix things. A conversation needed to begin with him, and it had to come from his heart. I was not the one choking a child. *Am I wrong, Helena? He has not apologized or made any attempt to make things better. Am I supposed to be the one to take the first step? I am not even sure I want to. I don't know this man anymore. He is angry and cruel every time I see him. Our time apart has not accomplished anything except to make him angrier. Does he even understand what he has done to my heart by putting his hands on my son?*

Until he seeks his truth, the anger will not subside.

I unpacked the groceries and then left the house to pick up a newspaper at the corner store. When I returned, I made myself a coffee and began thumbing through the Want Ads, with one in particular piquing my interest. "Are you looking for a career in catering? If interested, call and ask for Angie." I loved to cook so I dialed the telephone number. The woman on the other end of the phone was pleasant and invited me to her residence in Barrie for an interview in person. I was impressed when I pulled up in front of her home in a high-end neighborhood, but nothing could have prepared me for what I was about to walk into.

Angie was a heavy-set woman with a friendly demeanor, who reminded me of my Bubba (grandmother) right away. She invited me inside. As I stood in the doorway, she began physically sizing me up and down, which I found to be more than a little intimidating. Then she spoke. "You are extremely attractive with that long dark hair and your body. My customers would love you." *Huh? How does what I look like have anything to do with this job?* I learned quickly that Angie was a Madam and her "catering business" was catering to men's fantasies. She operated her business seven days a week, from 7:00 a.m. until 10:00 p.m. and her clientele were wealthy professionals. She must have been reading the shock and hesitation on my face as she spoke, so she quickly changed the conversation to money by telling me that her girls were earning $4,000 to $6,000 a week. I definitely needed the money, but I was still indecisive, as she invited me to take a tour of the home. When I followed her into one of the bedrooms, her bouncer, Scott, followed us as well. Without warning or a single word being spoken, he took off his clothing and climbed onto the massage table. "I want you to give Scott an erotic massage and finish the massage with a hand job." *Hmmm…he has quite the perks in his job if I say so myself.* I cannot tell you why I did not leave right in that moment. Perhaps, it was because I had fallen down the rabbit hole again. Or maybe, it was just a little too late to do the right thing now. I had already come this far.

When we returned to the kitchen, she poured me a cup of coffee, and we sat down to talk. "I take good care of my girls. I will provide you with your own cell phone, condoms, and I will buy you lingerie that is personal and yours to keep. While you are at work, the fridge is always stocked with food and beverages to which you are welcome to help yourself at any time. I do not tolerate alcohol, drugs, or any of my girls seeing clients on the side. If I find out, I will fire you. I pay my girls in cash every Friday, and I will look after any medical bills related to the job while you are working for me." Before leaving Angie's house that day, I agreed to work part-time for her, two evenings a week. I convinced myself that I would only do it long enough to land on my feet financially, but deep down, I knew differently. Steve's rejection and choice to end our marriage was fueling a fire inside of me. Maybe the fire inside can burn you alive if you don't give in to it. Whatever the true reason was, I did not hesitate to plunge right back into my addiction without a second thought of the repercussions. I was in survival mode.

When I arrived at Angie's the following night, I was totally booked for the evening. I was the new dish on the menu, and it took me less than a month to establish a regular clientele of my own. Men began asking for me personally and waiting for my shifts, instead of seeing another girl who was available. I was easily making $3000 a week, and I was out of debt. I had replaced the living room furniture, paid for with cash, and I had another $7,000 stashed away at home. You think I would have stopped at this point, but I could not. I had managed to take control of my life again, and I was nowhere near ready to relinquish that power. But I was about to find out soon enough that control was the last thing I had.

My son was none the wiser as to what I was doing, besides working a part-time job. He had a busy life, a life other than just staying at home. He was playing basketball at the gym and had become friends with a gym attendant named Steve. He was hanging out at the youth center with Jonathan or drinking in the woods with Brandon. I warned him what would happen if he got caught, but he failed to heed my warning. Truth be told, he was delighted with his new freedom. He had his first girlfriend, and he was enjoying the lack of parental supervision at home. Basically, the two of us had become ships passing in the night. I knew what he was up to, so I began leaving condoms in his nightstand, along with pamphlets on sexually transmitted diseases.

Three months had gone by. I had been juggling a double life successfully and concealing it from everyone. I was a soldier by day and an escort by night. I was shameless because I had stopped listening to the small voice inside me, and I was no longer talking to Spirit. I was actively living in the physical realm on my own terms, but my world was about to begin spiraling out of control.

It was a Thursday night when I arrived at Angie's, only to be told that one of my clients had hired me for my entire shift. "Scott will drive you to his residence. When you arrive, the client will hand you an envelope. Bring that envelope back out to the car to Scott, and then he will return to pick you up at 10:00 p.m. Enjoy your evening." I was nervous on the drive over to the client's house. It was one thing to have a bouncer on the other side of a door at Angie's and another to be walking blindly into a private home, alone. The potential for many things to go wrong was nagging at me, and for the first time, my behavior was speaking to me from a place of warning.

We pulled up in front of a magnificent stone mansion, surrounded by fountains, a pool, a basketball court, and acres of land without a neighbor in sight. After Scott pulled out of the driveway, the client took me into a gourmet kitchen that had a walkout to a large balcony overlooking a stunning view of the property. The smell of the food being prepared was teasing my taste buds as we passed through the kitchen. After enjoying the view from the balcony, we walked back inside. He pulled a chair away from the kitchen island and invited me to have a seat. He opened a bottle of champagne, poured two glasses, and then attempted to get to know me through conversation as he continued cooking. I was guarded about disclosing any personal information. He did not even know my real name. He knew me as "Onyx". All of Angie's girls had fictitious names after gemstones. The first day I met her, she handed me an onyx stone on a chain and told me to always wear it when I was working. "Ancient Indian cultures refer to this stone as a protector from evil," she said.

This client's pastime was cooking and, over the years, he had become a gourmet chef. The meal was savory, with interesting flavors I had never experienced before, and the plate presentation piqued my curiosity to, at the very least, try a taste. After dinner, he suggested we take the bottle of champagne to his indoor, king-sized hot tub - a tub surrounded by tropical plants with a perfect view of the sky above. I could smell the sweet scent of honeysuckle in bloom as I stepped into the tub. After an hour of soaking in a hydromassage bath and playfully exploring each other's bodies, he suggested we take the rest of the evening to his bedroom.

Scott was waiting for me in the driveway as I slipped my pumps onto my feet. The client thanked me for the evening, suggesting he would like to entertain me again in the future. Then he handed me an envelope saying, "This is a little something just for you. Thank you for such a charismatic evening." The envelope contained a $500 tip.

The next day at work, Susan asked me if I wanted to go to the "55 Special" for a few drinks that evening. I was game for a night of fun. When we walked in, the décor was similar to the "Cheers" sitcom set, with a large bar in the middle of the room, surrounded by booths along the walls. The waitresses were wearing billowy poodle skirts with bobby socks and saddle shoes. The front end of a 1955 Chevy car hanging on the wall over the dance floor added even more character, but it was the atmosphere in general that caught my attention. The place was high energy, the people were friendly, and the DJ impressed me with his talent for mixing music together. Susan and I grabbed a table beside the dance floor. This night was going to prove to be anything but dull or boring.

After a few drinks, a tall handsome man walked over to the table and asked Susan to dance. I continued to sip my drink while looking around the room. From where I was sitting, I could see the end of the bar with several patrons perched on stools. One patron in particular caught my attention immediately. I would recognize that mustache anywhere. It was Dave, my Airborne "Doc" from my Edmonton days. We both happened to be sweeping the room when our eyes connected for a split second and then we turned away. The double take was one of astonishment as our eyes locked, and we smiled at each other. Dave picked up his drink from the top of the bar and walked over to the table. "Laurie! Laurie! Laurie! You are a sight for sore eyes. Stand up, sexy lady, and give me a hug." He joined us at our table, along with Susan's new dance partner. The four of us had several more drinks before the DJ switched the music to the song "I Don't Want to Miss a Thing" by Aerosmith. Dave reached for my hand and led me to the dance floor.

All the walls I had put up to protect my heart from Steve and the double life I was leading came tumbling down with the touch of his hand. I wanted to spend the rest of the night lost in this sweet surrender. The real Laurie had come back to life. Through conversation, I learned that Dave was in Borden on his physician assistant course and staying in the transient barracks one block over from my house. Before Susan and I left the bar that night, Dave asked me for my phone number. "I would love to take you out for a bite to eat so we can catch up some more, but in a quieter atmosphere. How does tomorrow night sound, around seven o'clock or so?" It was a date.

When I awoke Saturday morning, I decided to drive into Barrie to look for a new car. The old jalopy I had bought to teach my son to drive was on its last legs and not worth putting any money into. Steve had taken the truck when he left, and the time had come to purchase some reliable transportation for myself. When I drove onto the car lot, I was following a 1997 Mercury Cougar. I parked my car and walked over to the showroom. When the salesman approached, I asked him what the story was with the forest-green-colored Cougar parked out front. He told me that an elderly gentleman was trading it in for a new car. "I really like that car. Can we talk numbers?" I asked. He returned saying that the car needed to have a mechanic go over it, and it needed to be cleaned. The price tag was $9,000, and it would take a few days before I could pick it up. My trade-in had no value, but they were willing to take it off my hands. Four days later, I returned to Barrie to pick up my new wheels, paying cash with a money order before driving it off the lot.

At 7:00 p.m. Saturday night, I picked up Dave from the barracks. The weather was threatening to rain so we decided to stay on the base and go to Bleachers Sports Bar for something to eat. I was excited as we settled into a booth, ordered drinks, and began catching up on the past ten years. Dave asked me why I had disappeared without saying a word to him. "When your wife asked me not to call anymore, I was respecting your decision to work on your marriage without any interference from me. Believe me, it was not easy. I was so hurt that you did not call to tell me yourself," I replied.

"Well, this is interesting news to me because it is bullshit. Obviously, my wife felt threatened by our relationship. When I returned home from an exercise in the field, I tried calling you right away, but your phone number had been disconnected. I was angry with you for a long time for not having the decency to say goodbye. As time went on, I tried to forget you, but your memory kept popping up at the weirdest times. When it did, I would fantasize about meeting up with you again one day, and here we are. It is so good to see you again," he replied. He noticed I was wearing my wedding ring and asked me if I was married.

"Separated right now," I replied. I learned that he was still with his wife, and they had an eight-year-old daughter. We continued our conversation through dinner, discussing mutual friends and where their lives had taken them.

After dinner, we ordered an iced Kahlua and coffee. The waitress had just brought our drinks when Steve approached the table. His cheek was twitching. He had walked into the restaurant with a few co-workers to have a beer when he noticed Dave and I sitting together. The first words out of his mouth were hostile and directed at Dave. "You really seem to be enjoying spending time with MY wife."

"Everyone needs to eat," Dave replied. Intimidating an Airborne soldier is next to impossible.

I stood up to direct Steve's attention towards me. "Steve, please don't do this. You are embarrassing yourself." His eyes were filled with hatred as he turned his stare towards me. "You know, Steve, I am going to do my absolute best right now to forget the way that you are looking at me. You need to go join your friends," I said.

Steve agreed to leave, but not before expressing one final thought. "She is crazy, you know. Good luck trying to figure her out!"

I was embarrassed and hurt but wearing a smile as Dave reached for my hand across the table. He began speaking. "You are always smiling, Laurie, but I can see the sorrow in your eyes. I know you too well. Talk to me. What is going on between the two of you?" he asked.

"This is not the time nor the place, Dave. Suffice it to say, Steve is more than a little angry right now, and he is choosing to express that anger every chance he gets. I apologize for his intrusion." Dave wanted to take a night off from studying and was not ready to return to the barracks, so he suggested we pick up a movie and go back to my place. I welcomed the thought. I was not ready for the night to end either. My heart needed his company.

We decided against picking up a movie on the way home, opting instead to have a few drinks and talk. As we walked into the house and were taking off our shoes, I lost my balance and fell against the shoe rack. Dave grabbed my arm to break my fall, pulling me back to a standing position. We were face to face. "I have been tasting your lips ever since I first laid eyes on you in the bar last night. Can I kiss you?" he asked.

"If you must," I replied with a giggle. I did not hesitate. I wanted to feel loved in that moment. The kiss was so passionate. Not wanting things to get out of control, I turned away from him, but my heart was beating wildly. *I need a distraction.* I cracked open a bottle of Jack Daniels and poured a few shots into two glasses filled with ice. We laughed, told a few jokes, and reminisced about the past for several hours. I was out of practice from my old days of drinking with the boys and by midnight, I was seeing three of him sitting across the table from me, even when I closed one eye. Trying to get up the stairs to the washroom was an impossible challenge as I took one step forward and two steps backwards. I had only accomplished three stairs when I collapsed on the first landing in a fit of laughter. Dave showed up at the bottom of the stairs and picked me up in his arms, carrying me up the flight of stairs. "I think you're done for tonight, you character. It's time to put you to bed."

"Not before I pee," I replied.

Dave was waiting for me outside the bathroom door and walked me to the bedroom. I fell backwards onto the end of the bed and began laughing.

Dave   What are you laughing at?

Me   I don't know. (more giggles) I think I'm drunk.

Dave   I never would have guessed. Let's get you under the covers.

Me?   I need my bra off. I hate bras. I think a man designed them so we would hate them and take them off. Sneaky little bastards! Pygmies have the right idea. Wanna come and run around the jungle with me

Dave   Maybe tomorrow. Right now, you need to go to bed before I lose control seeing you half naked.

Me   Please, don't go. I don't wanna be alone.

No sooner had I felt his arms around me when I passed out. I woke several hours later to a soft caress of fingertips tracing the outline of my body. When I rolled over, Dave was leaning on his elbow, and his eyes were misty as he continued touching me. "You are not the crazy one. Your husband is. You are every man's dream, Laurie. Compassionate, fun, loving, and sexy as hell." His energy was speaking to me from a place of divine love as I let it consume me. I had been trying to save what I had left of Steve, but Dave broke Steve's memory that night. He did everything just a little too right. When Dave left that morning, my smile turned to tears as I closed the door. I was more confused than ever.

The next day, I received a dozen red roses from Dave with a card attached that read, "Thank you for making me feel alive again. Love, Dave." *Ditto, Dave.* He called me a few days later to say goodbye and to let me know that he was being posted to Halifax. "Let's stay in touch this time. I will call you again once I get settled. Take care, sexy lady."

Shortly after the flowers arrived, Steve called and asked me to meet him at Dairy Queen in the town of Alliston, fifteen minutes south of the base. My double life was about to hit me right between the eyes, with a hard dose of reality.

Spiritual Beings on a Human Experience

Laurie has returned to her addiction, consumed with the need to control her life and ease her pain. Problems that seem too big or obstacles that seem permanent are a test for a soul to enter into rest. When a soul rests, the soul is in faith to allow the Creator's timing and restoration. Resisting the addiction will result in her resurrection.

God uses adversity and disappointment to move a soul towards its destiny. He uses rejection, betrayals, and delays in order to position a soul for a greater blessing. Laurie views the return of Dave into her life as adversity, causing confusion after their encounter. If this adversity were going to stop her destiny, her Creator would never have allowed it to happen. The Creator uses people to help a soul move towards its destiny. He is taking Laurie into her destiny through her reconnection with Dave.

CHAPTER 26

MY CREATOR'S TIMING AND RESTORATION

I was in a quandary at Steve's request to meet with him. Why did he want to see me? He was vague on the phone, only saying it was important that we meet and talk and doing it over the phone was not appropriate. *Does he want a legal separation or a divorce? Does he know I spent the night with Dave? Does he know about my part-time job?* As I made the drive to Alliston, my mind was racing with scenarios and how to appropriately handle them.

Your power is in the present situation, not in past behavior. Speak the truth.

Steve bought us each an ice-cream sundae and then suggested we sit outside at the picnic table to have a private conversation. This time, his demeanor was different from our former encounters. He seemed heavy hearted and troubled. When I sat down, he started the conversation by asking me who the guy was that he had seen me with at Bleachers. There was a vulnerability in his eyes, and my gut instinct was telling me not to hurt him, so I answered as casually as possible, without lying. "Just an old friend from Edmonton," I replied. *Please don't ask me if we were lovers.* He apologized for his behavior that night and then said, "You have no idea what it did to me to see you with him. Something snapped inside of me, and it made me realize just how much I love you." I remained quiet, letting him control the conversation at his own pace. He took a few bites of his sundae and then changed the subject.

"Where have you been working in Barrie?" was his next question. When I looked into his eyes, it was obvious that he already knew the truth. I hung my head in shame and took my Spirit Guide's advice, admitting to working as an escort for Angie. When I looked up, he continued to speak, "I don't know if I told you, but I have been working in the SIU Section (Special Investigation Unit) since January. Imagine my embarrassment when one of my co-workers took me aside yesterday and told me what you were doing. Barrie's Special Task Force has had her house under surveillance for several months. They have been taking pictures of cars parked there, and when they ran your license plate, they notified our unit. I could lose my job for telling you this, but a major sting operation is about to go down. I am helpless to protect you from the fallout of any of this, but I thought that you should know. If you are caught working when the bust goes down, you will be going to jail. I don't know what is going on with you right now, but because I still love you, I want to save you the shame and embarrassment of losing your career. Please take my advice and don't go back there again. This is really serious, Laurie."

I recognized the hurt in his eyes as he delivered the news, and I was remorseful knowing I was the cause of his pain. Me! His wife! I felt the warm tears slowly rolling down my cheeks, as I apologized to him and promised to heed his warning.

"Do you still love me?" he asked.

"Yes," I replied.

"Then what are we doing to each other? Our lives are out of control. It seems to me that we are both bound and determined to destroy each other. That is the last thing that I want. I miss you, and I really want to fix us." In that very moment, I felt the truth in his words. I was sure that it had not been easy to hear about my actions. Fewer men would not forgive such behavior, yet he was still willing to tell me what he knew and try to put our marriage back together. Had we finally arrived at a place where the anger and hurt were being replaced with compassion and love? As he hugged me goodbye that day, he asked me if we could start over again. "Maybe we could start with a date. I would like to take you to the movies on Friday night."

On the drive home, I felt my depression, loss, and grief of the past six months rear its ugly head. Is it possible that we can hide such feelings for months without any physical symptoms, but given enough time the feelings will eventually re-appear? Does our body hold our secrets until it just can't anymore and, once your secret is out, can you ever explain it away?

No mistake you have ever made is bigger than God's power to fix it.

I spent the night lost in thought. Steve had destroyed me with his behavior towards TJ, but I had destroyed him with my behavior with other men. Was it even possible to recover from such drastic actions on both our parts and return to a loving relationship again? Can a relationship survive once trust has been broken? He seemed zeroed in on fixing "us", but he had not said one word about his relationship with TJ. If his relationship with my son was not a priority for him, then the decision to fix "us" would be a deal breaker for me. I decided to stop bombarding myself with so many questions. It was futile. Time would tell.

I phoned Angie that night and was happy when she did not pick up her phone. I left her a message saying that I would not be returning to work. After the call, I immediately shut off my cell phone, placed it in a dresser drawer, and went to bed. I thanked Spirit that night for Steve telling me what was going on in order to protect me. He had been my saving grace in snapping me back to reality and realizing that I had lost control of who I truly was. I was also thankful for the fact that he still loved me, despite everything. For the first time in what seemed like forever, I felt hope return for a better tomorrow.

When I went to work the following morning, I was summoned to the School CWO's office. I was praying during the entire walk to his office that this meeting was not about my illegal activity. I was relieved when the following conversation ensued, "I have a request from Ottawa to immediately fill a MCpl billet in Halifax, and because I was not able to employ you as an instructor, I am coming to you first with the option to fill the position."

Destiny is in the palm of your hand.

My eyes fought back the tears, tears of joy, as the opportunity presented itself to leave the past behind and start fresh. "Before you give me your answer, I have spoken to your husband's Career Manager. You will be going to Halifax unaccompanied. He will attempt to co-locate you when he has a position available in Halifax to employ your husband. I will give you the evening to speak with your husband. I need your decision first thing tomorrow morning. The position requires you to be on the ground in Halifax and ready to work by July 15. That leaves you less than a month."

When I walked back to my desk, I was filled with relief, as well as apprehension. Was I really meant to move to Halifax? Leaving my illegal activity behind was enticing, for sure. A new start was also a welcoming thought. Running away and starting over had always been my way of coping when life was a mess, so I had no fear of the impending move. I had a girlfriend (Pheme) in the area, so I took comfort in knowing that I would not feel so alone once I arrived in Halifax, but the apprehension was still lingering. Maybe it was about having to make a move so quickly and having so little time to reflect on this decision and the effect it would have on my family. It was clear to me that my Spirit Guide was pushing me in that direction, pushing me towards a destiny in Halifax. Within less than two years, I would come to realize exactly "why" I was meant to be where I was. The Universe had opened this door for one very specific reason.

When I arrived home from work that night, my son was there. I told him that I was being posted to Halifax. Although the final decision had not been made yet, I wanted to see his reaction. He was not happy. "Mom, I don't want to move again. I have all my friends here. I'm not starting over again at another high school, and I'm not going with you." Initially, I was shocked. The thought of him not wanting to come with me had not entered my mind, but the more I thought about it, I could see his point. He had spent his whole life moving and starting over because of my career. He was sixteen years old, and the timing could not have been worse for him.

Stay true to your heart's desire.

I wanted a fresh start. I needed a fresh start. A feeling deep inside of me was telling me that I needed to find my own way in life, alone and without influence from anyone else. I had spent my entire life catering to the wants and needs of others in order to be accepted and loved. Perhaps the time had come to do what I needed to do for me. I told my son that if he wanted to stay behind, he needed to find a place to live right away and that we would discuss the details together once he had a plan. I was not about to selfishly abandon him to go off and do my own thing, without knowing he was safe and happy. He was my son and his welfare was just as important as my own.

After TJ left to meet up with his friends, I phoned Steve, asking him to stop by the house. His response to the news of the posting was one of shock as well. After a lengthy discussion, he felt the move was in my best interest given all that had transpired, so we agreed to spend the time apart. It would give us both the chance to figure out whether we wanted to stay married. The following morning, I accepted the posting to Halifax.

After my house-hunting trip was booked, I phoned my girlfriend, Pheme, to give her the news. The reality of the move had finally set in and was wreaking havoc on my nerves. I needed to hear a friendly voice. Being familiar with the area, Pheme offered to book my hotel and spend a few days helping me find a place to live. Knowing my crazy Newfie friend was along for the ride was calming, and I was looking forward to the trip as I hung up the telephone.

I arrived at the hotel Sunday night and called Pheme to let her know I was in town. The hotel she booked for me was beautiful, with several comfortable lounge chairs and tables set up in the lobby. We decided to meet in the lobby the following morning, and she would bring Tim Horton's coffee. A girl after my heart! My first night was restless and by 7:30 a.m., I had showered and was sitting in the lobby with a newspaper, looking for potential places to rent. When Pheme arrived at 9:00 a.m., her flamboyant personality lifted my spirits immediately. It was so good to see her again. I was surrounded by a reassuring energy that life was going to be okay.

I decided to begin looking for my new home on the Dartmouth side of the harbor. The rents were cheaper than in Halifax, and Dartmouth was the area where Pheme currently lived. After two days of searching and viewing several apartment buildings, I was totally discouraged. The rent for a two-bedroom apartment was close to $800 a month, and the buildings were old, run-down, and noisy. On Wednesday morning, I picked up another newspaper, hoping for some new prospects when an advertisement caught my eye. "Are you tired of renting? We can put you in a brand-new home for $650 a month." I called the real estate office and set up an appointment to meet with one of their agents that morning. The agent met me at the hotel, and we drove to Cole Harbor to a new subdivision with approximately twelve houses that had already been built. Walking through the show home, I was impressed and could picture myself living there, but there was a problem. I did not have time to wait for a house to be built. The realtor made a few phone calls and the developer was willing to sell me the show home given my time constraint. That day, I became the proud owner of a new home and a start to a new life.

Pheme met me after work on Wednesday in the lobby of the hotel. We were enjoying a cocktail and deciding where we wanted to have dinner together to celebrate, when the front doors to the hotel slid open and Dave walked in, with his wife and his daughter. He was in Halifax on his house-hunting trip, staying at the same hotel. When he saw me sitting in the lobby, he did a double take and then immediately walked over to where we were sitting, as his wife and daughter continued making their way to the elevators. He invited me to join him and his family for dinner the following night. He wasn't taking 'no' for an answer as he promised to call my room with the details. After he walked away, I told Pheme about our history together. Her response was, "Go figure. What are the odds? This could only happen to you, Laurie. You have to go to dinner with him, and I want to hear all about it."

Thursday was a busy day of details - finding a lawyer, securing a mortgage and house insurance, activating my cell phone again, and setting up accounts for my utilities. When I returned to my room, there was a message waiting for me to join Dave and his family at East Side Mario's for dinner at 6:30 p.m. The message was left by his wife. I was trembling as I hung up the phone. When I phoned Pheme to tell her about the message, she started laughing. "You have to go now, especially since his wife invited you. Maybe she wants to check out her competition in person. Whatever the reason, you need to eat, so why not. I am curious as hell. Phone me as soon as you get back to the room."

As I showered and got ready for dinner, my mind was racing as usual. This was no coincidence. What were the chances that we would both be in Halifax at the same time, in the same hotel, and run into each other? We had not spoken since he left Borden. This was kismet. *I have no idea what is going on right now, Helena, but I am trusting that this dinner is the*

Universe at work. Please give me the grace and the strength to attend this dinner and see it for what it is through the eyes of my Creator.

A true partnership will be revealed.

When I arrived at the restaurant, the hostess walked me over to a table. Dave stood up, hugged me, and then motioned for me to take a seat, as he slid into the booth beside me. I was sitting face to face with Dave's wife and his daughter. "Hi Laurie, I am Claudia and this is our daughter, Amanda. I am glad you decided to join us tonight. I finally get the chance to meet you in person, although I feel I already know you. Dave always speaks so highly of you." *Okay Helena! This is too bizarre!*

Embrace a learning moment.

His daughter was delightful and quite the conversationalist. I learned that his wife was a social worker by profession. They both put me at ease right away. As we all interacted throughout the meal, I realized that Helena had been right. Dave had a true partnership with his wife in raising their daughter. Even though they both stepped outside of their marriage, when they were together, they were a loving family in every sense of the word, with a focus on their daughter. There was a mutual respect between them that was very evident. When I left the restaurant that night, I was happy that I had decided to join them. After meeting Dave's family, I made the decision not to see him again. I knew that I would never be content being his mistress, and he would never be content to leave his family. Even though he had reappeared in my life again, it was one promise too late. I was still married to a man who had promised to love me forever, and we deserved a second chance to see if that promise was possible.

Little did I know at the time, but my relationship with Dave was far from over. Timing is everything in life, and the Universe had a different plan that was about to play out sooner, rather than later. On my flight back to Toronto, I felt comfortable in my decision to move to Halifax. Everything seemed to be falling into place effortlessly. Now I had two weeks left to face my reality in Borden. It was not going to be easy leaving my son and my husband behind, and I was dreading that very thought.

Steve was waiting for me at the Toronto Airport when my flight arrived. During the hour-long drive back to Borden, he wanted to know how the week had gone. I told him that I had bought a house. "You bought a house?

Wow! You really are moving on without me," he said with such sadness in his voice.

"It was a sensible financial decision. Nothing more. I am not moving on, just taking a detour. I think this move is going to be good for me, Steve. I need to discover who I am. I have spent all of my life afraid to be alone, afraid that I could not survive without someone else to lean on or to love me. I am almost forty years old, and I have no idea who I truly am as a person by myself. Maybe I will crash and burn with loneliness, but I need to try. This move is not easy for me either, but I want you to know that you can call me or visit whenever you want."

"I will hold you to that," he said. We still had so many hurdles ahead of us in order to put our relationship back together, my son being one of them, but we were finally in a place to let the healing begin and attempt to move forward. As I exited the truck and thanked him for picking me up at the airport, he asked me, once again, to go to the movies on Friday night since we had missed out on the opportunity because of my house-hunting trip.

My son was home when Steve dropped me off, and I was impressed when I walked through the door. He had been home alone for the week, so I was a little apprehensive as to what I would be walking into. The house was impeccable, and he was excited to see me again and tell me all about his week. After a hug, we sat down to talk. He had spoken to Brandon's mother, and she was willing to take him in so he could stay in Borden and finish high school. Brandon and TJ were best friends so they were together most of the time anyway. When I met with Brandon's mother, I agreed to give her $200 a month towards groceries, writing her postdated cheques, and then thanked her whole heartedly for accepting him into her home. "Those two are inseparable. It's not a problem," she replied.

My son had also found a job working for AMJ Campbell, a local moving company, as a "swamper". When moving vans arrived on the base to load or off-load furniture, drivers would hire swampers to help them. Due to the sheer size, strength, and work ethic of my son, he became popular with the drivers very quickly. He had found full-time summer employment, and I was proud of him. He had made a plan that was feasible and was working towards his independence. As I walked away from our conversation, it was with a heavy heart. For the first time in my life, I was letting him find his way in life on his own terms. His strength and resolve was impressive. Steve's opinion of him becoming a loser could not have been further from the truth.

When Steve picked me up for our date on Friday night, I was not in the mood to go to the movies. I had one week left before moving, so I suggested we go for something to eat and talk instead. We drove into Barrie, stopping to have dinner at the Crock and Block Restaurant. The air was melancholy as we both picked at our food. We had lost our appetite when faced with the reality that this was probably one of our last meetings before I would be thousands of miles away. In my heart, I could not leave before having a conversation about TJ, and since Steve did not seem to be approaching the subject on his own, I felt it was time that I brought it up. After I explained the plans that TJ had made, I said to Steve, "I am proud of his decision to stay and finish high school. His plan is solid, but he is still so young and has never been on his own before. If our relationship is important to you, then now is the time to prove it. I need you to have his back. I need you to be the father that will be there for him if he needs you, no matter what." Steve's reaction was far from reassuring as he agreed to my request, but his twitching cheek was speaking volumes over his words.

It was Thursday morning. My moving day had arrived. As the Allied Van Lines truck pulled up in front of the PMQ, I was jittery with nerves. The driver knocked on the door, paperwork in hand. "Hi Laurie, my name is Tom. I see from your paperwork that you are on your way to Halifax. Do you mind if I take a walk through the house to get an idea how to load the truck?"

"By all means, go ahead," I said. Tom was not your typical mover. He was tall, slender, and young with long, dark, feathered hair underneath a ball cap. Our personalities clicked immediately, and I quickly began to relax. Tom and his two swampers had the truck loaded within six hours. "When do you think you will be in Halifax?" I asked as I signed the final paperwork.

Tom replied, "I have ten days for delivery, and I won't know for sure until I talk to my dispatcher. He may reroute me for a smaller load to fill the truck before I reach Nova Scotia. I know that it is not common practice for drivers to speak to the clients directly, but if you have a cell phone number, I will call you with an exact delivery date in a few days." The protocol for a military move is for the service member to check in with R&D (Receipt and Dispatch) at the new location on arrival. The moving company speaks directly to R&D as well, and the timings for delivery are arranged through this third party. Tom and I exchanged cell phone numbers, and he was on his way. As I stood looking around the empty PMQ, tears filled my eyes. A chapter in my life was coming to an end, and I was embarking on a new one, totally alone. I was leaving Borden on a wing and a prayer to the unknown.

That evening, TJ and his friends met me at my hotel room in Barrie. We ordered takeout from Boston Pizza and sat around for a few hours talking and laughing. As I watched them interact, I realized that my son had chosen his friends well. When it was time for them to leave, my son and I had one final hug - a hug that I wanted to freeze in my mind forever. Letting go was more painful than I had anticipated. I slipped some money into his jacket pocket during that hug and then said to him, "You have my cell phone number. Call me anytime that you need anything. I love you and I will always be there for you, son. When I get settled in Halifax, I am going to call an airline and book a ticket for you to come and visit me at Christmas. Study hard and make me proud," I said, choking through the emotion as I tried to stay composed. After I closed the hotel room door, I burst into tears. *Please take this pain away. My heart is breaking leaving him behind.*

Before leaving town the following morning, I met up with Steve at Tim Hortons for one final goodbye. He looked so handsome in his suit and tie as he walked over to join me at the table with his coffee. Saying goodbye was not easy for either one of us. We both became emotional, so I quickly changed the subject by giving him my cell phone number and my plans for the drive. I made him promise not to call me while I was driving. I knew that hearing his voice would make me cry. "I will call you once I arrive in Halifax," I said.

After a hug and kiss goodbye, he reached into his suit jacket and pulled out a sealed envelope. "Read this when you get to Halifax. When you are ready to talk, call me. I love you, Laurie. I always have and I always will. You are my whole world. This letter will explain everything that I have not been able to say. Stay safe on the road." As I began walking to my car, he called me back. "I almost forgot. I made you a cassette of music to listen to while you are driving. These are songs that remind me of you and our life together." He kissed me one last time and walked away. As I settled into the driver's seat, I began to cry. *What have I done, Helena? I am walking away from my son and my husband, and I feel so worthless right now. I am nothing without them.*

Your value as a soul is not based on any relationship. Find your faith and travel this road with your Creator.

Spiritual Beings on a Human Experience

Laurie returned to grieving the losses in her life by choosing her addiction over discovering her value without other souls. In the physical realm, the greater the loss a soul experiences, the greater the addiction can become. Compounded losses throughout her life have resulted in escalating her addiction to a new level. Every soul has a choice when at a crossroad. It is a place of decision, spiritually designed with both opportunity and danger. Repetition of unhealthy behaviors will continually manifest at a crossroad until a soul learns the lesson being presented.

The still, small voice of the Holy Spirit is always present, communicating the need for true healing, self-realization, and spiritual awakening, but Laurie has stopped listening to Spirit after her marriage falls apart. Her Angel and her Spirit Guide continue to work behind the scenes to heighten her awareness that the path she has chosen is a result of unhealthy reasoning. In her Creator's perfect timing, Dave returns to her life, an authentic love from a previous lifetime, with the purpose to restore her soul. Once love is authentic, it is authentic for eternity.

The Creator chooses to speak to Steve's heart when he is confronted with Laurie's addiction. The result is Steve's decision to unselfishly approach her with a clarity of purpose (warn her of impending consequences) and unconditional love (non-judgment of her behavior). Another fundamental conscious awakening (shift of perception) takes place when she is offered a posting to Halifax. This new path is designed to give her the courage to overcome fear and self-doubt of being alone and to seek self-love.

CHAPTER 27

ALL ABOUT REDEMPTION

Have you ever made a mistake? Have you ever hurt someone that you love? Have you ever sabotaged your own happiness because easy and happy are so unfamiliar to you? I loved Steve, and I was the one who had asked him to leave, instead of working through our problems together. Had being happy with him become so foreign to me in Borden that I made the choice not to try and hold onto it anymore?

With Steve's final words of his undying love replaying over and over again in my mind, leaving him was unbearable as I drove away. I did not know how to stay and love him, nor did I know how to leave him.

Recognize where your true nourishment lies.

Father, please comfort me. Help me to be everything that You want me to be. I am so sorry for all of my poor choices. I have made such a mess of my life, yet again. Please, please forgive me. I need Your strength to leave my family. I feel so alone right now.

I am always with you, My child. Remember that I am your strength in your darkest hours.

After my Creator's presence, a wave of calm and confidence immediately returned as I began my drive.

When planning my trip, I had made the decision to drive as far as Windsor, Quebec and stop for the night at Linda's place (my girlfriend from Edmonton). We had not seen each other since her visit to Ginger's house in Laval, Quebec. I called her before I began driving to let her know

I was on my way. We were both looking forward to seeing each other again, and the thought of not having to spend my first night alone was a relief.

I had an eight-hour drive ahead of me before stopping for the night, so once I was on the other side of the traffic in Toronto, I decided to play Steve's cassette. I always loved listening to music, especially when I was driving. Something was telling me it was a good time to put my past into perspective and what better way than to begin with the cassette. It would give me a chance to reminisce about the good times in order to balance out the bad. The first song he recorded was by Patty Loveless called "When Fallen Angels Fly". I began singing.

> "On my journey through the darkness, I have finally
> seen the light… God will save his fallen angels and their
> broken wings he'll mend. When he draws their hearts
> together and they learn to love again."

When the song ended, I popped the cassette out and began talking to Steve in my mind. I thanked him for not judging me when he heard the news of my behavior; news that no husband should ever have to hear, let alone try to come to terms with. His grace was the last thing that I expected from him. I had been waiting for the anger to fly after I confessed, but instead, I felt forgiven.

I was realizing in my moment of reflection, that Steve had made a conscious choice that day to try and protect me - a choice filled with love and mercy, instead of anger and judgment. He could have reacted a multitude of different ways. *Thank you for that insight, Helena.* It had been over seven months since I had seen that side of him. I loved that side of him. I missed that side of him. That side of him was the man that I married.

I apologized to him for the pain I had inflicted, first by asking him to leave in my anger in the moment, and then for not reaching out to him once he left. I was an emotional wreck the day that I saw my son pinned up against the wall. My childhood resurfaced and my only instinct was to protect him. Instead of getting to the bottom of why Steve was behaving the way he was, I chose to ignore him and convince myself that the marriage was over. Although what he had done to my son had not been right, through my thought process now, I was remembering my father going through the same aggression with my two oldest brothers. Maybe what I witnessed had been nothing more than a rite of passage between a father and a son.

The Creator always spoke to me through music. Steve's choice in this song left the words speaking directly to my soul. Were we fallen angels with broken wings? Both of us had made some equally terrible choices. Burdened with so much guilt over my choices, was it finally time to forgive myself and let go of the shame I was continuing to carry? Was my sin being forgiven? On our journey through the darkness, had we both finally found the light? Was the Creator sending a message that He was drawing our hearts together so we could learn to love again?

I stopped for a coffee and washroom break just outside of Kingston. When I returned to the car, I decided to push the cassette back into the stereo. The second song he recorded was called "Love the Way You Love Me" by John Michael Montgomery.

> "I love the way you love me
> Strong and wild; slow and easy
> Heart and soul, so completely
> I love the way you love me."

Do you know, when you are sure that you have made the right decision, why you still end up questioning it? I began questioning my decision to leave Borden after the song ended. I knew in my heart that my destiny was to go to Halifax alone. My Spirit Guide had told me so, but what if I had decided to exercise my own free will and say "No" to the posting? Would it have changed anything or would it have changed everything? Debating the decision now was like closing the gate after the horses were out. There was no turning back, so I switched thought.

John Michael Montgomery's song took me back to the first five years of our marriage. We had an undeniable bond of love and compassion for each other. We had a mutual respect that never wavered, even if we were having an argument. There was no mudslinging, name calling, selfishness, bullheadedness or dredging up of the past. We were always in the moment, respectful and determined to reach a conclusion that satisfied both of our needs. Our relationship had been healthy, in every sense of the word. Everything fell apart when we moved to Ottawa.

Ottawa was such a strenuous time for our marriage. I was trying to balance an overly demanding career, trying to make time for my husband, and trying to make time for my son. Balancing all three demands had left me exhausted and unsuccessful. Steve and I had stopped communicating, probably because we rarely saw each other. When we had time together, we were usually arguing over something my son had done. I was in an impossible situation, and my choice to "hope for the best" had not been the right answer either. All that thought accomplished was leaving my son and my husband battling or ignoring each other, each with a seething undercurrent of disdain. Communication, or lack thereof, for the past four years had become the entire family's demise as a functional, cohesive unit. I wished I could have seen it for what it was at the time, but hindsight is always 20/20.

The time had flown by, and before I knew it, I had driven out of the province of Ontario and was now entering Quebec. In less than two hours, I would be stopping for the night. I decided to forego any more songs on the cassette for the day, especially since I had no idea what was coming next. I needed to leave the past behind and focus on happier thoughts before meeting with my friend, so I turned the radio back on.

Linda had married in 1993, so when I arrived at her place, I was introduced to Normand (her husband) for the first time. I immediately recognized how well suited they were for each other. You could tell they were happy together, and I was happy for my friend. Normand's thick French accent left his speech sounding strange or broken at times, which in turn became comical at points throughout the conversation. My French was not much better sounding than his English, so I tried hard not to laugh at his pronunciation, which was tickling my funny bone. Perhaps the funny bone had been named appropriately in relation to the upper arm bone known as the "humerus". He really was hilarious. The three of us chatted for fifteen minutes or so before Normand left the room to tinker with a project in the garage.

Linda and I proceeded to take a trip down memory lane for the next few hours. We talked about our days of drinking in Edmonton. "I loved when you drank tequila. You were always yourself, your real self so to speak. You were so affectionate, always hugging all your friends and telling us how much you loved us. We knew you had passed the point of no return when you turned into a dancing queen. Yup! Laurie is high now, and we have lost her to the dancefloor. You loved life and your friends, but most of all, you loved dancing when you had a tequila buzz," she said. We reminisced about decorating the Christmas tree with lingerie and all the fun we had attending lingerie parties over the years. We talked about former boyfriends and the crazy parties at my PMQ. We talked about our gang of girlfriends and where life had taken them over the years.

After reminiscing about Edmonton, Linda changed the subject to TJ and Steve. I explained to her what had happened between the two of them in Ottawa, and then Borden. "I am so surprised to hear that. They were getting along so well with each other when I saw the three of you in Montreal. I remember TJ being such a great kid. Everybody loved him. He did not have just you. He had this huge family of your friends around him, and we all treated him as if he was our own child," she said. It was reassuring to hear her words. For the past few years, I had been wondering if I had blinders on. Had my love for my son been clouding the reality of who he really was? Linda's words erased all my doubt regarding Steve's opinion. There was no shortage of conversation or laughter between us. That evening with Linda had been exactly what I needed.

Although Linda had made up the bed in the spare bedroom for me, I told her that I preferred to sleep on the couch if she did not mind. "As soon as I wake up, I am going to get back on the road, and I don't want to disturb either of you," I said. I gave Linda a big hug and said my goodbyes to her and Normand before they went to bed. I figured my night would be restless and I was not wrong. By 4:00 a.m. I was fully awake and decided to get up. *If I leave now, I can be on the other side of Montreal before the morning rush hour starts.* I folded up the blanket, placed it on top of the pillow at the end of the couch, packed my overnight bag, and made my way to the car. It was still dark outside and the streets were eerily quiet, not a soul in sight.

When I took the ramp onto the highway, there were very few cars. I began following an 18-wheeler truck in front of me. He was traveling at 110 kilometers and the lights on the truck made it easy to follow the curves in the road, roads that I was unfamiliar with. About twenty minutes into the drive, I realized that I had less than a quarter of a tank of gas left. I could not see anything for miles but fields and highway. No towns! No gas stations!

Continue to follow the truck.

A few more miles down the road, the truck turned on his right blinker. He was taking the next exit ramp. I still could not see anything but fields. I slowed down and hesitated. I had no idea where he was going. *Helena, he could be going anywhere. He could be pulling off to sleep or deliver his load.*

Follow the truck.

Okay! Just follow the truck. I'm listening and trusting you. The other alternative was being stranded on the side of the highway without gas.

As I took the exit ramp and crossed the highway overpass, I began driving into a foggy area. It was hard to see the road in front of me. Less than six kilometers from the exit, hidden in a heavily treed area, was a gas station in the middle of nowhere, one that was open 24 hours a day. I filled the car with gas, grabbed a coffee and a banana, and climbed back into my car, but not before thanking the truck driver. "Good thing for you I needed a bathroom break. Have yourself a nice day, pretty lady," he said climbing the steps to his seat in the truck. *Thank you, Helena! Thank you so much for this unscheduled trip into the Twilight Zone. I am so glad I listened.* I still wonder to this day if that gas station was really there or if it was provided by Spirit like experiencing a mirage in the desert.

The distance from Windsor, Quebec to Halifax, Nova Scotia is 1,200 kilometers. My goal was to try and make the entire drive that day. If I became too tired, I had the option to stop, but I was determined to drive until fatigue set in, and I no longer could continue. Once I drove through Montreal, the roads were quiet. Melancholy filled my spirit as the sun began to rise, filling the sky with shades of pink and orange. I wanted to hold my family again, cheek to cheek. I wanted to go back to the *before*, but the before was gone. I was in the *now*. I wondered if new beginnings often disguised themselves as painful endings.

When I lost a good radio signal, I decided to play Steve's cassette tape again. The third song he had recorded was "So Alive" by Love and Rockets. I had never heard the song before. "Your strut makes me crazy, makes me see you more clearly... I'm alive, huh, huh, so alive." The beat was addictive, but the voice of the singer and the lyrics were so spooky at the same time. I rewound the tape several times. It was like a drug that I could not get enough of, as my sorrow flew right out the half-opened window. Finally feeling upbeat, I removed the cassette tape and placed it in the glove box. I would not listen to it again for quite some time.

After stopping for another coffee and a bagel, my thoughts went to my sister Sharron as I continued driving. I had missed her wedding in 1998, but not because I did not want to go. I was such a mess at the time with everything going on in my life. A wedding is a time of love and celebration, and I was in a dark and morbid place. Anyone who knows me well will admit that I do not have a poker face. Although I had always been guarded in speaking my truth to others, I wore my emotions for all to see, especially with the people I loved. I did not want to be the one to put a damper on her special day, so I made an excuse not to attend, followed by a very heavy heart for not being true to my word to be there for her. Maybe one day, we would have the chance to reconnect in person again so I could tell her the truth and apologize. I trusted that the Universe would make that happen when the timing was right.

I thought about my final conversation with Dianne before leaving Borden. "Consider the gift you have been given. This is a path to a greater partnership - separate from Steve and your son. You are being prepared for union with your Higher Self and union with the Divine. God always takes a soul exactly where it needs to go. Trust that this move is in your best interest."

I pulled into the parking lot of the Dartmouth hotel at 7:00 p.m. that night. It had been a long fifteen-hour day, and my lower back was bothering me. I ran myself a bubble bath and climbed in the bathtub to soak for a half hour. My thoughts went immediately to my son. I knew without a doubt that our relationship would stand the test of time, apart or together. We had a special bond, and although life had suddenly changed my destiny entirely without him, I was amazed by the young man he had become when I was not looking. There were a million reasons why I loved him, his big heart being his most precious asset of all. He was my greatest accomplishment in life, despite my mistakes. I made a few phone calls, said my prayers, and then wrapped myself in the coziness of a featherbed. Surrounded by pillows, I drifted into heavenly bliss as I closed my eyes for the night.

When I spoke to Pheme the next morning, I invited her to spend the day with me. We went for a swim, enjoyed the Jacuzzi, and had a bite to eat. After she left, I called Steve to let him know that I had arrived safely and told him that I had not read his letter yet. I wanted to get settled first, so I promised to call him again in a week or so.

On Monday morning, I drove to Canadian Forces Base (CFB) Stadacona to begin my in-clearance to the base. The billet I had been posted into was the R&D (Receipt and Dispatch) Section, so I made it my first stop. The Corporal (Cpl) at the front counter took me into an office and introduced me to the Warrant Officer (WO) and Sergeant (Sgt) of the Section. Immediately, I learned from the conversation that the Section was in an upheaval. Four Cpls were off on stress leave, and the four remaining were burning out quickly doing twice the amount of work. "You have your work cut out for you, Master Corporal (MCpl). We are hoping a fresh set of eyes will help solve the problems we are having. When is your furniture arriving?" the WO asked.

"It will be here by next Monday at the latest. Hopefully sooner," I replied. I asked him if he would allow me a few days to sit with each of the Cpls to get to know them as individuals and to hear what they felt the problems were from their perspective. I would then report back to him with a diagnosis and recommendations once I had the full picture. He agreed to my request.

Wednesday, I received a phone call from Tom (my mover). He would be at my new residence on Friday morning to deliver my furniture, after delivering another load to Truro, Nova Scotia on Thursday. I thanked him for the heads-up. No sooner had I hung up the telephone when the lawyer called looking for my down payment to finalize my real estate deal. I made a trip to the bank, then to the lawyer's office, leaving with the keys to my new home.

I called Pheme on Thursday, asking her to meet me after work at the house. The house I bought was a split-level design with a living room, dining room, kitchen, and half bath on the upper level. The living room had a magnificent bay window and a propane fireplace. The dining room had sliding glass doors leading to a fourteen-foot-high terrace overlooking a greenbelt. The lower level was designed with three bedrooms, a full bath, and a laundry room. Pheme's reaction was the same as mine had been when I originally viewed the house. "This place is incredible. My home away from home," she said as we finished the grand tour.

As we were discussing where to go for dinner that night, my phone rang. It was Tom asking if I had any plans for the evening. We decided to meet up at a pub one block away from the motel he was staying at while in Dartmouth. There would be four of us because he was bringing along another driver. The meal and the conversation were entertaining to say the least. We laughed, told stories, had a few after-dinner drinks, and before we knew it, several hours had passed.

Around 10:00 p.m., Pheme headed back to her apartment and I drove back to the hotel for my last night in transient lodging. Tomorrow, I would be in my new home. Once inside the hotel room, I realized I had left my cell phone at the pub. I called them and asked them to put it behind the bar for me. Then I called Tom and asked him if he would be so kind to walk back and pick it up for me. "No problem. I will bring it with me tomorrow morning when I come to unload," he said.

Tom arrived at 8:00 a.m. the next morning, my cell phone and a Tim Hortons coffee in hand. He came inside, took a look around, and then went back out to the truck. I could hear him speaking to his two swampers. "Take your time and be careful with her things. Her furniture is solid wood and heavy, so watch the walls." By 5:00 p.m. the truck was empty and nothing had been damaged during the move. I signed off on the final paperwork. "Laurie, I have a suggestion. I am not reloading again until Monday morning. If you want, I can come back and help you unpack or move furniture around for you. Women always change their minds about where they want things," he said winking at me.

I laughed. "Call me later," I replied.

Pheme showed up at my place around 7:00 p.m. that evening with two passengers from the motel (Tom and his friend) and a few bottles of liquor for a housewarming party. I had most of the kitchen unpacked by the time they arrived, and my bed was made. The four of us cracked open a bottle, toasted to friendship, and then spent another hour finding blankets and pillows so that everyone had a place to crash for the evening. The guys set up my electronics and moved furniture, while Pheme and I unpacked several more boxes. It was time to let the party begin!

By midnight, we needed food and decided to order a few pizzas. When the deliveryman arrived, not one of us was sober. Pheme was at the front door, looking through the side window panel and begging the delivery-man to open the door and let us out. "We are locked in. Let us out, man," she kept repeating with her face pressed against the glass. The delivery guy kept trying the door handle, but it was locked. He had such a confused look on his face. I raced to the front door, afraid that he would leave with our food. Tom was right behind me and fell down the stairs on his way to the door to pay for the pizza. Now, he was lying sprawled out on the landing, and we still had not opened the door. I finally unlocked the door and apologized. That poor deliveryman! I am sure he must have gone back to the restaurant and had a good laugh with the other delivery drivers about the fools he had encountered on his last delivery. Tom gave him a twenty-dollar tip to compensate for all our clowning around. Then he went to find his friend who had passed out in my bed. What a wild night of drunken antics, followed by a brutal morning of hangovers!

Before Tom left the next morning, he asked me if he could make my home his home away from home. "I come to Halifax a lot, and it would be nice to have a friend here to do things with when I have down time," he said. I agreed to his request, and it would not be long before we would end up in a mutually beneficial friendship.

Spiritual Beings on a Human Experience

The soul needs to be nourished and energized on a regular basis, just as the physical body requires food and water. True nourishment of the soul, provided by the Holy Spirit, renews the mind, and replenishes the spirit. Without the Holy Spirit, a human will operate in the flesh, becoming shallow, self-absorbed, impatient, angry, and less gentle.

Redemption is a promise by the Creator to deliver souls from the power and presence of sin. Relationships can be restored. Tears can be wiped away. Through redemption, a soul can step into atonement, integrity, truth, and love. A soul is not held captive to mistakes because the spiritual path is always a journey in progress. When Laurie asks her Creator for forgiveness and guidance by acknowledging her sinful behavior, He rewards her with a journey of self-conquest, a journey of authenticity, a new way of being in the world. Laurie is undergoing another spiritual shift to becoming a Spiritual Warrior. A correct relationship with herself is at hand.

CHAPTER 28

KEEPING THE FAITH

After everyone left on Saturday morning, my immediate focus was to go grocery shopping. Waking up without coffee had definitely been challenging. At that time, there was no Sunday shopping in Nova Scotia. I needed to get groceries today or wait until Monday night after work. Extremely hung over, I forced myself to pick up the basics: coffee, milk, eggs, and bread. Then I returned home to continue unpacking. By Sunday night, my house looked like a home, filled with nostalgia and mementos. Finally feeling like myself again, I made a cup of coffee, a fried egg sandwich, and sat down to read Steve's letter.

> Laurie:
>
> I can't begin to describe what I am feeling right now knowing that you are leaving. Let me start by saying that I am sorry for everything. You are a beautiful person, and I have hurt you. Please forgive me for that. It was never my intention. I think in my pigheadedness over the past few years, I've hurt you a lot, and I am not very proud of that. No matter what happens between us, I want you to be happy because when you smile, it seems to make the world that much brighter. I know it does mine.
>
> I must tell you that I do not hate TJ. I can't really explain how I feel because I do not understand it myself exactly. I don't know what your previous relationships were

like with TJ, yourself, and whoever you were seeing at the time. Did they feel that they needed to date him in order to spend time with you? I don't know. But when I came along, I am sure I was a big disappointment to him because my focus was on you. I eventually turned the relationship between him and I into a competition for your affection which steadily got worse...well...until I moved out. Let me tell you something. Before I met you, I was always good with kids. That's why I did not hesitate to marry you even though you had a child. I never expected I would be jealous of him.

Laurie, when I met you, I was a virgin. I had never so much as kissed a woman, let alone been in a relationship. Maybe ten years ago I should have walked away, but I didn't. I couldn't. Here I had this beautiful woman who wanted to spend time with me and make love to me. She wanted me – the shy, awkward guy – so shy that I purposely avoided women. But you saw through that and saw that I had a huge heart with tons of love to give. My only mistake was that I kept all that love for you and did not share it with your son like I should have.

I AM SO SORRY FOR THAT!

I tried dating other women, but they were not you. I was always thinking about you or comparing them with you because my heart wanted you. If you feel our relationship still has a chance...GREAT. If not, I need you to know that I will always love you and will always be there for you in mind and spirit.

Love forever, Steve

Steve writing his personal truth in his letter changed me after I read it. I felt an energy emerge inside that had been blocked until now. I had a new clarity as he poured his heart out into words. I understood everything now. *Helena, now I know what you meant when you told me ten years ago that "PURE" love was what I needed. I was Steve's first love, an untainted, authentic love. Is that why a soul never gets over a first love? Is that why I struggled for so long to get over Lloyd and kept going back because my love for him was authentic too?*

Once love is authentic, it is forever embedded in the soul.

I made the decision to wait to talk to Steve. I was extremely emotional, and I needed to digest the contents of his letter before I spoke to him. He was expressing his remorse over his relationship with my son, and that was monumental for me. I needed to sit with that thought. I would call him tomorrow night.

I was learning to pay attention to my Spirit Guide, to ponder the meaning in her words, and to trust that all my challenges were designed to keep me connected to my blueprint. The Universe knew the bigger picture, and those timely conversations were becoming a gift. I was expecting the unexpected while realizing that each message was a call to help me or to evolve my soul.

At the same time, I was experiencing the reality of a physical existence and all the emotions that were inevitable. I was reliving the loss of intense emotional bonds that had been severed and profound relationships that had been radically changed, with both my husband and my son.

Everything a soul experiences has a beginning, a middle, and an end. It is always followed by a new beginning. Take heart.

When I went to bed that night, I was lost in deep thought. Is it necessary for the Spiritual Self to balance with the physical self in order to be in the world, and not of it? Is it how souls find their true direction and steadily grow through numerous shifts and changes? Like a game of chess, does the Universe always have the first move based on our blueprints, whether we choose to connect to our Divine Self or not? Then I wondered: Are the obstacles we face in our lives conquered in victory by our faith? Faith is not always easy, and perhaps, for a reason. Maybe if it were too easy, it would have no value. Through my faith, I had finally found a new hope for my marriage and my family as I drifted off to sleep.

My first priority, when I returned home from work on Monday night was to call my son. I needed to hear his voice. I was still haunted by all my failures as a mother, and I needed to know that he was alright. He sounded happy as we made plans for him to come to Halifax for Christmas. Before hanging up, we promised to speak to each other at least once a week.

Later that night, I called Steve. We talked about his letter, and I thanked him for his honesty. After a lengthy conversation, we decided to give the relationship another chance, but we discussed taking things slow, one step at a time. Before the conversation ended, he dropped a bomb on me. "The SIU (Special Investigation Unit) in Borden has transferred your file to the SIU in Halifax. I read the file before it left. There is nothing in it that implicates you being involved in illegal activity, other than your car being parked at Angie's residence. They have no solid evidence to press charges. Having said that, expect a visit. They need to follow through before closing the file. Don't admit to anything! Just figure out a feasible explanation as to why your car was parked there." I was more than grateful for the heads-up.

By the end of my first week at work, I had figured out the challenges the R&D Section was facing, along with several viable solutions. The biggest hurdle the Section had was the fact that the four remaining staff felt unappreciated, overworked, and burnt out. There was no control system in place to know where "moving claims" had ended up once we accepted them over the counter. Claims were being misplaced or lost, and the staff was spending countless hours trying to figure out where they were, losing valuable productive work time in completing other claims. Military members who were submitting claims were annoyed and often times hostile because those claims represented spent money they were waiting to be reimbursed for.

While sitting with one of my Corporals that week, I learned that he was designing computer programs at home as a hobby. I asked him if he would be willing to design a program to control the whereabouts of claims coming into the R&D Section. It would need to include whose desk the claim went to for processing, when it was sent for final approval, when it was sent to the "cash cage" to have a cheque issued, and when the final payment was picked up by the member who had submitted the claim. He was excited by the challenge and agreed to design the program in his own spare time.

Then I revamped the filing system. During that process, I found many misplaced claims that had been hidden away in the back of filing cabinet drawers. I gathered my four Cpls together and told them that I wanted to have a fifteen-minute meeting once a week to discuss any concerns they might have, to which they were all very receptive. They were the workers and their opinions were the most valuable of all. I expressed that it was important for them to work as a team and not as individuals. In order to accomplish that, they needed to be cross trained in all functions of the Section, not individualized in specific jobs. They had been avoiding taking vacation time because the work that piled up while they were away became so overwhelming when they returned. That alone was the reason four of my staff were off on stress leave.

I reported my findings and plausible solutions to the Section WO. I also recommended that a reward system be put into place to acknowledge performance. I suggested the Cpl who was designing the Section Control Program be recommended for an Innovation Award. I also suggested that the Section should go down to "minimum manning" on Friday afternoons, allowing 2 Cpls each week to have a Friday afternoon off, workload permitting. He agreed.

Before leaving his office, we discussed my job. "The main function of your job is reviewing all completed claims prior to sending them for payment to the cash cage. You are the signing authority that all expenditures are legitimate and reimbursable. With that authority comes tremendous responsibility. You will be held accountable for any fraudulent claims and punished accordingly. I cannot emphasize enough the importance to detail in your job. There is no room for error. If you are questioning an entitlement and the regulations are not clear, bring that question to me for a second opinion." I left his office that day knowing I had a steep learning curve ahead of me, but I felt confident I could achieve it. Within a year and a half, I would be under investigation by the SIU for fraud and my signing authority would be revoked.

I had not taken any summer vacation because of the move to Halifax, so when Caroline (my friend from Montreal) called to tell me she and Peter were getting married in the middle of September, I booked a week of holidays. I had been working long hours and the timing of a road trip to see an old friend sounded perfect.

While I was packing the night before my trip, Tom called and invited me to join him for dinner. During our conversation, I learned that he had a load on his truck for delivery to Ottawa, and then he was re-loading in Quebec City and returning to Halifax. The timing could not have been more perfect. "Can you take passengers with you?" I asked.

He replied, "Yup! What did you have in mind?"

"How would you like to go to a wedding with me in Ottawa?" The next morning, I was a passenger in an 18-wheeler for the first time in my life, and my stomach was doing cartwheels with excitement. *Let the adventure begin!*

We drove out of the Maritimes and into the Province of Quebec before Tom decided to stop for the night. Tired from the day's drive, we both crawled into the two bunks in the sleeper cab. Less than an hour later, another long-haul trucker arrived and parked beside us. His cargo was a livestock hauler containing pigs. The smell and the noise were appalling. Frustrated and unable to sleep, two hours later we were on the road again. I called Linda and Normand that morning, asking if they wanted some company. Tom was not scheduled to deliver the load of furniture to Ottawa until Sunday morning, and it was only Friday afternoon. Even though it was such short notice, Linda insisted that we stop and spend the night with them. Tom dropped the trailer in a truck stop nearby, and we bobtailed over to Linda's place, arriving around 2:00 p.m. Tom and Normand hung out at the truck, engrossed in conversation for half an hour while I went inside. Linda's parents were visiting, and her mom was busy in the kitchen preparing salads.

The guys grabbed a few beers, and the girls opened a bottle of wine as we exited outside to the patio to relax. That night, the barbequed chicken dinner was delicious, but the best part of all was the conversation. We laughed so much when Tom retold the story of sleeping with the pigs the night before. He was a very animated storyteller and sounded just like a pig as he imitated the noise he had been trying to sleep through.

Tom slept in the truck that night, and I stayed inside the house. The next morning while having coffee, Normand said to Tom, "Aren't you glad you didn't have to sleep with the pig last night?"

Tom choked on his coffee as Linda began laughing. Being a smart ass, Tom replied, "That's not a very nice thing to say about Laurie."

Linda shouted, "Pigs, Normand, not pig. You forgot the 's' and it changed the whole meaning." Linda and I still laugh about that conversation to this day.

We left Linda and Normand's home after breakfast, arriving in Ottawa early Saturday afternoon. I offered to pay for a hotel room for the night so we could shower and get ready for the wedding. It was the least I could do for payment for the free ride to the wedding. I could not have chosen a better date for that evening. Tom was relaxed, fun, a great conversationalist, and an even better dancer. I did not have much time to spend with Caroline. A bride is always busy making rounds with her guests, but I promised to call her when I got back to Halifax. I was simply happy that I had been able to see her get married and share her joy.

When I awoke early the next morning, I took a quick shower, dressed, and went to the lobby to pick up two cups of coffee and some fresh fruit. When I returned to the room, it was 6:15 a.m. and Tom was in the shower. Less than an hour later, we were at his delivery destination. I spent the day offloading boxes from the moving truck. The exercise felt good and the extra set of hands resulted in us finishing two hours earlier than expected. We spent that night in a truck stop outside Quebec City ready to re-load the following morning. By Tuesday, I was back home. Five days on the road with him, along with seeing Caroline again, had been so uplifting. That vacation had been just what I needed.

I returned to work on Wednesday morning, burying myself in a pile of claims that were awaiting approval, when the SIU showed up at the R&D counter. "MCpl, the SIU is here to see you."

"Take them into the conference room and tell them I will be with them shortly," I replied. I took a few deep breaths and composed myself for what was coming.

You can tell someone's intentions by the tone of their voice and the words they are speaking. Pay attention.

When I entered the conference room, there were two gentlemen seated, one with a manila folder in front of him. "Good morning, MCpl. I have a file in front of me that has been transferred from Borden, so I will get straight to the point of this visit. Your vehicle was spotted parked in Barrie at a house known for illegal activity. Suppose you tell me exactly what you were doing there." *Wow! They are shooting straight from the hip with intimidation and accusation. Stay composed.*

He proceeded to show me a picture of the house, and there was no doubt that my car was parked there. "I had a girlfriend who was working there as an escort, and I stopped to pick her up one evening after her shift. Her car was at a garage for repairs, and I was taking her to pick it up. Is there a problem?" I asked. I kept my answer short and sweet. I offered nothing more than a few sentences. They both looked at each other and then at me again. The silence was awkward.

"You are well aware that you have a security clearance and that clearance can be revoked very easily just by who you choose to associate with. Without a security clearance, your career is finished. I have the power to make that happen today," he said.

Now they are threatening me. Remain calm, Laurie. They have no proof of anything. Appease them. "I never thought of it that way, but you have a very valid point. Lesson learned. I will definitely choose my friends more wisely from now on," I replied.

"For your sake, I hope so," he replied. They stood up, thanked me for my time, and left the conference room. *Crisis averted. Thank you, Steve, for the heads-up.* The file from Borden was closed that day. My career was still intact, for now anyway.

Christmas had arrived and I was on my way to the airport to pick up my son. It was difficult to contain my excitement at the thought of seeing him again. When we met at the baggage carousel, his excitement was just as evident. We spent hour after hour catching up on all the news of the past four months. We went out to dinner with Pheme to Crawdad's Crab Shack and Oyster Bar in Halifax to celebrate my birthday. From there, we went to the casino. We spent another day at the Mic Mac Mall in Dartmouth doing some Christmas shopping. Our time together was over before I knew it, and I was on my way back to the airport. There was no excitement this time. My son was going back to Ontario, and I was trying so hard not to cry. Before going through security screening, TJ gave me one final hug. I could no longer stay composed and began crying when he joined the other passengers in the lineup. Every time he looked back at me, the crying became intensified. Now I was gasping for air.

Watching me struggle, he left the lineup and wrapped his arms around me. "Mom, please don't cry. I can't leave you like this. You are a mess! I am coming back again. I promise. You can't get rid of me that easy, so please stop crying," he said. His words were the logic that I needed to hear. I apologized, told him one last time that I loved him, and immediately left the airport for the parking lot. *My poor child! His mother is such an emotional wingnut!* During the walk to my car, I consoled myself with the thought that it was better to hurt than to feel nothing at all. Perhaps, I was just trying to justify being a wingnut.

By the time the new year rolled around, I had a full staff of eight Cpls again. The R&D Section was running like clockwork. Moving claims had less than a week turnaround time for payment, nothing was being misplaced, and the staff was happy. Cross-training had been completed, and the staff was enjoying their vacation time. Our fifteen-minute meetings always ended with a joke, and those meetings accomplished more efficient ways of doing things or solving problems at the onset. Everyone was invested in the success of the Section. The Cpl who had designed our computer program won the Innovation Award, accompanied by a cheque for $5,000. By the end of the following year, the R&D Section would finish in the number-one spot on the base for exemplary customer service. That success was due to a team of hardworking and dedicated individuals.

I cannot tell a lie. I had my moments of loneliness when I was not at work, but I had learned that loneliness was not fatal. It was just a temporary state of mind that was easily remedied. I would solve that feeling by making a phone call to Steve or reaching out to a friend that I had not spoken to in a while. When I needed to get out of the house, I would go to the Cole Harbour Recreation Center to take a water aerobics class. On Sundays, Pheme and I would get together and prepare a meal, a hearty meal like roast beef. Making a roast for one person to eat was hardly worth the effort. Then we would split the leftovers for lunches the following week. Occasionally, we would go out to brunch together for a change of scenery or out to a pub on a Friday night for a bucket of steamed clams and a drink. My home had truly become Pheme's home away from home on weekends, and I welcomed her company with enthusiasm. All in all, living alone was becoming a comfortable place to be in my life. The fear of loneliness had definitely been a waste of time and energy.

By February of 2000, Steve decided to fly out to Halifax for a four-day visit. His pending arrival was nerve-wracking for both of us. It had been well over a year since we had co-existed under the same roof for more than an hour at a time. Were we crazy to commit to four days? Steve was impressed by the house after I gave him a tour. "This home is beautiful, but not as beautiful as you in this moment. It is so good to see you again. I have missed that smile of yours. Can I have a hug?" he asked. My body melted into every muscle of his body, as I bathed in the scent of his aftershave. That hug was the perfect gesture of affection. Perhaps it was the fragile beginning to love returning.

Neither one of us had eaten that day, so we decided to take a walk down the block and stop for lunch at Jamieson's Irish Pub and Grill. I was basking in the cold fresh air as I held Steve's hand. It reminded me of old times, as memories came flooding back during the walk. Once we had ordered lunch, Steve told me that he had spoken to his career manager and that the intention was to post him to Halifax in the summer. "You might want to wait on that decision, Steve. I was told yesterday that I will be going to the Golan Heights in Israel for a six-month tour from the end of September until March of 2001. Maybe the Spring of 2001 would be better timing," I said.

He was disappointed to have to wait longer, but he agreed that delaying the move made perfect sense. "I don't want to move to Halifax only to have you leave for six months," he said. The four days we spent together were as natural and casual as when we first started hanging out together in Montreal. When I dropped him off at the airport, I was sad to see him go. During one final hug, I whispered in his ear, "We have been separated for so long, but look at us now. Love wins!"

In late spring, I got a call from Linda. They were planning a vacation to the East Coast and wanted to stop by for a quick visit. We spent a fabulous two days enjoying each other's company. I always laughed so much when I was with her and Normand. Eileen (my co-worker from Borden) knew Linda well and happened to be on a course in Halifax at the time, so imagine my surprise when she showed up at my front door. Eileen was meeting up with Linda and Normand to continue their trip to Prince Edward Island. It had been such a wonderful two days.

The summer flew by and before I knew it, I was on my way to Kingston, Ontario for pre-deployment training to Israel. It had been a mad rush putting my life in order to leave the country for six months. During one of my conversations with Caroline, she mentioned that she and Peter wanted to move to Halifax so I offered them my house as their residence for the six months I would be gone. All they needed to do was pay the hydro bill and the gas bill. That would give them lots of time to save some money and find their own place to live before I returned. On the flip side, I would not need to find someone to check in on my property throughout the winter. It was a win/win situation. They were helping me and I was helping them. They would be arriving in Halifax when I returned from Kingston.

Before a military member leaves the country, they are required to review all their official paperwork such as wills, emergency contacts, etc. When I filled out a new NOK (Next of Kin) form, I put Steve as my primary contact and my mother as my secondary contact. Unbeknownst to me, the Windsor Police Department showed up at my mother's door one day asking her to confirm that she was my mother and that the information on the NOK form was correct. I would have loved to have been a fly on the wall for that visit. That day, my mother became aware that I was leaving on a peacekeeping mission. After ten years of refusing to acknowledge that I existed, she had finally let go of her stubbornness and picked up the phone to call me. The timing of her call would be too late for us to speak.

Spiritual Beings on a Human Experience

Faith in a physical life is lived in the face of uncertainty, where a person is unquestionably certain of things they cannot see. It is a natural state of existence that allows inner peace to emerge, an inner, quiet confidence where a soul no longer feels the need to control anything. During a soul's physical journey, faith is trust and assurance in the Creator's presence and His timing. Laurie leaving her family behind is not without sorrow. It is emotionally difficult for her to bear. The inner peace and strength that the Creator provides for her to make the journey alone appears because of her faith.

Faith is something given to a soul by the Creator, not something a soul is born with or can achieve through willpower. It comes from hearing the word of Spirit and believing. Laurie has maintained a relationship with her Creator from a young age. She no longer questions the direction of her life, choosing instead to reach for His comfort when the emotions of her personality surface.

The only control a soul has in any relationship is control over how that soul chooses to be in the relationship. The expression of love, compassion, respect, and kindness is the foundation of any relationship and needs to be reciprocated for the relationship to achieve success. Laurie and Steve's relationship has returned to a place where it is no longer taking on roles or playing out with a dynamic of power through their personalities. They have restored trust through honesty. They have restored love through equality and forgiveness. Their union has come full circle and returned to its beginning.

Laurie's mother has spent ten years denying Laurie's existence through stubbornness, a behavior that has become a habit when not getting her own way. Her need to control her daughter's choices, coupled with the inability to do so, has resulted in a need for vengeance. It has blinded this mother to her daughter's love through her own bitterness. In the Creator's timing, he sends the Holy Spirit to speak to her mother's heart when she receives the news of Laurie's peacekeeping mission. Her heart experiences a moment of compassion, resulting in her decision to reach out and connect with her daughter. The inability to reach her daughter is a powerful teaching moment. She is faced with the potential that she may never have the opportunity to speak to her again.

CHAPTER 29

TOMORROW IS NEVER PROMISED

Some humans are afraid of the dark, so they create a thing called *faith* that they believe will get them *around* trouble. My belief was that faith would get me *through* trouble. Without faith and hope, would it have been possible to survive the things that seemed unbearable in my life or to recover from the losses I had already endured? As if my life had not already been filled with enough trauma, my faith was about to be put to the test one more time.

The night before leaving for Israel, I made several phone calls, the most important of all to my son. I had not told him about my peacekeeping mission and that it would preclude us from our weekly conversations on the telephone. I still felt remorseful that he had been at the center of all my trials and errors in life, and I wanted to get things right this time. I wanted to spare him from worrying as long as possible but delaying the inevitable was no longer an option. When I gave him the news, he was shocked and upset. After a lengthy conversation, I had managed to reassure him that everything would be okay. I also gave him my mother's phone number and told him to reach out to his grandmother if he needed help with anything. I would be too far away, but she would come to his rescue for sure. After all, he was her grandson and they had a loving history. My heart was telling me that Steve was not a viable option.

My next call was to Steve. After talking for half an hour, his final words to me were: "There are so many people who have never had to face real difficulty in their life. You are not one of those people, Laurie. You are strong, intelligent, and a professional soldier in every sense of the word because of those difficulties. Not to mention the fact that you seem to be connected to the Other Side. Trust your instincts, pay attention to your environment, and you will be fine. You have never let any challenge in life stop you, and this one shouldn't either. Send me an e-mail when you arrive in Israel and give me a telephone number so that I can call you occasionally. I promise to help you through any days of adversity and, trust me, you will have such days. I love you with all of my heart. Be safe, sweetheart."

My final phone call was to Dianne; probably not one of my better ideas in hindsight. Her final words left me bewildered. "You are going to have a life-altering experience while you are in the Holy Land. Remember to walk with the Creator though your darkest moments. Be bold, hold on tightly to your faith, and never forget that you are His child." Perhaps there is a day, as sure as the sun rises each morning, that will forever change *any* soul's life. I had no idea what Dianne meant by a life-altering experience, and she refused to elaborate. I figured at some point, her words would make perfect sense. They always did.

The trip to Israel was grueling. It began with a four-hour flight from Halifax, Nova Scotia to Toronto, Ontario. A military shuttle bus picked up twenty-five soldiers who had flown in from across Canada and drove us to CFB Trenton, two hours away. Once in Trenton, we met up with another eleven soldiers already at the AMU. Four hours later, we had cleared customs and were boarding a Military Boeing destined for Tel Aviv, Israel. The in-flight duration was another twelve hours. On our arrival in Tel Aviv, a United Nations bus was waiting for us on the tarmac. We boarded the bus for a five-hour road trip to a military camp that had been established in the Golan Heights, a camp of strategic importance. The Golan Heights was an area seized from Syria by Israeli Forces in 1967 and was still being disputed.

Due to a combination of jet lag, lack of sleep, the time change, and a scorching temperature over 100 degrees Fahrenheit, we were extremely fatigued on arrival at the Camp. We were Rotation (Roto) 64, thirty-six soldiers in total, and had just arrived to replace Roto 62. Roto 63 had three months remaining in their six-month peacekeeping tour. Staggering the rotations allowed for continuity in the role being provided by the Canadian

Contingent (CANCON) to the Israeli and Syrian Governments. The camp was also comprised of a Japanese Contingent (JAPCON) and a Polish Contingent (POLCON).

Roto 63 soldiers were waiting for us as we stepped off the bus. We formed a platoon waiting for instruction from the Regimental Sergeant Major (RSM). He proceeded with a roll call. As I came to attention when my name was called, a person from Roto 63 stepped forward. We grabbed my luggage from the bus and walked to the barracks. I had two hours to become familiarized with the camp and grab a bite to eat before all personnel from Roto 64 were required to meet in the camp theatre for a briefing by the RSM.

When we arrived at the camp theatre, we were each handed a two-liter bottle of water and instructed to drink a minimum of four liters a day for the first week. It would help us acclimatize and avoid dehydration. We each took a bottle of water and found a seat inside. I was sweating so profusely that my combat clothing was drenched with perspiration, and I was not the only one. My first priority was a shower and dry clothing as soon as time permitted. When the two-hour briefing had been completed, we were instructed to report to clothing stores to draw our desert kit. From there, the rest of our day was our own to settle into our rooms and sleep. We were instructed to report for duty the following morning.

That night, I became friends with the girl rooming next door to me in the barracks. Her name was Ginnie, and she was from Halifax. Ginnie always had a smile on her face, a smile that made you wonder what she was up to. She had such a fun, crazy side to her. Being as she was part of Roto 63, I would only have three months with her before she would return to Canada, but our friendship would not take long to rekindle once I returned home.

My billet in the camp was as the "Welfare Clerk", a job that would entail arranging R&R (Rest and Recuperation) for all Canadian occupants in the camp. When I arrived at the office the following morning, I was greeted by a Warrant Officer named Sandy. She was pleasant, relaxed, and easy to work for because she put rank aside and viewed us as a team. A local civilian was also employed in the office, whose job was to arrange all international flights because she spoke the local language. When soldiers deploy to Israel, they are given three weeks' vacation time that must be used during the mission or forfeited. Soldiers have the option to bring someone to Israel to join them on a vacation or to use the three weeks to return to Canada. *How lucky am I? I am a tour guide, exploring foreign lands halfway around the world while getting paid for it.* Each tour that was organized required Sandy or me to accompany the tour, along with a local tour guide. We decided, by a consensus between the two of us, who wanted to accompany which tours. We set up short tours and week-long tours. Both left the option for soldiers to visit several areas during their six-month tour of duty. However, there was always the possibility of tours being cancelled if the zones we were scheduled to visit became hot spots of fighting.

I hit the ground running. A tour had been scheduled to Latakia, Syria, the following week and I was about to experience the local culture first-hand. It gave me a whole new appreciation for the freedom and mindset we have as Canadians. The camp sits on a border between Syria and Israel. In order to cross from one country to the other for the tour to Latakia, I needed to go to the Embassy in Damascus and have all passports of traveling soldiers stamped prior to the trip.

My driver arrived first thing the next morning. United Nations (UN) soldiers are forbidden to travel alone while on duty. Going through the Israeli border, we were motioned by heavily armed soldiers to drive over a large hole in the ground. It reminded me of having your oil changed in Canada. We were instructed to exit the vehicle so it could be inspected inside and out for bombs. We were searched, our paperwork was inspected, and then we were instructed to return to the vehicle. A few miles down the road, we crossed a United Nations border manned by Military Police. We crossed that border with ease by driving straight through with a hand wave. The next stop was the Syrian border and that experience was the same as the Israeli border.

Twenty minutes later, we were finally free to carry on to Damascus. I noticed the town of Quneitra off to my left about six kilometers down the road. The town had been destroyed by Israeli tanks during the Yom Kippur War in 1973. The survivors were still living amongst the rubble, and they were lined up along the roadside begging for food and water. The children were wearing nothing but underwear; no shoes, no clothing, no toys. We had been briefed to drive past them slowly because it was not unusual for them to shove their children in front of a moving vehicle. The United Nations pays a sum of money to a family whose child has been injured or killed by UN soldiers. For them, that money would equate to us winning a lottery in Canada. I could not believe what I was witnessing. They were fellow human beings living in a pile of rocks, without food or water, challenged by survival on a daily basis, and desperate enough to sacrifice a child for money in order to stay alive.

Driving in Syria was a nightmare all of its own. Road rules appeared to be non-existent. Stopping at a traffic light resulted in three or four cars being huddled together side-by-side on a road meant to accommodate two cars. There were donkeys with carts, people on bicycles, and everyone drove by honking their horn. The noise of the horns was nerve-wracking. More often than not, traffic lights were ignored. If you proceeded to slow down for a red light, it angered the locals. The idea was just to follow the flow of whatever the traffic was doing at the time. As we approached Damascus, we had to enter the city using a traffic roundabout. Access to the roundabout was controlled by a person standing in the street with a stick and a whistle, a person highly ignored by drivers. He was playing Russian roulette with his life just by standing there. Cars were seven or more abreast inside the circle, and it was mayhem trying to reach an exit without getting hit by another car. The traffic circle was often referred to by UN soldiers as the "Holy Fuck Roundabout". Those swear words had become the notorious reaction of every UN driver approaching the roundabout for the very first time.

On our return from Damascus, the driver stopped a kilometer away from the Quneitra people along the side of the road and told me to place our box of water, fruit, and crackers on the roadside. UN soldiers never traveled without their own food and water. It was a necessity in order to avoid sickness due to consuming unsafe local food and water. The level of hygiene in certain places in these countries was different from Canada's, and the foreign parasites made Canadians extremely sick, often requiring hospitalization. When I climbed back into the vehicle, the people of Quneitra began running towards us, focused on the box. Once we passed the locals, I thanked the driver for stopping to put the food out. "You cannot take it back across the Israeli border. It has been contaminated because it has been on Syrian soil. They will make us throw it in the garbage when we get there. This way, it helps to feed the town," he replied. The people of Quneitra were surviving on the generosity of the United Nations. *Helena, I cannot imagine what it must be like to wonder whether you will have a drink of water in a day or if you will starve to death. Obviously, the Syrian government does not look after its citizens. How incredibly sad! Not to mention the level of hatred between these two countries.*

Rectification must come before progress.

One month into the tour, my driver would end up running over a three-year-old girl and killing her after she was shoved in front of our vehicle at the last minute. The Post Traumatic Stress (PTSD) would result in him being returned to Canada because he was unable to continue in his capacity as a UN driver. For several weeks, I relived the nightmare sounds of hitting that little girl every time I closed my eyes. The saddest result of this tragedy was a directive that we could no longer drop food for these people. It was the only way to prevent them from gathering on the side of the road. Perfectly good food was now being trashed at the border once again.

I did not have set working hours per se. Seven days a week, I showed up at the office for 8:00 a.m. and left at various times throughout the evening, depending on the workload left that needed to be accomplished that day. Sometimes I would spend my evenings writing e-mails home. Sometimes I would stop at the Junior Ranks Mess for a nightcap with Ginnie before retiring to the barracks for the night. Other times, I showered and went straight to bed. Desert temperatures in the day were averaging 90 degrees Fahrenheit and falling to 29 degrees Fahrenheit in the evenings. That drastic drop in temperature was such a relief in order to sleep.

The entire barracks was awakened one night during my first encounter with a camel spider at 2:00 a.m. It was not a camel, nor was it a spider like I had ever seen before. When I flicked on the washroom light, I was met by a spider the size of my hand. It began screaming like a banshee and so did I. I do not know who was more afraid. Me or it. Camel spiders can move up to 25 miles per hour, so it was gone in a matter of seconds, but I was too spooked to sleep for the rest of that night. Now I know why they briefed us to check inside our boots before putting them on.

In the middle of October, my first tour group was destined for the Dead Sea, a salt lake situated between the shores of Israel and Jordan. The Dead Sea is 400 meters below sea level and the lowest body of water on Earth. It is also renowned for its health and healing properties. When we arrived, we changed into our bathing suits and covered ourselves in a mineral-rich mud. In actuality, we had a mud fight that resulted in us being covered in mud and then we baked in the sun for several hours. Caked with dried mud, we entered the salty waters of the Dead Sea. The high concentration of salt keeps bathers buoyant from the moment you enter the water, so we were warned to lean back and allow our feet to rise. Leaning forward would result in us tipping forward and ending up with a face full of salt water. Being weightless in the Dead Sea water was definitely therapeutic, especially when it required absolutely no effort to stay afloat. It felt invigorating and I could have stayed there for several more hours.

For the second day of the tour, we were heading to the ruins of the Masada Fortress. Masada is located on a high plateau above the Dead Sea, on a mountain that is one of the great archeological sites in Israel. Israeli soldiers are still sworn into service at the Masada Fortress to this day. The Fortress was built in the year 30 BCE by King Herod. I was most impressed by the remains of King Herod's Palace built on three rock terraces overlooking a gorge below. Our guide was full of historical information, but my interest was the landscape. There was something magical and unforgettable as I watched the sunset over the Jordanian Moab Mountains and the Dead Sea. It was such a spectacular view, second only to the Northern Lights.

That evening, the tour took us 228 kilometers further south to Eilat, Israel, where we checked into another hotel for the night. The following morning, we arrived at the Red Sea for a day of swimming with the dolphins. The area was caged off, but the dolphins were not kept captive. They were free to live in their natural habitat and come and go as they pleased. They came into the area to feed and then remained to play, unfazed by humans. There were schools of bottle-nosed dolphins, along with their babies, and they were some of nature's most magnificent creatures as we swam alongside them. One of them even allowed me to hold his back fin as he playfully tossed me through the water. At another point, a dolphin approached me from behind, stuck his nose between my legs, lifted me out of the water, and flung me through the air. If you have ever considered swimming with dolphins, I highly recommend it.

Next, we headed for a botanical garden containing three relaxation pools - a fresh sweet water pool, a sulfur water pool, and a seawater pool. The calming underwater music provided the perfect haven of tranquility and luxury to end the day. Those who were tired of swimming decided to enjoy refreshments and food on the beach. The bus ride back to the Golan Heights was quiet. Most people were exhausted and fell asleep. Those three days away from the camp had given me a chance to get to know fellow soldiers on a more personal level. Within a month, many of them would become my military family, and others, lifelong friendships.

The following morning on my way to the office, the camp sirens sounded. The protocol was to proceed immediately to the nearest bunker where we would be further briefed on what was happening. The sirens turned out to be nothing more than a dry run to assess actual response time in the event of a real emergency. Two hours later, we resumed normal routine. After such a relaxing vacation, that trip to the bunker jolted me back to the stark reality of where I was and the potential looming danger surrounding us.

The following week, Sandy sent me to the Horizon Spa in Tel Aviv to replenish our spa tickets. I was on edge that day as I climbed into the vehicle. I attributed the feeling to a restless night of sleep deprivation. While driving down Ha Yarkin Street in Tel Aviv, my Spirit Guide spoke to me with alarming force. She was shouting at me, something I had never experienced before.

Turn right, NOW!

I immediately bellowed to my driver, "Turn right, NOW!" She took an alley alongside a brick building and stopped in a parking lot at the back of the building.

"What the hell is wrong with you, Laurie?" my driver asked annoyed. No sooner were the words out of her mouth when we heard rapid machine-gun fire for several minutes on Ha Yarkin Street. We both looked at each other without uttering a single word, as we let the reality of what was happening sink in. After several minutes she spoke first, "Holy shit! Are you psychic or something?"

"No, I just have friends in high places," I replied.

"I would say so. I am sorry I yelled at you now," she said. *Thank you for the warning, Helena.* We left that day without picking up the spa tickets. I shuddered to think what might have happened had I not responded to my Spirit Guide's message the way I did. Within the hour, Tel Aviv became out of bounds for R&R for the next five days.

I spoke to Steve a few days later when he called me at the office. The phone call did not last more than five minutes. He wanted to tell me that he was working undercover, and he did not know when we would have the chance to speak again. Steve had always been secretive about his job, and I never pressed him for any information. I just listened to what he was willing to offer.

My son and I were connecting through e-mails, and I would send him postcards as I traveled. He seemed happy in the e-mails and was not letting on that anything was wrong in his life. Nothing could have been further from the truth. Perhaps, he was not telling me what was going on because he did not want to worry me. Or perhaps, he was attempting to be an adult and sort things out on his own. Either way, I was none the wiser to what he was going through at the time.

I quickly made several close friends, most of them from the Construction and Engineering Section. Whenever they found out that I was taking a tour group out, several of them would sign up for that specific tour. One of them, in particular, was named Jamie. He was the water and sanitation expert in the camp. We connected for the first time during a trip to the Sea of Galilee, the body of water Jesus had walked on. Twenty of us boarded the bus for a Saturday afternoon of swimming, followed by a barbeque supper and a campfire in the evening. Jamie played the guitar, and when he boarded the bus with it over his shoulder, I knew we were going to have a fun trip. While everyone was swimming, one of the girls on the tour stayed behind, helping me set up and prepare the supper meal. The bus driver offered to help out by lighting the barbeques. Little by little, people wandered back to the bus from the beach and helped as well. The camp kitchen had provided us with hot dogs, hamburgers, potato salad, macaroni salad, and baked beans. They also threw in an apple pie and a cherry pie. Due to a full team effort, we had cooked, eaten, and had everything cleaned by 7:00

p.m. With a roaring bonfire set ablaze on the beach and several bottles of liquor, everyone gathered around the fire, drinking and singing. We were scheduled to be back at the camp by 11:00 p.m., but no one wanted to leave, not even the bus driver. I radioed back to Zero Bunker asking for an extension. They graciously provided us with another two hours. That trip was the beginning to a special friendship with Jamie. He became the big brother looking out for his little sister.

My next tour group was departing to Egypt's Capital City of Cairo for a week. The tour was scheduled with plenty of activity and included a trip to visit the Great Pyramid of Giza and the Great Sphinx, an evening supper cruise along the Nile to enjoy the spectacular view of the pyramids lit up at night, a day at Cairo's Medieval Corners (the history of Egypt from the 13th to the 19th centuries), an afternoon at the Royal Mummies Hall (mummies excavated from the Valley of the Kings), the Museo Egizio (the world's oldest museum devoted to ancient Egyptian culture), and a day of souvenir shopping.

The pyramid blocks were a truly breathtaking example of stone masonry. Each block was approximately 28 feet high and 150 feet long, comprised of granite and limestone. They were massive in size and moving them into place by stacking them could not have been an easy feat. One of the things on my bucket list in life had always been to ride a camel, so when the opportunity presented itself after touring the Pyramid of Giza, I jumped at the chance. The people in the tour group who did not want to partake in the unique experience went to the gift shop to browse and wait for the rest of us.

Before getting onto the camels, we were provided with "nemes" (pieces of striped headcloth worn by the Pharaohs). When the camel handler motioned for me to approach the kneeling camel, I followed his instruction to the tee. I held tightly to the handle on the saddle and threw one leg across the camel's hump. As soon as I did, there was a sudden upward movement as the camel stood up; hissing, spitting, and trying to bite me. *Easy, boy, easy! I don't taste good, honestly.* Camel bodies are extremely wide and their swaying gate gives a human body a vigorous workout. By the time we dismounted the camels, none of us could walk properly. We were all painfully walking bull legged after a short twenty-minute ride. I could not imagine taking a day's ride across the desert.

It would take another book entirely to write about my experiences that week, but my most enlightening memory, besides the pyramids, was seeing the Pharaohs of Egypt mummified and placed in a sarcophagus that was painted and inscribed in hieroglyphics. The tombs were remarkably intact. Royalty was buried in seven or more tombs, one within the other, along with their most prized possessions. Mummies of less importance that had been unwrapped were on display in a darkened room. They were encased inside a dry, temperature-controlled glass box for perfect viewing close-up. Imagine seeing a body that has been dead and preserved for over 3,000 years. Nothing compares. Egypt will be forever imprinted in my mind.

My next tour group set off to experience a Bedouin lifestyle. Bedouin people are desert tribes who are nomadic by nature. They share a common culture of herding camels and goats. This particular night, a Bedouin clan in Palmyra, Syria had invited UN soldiers to experience their culture with a traditional meal, sword fighting, and dancing. We were ushered into a huge tent and offered a small glass of a milky liquid. We were told it was camel milk, and it had one wicked punch. Just a sip made you feel like you had consumed a half a dozen drinks of alcohol. Many of us stopped after one sip because we were so lightheaded. The food was fabulous, consisting of goat meat, rice, spices, and bread. We sat on carpets and ate out of wooden bowls. The meal finished with Turkish coffee.

After dinner, the other female in the tour group, along with myself, were invited to sit on the floor, one on each side of the Sheik. A Sheik is the head of a tribe and the wealthiest member of the tribe. The entire clan caters to his every request. I did not want to go sit with him. I wanted to stay with my fellow soldiers, so I politely refused. The tour guide came over and sat down beside me explaining how insulting and disrespectful it was for me not to accommodate the Sheik's wishes. "He is offering you twenty of his camels if you will join him," he said. *What am I going to do with twenty camels? I live in Canada. Good grief! This is just crazy talk.* After confirming that all I had to do was sit beside him and nothing more, I agreed to his request. Middle Eastern men can be overly aggressive with women, and I had no intention of becoming his prize for the evening. Following the entertainment portion of the tour, I stood up, thanked the Bedouin people for their hospitality, and began a head count as we returned to the bus. Once the bus was underway, the tour guide handed me a note written by the Sheik. It was asking for my hand in marriage. "He is too late. I am already married," I replied returning the note to the guide.

Mid-December had arrived. Roto 63 was returning to Canada and Roto 65 was arriving for their six-month tour of duty. I was sad to see Ginnie leave. I was going to miss our moments of laughter together. After bidding everyone farewell, I returned to the office just in time to answer my phone. It was Steve calling. The conversation began with us discussing his upcoming visit in February for a vacation. We had always wanted to travel to Greece so the timing was perfect for us. After discussing our plans, the conversation turned to the undercover work he was doing. He did not say much, but what he did say frightened me. "I need you to know that if anything happens to me, the military is responsible. I love you," were the very last words I would ever hear him speak.

Several nights later, I had an extremely restless night. I kept kicking at the darkness hoping it would bleed daylight. I finally awoke in tears and I could not get Steve out of my mind. *Helena, what is wrong with me?*

A difficult passage is at hand. Seen in its true light, everything is a test.

My heart was overwhelmed with an indescribable aching, and I could not stop crying. *Stop it, Laurie! You are acting ridiculous. Pull yourself together, wash your face, and go to work.*

I took my sweet time as I walked to the office that morning. I needed to feel something besides the devastating despair of the past two hours, so I stopped for several minutes to feel the warmth of the sun on my face and smell the fresh air. I filled myself with the White Light of the Holy Spirit before I began walking again. When I finally arrived at work, Sandy was in her office speaking with someone behind a closed door. As I settled into preparing the paperwork for an upcoming tour to Lebanon, the door opened and I was summoned into her office. The Padre (Military Chaplain) was standing there as I entered. There was an awkward silence for several moments. Then he spoke, "Laurie, there is no easy way to say what I have to say. In fact, there is no way to even cushion the blow." He paused to gather his next words. "At 5:00 a.m. this morning, I received a phone call from the Padre in Borden. Your husband is dead."

Spiritual Beings on a Human Experience

In order to truly flourish and advance, a soul must face spiritual challenges. Instead of allowing trials to turn a soul away from the Creator in anger, trials are meant to strengthen a soul's faith. Faith is a resilient hope that a soul must choose despite the situation. A spiritual challenge is achieved by calling on the Creator for help and then relying on His strength to bring you through the darkness. Laurie's faith is being tested once again. Will she choose to handle her husband's death with faith or return to her addiction to cope? A challenging passage is at hand.

CHAPTER 30

THE BALANCE OF LIFE

The best way to describe the last twenty years of my life is to equate it to riding a roller coaster. At times, life had been filled with fear of the unexpected, one of the hardest things to experience emotionally. It had also been exhilarating, with adrenaline racing through my heart. Other times, it had been a disconnect between my soul and my personality as my Spirit World intervened to guide me on my journey.

Each time I climbed to the top of the roller coaster, there were moments of perfection, filled with love, peace, and joy. When I reached the peak, there were subsequent moments in the stillness where I anxiously felt the panic of it all ending abruptly. After all, life is about balance. When I began my descent on the roller coaster of life, it was swift with a debilitating decline - heart breaking, stomach churning, upside down blows that felt impossible to recover from. There had been big climbs and big falls, filled with acceleration and deceleration, and many twists and turns.

Is there a secret to getting through life, getting through a physical experience? Should we control our own narrative about who we truly are by being true to ourselves? Will other souls accept us no matter what we do or will they make assumptions about how unworthy we are and choose not to be part of our life? I had experienced both, the balance. Should the rejection by another soul even matter? Perhaps the truth is that other souls have different beliefs and opinions based on their own experiences and that every soul is in the precise place they need to be on their journey.

Perhaps two souls cannot walk together when they are traveling on different paths of learning. Maybe every encounter is always about timing and not rejection.

Is there a mystery to happiness in life? Seeking happiness seems difficult to find for yourself, yet when you do things for other souls that make them happy, happiness fills your own soul automatically. It always had for me anyway. But what happens when you live to make others happy, disregarding your own soul's desire and fulfillment? If we seek happiness through opinions of others and weak eyes, are we fooled and misled? If we seek happiness through self-advancement and strong eyes, are we actually facing a truth that results in happiness?

Are we all self-destructive to some degree? Does negative conversation in our minds (imposed by other souls) limit our potential and the ability to see ourselves for who we truly are? Do we adopt risky behavior to deal with the pain of life and then become that very behavior? By seeking refuge in the short term of my pain, my addiction had not served any purpose other than to leave me with low self-esteem and a lack of self-love. The behavior had kept me disconnected from the pain that I was meant to be feeling. Perhaps experiencing the pain allows you to free yourself from your compulsions or obsessions. Are painful emotions nothing more than messages from the soul in the moment? Are they worth listening to in order to evolve the soul?

Is there a purpose to being still and living in the present moment? Does it strengthen our ability to wait and listen for wisdom from the soul? Do hasty decisions to move forward cause regret and tempered impulses? Maybe we are designed to be still in order to reconsider the old and to integrate the new through a spiritual lens to achieve growth. Soul searching, so to speak. When leaving Edmonton, I had learned that by viewing my past, it was balanced; filled with joy, victory, defeat, and sorrow. Perhaps it is necessary to observe it all, bless it all as a learning experience, and then release it all before we can move forward in a constructive manner. Maybe we choose not to do so because it is emotionally hard to deconstruct a human story, to go back and deal with past trauma, limiting beliefs, or destructive triggers and behaviors. Perhaps, it is easier just to move towards the future hoping for a better outcome.

What about choice or free will? Do we view our life through an "ego need" as a human - looking for outward success or recognition, fulfilling material desires, or acknowledging others in the quest for something in return? Or do we view life through a "spiritual need" as a soul seeking a deeper meaning to life and selfless giving? When we experience a loss of security, a relationship, or a loved one and life is challenging and lonely, do we understand that the darkness happens just before a spiritual shift, just before a deeper understanding of what life is all about and how we want to continue?

I had experienced several spiritual shifts in the first forty years of my life. The first shift happened in Montreal at eighteen years old when my relationship ended with my first love, Lloyd. I had absolutely no idea who I was as a soul and was desperately searching for someone to love me, to validate me as worthy of being loved. His rejection was devastating, and I was determined to live my life without love. Perhaps the timing of that spiritual shift was my soul providing me with new insight and reflection into discovering what I genuinely wanted out of life. I had a choice to sit and wallow over Lloyd or to pick myself up, go out into the world, and discover for myself what was going to make me happy. I would not discover that happiness throughout my first marriage, but I would definitely discover it after meeting Mark. It was a journey that took seven years to accomplish. I had finally found authentic love, someone who loved me for me - flaws and all. For the first time in my life, I had experienced the true meaning of love in a healthy adult relationship.

My second spiritual shift happened when my marriage to Tim ended. From a spiritual perspective, I was given a new beginning filled with grace from the Creator. Through all my devastation with Tim, I had learned to let go of what was not meant to be and to leave another soul without guilt or regret. Perhaps traveling together, out of a commitment to a child, would never have changed the inevitable. Perhaps that journey was not meant to continue without destructive results being repeated over and over again.

My third shift happened when I was posted to New Brunswick. After my father's death, my mother's rejection, and my son being temporarily schooled in Ontario, I had never felt more alone. By fixating on successful completion of my combat leader's course, I developed self-efficacy, a confidence in my ability to exert control over my motivation and behavior in a demanding environment *without feeling overwhelmed*. I had learned to be still in the moment and let life take me where I was meant to go.

My posting to Halifax is the beginning of a fourth spiritual shift, one of being alone and learning to love myself. None of these shifts are easy because the personality is continually conflicting with the soul's desire to advance. Spiritual shifts usually involve life changing from how we originally perceived it. It is journey with extreme highs and extreme lows, with deep wounds and heavy emotions surfacing, until we reach a new clarity of how we wish to continue in the world. Perhaps that is why there is always a greater source of power available, a power that is beyond earthly conditions and earthly possessions. The choice of advancement is ours to make with tremendous blessings just around the corner.

During a physical experience, the timing of death is a great mystery for all of us. There are souls who wish to die, but do not. There are other souls who have horrific health issues or accidents who wish to stay, but do not. Perhaps, the purpose of an exit point in a blueprint is a moment of choice. Is an exit-point a re-birth of sorts without having to go through the physical dying process? Does life return in a new infancy stage if we make the choice to stay? Maybe we reinvent ourselves with a new clarity of purpose and look at life differently. Maybe it is designed to help us accept new challenges with a new heightened purpose. Perhaps it is nothing more than a gift from the Creator that offers a soul release from its current life path of challenges and struggles. Maybe, just maybe, it might be a true calling for the soul to decide if it wants to remain or leave, not a calling of the personality.

I have bypassed three exit points in my blueprint so far. The first was a near drowning at sixteen years old. By listening to Spirit and relaxing, I was released from the undertow. Was this exit designed to alleviate the pain of my childhood by allowing me to return home? My second exit point occurred after Mark's suicide. I had been introduced to authentic love with a Twin Flame. Losing that kind of love was insufferable as I begged Spirit to take me home too. My blessing was that Spirit allowed me the time to grieve and remain with my son, in lieu of granting my request in the moment. A true blessing! At my third exit point, my Angel intervened during my suicide attempt. I could not see past the physical pain of the personality, but in hindsight, I am eternally grateful for the intervention. Perhaps instead of looking at how big our obstacles are in life, we need to look at how big our Creator is to see us through anything.

Thank you to all my readers for taking the second part of this journey with me. Hopefully, you will decide to spend the next twenty years with me through my third book. I can assure you that we never stop experiencing life or learning. It is necessary to the evolution of the soul and the reason we decided to make the journey in the first place. Like a roller coaster, perhaps *balance* is the very blessing that helps us endure the entire process - the good and the bad, the ups and the downs, the highs and the lows, and all the twists and turns.

ACKNOWLEDGMENT TO JOURNEYING SOULS

To my son, Timothy (TJ), my pride and joy and my greatest accomplishment in life. Our journey together has been both challenging and rewarding with unfaltering love throughout. I hope that by writing my memoirs, I have accomplished what I set out to do when you encouraged me to leave a legacy for generations to come. It was important to me to be brutally honest and to write my truth. Hopefully, my words have allowed you to understand me a little better and feel closer to me for the choices I made along the way, especially the ones that affected you. Never forget, my son, wherever I am or whatever I am doing, you are with me in my heart and in my thoughts always.

To my father, thank you for leaving an imprint on my heart for the rest of my life. You were my first love in life. Although you left the physical world far too soon, the journey to discovering love between a father and a daughter knows no absence. I am continually blessed to feel the energy of your presence from the other side as I experience my journey on this side. I love you, Dad, and always will.

Thank you to my family. You have tried to be my cornerstone with love and support as I made mistakes and struggled to find my way in life. A special thank you to my brother, Steve, for your sacrifice of going out of your way during an extremely critical juncture on my journey. You have seen me at my worst, but always remained steadfast and honest with me. Because of you and our shared history, I am who I am today.

To my deceased husband, Steve, death ended your life, but not our relationship. I live on as an evolved soul because of your compassion and love. Thank you for teaching me how to *be* love instead of being in love.

To my psychic girlfriend, Dianne, you were my saving grace during pivotal moments throughout my journey. Your ability to hear, perceive, and connect with souls who had left their physical bodies brought peace and healing during my many frozen points of grief. Most of all, thank you for allowing me to discover with absolute certainty that the afterlife is real. Sadly, you went home to be with the Creator while I was writing this second book, but you will live on through my memoirs. Thank you, dear friend, for a remarkably different connection, unique only to the two of us and for sharing your wisdom to help me evolve.

To all my forever friends, some of my deepest connections, thank you for criticism that was constructive and not destructive. I trusted many of you with my darkest secrets, without betrayal or judgment. You were instrumental in reminding me of my inner beauty and capability, always seeing the best in me. Most of all, thank you for being my most loyal and compassionate companions to this day. I am truly blessed for the journey together, side by side.

Finally, to my friend Donna, thank you for returning to my life. You have been the gatekeeper between my writing and my audience for the past two years. I remain forever grateful to you for my emotional well-being, your understanding without judgment during the editing process, the laughter when needed, and for the pure joy of embarking on this journey together.

CPSIA information can be obtained
at www.ICGtesting.com
Printed in the USA
BVHW030118140721
611689BV00004B/5